M000316965

Roving Revolutionaries

The publisher and the University of California Press Foundation gratefully acknowledge the generous support of the Constance and William Withey Endowment Fund in History and Music.

Roving Revolutionaries

*Armenians and the Connected Revolutions
in the Russian, Iranian, and Ottoman
Worlds*

Houri Berberian

UNIVERSITY OF CALIFORNIA PRESS

University of California Press, one of the most
distinguished university presses in the United States,
enriches lives around the world by advancing scholarship
in the humanities, social sciences, and natural sciences. Its
activities are supported by the UC Press Foundation and
by philanthropic contributions from individuals and
institutions. For more information, visit www.ucpress.edu.

University of California Press
Oakland, California

© 2019 by Houri Berberian

Library of Congress Cataloging-in-Publication Data

Names: Berberian, Houri, author.
Title: Roving revolutionaries : Armenians and the
    connected revolutions in the Russian, Iranian, and
    Ottoman worlds / Houri Berberian.
Description: Oakland, California : University of
    California Press, [2019] | Includes bibliographical
    references and index. |
Identifiers: LCCN 2018035605 (print) | LCCN 2018037761
    (ebook) | ISBN 9780520970366 (ebook) |
    ISBN 9780520278936 (cloth : alk. paper) |
    ISBN 9780520278943 (pbk. : alk. paper)
Subjects: LCSH: Revolutionaries—Armenia—History—
    20th century. | Russia—History—Revolution,
    1905–1907. | Turkey—History—Revolution, 1908. |
    Iran—History—1905–1911.
Classification: LCC DS195 (ebook) | LCC DS195 .
    B47 2019 (print) | DDC 950.4/1—dc23
LC record available at https://lccn.loc.gov/2018035605

Manufactured in the United States of America

28 27 26 25 24 23 22 21 20 19
10 9 8 7 6 5 4 3 2 1

To Sebouh

Contents

List of Illustrations

Preface

In 1907 skilled bomb maker and revolutionary Stepan Zorian (1867–1919)—known to his comrades as Rostom—sat with Iranian constitutionalist leaders and consented to place the Armenian Revolutionary Federation, which was the leading Armenian party at the turn of the twentieth century, at the service of the Iranian Constitutional Revolution. Soon after the meeting, they took up arms together against royalists who were trying to halt the progress of the constitutionalist struggle. Two years earlier, during the Russian Revolution, Rostom had been far from the Iranian scene, stirring things up in the South Caucasus, where he convinced his party comrades of the importance of including the South Caucasus in their revolutionary struggle. Four years later, Rostom turned up again, this time in the Ottoman Empire after his party's involvement in the reinstatement of constitution and revolution.

Rostom's geographic mobility, his appearance at pivotal moments in three different revolutionary struggles, and his remarkable ease when operating in varied milieus point to a fascinating but heretofore unexamined and central feature of these modern revolutions: the critical circulation of revolutionaries as well as ideas, arms, and print. Rostom was one among many roving revolutionaries who made their way through these early twentieth-century revolutions and whose itinerant global ideas about constitutionalism, federalism, and socialism traveled with them and were appropriated according to local and regional circumstances.

These roving revolutionaries are at the core of this book. The book situates the revolutions and the movements of revolutionaries through them in a global context that focuses on the unprecedented technological transformations in transportation (steamship and railways) and communication (telegraph and print) that help reveal the circulation of not only revolutionaries but also weapons, print, and prevalent ideologies. My study takes a connected histories approach by highlighting circulation and mobility through the struggles in three empires to show the way in which the revolutions were connected by these transimperial crossings. The fervent idealism of revolutionaries as they made their ideological and physical journeys through revolutions takes on particular relevance in today's world of ever-increasing globalization, transnational movements, and communications, especially in light of their role in connecting the Arab uprisings that began in 2011.

The rising interest of world historians in tracking individuals across borders as a way of writing global, transnational, and connected histories makes this study especially timely, as it speaks to the larger concerns of the world history movement and, I hope, will inspire similar studies in other revolutionary periods. The story I tell in this book is a story of "connected revolutions"—a story of peoples and ideas in upheaval and in collaboration with each other, a story of revolution as a concept and revolutions on the ground and the promise they held for imperial subjects. This story spans three empires and brings to the fore historical processes and actors through a conceptual approach to historical writing informed by world history and connected histories.

My fascination with these revolutionaries dates back to my first book, which, although focused more closely on Armenians and the Iranian Constitutional Revolution, nevertheless indirectly addressed connections and crossings in the triangulated frontier empires of the Russians, Ottomans, and Iranians. I continued to develop my interest in early twentieth-century revolutions and revolutionaries and delved into world history in my teaching. Starting in 2008, I began having conversations with my partner, Sebouh Aslanian, in which he introduced me to the possibilities of connected histories, especially in relationship to the history and historiography of Armenians. Thanks to my participation in 2008 in a conference on the centenary of the 1908 revolution in the Ottoman Empire, I put my preliminary thoughts on paper and became energized by the prospect of connecting revolutions, revolutionaries, and histories. The graduate seminar I taught on comparative revolutions in 2012 and the animated discussions we had in that seminar served to cement in my mind the necessity of a connected histories study on revolutions, and I am more convinced than ever that expanding our lens to explore larger regional and global contexts opens up multiple worlds of richness, possibilities, and interconnections. This book is a product of my deepening commitment to excavating and examining the myriad connections and the meaningful ways in which those connections shape lives and histories, ties that may seem invisible at first, until we look closely and realize how ubiquitous and powerful they are. Through the book, I hope to make interventions in various fields, from global history—especially comparative and connected revolutions—to the narrower fin de siècle Russian, Ottoman, and Iranian imperial worlds and the closely bound Armenian history. In a modest way, this book also aims to bring world history to the Armenians and Armenians to world history.

Acknowledgments

This book is the product of multiple circles of assistance and support, of relationships and friendships with loved ones, friends, colleagues, and professionals. Their influence has often taken place behind the scenes in both minor and extensive ways related to my process of thinking, researching, writing, revising, or taking a break from all of that. They have my deepest gratitude, and thanking them is a joyful pause at the end of this long journey. If I forget to acknowledge some individuals, it is neither from a lack of appreciation nor a lack of trying to remember all acts of help, small and large; I hope that anyone I may have overlooked will be forgiving.

Thanks to the University of California Press team, especially Niels Hooper, Bradley Depew, and Francisco Reinking. My appreciation extends also to Erica Olsen for her meticulous copyediting and Ruth Elwell for her thorough indexing.

Several people helped me collect sources and prepare or acquire maps, or made well-timed interventions. For their contributions and assistance in this regard, I would like to thank Dzovinar Derderian; Nile Green; Kristine Kostikian; Monica Ringer; Father Boghos Kodjanian, abbot of the Mkhitarist Monastery in Vienna; Meruzhan Karapetyan of the Digital Library at the American University of Armenia; Boris Ajemian, director of the Nubar Library in Paris; Vahan Ter-Ghevondyan, director of the Matenadaran; Tigran Zargaryan, director of the National Library of Armenia; Amatuni Virabyan, director of the National Archives of

Armenia; cartographer Bill Nelson; Marc Mamigonian, director of academic affairs at the National Association for Armenian Studies and Research; and David Igler, former chair of the Department of History at the University of California, Irvine. I owe a special acknowledgment to Peter Holquist, who came across my project near its end. His suggestions for readings at a symposium on the Russian Revolution at Hokkaido University in Sapporo, Japan enhanced my treatment of the larger Russian context. I am grateful to him and to the organizers and participants of the symposium for their generosity, professionalism, and collegiality, all of which validated my project and left me with fond memories.

Viken Hovsepian and Vatche Proudian were instrumental in granting me access to the Armenian Revolutionary Federation Archives. Daron Der Kachatourian was key to granting me permission from the ARF to reproduce certain images in this book. Sako Berberian and Viken Yacoubian facilitated this process. Hampig Sarafian also allowed for the reproduction of an image from a Social Democratic Hnchakian Party publication. Harut Der-Tavitian and Sevak Khatchadorian facilitated that process.

Many thanks to anonymous readers, as well as Bedross Der Matossian, Houchang Chehabi, and especially Sebouh Aslanian for their astute interventions. It is because of their suggestions for revisions that this is a stronger book.

It is an honor to call UC Irvine my new intellectual and teaching home, and I am grateful to my new colleagues in the Department of History. I am also privileged to hold the Meghrouni Family Presidential Chair in Armenian Studies, and I remain profoundly beholden to the Meghrouni family, especially Vahe and Armine. Some of the research travel and other preparations for this book were made possible by the Meghrouni Family's endowment.

Portions of this book were presented at various venues throughout the years, including the Collège de France in Paris, where the seed for the book was planted; University College in Dublin; SOAS University of London; the Association for Iranian Studies Biennial Meeting in Vienna; Hokkaido University in Sapporo; Columbia University in New York; the University of Michigan in Ann Arbor; the University of California, Los Angeles; UC Irvine; and others.

Earlier versions of some sections of the book were published in essay form in *Russia and Iran: Ideology and Occupation*, edited by Rudi Matthee and Elena Andreeva (London: I. B. Tauris, 2018) and *"L'ivresse*

de la liberté": La révolution de 1908 dans l'Empire ottoman, edited by
François Georgeon (Louvain, Belgium: Peeters, 2012).

On a more personal note, I owe special gratitude to cherished friends
for their care, patience, sustenance, continued support, and even necessary distraction during this journey. Thanks especially to Jasamin
Rostam-Kolayi, Afshin Marashi, Mimi El-Zain, Zaid Omran, and Laila
Halaby. Laila, a writer herself who offered insightful comments on the
preface, has been a trusted confidante. I thank her for listening with such
generosity, for reminding me of what is important, for long conversations that often left me with the same benefits to the mind and soul that
yoga does. Some friends have been longtime colleagues as well at California State University, Long Beach, my intellectual and teaching home
until recently and the birthplace of this project. I want to thank, in particular, Pat Cleary, who has been a reliable reader of all kinds of applica-
tions and proposals throughout the years and whose sharp eye and mind
helped perfect a passage that has morphed into the opening paragraph of
my preface. Ali İğmen, who became like family at some point during our
friendship, was especially important at the beginning of the writing process, when he critiqued the first, very rough draft of the first chapter.

A special nod to the spring 2016 history MA students at CSU Long
Beach: I was deeply moved by "the clock" and will never forget it
or you.

Ethel Daniels and David di Francesco have also played an important
part in the writing process, although they might not be aware of it.
Thanks to Ethel for helping me find my way back to me and to my
project, and to David for guiding me through burpees and weights and
often serving as a literal punching bag to release my stress.

I remain most indebted to my family, of birth and of marriage, who
have my profound love, gratitude, admiration, and respect. There is
absolutely no doubt in my mind that this book or anything else in my
life would not have been possible without my family's unconditional
love, steadfast support, and their much appreciated and perfectly timed
sense of humor throughout the journey of this book and the journey of
my life. I am grateful to them, especially my mom, Maro, and my sister
Sanan, more than I can ever express. The time I spend with them and
with my nephew Christoph, our weekly meetings and discussions from
the weighty to the mundane, are like booster shots that help me make it
through the week and beyond. Mom's question, sometimes at the most
inopportune time, of "Kirkt verchatsutsir?" (Did you finish your book?)
would unnerve me when things were going slowly and would also

propel me to work harder and faster. Sanan has always been there for me as my sister and as my closest friend and ally.

Sebouh has been a fountain of intellectual inspiration and stimulation, a trusted critical reader of my work, and the one who first introduced me to connected histories and invited me to consider its application. His love, generosity, integrity, and good heart, as well as his unwavering encouragement of this project and of me, have been vital and have buoyed me throughout the process. This book is dedicated to him.

A Note on Transliteration

I have followed a modified version of the romanization system of the Library of Congress for Classical Armenian except for personal names, for which I follow the phonetic values of Western or Eastern Armenian as applicable to the individual unless the personal name is part of a publication's title. Some terms have varied and inconsistent spellings; I have transliterated according to the text in the original source. For Persian, I have used the simplified transliteration system of the *Journal of Persianate Studies,* and for Russian, a modified Library of Congress system.

All translations are my own unless otherwise noted.

CHAPTER I

Connected Revolutions

Local and Global Contexts

No doubt, too, the universality of revolution owed something
to mere contagion: the fashion of revolution spreads. But
even contagion implies receptivity: a healthy or inoculated
body does not catch even a prevailing disease. Therefore,
though we may observe accidents and fashions, we still have
to ask a deeper question. We must ask what was the general
condition of Western European society which made it, in the
mid-seventeenth century, so universally vulnerable—
intellectually as well as physically—to the sudden new
epidemic of revolution?

Controversial British historian Hugh Trevor-Roper refers to seventeenth-
century Western European revolutions as "contagion," "epidemic," and
"fashion"; whether one agrees with these general observations or not, his
plea to delve deeper into the revolutionary context is certainly welcome.[1]
To explore revolutions not only with their local and regional constraints
as well as freedoms in mind but to view them as part of the global context
remains the most meaningful approach. This book is a study of three con-
tiguous and overlapping revolutions, the Russian (1905), Ottoman (1908),
and Iranian (1905–11), through the lens of Armenian revolutionaries
whose movements within and across these frontiers contributed to connecting the struggles as well as illuminating their study. It seeks to explore
the interconnectivity of the Russian, Ottoman, and Iranian revolutions in
several ways that interweave global and local. First, the study advocates a
novel approach to the three revolutions, previously studied in isolation
and, to a lesser degree, in comparison, that draws on a "connected histories" approach to the study of world or global history, which has, over the

last decade, become influential in how historians study the past. A connected histories approach goes beyond an examination of the similarities and differences of revolutions and allows a more revealing understanding of how the revolutions are connected. It does this through an archivally grounded analysis of the circulation of revolutionaries, ideas, and print. The protagonists of our analysis are the roving Armenian revolutionaries and intellectuals who, because of their participation in all three revolutions, their border crossings within the region and beyond, their adoption and interpretation of and adaptation to such influential and global ideologies as constitutionalism, federalism, and socialism, become ideal subjects for a retelling of the complex story of the revolutions—a story of revolutionary linkages, of local and regional actors with global ties to big ideas. This brings us to another aim of this book: to view the revolutions not only within their local and regional milieus but as part of the global context. This approach takes into consideration the interplay of "facts on the ground"—that is, phenomena particular to the region—with larger historical processes, such as revolutions in communication, transportation, and ideology that had deep and wide-ranging ramifications across the world. A consideration of these global factors helps to explain the deceptively narrower world of our revolutions.

Chris Bayly's astute observation that global philosophies, like liberalism and socialism, originating in the West "had left an indelible imprint on most human communities by 1914" certainly resonates for the Middle East and South Caucasus, where these ideas spread and indigenized according to local conditions, objectives, and aspirations. Bayly notes that often ideas and ideologies took on a discernibly distinct form as they disseminated.[2] In chapters 3 and 4, this kind of adaptation and appropriation becomes apparent. Several ideas or ideologies became malleable in the minds and writings of our revolutionaries and intellectuals, as they selectively applied aspects of anarchism and socialism and synthesized them into an eclectic blend that suited their reality and served their political and social interests. Revolutionaries were keenly aware of and familiar with European (including Russian) social scientific and socialist literature, as well as with leftist movements and revolutionary stirrings, not only in their backyard and in Europe but also farther afield—for example, in Cuba and China. As such, they shared much with each other but also with the world around them, which had, in the course of the nineteenth century and early twentieth century, been experimenting with such ideas as constitutionalism and socialism and had witnessed constitutionalism succeed in parts of Europe and socialism thrive in Western and Central European and Russian political movements. They drew inspiration from such activities and applied their understanding and familiarity to the Russian, Ottoman, and Iranian revolutionary environment.

It is within this larger global context that the Russian, Iranian, and Young Turk Revolutions, occurring almost simultaneously in regions bordering each other, may be understood in fresh and revealing ways. All three revolutions under discussion involved the participation of Armenian revolutionaries and intellectuals who contributed in differing ways and degrees and with varying rates of success to revolutionary preparation, process, and development. Whatever the parallels and dissimilarities among the revolutions, neither the revolutions nor the participants were isolated from each other. In fact, they were inextricably connected, a concept not yet fully explored in the study of revolutions. Activists of all three revolutions knew of and about each other and their actions; they were not operating in a vacuum. Therefore, it is essential that such contemporaneous, geographically close revolutions be considered in conjunction and with reference to the larger contemporary context.

With these concerns in mind, this introductory chapter aims to accomplish several goals. It seeks to introduce the local, regional, and global environment and lay out the methodological concerns that drive the study. It begins with the main protagonists of the study, the roving Armenian revolutionaries and their milieu. Following Roper's advice, the chapter then moves to the "general conditions," not only in terms of the wider regional and global context but also the larger methodological issues. It examines comparative, world, and related histories as well as more specifically comparative revolutions to make a case for applying a "connected histories" approach to the study of the early twentieth-century Russian, Ottoman, and Iranian Revolutions—that is, for viewing them as "connected revolutions." It then explores these revolutions on their own and compares them to each other in order to provide the necessary historical background and, thus, move to a discussion of the fin de siècle, 1880s and 1890s, and global transformations that smoothed the way toward revolution. The introduction ends with an overview of the sources and the structure of the book. It seeks to lay the crucial foundations for the rest of the study, which explores the finer points of the circulation of men, arms, print, and ideas that justifies a connected histories method for the study of these revolutions and of the interaction of global, regional, and local contexts that explain circulation and connections.

Before moving on to a discussion of connected histories—and given the considerable importance of Armenian activists and intellectuals in the connected history of the revolutions under discussion here—it is necessary to provide briefly some background on the communities and conditions that produced these historical actors on the move.

ARMENIANS AT THE TURN OF THE TWENTIETH CENTURY

At the turn of the twentieth century, Armenians constituted a minority in three empires: the Ottoman, the Russian, and the Iranian. The largest number of Armenians lived in Asia Minor, or Eastern Anatolia, in the six Ottoman provinces of Van, Bitlis, Erzurum, Diyarbakır, Van, and Harput, with a smaller, commercially and intellectually developed minority in the urban hubs of Istanbul/Constantinople and Izmir/ Smyrna. It is an impossible task to establish the exact number of Ottoman Armenians at the turn of the twentieth century, partly because the demographic issue has been closely tied to the politics of the "Armenian question," but according to the Armenian Patriarchate's census of 1913, the number of Armenians was slightly under two million.[3] A smaller Armenian community existed in the Araxes valley and Ararat plain, as well as the South Caucasus—specifically Tiflis/Tbilisi, Yerevan, Kars, Elisavetpol, Batumi, and others—and hovered above one million.[4] Relative to the number of Ottoman and Russian Armenians, a rather minuscule population of about seventy thousand Armenians resided in the provinces of Azerbaijan and Isfahan in Iran.[5]

The latter half of the nineteenth century was a particularly transformative period for the region and for all three communities of Armenians but was notably more so in the case of the Ottoman and Russian Empires, where most Armenians lived. The period was punctuated by advances in and greater access to education, a journalistic and literary revival, and a changing political landscape at home and abroad, which simultaneously included reforms as well as persecution.[6] Women in both the Ottoman and Iranian Armenian communities were instrumental in the spread of education, especially but not exclusively of girls, starting in the second half of the nineteenth century. Women formed charitable organizations; helped to establish kindergartens, primary schools, and secondary schools; and often provided students with tuition, clothing, and school supplies. One of the key driving forces behind the opening of secular Armenian schools starting in the late nineteenth century was the cam-

MAP 1. Connected empires. Map created by Bill Nelson.

paign to offset the influence of missionaries and curb the opportunities of assimilation.[7] In the early twentieth century and in particular during the revolutionary early twentieth century in Iran and the Ottoman Empire, Armenian women of the uppermiddle and upper classes expanded their activism to the women's movement in an attempt to bring women's issues to the attention of women themselves and to raise their consciousness. Their organizations tried to educate women in politics and in Ottoman and Iranian constitutionalism, as well as inheritance rights, hygiene, and so forth.[8] Especially significant were women writers Srpuhi Dussap, Sibyl (Zabel Asatur), and Zabel Yesayan, whose writings promoted justice and equity for women in the public and private spheres and educational and employment opportunities.[9] Beginning in the late nineteenth century and early in the twentieth century, women's journals began to appear in Istanbul, Cairo, and Beirut. For example, journals such as Marie Beylerian's *Artemis*, which appeared in Cairo in 1901–3, and Hayganush Topuzian-Toshigian's *Dzaghig Ganants* (Women's flower), published in Istanbul in 1905–7, focused on women's issues. They encouraged girls' education and women's full participation in public life as a crucial part of national development.[10]

The changes taking place among women and women's increased participation in public life were taking place in conjunction with other trends, especially in the Ottoman Armenian communities. In the mid-nineteenth century, a younger generation of Ottoman Armenians, mainly from Istanbul, returned from Europe, where they had pursued their education inspired and motivated by the French revolutionary ideals of liberty, equality, and fraternity. The struggle they waged along with guild members *(esnaf)* against the power of the Armenian Apostolic Church and the class of magnates *(amiras)* for control over the affairs of the community resulted in the adoption of the Armenian National Constitution in 1860.[11]

The internal cultural and political awakening of the Armenian communities paralleled the Ottoman Empire's administrative, financial, and military breakdown and subsequent attempts to revitalize and preserve the Ottoman state. The Tanzimat (Reorganization) reforms, promulgated during the reigns of Ottoman sultans Abdülmecid I and Abdülaziz between 1839 and 1876 in an effort to safeguard the integrity of the empire and win over the loyalty of its subjects, promised among many other things that subjects would have equal obligations and opportunities regardless of religion. The reforms culminated in the promulgation of a short-lived Ottoman Constitution in 1876.[12] However, the disparity between expectation and actual implementation and even increasing mistreatment and violence against the empire's Armenian population, most evident in the 1894–96 massacres of Armenians, led some Armenian leaders, like their Greek and Bulgarian counterparts, to seek assistance from Western European powers as well as from Russia.[13] In fact, the Bulgarian case proved to be quite inspirational for Armenian activists despite the obvious differences in their situations. The majority of the Armenian population was dispersed between two empires, where Armenians remained a minority.

The internationalization of the Armenian question achieved by the Berlin Congress of 1878 did not bring about the implementation of reforms requested by the Armenians—that is, local self-government, civil courts of law, mixed Christian and Muslim militias, voting privileges for adult men, and the allocation of a large portion of local taxes for local improvement projects. Instead, the European powers—Great Britain, France, Austria-Hungary, Italy, and Germany—entrusted the Ottoman sultan to carry out reforms and report the empire's progress to the European states at the same time that they forced Russia out of the equation.[14] Starting in the 1880s, Armenians no longer fully entrusted their fate to Europe, although hopes and efforts continued. They began to look outward for inspiration to their Bulgarian and Greek neighbors, who had been successful in carrying out revolutionary movements against the Ottoman Empire, and inward to themselves for the solution to the Armenian question. They began by organizing small self-defense groups (for example, in Van and Erzurum) and soon after coalesced around revolutionary political parties with the purpose of achieving reforms and local autonomy for Ottoman Armenians.

It was the South Caucasus, however, that produced the two most important and long-lasting Armenian political parties. Caucasian Armenian youth, unlike their counterparts in the Ottoman Empire who studied in France, pursued their education in Moscow, Saint Petersburg, Dorpat/ Tartu, Leipzig, and Berlin. Also, unlike their fellow Ottoman Armenians—the majority of whom, with the exception of residents of Istanbul and Izmir, worked on the land—Caucasian Armenians formed a substantial segment of the working class in the urban centers of Tiflis/ Tbilisi (which was also a critically important intellectual center), Baku, and Batumi. Even Caucasian Armenian peasants had better access to all the advantages and drawbacks of urban life as these cities became the destination for those seeking work in factories. At the turn of the century, Caucasian cities grew and became transformed by market economies and industrialization, as well as railroads, telegraphy, and improvement of roads, forces of turn-of-the-century globalization to which we will return below. In turn, the growth of the Armenian bourgeoisie in the South Caucasian cities of Tiflis, Baku, and Batumi reflected a disparity between population size and dominant economic position, thus raising tensions between the Armenian bourgeoisie and the larger population of Georgians and especially Muslims, as manifested in the bloody clashes between Armenians and Azeris in 1905–6.[15] These developments paralleled the enactment of Russification policies in the late nineteenth century and increasing Russian concerns about separatist movements in the provinces. The policies enacted under Tsar Alexander III (r. 1881–94) and Tsar Nicholas II (r. 1894–1917) led to restrictions on Armenian cultural, philanthropic, and political institutions as well as schools, and they culminated in the 1903 seizure of Armenian Church properties. The Russification policies and closure of schools also affected Armenian schools such as the Nersisian, Gevorgian, and Lazarian Academies, which had served the Caucasian Armenian community and contributed to producing Armenian literati as well as activists and revolutionaries, some of whom continued their education in Germany and Russia.[16] Like their counterparts in the Ottoman Empire, Caucasian Armenians returned from their European sojourns strongly influenced by German and Russian intellectual trends and took leadership of the South Caucasian Armenian communities and, more important for us, the revolutionary movements.

It is within this Ottoman and Russian context that the Armenian revolutionary movement emerged, as some Armenian youth, disillusioned with failed legal appeals and inspired by Bulgarian and Greek movements, began in the 1870s to form small and secret local groups in the eastern provinces of Anatolia to protect unarmed Armenians from acts of violence and extortion by fellow Ottoman subjects, Turks and Kurds. Two such groups were the Black Cross Organization (Sev Khach' Kazmakerput'iwn), formed in Van in 1878, and the Protectors of the Fatherland (Pashtpan Hayreneats'), formed in Erzurum in 1881.[17] Other active "small clandestine groups" that "aimed at national and cultural revival" included Miut'iwn ew P'rkut'iwn (Unity and Salvation) and Bardzr Hayots' Gaghtni Ěnkerut'iwn (Secret Society of Upper Armenia), both formed in Erzurum in 1872 and 1882 respectively, and P'ok'r Hayk'i Kazmakerput'iwn (Armenia Minor Organization), formed in Marsovan/Merzifon in 1885.[18] These organizations were soon followed by much larger and transimperial revolutionary parties, represented most visibly by the Hnchakian Revolutionary Party, founded in Geneva in 1887 (known as Sots'eal Demokrat Hnch'akean Kusakts'ut'iwn/ Social Democratic Hnchakian Party, or SDHP, following its Sixth Congress in 1909), and the Armenian Revolutionary Federation, or ARF (Hay Heghap'okhakan Dashnakts'ut'iwn), established in Tiflis in 1890. The ARF emerged, at first, as an unsuccessful attempt to organize the rather divergent members of the SDHP, the Russian populist Narodnaya Volya (People's Will), and liberal nationalists.[19] As chapter 4 discusses in detail, both parties attempted to combine the national question and socialism and sought solidarity and collaboration outside Armenian circles. Unlike the SDHP, however, the ARF did not advocate independence or separation from the Ottoman Empire. The SDHP, as its name reflects, leaned toward social democracy, although it never gave up national aspirations. As a socialist party, it had joined the Second Socialist International (1886–1914) by 1904 (perhaps earlier) and participated in its congress in Amsterdam, where it was represented by Marxist theoretician and founder of the Russian social democratic movement, Georgi Plekhanov.[20] The debate over the national question— that is, the idea of the nation-state, national or cultural autonomy, and self-determination, and especially the way the last two played out in multiethnic or multinational empires—continued to be discussed in the Second International. The ARF espoused a socialism that most closely resembled moderate European reformist socialism, although it borrowed and appropriated quite broadly from a wider array of West and Central European and Russian intellectual and political currents. Although the ARF participated for the first time in the Congress of the Second International in London (21 July and 1 August 1896) and its delegate presented a report of party activities, the issue of membership came up only in 1905, after the party committed itself to opposition to tsarism, solidarity with Russian socialist parties, and renewed commitment to socialism.[21] Membership came in 1907, although the Socialist International Bureau recognized the party's operations only in the Caucasus and as part of the Russian Socialist Revolutionaries. The ARF's demand to create an Ottoman section was accepted after some deliberation and appeals by the ARF in December 1908, and the party went to the 1910 Copenhagen congress with two delegations representing Caucasian and Ottoman branches.[22] Perhaps taking into account the SDHP's reluctance to carry out socialist activity in the Ottoman Empire, the ARF argued that it was the only socialist organization in Anatolia.[23] In addition to these revolutionary parties, there existed also a number of smaller organizations of Armenian leftists of varying degrees of commitment to orthodox Marxism, social democrats, socialist revolutionaries, internationalists, and others who were not aligned with the two parties. They either acted under an Armenian social democratic banner or joined larger parties such as the Russian Social Democratic Party. Unlike the ARF, which operated in three revolutions, and the SDHP, which operated in two (Russian and Iranian), very few of these smaller organizations operated in more than one or in all of the revolutionary movements. They contributed, however, to the intellectual and ideological milieu of the revolutionary period and, therefore, appear in relevant discussions in the following chapters.

Both the SDHP and the ARF spread their influence by establishing cells throughout the South Caucasus, the Ottoman Empire, and even Iran, whose Armenian community began to experience an increase in the number of schools in urban and rural areas starting in the 1870s.[24] This development, especially in northwestern Iran, was quickly followed by politicization, in large part because of Caucasian Armenian influence with the influx of teachers and political activists. Northwestern Iran, bordering Anatolia and the South Caucasus, served as a point of passage or layover for militants, arms, and print crossing imperial

(Russian to Ottoman) frontiers. Just as northwestern Iran, the South Caucasus, and the Ottoman Empire were all linked in the Armenian revolutionary struggle, they continued to act as interlocked loops in the same revolutionary chain during the Russian, Ottoman, and Iranian revolutionary movements. Armenian revolutionaries, therefore, struggled on multiple fronts and brought their expertise and broader vision of the future of the empires into the service of the three revolutions.

The ARF takes center stage in this study for three key reasons: first, it was the leading Armenian party in the late nineteenth and early twentieth century in the Russian, Ottoman, and Iranian states and even in Europe; second, it was the only organization that took part in one degree or another in all three revolutions; and third, it is the only party that has maintained a very rich private archive. The SDHP is second in importance, followed by Armenian Socialist Revolutionaries and Social Democrats affiliated with the larger Caucasian and Russian Socialist Revolutionary and Social Democratic movements. However, the others pale in comparison to the ARF when it comes to revolutionary participation, sheer numbers and strength, and sources. After all, as the Polish socialist paper *Naprzód* (Forward) in Krakow remarked, the ARF was a "tough walnut"—that is, difficult to rein in.[25] Nevertheless, all play an important role in the history of this period and therefore help us understand the variety of ideas and ideologies that Armenian revolutionaries espoused.

Momentous changes in the nineteenth and early twentieth centuries not only shaped the making of these revolutions but also contributed to creating the subjectivities of the revolutionaries who connected all three. Drawing on a large arsenal of internal and external political, social, and economic developments and "pull and push" factors, Armenian revolutionaries and intellectuals took part in the Russian and Young Turk Revolutions and were instrumental in the Iranian Revolution. Key among the factors driving Armenian participation was the revolutionaries' conviction that the fate of the Armenian populations living in all three empires would benefit from the victory, the establishment of a constitution that promised the end of autocracy and arbitrary rule, and the realization of representative government, social and economic justice, harmonious coexistence, and equality of all citizens regardless of religious and ethnic differences. Therefore, the wider participation and collaboration in these revolutionary and constitutional movements must also be seen as part and parcel of the more limited Armenian struggle in the Ottoman and Russian Empires, as the campaigns and their participants were intertwined and informed by each other. As this study shows, revolutionary participation became possible only because of the ground that had already been set—that is, the transport of arms, circulation of activists, and dissemination of newspapers, all of which served both the larger (Russian, Ottoman, and Iranian) revolutionary goals and methods as well as the kindred Armenian revolutionary movement. Our revolutionaries saw the movements as connected and part of the same fight.

THE CASE FOR CONNECTED HISTORIES

In recent historiography, comparative history has faced a formidable challenge for a number of reasons and from a number of academic quarters, especially from those advocating transnational, entangled, *histoire croisée,* or connected histories.[26] What is the relationship of these approaches to each other and to world history, and what case can be made for adopting a connected histories approach in this study?

Historians' views on comparative history, although often cautious and sometimes critical or even censorious, have progressed significantly from those expressed by Raymond Grew in a 1980 essay. Grew opines, "Not only is comparison not a method, but 'comparative history' is a term better avoided . . . "[27] Writing during a time when he believed that the term had been overused and therefore "compromised," Grew wittily cautions, "for many professional historians comparative study evokes the ambivalence of a good bourgeois toward the best wines: to appreciate them is a sign of good taste, but indulgence seems a little loose and wasteful."[28] Writing twenty-five years later, Micol Seigel wonders whether the time has come for a "moratorium." Writing in an exceedingly globalized world, Seigel explains, "It is the charge to illuminate the complex, global network of power-inflected relations that enmesh our world, including those connections generated by academic engagement and observation. For scholars committed to this radical legacy, comparison serves as a better subject than method."[29] Contemporary historians of comparative history advocate a particular and systematic methodology and one that emphasizes complementarity to other approaches—such as transnational, world, and connected—but attempts to avoid the common tendency to conflate them.[30]

Critics challenge a number of additional issues often associated with the comparative approach, ranging from its close attachment to the nation-state and national histories and its universalist or presentist tendencies to its reliance on secondary sources.[31] While herself cognizant and critical of these attributes, Philippa Levine advocates for comparative studies and criticizes entangled and connected histories, using examples from Eliga Gould and Sanjay Subrahmanyam, respectively, precisely because they seek to sever their ties to the comparative. As Levine points out, for Gould, the main issue with comparative history is its reliance on the necessity to have two distinct and "geographically and temporally remote" wholes.[32] In his study of the English- and Spanish-speaking Atlantic worlds, Gould argues that far from being separate, it is "an interconnected yet porous and open-ended whole," and its "intertwined" history, therefore, must be studied not comparatively but as entangled.[33] When discussing Subrahmanyam's plea for connected histories, Levine does not seem to do it justice. What distinguishes Subrahmanyam's connected histories approach is not some obscure "connectedness" that explores "common salient elements" but a systematic exploration of the circulation of ideas, individuals, and objects. It goes beyond "entangled" by offering circulation as a mode for understanding entanglements. Therefore, comparison may be insufficient compared to the more direct and dynamic circulation as a way to explore and understand connection.[34] While Levine sees these methods as belonging within the larger framework of comparative history, Heinz-Gerhard Haupt argues that transnational history, connected histories, or *histoire croisée* are substantially different from comparative history. He fairly concludes, "Those approaches . . . choose circulation of models, the appropriation of transfers, and hybrid structures more than they choose comparative history." For Haupt, they are a welcome intervention, even a "provocation," to comparative scholarship.[35] While recognizing the promise that studies of "transnational entanglements"—including entangled history and *histoire croisée*—hold, Jürgen Kocka seems rather dismissive in his final assessment, warning that the absence of "rigorous comparison" may lead to "speculative or feuilletonistic" studies, an indictment that, one can argue, equally applies to any scholarship that lacks rigor.[36] Levine argues for a "remak[ing of] comparative history through an attentiveness to the interplay of local and global, to the meaning of rupture as well as commonality, and always with an eye to the teleologies of essentialism that plague not just comparative but all forms of historical endeavor."[37] Much like Jerry Bentley in his explication of world history, she calls for a comparative method that explores and explains "interactions" that make history, thus "comparing 'across' and 'in spite of.'"[38]

This brings us to the question of the relationship of world history, comparative history, and other approaches like *histoire croisée* or connected histories. In several of his essays on the significance and contributions of the world-historical approach to our historical understanding, Bentley addresses comparative history and world history in the same breath, as world history clarifies relationships between societies "by placing them in comparative perspective."[39] The approaches have much in common, including an effort to think beyond the nation-state and to reject Eurocentrism.[40] Similar to the aims of contemporary historians practicing a form of comparative history or, even more so, connected histories and transnational history, world history emphasizes encounters, interactions, and "large-scale processes that transcend national, political, geographical, and cultural boundary lines."[41] For Bentley, the commonalities of connected, transnational, and entangled histories with world history warrant treating them as approaches that "overlap."[42]

Much of world history and comparative history methods, perhaps until recently, have suffered from the same drawback: a reliance on secondary sources in place of rigorous primary source investigation.[43] This drawback is also the case, more specifically, with comparative studies of revolution, which are characterized by yet another trait: social scientists—not historians—dominate comparative studies of revolutions. This may be partly because, on the one hand, social scientists, particularly sociologists or historical sociologists, have been the initiators of the comparative approach, and, on the other hand, because much of the comparative revolution scholarship concerns itself with creating somewhat all-embracing theoretical models to explain revolutionary causes, processes, and outcomes—a methodology that unnerves historians.[44] Whether we see entangled and connected histories as "shar[ing] some of the characteristics of historical comparison," as does Haupt; as "forms of comparative history," as does Levine; in combination, as does Kocka; or "overlap[ping]" with world history, as does Bentley, it is crucial to distinguish more explicitly the unique contribution of the connected histories approach and acknowledge its departure from comparative history.[45]

REVOLUTIONS: A BRIEF DISCUSSION

In this section, I provide a brief overview of some of the debates in the scholarship on revolution and comparative revolutions, especially on what Jack Goldstone calls comparative historical analysis (CHA) of revolutions, as a necessary theoretical backdrop that will lead to considering a connected histories approach to revolutions.

Debates regarding the definition of revolution, the role of structures and ideas, the question of why individuals take part, outcomes, and even theories to predict revolutions still continue, largely among social scientists but also among historians of revolutions.[46] No single definition applies to all types and cases of revolution.[47] Social scientists' dizzying array of definitions range from narrower ones that insist on regime change accompanied by mass mobilization to more open-ended ones whose focus lies in the *attempt* to overthrow or transform a regime rather than the actual realization of those goals.[48] In the latter case, one could argue that the process is just as important as the outcome, thus opening the way for a more inclusionary definition that emphasizes not merely successful social revolutions that completely transform states and social structures in the short and long term but also others that initiate significant changes that affect the future course of society. Ultimately, however, as Eric Selbin notes, "While definitions and explorations of revolution come and go, decades of social science research have done little to bring us closer to understanding why revolutions happen here and not there, now and not then, among these people and not those."[49] A rather limited definition that insists on a complete and enduring political and social transformation may exclude one or more of the revolutions in this study. However, on the whole, current scholarship treats all of them—Russian, Ottoman, and Iranian—as revolutions. Our revolutions have not been complete successes; however, it would be just as imprudent to dismiss revolutions because they do not measure up to the few classic social revolutions such as the French (1789) and the Russian (1917) as to dismiss twentieth-century genocides because they do not meet the criteria of the Holocaust. Are the revolutions we are looking at successful? What is a successful revolution? Can a failed revolution still be a revolution if one considers process and effort as important as outcome? Should the focus be on process? All are noteworthy questions, but they are not necessarily crucial to our understanding of how these struggles are connected by a larger global context and regional and local circulation of transimperial revolutionaries and global ideologies.

The role of revolutionaries and ideas brings us to the question of the degree of importance of agency and structure in comparative analyses of revolution, a debate inspired by Theda Skocpol's work in the 1970s. The debate over structure versus agency has been a central part of the scholarship on the comparative aspects of revolutions in the early modern and modern periods, whether in Europe or Eurasia. Jack Goldstone's essay on CHA of revolutions provides an insightful examination of CHA methods as practiced by social scientists and some historians. What is clear from his study is CHA's privileging of patterns of events—and, even more so, causal relationships—in most studies but especially in the influential and hotly debated work of Skocpol.[50]

In the 1920s and 1930s, studies on revolutions (mainly by Crane Brinton, Lyford Edwards, and George Pettee) focused on similarities in patterns of events and contributed little to our understanding of causes.[51] That focus began to change in the 1950s, and the change intensified throughout the 1960s and 1970s, as scholars sought causal explanations in the uneven relationship between traditional and modernizing elements within society. They were quickly critiqued by the giants in the field of revolution studies, Charles Tilly and Barrington Moore, who challenged the very foundation of modernization theory, which attributed the occurrence of revolutions to society's modernization.[52] Skocpol's intervention, as Goldstone explains, moved modernization from the national to the global level.[53] Although Skocpol's conclusions were, in turn, challenged by new revolutions in places such as Nicaragua, Iran, and Eastern Europe and by scholars who reminded us of the significant role of actors and ideology, nevertheless they left a lasting impression on the scholarship on revolution.[54] Goldstone succinctly describes Skocpol's structural theory as one that insists on three conditions that affect the social and political structures of society and that are necessary for revolution: "international pressure from a more advanced state or states; economic or political elites who had the power to resist state-led reforms and create a political crisis; and organizations (whether village or party) that were capable of mobilizing peasants for popular uprisings against local authorities."[55] As the numerous CHA-inspired studies of revolutions have also clearly proven, there is neither a single cause nor a combination of causes that guarantee the occurrence of revolutions. A number of interrelated and sometimes seemingly unrelated factors on the global, regional, and local level combine to cause revolutions to flare up.[56] For example, in his study on third-world social revolutions, John Foran, who adopts Skocpol's definition of a social revolution—that is, "rapid, basic transformations of a society's state and class structures"—points to five factors, which, occurring in conjunction, result in successful revolutions in the third world.[57] They are "1) dependent development; 2) a repressive, exclusionary, personalist state; 3) the elaboration of effective and powerful political cultures of resistance; and a revolutionary crisis consisting of 4) an economic downturn; and 5) a world-systemic opening (a let-up of external controls)."[58] Foran brings in agency and ideology—in the form of a culture of resistance—to supplement an otherwise structural approach.

Therefore, some scholars have attempted to consider agency—the role of individuals and ideas—in combination with structure to understand revolutions, whereas others have given agency priority. Many scholars have questioned, to one degree or another, Skocpol's and other structuralists' insistence on the primacy of structure as the key component of revolutionary action and their downplaying of agency and ideology; instead, these scholars have allotted individuals and ideas formidable influence on revolutionary mobilization.[59] For example, in his comparative study of the Iranian, Nicaraguan, and Philippine Revolutions, Misagh Parsa extensively analyzes the collective actions, interests, and ideologies of major social groups, classes, and individuals; he shows that they are "at the heart of revolutionary struggles but are given short shrift" in the scholarship.[60] In a more recent and provocative analysis that offers an antidote to the privileging of structural theories, Eric Selbin calls for "bringing story back in" by delving into the role and power of myth, memory, mimesis, "stories and narratives of popular resistance, rebellion, and revolution which have animated and emboldened generations of revolutionaries."[61] Selbin has long been a strong critic of structuralism, arguing that the role of individuals cannot be excluded from explanations of why revolutions take place and that indeed individuals are central to why revolutions emerge and how they proceed. He emphatically contends that revolutions are "created by people, led by people, fought and died for by people, consciously and intentionally constructed by people."[62] To this, he adds individuals' stories and how the stories contribute to the making of revolution. This aspect of Selbin's analysis relates to the aim and approach of this study, which focuses on the stories of roving revolutionaries and circulating material and ideas and their contribution to connecting revolutions.

The question of agency and the contribution of ideas and individuals to creating revolutions ties in very closely to the reasons that actors participate in revolution. Theories about what propels individuals and groups include, for example, "relative deprivation," when expectations go unmet and people instead encounter deprivation; rational choice theory, when self-interest dictates the decision to become active, and its opposite, when group interests override individual ones; and even "bandwagoning," whereby people join because they see others taking up arms or taking to the streets.[63] In the case of this study of circulating Armenian revolutionaries, the matter of agency and the reasons individuals chose to venture into three simultaneously and/or consecutively occurring and bordering revolutions is particularly important. What ideas and promises drove these actors? What practical circumstances on the ground contributed to action? How did the regional, political scene and global transformations in technology and ideology encourage and make possible the choices they made regarding collaborative struggle with other revolutionaries? It is these kinds of questions that drive this study. While the debates on revolutionary theory, definition, and and other related matters remain admittedly important and may provide breadth and backdrop, a primary-source-driven and historically grounded treatment of the three revolutions that goes beyond comparison and instead highlights connections through circulation and context—local, regional, and global—takes precedence here. Thus, this study departs from earlier comparative approaches and brings a fresh perspective to the scholarship on revolutions. From where does such an approach draw inspiration? What are its foundations and rationale?

CONNECTED HISTORIES APPROACH AND ITS POTENTIAL CONTRIBUTION TO THE STUDY OF REVOLUTIONS

Unlike insular studies of revolution, and unlike comparative scholarship, which compares the common historical traits of revolutions, a third approach occupies itself with revolutions' "horizontal continuity," to use a term introduced by Joseph Fletcher. According to Fletcher, "horizontal continuities" are said to exist when an "economic, social, or cultural historical phenomenon experienced by two or more societies between which there is not necessarily any communication . . . result from the same ultimate source."[64] In our case, of course, there is indeed communication between societies; therefore, Fletcher's "interconnection"—that is, "historical phenomena in which there is contact linking two or more societies, as, for example, the spread of an idea, institution, or religion, or the carrying on of a significant amount of trade between societies"—becomes far more apt.[65] Whether one searches for horizontal continuities or interconnection, Fletcher makes a point similar to that of Bayly but much earlier and for an earlier period, recommending that we look for the larger patterns connecting disparate or related societies.[66] While Fletcher prefers comparative history to area studies or a "parochial outlook," he finds it lacking and inferior to integrative history that explores interrelated historical phenomena.[67] Like Fletcher, Bayly focuses on interconnections and globalization but in the nineteenth century. He observes, "As world events became more connected and interdependent, so forms of human action adjusted to each other and came to resemble each other across the world." These connections, in turn, "created many hybrid politics, mixed ideologies, and complex forms of global economic activity" at the same time that they amplified areas of divergence as well as animosity.[68]

What distinguishes this school of "integrated" histories of revolutions from comparative histories is its emphasis on integrating, as opposed to isolating or comparing, the study of different revolutions in relation to an underlying common causal mechanism, such as population growth (to name just one example). Fletcher's integrative approach, in which he emphasizes searching for interrelated causes for "historical parallelisms (roughly contemporaneous similar developments in the world's various societies)," is associated most with the work of Jack Goldstone on early modern revolutions and rebellions in Stuart England, Ming China, and the Ottoman Empire.[69] Goldstone studies early modern revolutions or rebellions in Stuart England, Ottoman Turkey, and Ming China in an integrated fashion by focusing on common demographic growth and its role in causing revolutionary breakdowns in these seemingly isolated places. He is particularly interested in exploring "a common causal framework rooted in a wide-ranging ecological crisis." He shows how population growth in a period of stagnant agricultural growth led to a number of economic, social, and political problems—"decline of traditional systems of taxation, overloading of institutions of elite training and recruitment, and decay in popular living standards"—that culminated in revolution.[70]

A related approach to Fletcher's notion of interconnection is *histoire croisée*, promoted by Michael Werner and Bénédicte Zimmermann. For Werner and Zimmermann, "The notion of intersection is basic to the very principle of *histoire croisée*," and "Accordingly, entities and objects of research are not merely considered in relation to one another but also *through* one another, in terms of relationships, interactions, and circulation."[71] This approach is similar to Fletcher's concept of interconnection: linking societies through related phenomena. Benedict Anderson's *Under Three Flags: Anarchism and the Anti-Colonial Imagination* is an important study of interconnection that focuses on the connections and coordination between subjects of the late nineteenth-century Spanish Empire (Cuban, Puerto Rican, Dominican, and Filipino anarchists) and the cross-pollination of anarchist and revolutionary ideas and ideologies in the last few decades of the nineteenth century.[72] While Charles Kurzman presents a notable comparison of early twentieth-century democratic revolutions and their consequences in Russia, Iran, the Ottoman Empire, Portugal, Mexico, and China, his approach remains a comparative, not connected, history of the role of intellectuals.[73] Ilham Khuri-Makdisi's

The Eastern Mediterranean and the Making of Global Radicalism demonstrates the connections between global transformations and radical networks in the Eastern Mediterranean, particularly in Beirut, Alexandria, and Cairo between 1860 and 1914.[74] More recently, but for an earlier period, Janet Polasky's *Revolutions without Borders: The Call to Liberty in the Atlantic World* focuses on itinerant revolutionaries and ideas that traversed the Atlantic world before the advent of an international postal system or the technological transformations in transportation and communication.[75]

My approach, which I call "connected revolutions," owes its conceptual or theoretical debt to Fletcher's interconnection and Werner and Zimmermann's *histoire croisée*. In addition, the idea behind connected revolutions is inspired by Sanjay Subrahmanyam's studies of early modern Indian Ocean and European history, where Subrahmanyam presents his approach as an alternative to historical writing inspired by either area studies, comparative, or nationalist approaches, all of which tend to *parochialize* the study of history by severing the rich and complex connections between historical developments occurring in seemingly dissimilar regions.[76] As Subrahmanyam points out, "Contrary to what 'area studies' implicitly presumes, a good part of the dynamic in early modern history was provided by the interface between the local and regional (which we may call the 'micro'-level), and the supra-regional, at times even global (what we may term the 'macro'-level)."[77] One way in which Subrahmanyam proposes to deparochialize or deprovincialize the study of the past is by focusing on real connections between regions that otherwise have been studied in isolation. He does this by highlighting the role of the circulation of cultural forms, ideas, capital/commodities, and elites. Similarly, one way of deprovincializing the study of the Ottoman, Iranian, and Russian Revolutions is to explore them through the circulation of Armenian revolutionaries who simultaneously operated in each of these political and social upheavals. The Armenian activists were some of the most active and dynamic of their kind to connect all three revolutions at the dawn of the twentieth century. They were themselves "connectors," much like Malcolm Gladwell's Paul Revere but perhaps much less dramatic and much more constant.[78] In studying the circulation of the Armenian revolutionaries and political activities in Russia, Iran, and the Ottoman Empire, this book contributes to the project of connected histories through the study of the connectedness of all three revolutions and, in doing so, sheds light on the tumultuous events at the beginning of the twentieth century that have helped shape the history of the states and societies in which they occurred. It also seeks to contribute to the concerns of world historians, whose growing interest lies in border crossers. Therefore, what follows in this book both is informed by and aims to give back to world-historical and connected histories approaches and scholarship through the telling of the revolutionary drama that unfolded in the early twentieth century in the Middle East and the Caucasus, as transimperial subjects conceived, espoused, and spouted revolution in both words and deeds.

COMPARING THE RUSSIAN, IRANIAN, AND YOUNG TURK REVOLUTIONS

Having briefly touched upon some of the comparative historical analyses of revolutions, I now turn to the constitutional revolutions at the core of this study: the Russian, Iranian, and Ottoman. What common threads and aspirations did they share? How can we understand these revolutions beyond their particularities and in global perspective? How do they reflect not only the local and regional but the global context? How can we approach them in an area that triangulates three bordering empires? Why are they important in the larger scheme of world history?

At the risk of simplification, one can say that there have generally been three schools of thought on how the Russian, Iranian, and Young Turk Revolutions have been explored. The conventional school studied revolutions in a rather insular fashion, producing scholarship on each revolution and treating each in isolation from the others. To some extent, although not entirely, this approach may be seen as emanating from the conventional concerns of national historians and area studies specialists in each of these regions, who have privileged the study of the history of nation-states at the expense of exploring shared histories with other states or societies. Nevertheless, the important contributions and foundational knowledge produced by this kind of scholarship, which has been the dominant form until recently, must be acknowledged. Another approach to the study of revolutions in general has been the comparative scholarship that has set for itself the agenda of comparing the common historical traits of otherwise seemingly disparate revolutions.[79] Nader Sohrabi's study comparing the three revolutions is without doubt the only serious sociological and historical study on the subject.[80] Here, Sohrabi compares what he calls two successful constitutional revolutions, the Ottoman and the Iranian, with a failed one, the Russian, arguing that "the support of extraparliamentary resources, including the military," determined short- and long-term success.[81] Sohrabi's structural approach also takes into consideration ideology.[82] His discussion of the impact of the dominant "revolutionary paradigm"—that is, the French Revolution of 1789—as the revolutionary and constitutional model points out France's premier position in the minds of the revolutionaries of all three revolutions.[83]

Sohrabi picks up on the theme of the revolutionary paradigm of the French Revolution in his recent valuable and lengthy study. Here, however, he is particularly interested in comparing the Ottoman and Iranian Revolutions "in the spirit of" Clifford Geertz's "commentary on one another's character."[84] His study is an example of what Levine calls "comparison to," which "sets up a hierarchy with the lead comparison as the normative entity [Ottoman] against which something else [Iran] will be compared."[85] Sohrabi's analysis serves the dual purpose of exploring why and how these revolutions took place and, therefore, what makes them constitutional, as well as historicizing the study of revolutions through a comparative examination of the ideologies and the revolutionaries that supported them.[86] One of the key aspects of Sohrabi's study is the connection he makes among the global, regional, and local, solidly grounding the ideology of constitutionalism at all three levels.[87] As Sohrabi asserts, while constitutionalism was a global phenomenon, it took a different shape in the Ottoman and Iranian Revolutions because of negotiations with the regional and local and, therefore, what he finds in both cases is a specific "domesticated constitutionalism" rather than an abstract one.[88] His study benefits from a more inclusive methodological approach that takes into account structuralism, causal relations, and patterns of events, as well as agency and contingency, in order to provide the single most comprehensive comparison of the two revolutions.[89] Although Sohrabi's study falls into the category of comparative history, his global framing of the revolutions makes it a vital and original contribution to that approach.

Sohrabi's analysis of the local in relation to the regional and the global is evidence of Bayly's observation about the impression made by Western ideologies on global communities. What Iranian and Ottoman communities did with these concepts, as Sohrabi demonstrates, however, was clearly dependent upon their own local conditions. As Bayly explains, "In the process, intellectuals and popular audiences the world over had rapidly transformed their meanings into a variety of doctrines, often very different from their exemplars."[90] For example, constitutionalism—the concept that a state's authority is limited by a set of rules and regulations agreed upon by the populace through a constitution and, furthermore, that the state's authority is dependent upon its observation of those limitations—traveled from Europe east to the Middle East and Japan. In fact, constitutionalism made its way to Japan before it got to the Middle East and even to the Caucasus. For constitutionalists in the region, Japan's victory over Russia signified the perceived promise and strength of constitutionalism. After all, had not the only decaying nonconstitutional Western empire lost to the only constitutional power in Asia?[91] Revolutionaries in all three cases, Russian, Ottoman, and Iranian, may have disagreed on the form of government or the economic stage of their societies in the evolutionary process or the way in which to reach their goals or even the contents of their constitutions, but what they all thought in unison was that constitution was the "secret of strength" of any society.[92] In that sense, the revolutions shared much in common with each other and also with the world around them, which had, in the course of the late nineteenth century, seen constitutionalism succeed, in one degree or another, in Western Europe. In chapter 3, I discuss the complicated relationship that Armenian revolutionaries had with constitution as principle on the one hand and real constitutions in the Russian, the Iranian, and especially the Ottoman case on the other—in a sense, that is, the global and the local. Constitutionalism was only one of a myriad of ideas, including most importantly socialism and federalism, that inspired our revolutionaries, leading them to adopt and appropriate such global ideas through a number of means, including print in the original or translation and personal and professional encounters through imperial frontier crossings.

Revolutionaries and observers were very much aware of their own recent history, of the wave of revolutions from 1765 to 1830—the age of revolutions—and from 1847 to 1865, in particular, and they may have soon become deeply conscious of their role in the third wave, from 1905 to 1912. As Jürgen Osterhammel explains, unlike earlier revolutionary waves, "this time the mutual influences were more intense than in the mid-nineteenth century; the revolutionary events were expressions of a common background in the times."[93] In all cases but in varying degrees, revolutionaries opposed autocratic, personalist rule, reforms kindled revolutionary potential and action, and intelligentsia drove the coalitions that brought about change, even if at times temporarily.[94] The revolutions all involved, to some extent, the collaboration of linguistically and ethnically diverse imperial subjects and adaptation of European Enlightenment ideas as well as socialism in its many variants. More importantly, however, the military and international setting, whether military defeats and setbacks or concessions and capitulations, permitted the revolutionary context.[95]

All empires faced financial problems, although the Ottoman and Iranian Empires were much worse off than the Russian, which experienced economic development and modernization before the turn of the twentieth century. Most importantly, though, they all felt the heavy blow of the worldwide economic depression that began in 1873 and may have lasted until 1896. As James Gelvin succinctly explains, "In the Middle East, the collapse of international trade and commodity prices bred discontent among merchants and farmers. It also resulted in Ottoman and Egyptian bankruptcy and foreign supervision of the finances of each. Money that had gone into public works, military salaries, and the expansion of services vital to the functioning of modern states now went to repaying European creditors. Many in the region were resentful."[96] That resentment intensified the already vulnerable situation to such an extent that popular uprisings erupted in the triangulating and frontier-sharing region.

The three revolutions were similar to earlier revolutionary waves in the Atlantic world before and after the French Revolution of 1789 and in Europe in 1848 and also coincided with revolutions in Portugal (1910), Mexico (1911), and China (1912).[97] The revolutions in the Russian, Ottoman, and Iranian states drew strength from each other's successes and attempted to effect change in their own particular environments. Even as far away as Portugal, for example, Portuguese revolutionaries, inspired by the Young Turk Revolution, began to call themselves "Young Turks."[98] Our three revolutions shared a great deal with the others and took markedly similar paths. Progressive movements toppled autocratic states and initiated the beginnings of popular sovereignty—constitutional rule, parliaments, and freedoms—but they did not successfully implement or guarantee them. All revolutions were followed by coups d'état initiated by more conservative forces.[99] While one may quibble about the degree of success of each revolution and the degree of political and social transformation, none reverted back to the old order.

Russian Revolution, 1905 (1904–1907)

The Russian Revolution was characterized by a series of protests, worker strikes, and mutinies in parts of the Russian Empire, including the Caucasus. It marked the culmination of decades of both liberal and radical (and everything in between) opposition to the tsar's unchecked authority and attempts to limit the autocracy's powers through constitutional limitations. Tsar Nicholas's response to demands oscillated from inaction and empty promises or concessions to violent repression. The promise of reform and the concession to form a *duma* (parliament) did little to meet the demands of constitutionalists, who were disappointed by the limits placed on the electorate. The struggle continued between the oppositional forces and the tsar and among constitutionalists themselves until 1907, when the autocracy restored its authority, which it had conceded in 1906, in direct violation of the constitution. As the foremost scholar on the revolution, Abraham Ascher, concludes, the revolution left behind "an enduring legacy: it initiated a process of political, economic, and social change that even now still has not run its full course."[100] Moreover, the Russian Revolution had a tremendous intellectual, ideological, and political impact on the Ottoman and Iranian Revolutions, especially on the latter.

Ascher makes a case that the revolution actually began in late 1904, with liberal agitation against the autocracy aroused by Russian military defeats in war with Japan, and ended with the dissolution of the second duma in early June 1907.[101] Scholars have disagreed on the key protagonists and the event that marks the start of revolution, many arguing that workers spearheaded the struggle and that it began with Bloody Sunday.[102] Ascher, instead, supports what he calls the "liberal" view, which "depicts the revolution . . . as a critical juncture that opened up several alternative paths" and at first involved liberals from the nobility and professional classes with political demands and later "workers, peasants and national minorities—who were additionally interested in economic and social change. . . ."[103] While there have been some rumblings by Marxists and non-Marxists alike against labeling the Russian Revolution a revolution because it did not culminate in a complete social and political transformation, as did the later 1917 revolution, a number of factors—including large-scale popular protests, organized opposition, and broad-based coalitions, as well as new social and political institutions—warrant considering this movement as a revolution, one that stood on its own and was not merely, as Lenin claimed, a "dress rehearsal" for 1917.[104]

A number of economic, political, and social factors acting in conjunction led to the Russian Revolution. Beryl Williams raises Alexis de Tocqueville's contention that revolutions occur not in times of impoverishment but during periods of accelerated economic and social development that benefit some but not others. Just as the abolition of serfdom in the 1860s raised the hopes of peasants about land ownership and autonomy, industrial modernization raised the expectations of workers in the late nineteenth century.[105] These expectations and hopes then came face to face with an economic depression in 1900, which caused lower wages, higher prices, and increased unemployment and was exacerbated by the Russo-Japanese War only four years later. Franziska Schedewie argues that peasants tended not to be revolutionary and that when they were, they were not motivated by increasing poverty but were responding to the consequences of modernization.[106]

The results of industrial growth and urbanization hastened by railways and telegraphy included horrid conditions for workers in towns and in workshops and factories, long hours, and arbitrary penalties and fees. Worker unrest began in a rather disorganized way, with limited demands, but later became more organized and espoused political objectives. This unrest was made possible by railways, "the motor of industrial development, not only creating a large new demand for coal, steel rails and rolling stock but also facilitating the movement of raw materials and finished goods. They accelerated urbanisation as expanding trade and new industries were supported by a flood of migrants from the countryside both into existing towns and into new urban settlements."[107] In the countryside, although serfdom legally ended in the 1860s, emancipation was not fully realized. Peasants received some land, but they did so not individually but collectively; this system of land distribution was inefficient. Moreover, because of increased rural populations, land remained limited, and peasants had to pay for it by buying or leasing. Peasant disturbances began as early as 1902 in the provinces of Kharkov and Poltava (in today's northeastern and central Ukraine, respectively).[108]

Another aspect of modernization was the legal and social advances in the form of judicial (1864) and local government reforms, resulting in new elected *zemstvo* (local self-government) institutions, advances in education and public health, and a new class of lawyers and educated professionals interested in fighting injustice and arbitrary actions as well as advocating for political change. New professional groups with fresh visions and demands were joined by students and unions as growing radicalization altered the initial aspiration for a national consultative assembly to one that included a legislative consultative assembly elected by universal suffrage in 1905. A similar acceleration of demands took place in the Ottoman Empire and in Iran, as we shall see below.

The Russo-Japanese War may have been one of the straws that broke the camel's back, as defeat and disillusionment turned into discontent and disorder. As Russian losses intensified and over a million reservists were called to fight, the practical economic and political effects, as well as the psychological and social ones, became palpable and helped fuel the growing view that the nonconstitutional tsarist state had become vulnerable not only to constitutional Japan but to its own people, Russian and non-Russian. Russia's defeat by Japan struck a hard blow to the autocracy's legitimacy. The Russian Empire's linguistically and ethnically diverse non-Russian populace experienced the same situation as its Russian subjects, with an added twist. The vast and varied land empire required local, often ethnically and religiously non-Russian and non-Orthodox administration to function. Through the creation of local officials and functionaries—and challenged, as we shall see in the next chapter, by increasing Russian nationalism and Russification policies that imposed Russian culture, language, and religion in places like the Caucasus and elsewhere in the far-flung empire—an ethnic/national consciousness began to develop. This consciousness added not only to local rivalries with national and religious expressions among different groups (e.g., Armenians and Azeris in the Caspian oil-producing port city of Baku and surrounding areas) but also to the economic and political grievances that the ethnically diverse peoples of the empire shared with their fellow subjects.[109] Subjects' demands ranged from basic civil rights like freedom of assembly and press to a thorough constitutional system that would rein in the arbitrary powers of the tsar. As political consciousness grew, the dominant call became one for a constitutional system and assembly. Williams argues that what all groups in Russian and national minority areas shared was the desire and demand for a say. She writes, "In many ways this demand for autonomy, whether from national minority areas, or from individual towns and districts, was what characterised 1905 as a revolution." She quotes the workers joining the assembly organized by Father Georgy Gapon: "Russia is too great, its needs too varied and profuse, to be governed by bureaucrats alone. Popular representation is essential. The people must help themselves and govern themselves."[110]

Popular grievances found expression in protests, strikes, and mutinies starting in December 1904. The tsarist regime's response here and elsewhere oscillated between concession and repression. At first, in response to protests, the state made concessions through zemstvo congresses and meetings modeled after the private political meetings, *cam-*

pagne de banquets, of the French Revolution and set up to bypass laws against public assembly. However, people's demands by this point included a legislative assembly and constitutional regime. Concessions in many ways encouraged and stimulated continued or further opposition, but so did repression. In fact, the bloody crackdown on Father Gapon's peaceful march on 9 January 1905 to present a rather modest petition to the tsar took on immense significance, symbolic and real. Gapon and his followers had looked to the tsar to solve their problems. In some ways, as their view of the tsar as a benevolent father changed and their reverential relationship to the tsar broke down, the revolution began to radicalize. The realization of complete loss of face against Japan led to more popular protests—peaceful and otherwise—in May 1905, labor organization and strikes, and worker demands for better working conditions, better wages, an eight-hour day, and so forth, as well as assassinations of officials. Peasants demanded the right to the land on which they worked and expressed their grievances in ways available to them: for example, withholding rent, illegally gathering wood, and attacking the property of the gentry. Strikes by railway, telegraph, gas, electric, and postal workers paralyzed important sectors of the empire, and as soviets/councils began to rise and take over local leadership, they acted as a direct challenge to the tsarist state.[111] Both the demands and the activities crossed imperial boundaries as revolutionaries expressed parallel demands and acted out in similar ways in the Ottoman Empire, Iran, and beyond.

The October Manifesto authored by the new prime minister (and former director of railway affairs and finance minister), Count Sergei Yulyevich Witte, which promised a constitution, basic freedoms such as freedom of expression and of the press, and legislative assembly (duma) with limited suffrage, as well as other concessions to peasants in the form of canceled redemption payments, succeeded sufficiently to satisfy a large segment of the opposition. Others continued protest and agitation and faced counterprotests and the state's repressive measures. Although the anti-autocratic struggle persisted until 1907, the strikes and uprisings had by that time lost their verve. Disunity within the duma between liberal and radical groups facilitated its dissolution in June 1907. On the left were the Marxist Social Democrats and the Socialist Revolutionaries, who were very much influenced by the Russian populist movement of the late nineteenth century and had diverse approaches to workers, peasants, and class struggle, as well as diverse tactics. They remained most unsatisfied with the October Manifesto, believing that it had not gone far enough. The liberal Kadets (Constitutional Democrats) and centrist Octobrists, especially, were most satisfied with the October Manifesto and occupied the political center. To their right were the conservative nobles and traditional elements who supported the tsar fully and—unlike the center, which considered the duma a positive step toward democracy—tolerated the duma only as a safeguard against further revolution. Minister of Internal Affairs Pyotr Stolypin (Witte's replacement as prime minister in 1906) saw to the hunt for revolutionaries and the transformation of the duma's composition from foe to collaborator through restrictions on the franchise.[112]

Tsar Nicholas II's regime survived as a result of the subduing of the duma as well as a number of other reasons: on the whole, troops remained loyal (despite some mutinies) and restored order; the opposition, with differing visions and commitment to action, remained divided and became more so because of concessions to peasants and liberals, leaving the radicals to fight among themselves, with limited popular support. As Anthony Heywood explains, the alliance between liberals, workers, and peasants was key to their success and what the tsar feared most, but ultimately, they were unable to maintain it, as "class rivalry" based on very different worldviews won out.[113]

Despite its seemingly limited gains, the Russian Revolution of 1905 fundamentally altered Russian society and the Russian state, developed far more conscious classes at all levels, and brought forth a new Russian identity and relationship to the tsar, who was no longer viewed with fatherly reverence, as he had been before the revolution. This transformation in the relationship made possible revolutionary opposition by large portions of the Russian populace in this revolution and in the one that followed a little over a decade later.

Young Turk Revolution, 1908

The Young Turk Revolution shared some key elements with the Russian case discussed above, yet it differed in some critical ways. For example, the Young Turk Revolution did not have the intense popular participation of the Russian Revolution, nor was the Ottoman Empire as economically developed and modernized, with an industrial proletariat, as the Russian Empire. This is certainly not an exhaustive list; the discussion below should lay bare some critical differences as well as the particularities of the Ottoman case.

The Young Turk Revolution involved a coalition of forces—including the exile community in Geneva and Paris, discontented civil servants, students, nondominant ethnic and religious populations, and army officers—and was preceded by strikes and tax rebellions. Unlike the Iranian Revolution and especially the Russian Revolution, there was no perceptible organized socialist movement in the Anatolian heart of the Ottoman Empire, at least not at this early stage. There were, of course, socialist organizations among non-Muslim subjects of the empire, particularly Bulgarians who had achieved autonomy through the Berlin Congress in 1878 but remained formally within the Ottoman Empire. Although they varied in background, outlook, and demands, most oppositional groups agreed on the restoration of the 1876 Ottoman Constitution and parliament, both of which sought to limit the autocratic powers of the sultan. In the face of coordinated military campaigns by the Second (Thracian) and Third (Macedonian) Armies, demanding the restoration of the constitution, Sultan Abdülhamid II (r. 1876–1909) acquiesced. Multiethnic and multireligious celebrations in the streets greeted the news, followed by elections, assembly meetings, and numerous strikes in cities throughout the Ottoman Empire. The attempted coup in 1909 was opposed by the Third Army and resulted in the deposition of the sultan, but it laid bare the constitutional authority's tenuousness.[114]

A number of factors acting in conjunction led to revolution in the Ottoman Empire. The Tanzimat reforms (1839–1876), culminating in a short-lived constitution, provided vital impetus in two key ways. First, the Tanzimat decrees, which aimed to reform the Ottoman state in order to ensure its preservation and longevity as well as its diverse population's loyalty and further integration, not only targeted agriculture, manufacturing, transportation, and communication, as well as legal and educational sectors, but also guaranteed all subjects regardless of religion the same rights, opportunities, and obligations as Muslim subjects, thus ushering in a reordering of society that challenged the status quo and made inroads into institutional modernization. Young Ottomans (predecessors of the Young Turks) like Namık Kemal became the key critics of the reforms in the 1860s and 1870s (before the ratification of the constitution in 1876), believing them to be insufficient. They advocated, instead, for broader political participation and rule of law through constitution and parliament. For Sultan Abdülmecid I (r. 1839–1861), these changes were enacted with the purpose of consolidating his own authority, preserving the Ottoman state under intense Great Power pressure as well as in response to internal liberalizing forces for reform. For the reformers, the Tanzimat—despite its imperfect implementation and even after Sultan Abdülhamid II's dismissal of the constitution and parliament only two years after promulgation—held great promise. The reforms themselves also created a new class of Ottomans who continued to struggle against autocratic rule and for the realization of true constitutionalism and did so in an environment of increasing financial and territorial encroachment by European, especially British and Russian, powers.

The year of the dismissal of the constitution, 1878, was also the year of the Congress of Berlin, which met after the Russo-Turkish War of 1877–78 and revised the San Stefano Treaty of a few months earlier. The Treaty of Berlin stacked the cards in favor of the Great Powers, particularly Britain and Austria-Hungary; saw to the independence or autonomy of a number of Balkan provinces; and reduced the territorial expanse of the Ottoman Empire, thus sowing the seeds, or fertilizing the seeds already sown, for further internal and external conflict within the Ottoman Empire. For instance, the Berlin Congress redrew the map created at San Stefano, reducing Bulgaria to less than half the size of the expansive Bulgarian state that had been established, and demoted Macedonia from autonomy, returning it to full Ottoman rule. Moreover, of especially central importance for non-Muslim Ottoman subjects, as Michael Reynolds notes, the Berlin Congress "acknowledged ethnicity as an attribute of human identity carrying distinct political claims."[115]

Further military and territorial losses in Tunisia and Egypt in 1881 and 1882, the threat of losing Macedonia (confirmed by a meeting in 1908 between Russia and Britain on the Bay of Reval, on the Baltic Sea in today's Tallinn, Estonia), and a brewing financial crisis acting in conjunction with other factors helped set the stage for revolution.[116] The Ottoman Empire had procured its first loan during the Crimean War in 1854 and by 1875 had secured fifteen loans totaling a debt of 200,000,000 Ottoman lire. Inability to keep up with payments led the empire to declare insolvency in 1876, resulting in the surrender of Ottoman financial independence to European interests, as representatives of creditors in the Ottoman Public Debt Administration collected state revenue to pay off the debt. As losses hit the empire from many directions, Sultan Abdülhamid II, whose responsibility was to protect and preserve the integrity of the empire, began to lose support. His inefficient and incompetent rule, reflected in military and territorial forfeiture and financial fiasco, further galvanized those who already found fault in his autocratic and repressive rule and drew the army and administration into the ranks of the discontented opposition at home and abroad. They called for constitutional monarchy and representative government; through these demands, they sought the preservation of the empire—and not only its survival but its flourishing.

Jürgen Osterhammel brings up the Ottoman example in passing when he discusses the complicated links between exile and revolution.[117] The opposition that ultimately brought the 1876 constitution back and forced Sultan Abdülhamid II to acquiesce had its proponents in Geneva and Paris, where some Ottoman elites lived in exile. At two congresses in Paris in 1902 and 1907, Ottomans representing the diversity of the empire, including Armenians, met to consider their options and discuss their demands and ways in which to proceed. The program on which they settled called for the restoration of the constitution of 1876, which had been summarily shelved since 1878, in order to curb the power of the sultan and preserve the integrity of the empire. Furthermore, the participants promised to work together to bring down the sultan. According to the preeminent historian of the revolution, Şükrü Hanioğlu, the opposition unanimously agreed to force the sultan's abdication, to transform the administration, and to put in place a consultative government and constitutional system and to do so by whatever means were deemed appropriate, not limited to armed and unarmed resistance (e.g., labor boycotts, strikes, nonpayment of taxes), propaganda within the army, and general rebellion. As evidence of the revolutionaries' awareness of regional movements, shared circumstances, and the now-ubiquitous telegraph system, "the congress sent a telegram of solidarity to the Iranian parliament expressing Ottoman opposition groups' desire for collaboration between the future Ottoman constitutional government and Iranian constitutionalists."[118] While the congresses and the Paris-based Committee of Progress and Union (CPU) had very little authority, their demands signified the import of constitution, the commitment to preserve the empire, and the public identification with Ottomanism—that is, the view of "all Ottomans as equals . . . [although] CPU publications . . . attributed a dominant role to the Turkish element in the Ottoman empire by claiming that 'reform of the Ottoman administration depends on a rebellion by the Turks, the dominant element in the empire, and not on insurrections by a bunch of Armenians or Bulgarians.'"[119]

Much earlier and closer to home, within the empire itself, civil servants and students from the military and medical academy founded a secret society in 1889 that came to be called the Committee of Union and Progress (CUP). The group was particularly strong in Salonika (present-day Thessaloníki) among the Third Army, which believed that the sultan's policies were undermining the military and the Ottoman Empire's security. The CUP came out of secrecy in 1908 after discussions between internal headquarters in Salonika and external headquarters in Paris and was quickly placed under surveillance by Ottoman authorities. The CUP extended its activities, forming groups of fighters all over Macedonia. By early July 1908, with support and numbers on the ground and facilitated by the empire's extensive telegraph system, CUP leaders made their intentions and demands to reinstate the constitution explicit and even offered an ultimatum at the end of July, threatening to march to Istanbul; they moved—without having received a response—to declare the restoration of the constitution on 23 July. The sultan's acquiescence and the reopening of parliament quickly followed. As newspapers and word of mouth spread the news on 24 July, the multilingual, multiethnic Ottoman populace spilled into the streets to celebrate.[120] Elections for parliamentary representatives, challenge to the status quo, and the promise of a new era did not sit well with all, culminating in 1909 in an attempted coup by common soldiers and theological students to restore the sultan's powers and authority, and the accompanying destruction of churches, schools, and "the entire Armenian residential quarter" and massacre of Adana's Armenians.[121] The revolt did not fare well, as the Third Army quickly secured the survival of the new government and deposed the sultan in a manner that combined old and new forms of rule: the Shaykh al-Islam decreed the deposition and a four-member delegation, including an Armenian and a Jew, was dispatched to inform the sultan of his removal from the throne. The figurehead Sultan Mehmet V (1909–1918) replaced Sultan Abdülhamid during a period of power struggle but also an expansion of the educational system (particularly primary and secondary schools) and of civil liberties like freedom of press and assembly, improvement of the military, and a reduced bureaucracy. By 1913, however, the CUP was able to gain the upper hand and consolidate its rule. The coup carried out in January 1913 by a group of CUP members secured the party's grip on power, in particular that of the triumvirate (Enver, Talat, and Cemal Paşas).

For much of its history, the scholarship on the Young Turk Revolution has dealt with it as a coup rather than a revolution—or, at the most, as a kind of top-down revolution. To a great extent, the thrust behind the actual collapse of the sultan's autocracy came from the military. However, the Ottoman case also had the components that we associate with revolution (including popular mobilization that predated the actual takeover in July 1908) and that prepared some elements of the populace for 1908. For example, as Hanioğlu explains, political activity in eastern Anatolia from 1905 to 1907 "successfully turn[ed] dissatisfaction among various classes of people, which was rooted mainly in economic difficulties, into revolutionary movements demanding the reopening of the parliament and the restoration of the constitution."[122] The rebellion was fomented through an alliance between the ARF, the Young Turks, and the League of Private Initiative and Decentralization (LPID), led by Prince Sabaheddin Bey, which, unlike the Young Turks, sought European assistance to enact reforms in the empire and sought administrative decentralization.

Peasants' dire economic situation reached the tipping point with the enactment of two new taxes. When their petition met with indifference, Muslim, Armenian, and Greek peasants resorted to demonstrations and even the occupation of the telegraph office in Kastamonu and Erzurum. They were joined and supported by shopkeepers, merchants, and even the mufti, who was called on to mollify the masses.[123] Tax revolts and unified Armenian and Young Turk action spread throughout eastern Anatolia in such places as Trabzon, Bitlis, Van, and many others; these actions turned, according to Aykut Kansu, from calls to repeal "unjust taxation without representation to an outright and widespread rejection of the existing regime."[124] Moreover, while Hanioğlu recognizes that the Russian and Iranian Revolutions had a role to play in motivating "dissidents in their attempts to stir up the masses," he insists that the driving force that caused the "metamorphosis of these local disturbances into full-fledged political movements demanding the reopening of the parliaments" was the alliance of Young Turks, ARF, and LPID and not the other revolutions or revolutionaries.[125] Kansu also acknowledges the influence of the Russian and Iranian Revolutions on the participants in the March and October 1906 revolts in Erzurum and elsewhere, as they came across revolutionary pamphlets printed in Europe and discussed the possibility of revolution as a "remedy for the current situation in Turkey."[126] For Kansu, the tax revolts of 1906–7 "involved such profound social, political and economic changes that . . . [they must] be considered as nothing less than a revolution."[127]

It would seem impossible to talk about the aftermath of the Young Turk Revolution without mentioning the Armenian Genocide (1915–18)—although some authors have managed. None of the revolutions or their aftermaths were bloodless; however, neither the Russian nor the Iranian Revolution was followed only a few years later by such horrific violence, questioning the very principles and promise the revolution had held for many.[128] The revolution accomplished much, ultimately ending not only the Hamidian regime but monarchy itself, replacing old institutions with new ones, creating a new governing elite and new political organizations, laying the foundations for a modern state, breaking out of the shackles of imperialism, making strides toward greater gender equality, and so forth. Therefore, in some ways, genocide is even harder to comprehend if we are to accept Kansu's contention that "the Unionists' intention was the establishment of a *truly liberal democratic* regime."[129] Yet, if we adopt Hanioğlu's argument that "they were not constitutionalists or advocates of the reinstatement of the constitutional regime for the sake of establishing a constitutional political system; rather they thought that having a constitution in effect would help them to overcome many of the internal and external problems of the empire," and that they leaned toward "authoritarian theories" and Turkism, then we get an important piece of the puzzle.[130] It would not be out of place to say that both tendencies and visions existed among Young Turk revolutionaries and their collaborators. However one looks at it, there is no question that the Young Turk Revolution was, as Hanioğlu writes, "a watershed in the history of the late Ottoman Empire," but a watershed not only for its dominant Turkish citizenry but also for its diverse population of Kurds, Greeks, Assyrians, and Armenians, for whom the great potential and expectations of revolution were crushed by assimilationist policies, population transfers, and genocide.[131]

Iranian Constitutional Revolution, 1905–1911

Much like the Russian and Ottoman cases, the Iranian Constitutional Revolution sought parliamentary representation, constitutional government, limits on the authority of the shah, and other reforms. In the Iranian case, however, and more like the Ottoman than the Russian, an increasingly threatening European imperialism also played a role in the unfolding of revolution and its consequences. Oppositional forces in the revolution ran the gamut from *ulama* (clerics) and *bazaaris* (merchants) to secular intellectuals, progressives, and even socialists, and they found strength in Russia's defeat in the Russo-Japanese War (1904–5), as well as in the Russian Revolution. Although the revolutionary struggle continued for several years, its initial success came in July 1906 when the

Qajar monarch Mozaffar al-Din Shah (r. 1896–1907) conceded to a *majles* (assembly) and constitution. His son, Mohammad 'Ali Shah, attempted two coups, of which the one in June 1908 had a successful outcome. *Mojahedin* (popular troops), Bakhtiyari tribal forces, and Armenian revolutionaries joined in battles against royalist forces and restored the constitution in July 1909. Financial, factional, and other problems plagued the constitutional government, but ultimately Russian interference, supported by the British, led to the dissolving of parliament and the end of the revolution in December 1911.[132]

A variety of developments in the nineteenth century led to the Iranian Revolution: military defeats by the Russian Empire, European economic penetration in the form of commercial capitulations and concessions to Russia and Great Britain, autocratic and incompetent rule leading to— among other things—loans to cover three extravagant voyages to Europe by Mozaffar al-Din Shah and his entourage, and subsequent social discontent. Loans became a particular thorn in the side of the Iranian economy. As James Gelvin explains, unlike the Ottoman Empire, which was equally affected by the global depression in the late nineteenth century, Iran experienced the added impact of a decline in the value of silver, along with China, Japan, and India, all of whose economies were bound with silver. Although brief, Gelvin's integrative approach focuses on overriding causal mechanisms—that is, decline in the value of silver and stock market collapse—to explain similar consequences despite regional variations. Much like the devaluation of silver in the sixteenth century, the nineteenth century experienced the flooding of silver in large part because of the increase in the number of countries on the gold standard and "the discovery of new deposits of silver, such as the Comstock Lode in Nevada and the Albert Silver Mine in South Africa." The flooding caused a rise in prices of basic commodities and inflation in Iran between 1850 and 1890, leading to loans to pay the debt acquired by earlier loans.[133] Moreover, the shah's relationship to Britain and Russia, a relationship that many of his subjects viewed to be one of subservience, added to prior economic and political grievances and helped fuel opposition. Like the Ottoman Empire, Qajar Iran was deeply affected by its unequal relationship with Europe and semiperipheral integration into a European-dominated world economy, as local market economies that produced crops for local consumption were transformed into market economies producing cash crops. Thus, the Middle East entered the global economy as a dependent region, a supplier of raw materials (e.g., cotton, tobacco, opium, silk) to Europe and a consumer of goods manufactured in Europe.

European loans and concessions that became commonplace in nineteenth-century Iran, and to some extent in the Ottoman Empire, drew much critique. At first, the opposition made up of *ulama*, courtiers, and secular progressives targeted the shah's ministers—for example, his chief minister Mirza Ali Asghar Khan, known by his two titles Amin al-Soltan and Atabek—whom they blamed for the loans and concessions, which were viewed as leading to Russian control of Iran. As secret societies within Iran began to form and multiply, members of the opposition read and disseminated the writings of critical Iranians abroad in the Russian and Ottoman Empires as well as in Europe (for example, Malkom Khan, Mirza Fath-Ali Akhundzadeh, Mirza Agha Khan Kermani, and Seyyed Jamal-al-Din Afghani, among others) who were calling for reform and who included the shah among the targets of their criticisms. Concessions served as another focus for the opposition.

Two economic concessions stand out in the context of popular reaction and its significance for the constitutional revolution. Iran had been granting favorable commercial terms to Europeans since the sixteenth century; however, the nineteenth century witnessed the beginning of a number of agreements that had a profound effect on the Iranian economy, sovereignty, and therefore the populace's view of the monarchy. Following the 1828 Torkamanchay/Turkmenchai treaty, which settled a Russo-Persian war and resulted in the annexation of Caucasian provinces by Russia, both Russia and its main rival in Iran, Britain, began to extend and consolidate their grip over Iran's economy. Increasing European economic encroachment had a number of destructive consequences: agriculture was oriented toward export crops, domestic craft industry was hit hard by European imports, and prices of Iranian exports fell—all contributing to unemployment and insecurity for many, although some, of course, did profit. In the late nineteenth century, further agreements between the Iranian monarchy and Europeans led to a number of concessions for telegraph, banking, fishing, railway, as well as other resources and enterprises.[134] The Reuters concession of 1872 and the tobacco concession of 1890 garnered the most strident resistance. The first gave the founder of the Reuters news agency, Baron Julius de Reuter, an unprecedented grant of control over Iran's resources: the right to build a railway from Caspian ports to the south and exclusive rights to factories, irrigation, minerals (except those already being worked), and so forth. Iranian popular resistance as well as Russian opposition stopped the concession. The second concession, almost twenty years later, brought about even more opposition. In another ill-advised move, the

Qajar monarch granted a monopoly over the production, sale, and export of Iranian tobacco to a British subject, Major G. F. Talbot. Unlike the Reuters concession, which focused on previously untapped areas, this concession targeted a product extensively produced and exported by Iranians. An alliance of merchants, *ulama,* and intellectuals and popular protest in 1891 brought about a nationwide boycott of tobacco sales and use. This concession, too, failed because of its ardent rejection by the populace and its leadership, which emboldened those who made greater claims for justice a decade later.[135]

Grievances and demands varied in the constitutional revolution but reflected some of the earlier concerns as well. Urban classes had important economic grievances ranging from merchant dislike of new customs administration and concern over loans and concessions to rising prices and taxes and continued undermining of all crafts, except carpets, which benefited from increasing European demand and a subsequent boom in the late nineteenth century. Some Iranians felt threatened by the growing presence and role of foreigners, whether through influence and encroachment on Iran's sovereignty or business, or the spread of missionary education. Unlike the Russian case and more like the Ottoman one, anti-imperialist sentiment became a critical force driving revolutionaries. Their awareness, however, that their much more powerful and close neighbor Russia could and would easily intervene to prevent serious reform and, of course, revolution kept them from taking action. Only after Russia's involvement and ultimate defeat in the Russo-Japanese War and the Russian Revolution itself did decisive action become a possibility. The Russian Revolution and Japan's victory encouraged the shah's opposition, which saw the sole Asian constitutional power humiliate through military defeat the lone nonconstitutional European empire, giving hope to Iran as an Asian state and proving the virtues of constitution.[136]

The opposition, which came to comprise intellectuals, clerics, and merchants, found an opportune moment in December 1905 when the governor of Tehran bastinadoed sugar merchants for not lowering their sugar prices, which had risen even further since the devaluation of silver by wartime conditions—that is, the Russo-Japanese War. Mullahs and merchants took sanctuary *(bast)* in the Royal Mosque of Tehran as a form of protest. These *basts* were followed by many more, attracting thousands of *ulama,* religious students, mullahs, merchants, and others. Demands quickly escalated from a vague house of justice to a constitution and a *majles.* The shah acquiesced, granting constitution and parliament in August 1906.

As was the case in the Russian and Ottoman Empires, constitutional monarchy as imagined by the constitutionalists was to be a radical break in Iranian governance. Their intention was to set up a true constitutional state with a strong position for the *majles,* giving it the authority to weigh in on all critical state matters—including, for example, foreign loans and treaties—in an attempt to create an independent state and rein in ministers and the shah. The constitution that resulted called for compulsory public education and a new legal system; it promised equality to all its citizens regardless of religion, and it promised civil liberties like freedom of speech at the same time that it made Islam the official religion of Iran and qualified freedoms of press and speech by barring statements deemed anti-Islamic. As in the Ottoman Empire, new freedoms of press and assembly brought about the sudden flourishing of newspapers and popular and revolutionary associations, *anjomans.*[137]

The years that followed the institution of the new constitution were tumultuous and threatened the new constitutional regime. In 1907 the British and the Russians signed a treaty settling their differences in Tibet, Afghanistan, and Iran. The agreement divided Iran into spheres of influence, with northern and central Iran going to Russia and the southeastern region to Britain, in direct violation of Iranian sovereignty.[138] Early in the same year, Mohammad 'Ali Shah (r. 1907–9) succeeded his father, Mozaffar al-Din Shah, and attempted to regain autocratic powers through two coups, the latter assisted by the Cossack Brigade in June 1908. Robust and consistent resistance came from Tabriz, in Iran's northern Azerbaijan province. Constitutionalists received arms and fighters from the South Caucasus, as Azeris, Georgians, and Armenians collaborated and struggled against royalist forces and Russian troops and successfully reinstituted the constitution in 1909. These Caucasian revolutionaries, along with Iranian workers returning from jobs in the oil refineries of Baku, also became important conduits in the transfer of socialist ideas and labor organization that influenced Iranian revolutionaries more than in the Ottoman case.[139]

Constitutionalist *ulama* continued to offer their support for the constitution and *majles* while conservative *ulama* opposed both. For some conservative *ulama,* representative government—however limited— flew in the face of God's sovereignty and the Quran and challenged their own position, or at the very least was superfluous. Progressive *ulama,* however, contended that the constitution was an acceptable—if not the only possible—means by which to rein in arbitrary rule in the absence of the Hidden Imam, who, according to Twelver Shi'ism, was eleventh in line to Imam Ali and the twelfth imam, and who had gone into hiding in the ninth century and would one day return as the Mahdi.[140] As the proconstitutionalists reasoned, after all, were not popular sovereignty and legal equality the foundations of government set up by Prophet Muhammad himself?

Division and conflict became further pronounced in 1910 among constitutionalists on different sides of the political spectrum; the more liberal Democrat Party (founded in 1909 and made up of liberal and social democratic elements) and the not so aptly named conservative Moderate Party fought it out in the *majles* and the streets. Financial troubles and insolvency added to the internal disunity and conflict, and the constitutional government brought in an American lawyer, William Morgan Shuster, to set Iran's finances in order as treasurer-general. His attempts encountered opposition, especially from Russia but also from Britain.[141] In November 1911, Russia's ultimatum demanding Shuster's dismissal and the government's agreement to refrain from any deals with foreigners without British and Russian consent met with popular protests calling on the *majles* to stand firm against further violations of Iran's independence. The defiance of the *majles* led to its dissolution and Shuster's dismissal as Russian troops moved into Tabriz in December 1911, striking the final blow to the constitutional revolution already writhing with internal problems.

Although there were signs of popular revolt against concessions, particularly against the tobacco concession in the later nineteenth century, the Iranian Constitutional Revolution turned out to be the explicit expression of anti-autocratic and anti-imperialist movement—more so than anything else in its past and certainly in relation to either the Russian or the Young Turk Revolution. Despite its rather disappointing end, it left an enduring legacy. Revolutionaries sought representative government, resisted imperialism, attempted economic independence, made inroads into secularism, reformed education and the judiciary, and fostered popular activism through associations. The revolution held both the promise of inclusivity for its citizens and the strengthening of Iranian nationalism.

Revolutionaries in all three cases, much like their counterparts around the globe, sought the cure to what ailed their societies and governments in constitutionalism, parliament, and some degree of popular sovereignty. In one sense or another, all revolutions may be perceived as having failed, at least in the short term (some more palpably than others); however, they also have succeeded in many ways, leaving an important legacy of organized opposition, constitution, and (even more important for us) a dynamic history of connections, which this study reveals. Equally critical to a meaningful understanding of these revolutions is an appreciation of the global context or conjuncture that allows us to see them beyond their regional setting and local particularities and in light of larger transformations, not only in terms of the worldwide dissemination of an ideology such as constitutionalism or, as Sohrabi characterizes, "ideological 'world time'" but also in terms of radical and far-reaching advances in technologies of transportation and communication that effectively shrank time and space.[142] In chapter 2, I explore the critical developments of technology in the form of steamships, railroads, and telegraphy, which noticeably facilitated the crisscrossing of revolutionaries and activists across imperial frontiers. They circulated throughout and across the Russian, Ottoman, and Iranian borders and beyond into Western and Central Europe during revolutionary upheavals. They also carried with them or saw to the transfer of weapons, explosive elements, and devices, as well as revolutionary print in the form of newspapers, pamphlets, and books in translation or in the original. These circulations in support of revolutionary movements are at the heart of their connectivity.

"THE WORLD AS A CONTINUOUS BLUR": THE GLOBAL CONTEXT AND TIME-SPACE COMPRESSION

The movement and participation of Armenians among others in these revolutions tells us a great deal about their particularities and also signals the global transformations that had begun to take shape in the last half of the nineteenth century, leading, as Bayly writes, to the emergence of "a kind of international class structure . . . [that at] the very least . . . could perceive and articulate common interests which breached the boundaries of the nation-state . . . "[143] Easier and faster transportation and access to communication (through the telegraph, for example) and news from different parts of the world through the movement of people and print, especially in the form of periodicals, all helped produce, as Ilham Khuri-Makdisi argues in her book on Eastern Mediterranean radicalism, "local, internal reconfigurations triggered by both state and society . . . Dramatic changes, simmering discontent, and great expectations triggered contestation as well as the 'experimentation with new forms and ideologies of collective action,' both rural and urban, which historians have identified as a 'key feature' of the 1880–1925 period."[144] These global developments had an unmistakable impact on the three empires bordering each other and effecting revolutionary movements through the increased mobility of border-crossing activists as well as revolutionary accoutrements like arms, print, and concepts. The extent of circulation of roving Armenian activists, arms, and global ideas that we witness at the turn of the twentieth century only becomes possible when we consider the role of new technologies like railways and telegraph and the proliferation of periodicals and books, all of which had a powerful effect on revolutionaries taking part in multiple struggles against autocracy. The 1880s and 1890s were an especially critical period of globalization characterized by capitalist development, growing overseas markets, escalating industrialization and imperial expansion, and record use of fossil fuels, as well as the vastest surge in migration, unrest, and self-assertiveness by workers, women, and anticolonial groups.[145]

The revolutions occurred at a time and in a world that may have seemed to be on speed—as in amphetamine sulfate—with all the implied effects associated with the high and with the risks, including the "comedown." The revolutionary period itself produced a whirlwind of ideas and activities, exhilaration, and hope, as well as violence followed by anxiety, dejection, and disillusion. Historian Eric Hobsbawm has labeled the early twentieth century, which experienced all these revolutions, the "little age of revolutions."[146] The century that preceded it and overlapped with it, the long nineteenth century (1750–1914)—a phrase also coined by Hobsbawm—seems to be the age of a number of phenomena: age of fossil fuel, age of uniform time, age of the speed revolution, age of migration, age of urbanization, age of revolution, age of the telegraph, and age of industry and empire.[147] The nineteenth century witnessed dramatic changes, but the turn of the century was an especially radical period that, as Osterhammel notes, "brought a surge in globalization that for the first time linked all continents into economic and communications networks."[148]

In his influential *The Condition of Postmodernity,* David Harvey notes that the period in which these revolutions took place, particularly from the late nineteenth to the early twentieth century, witnessed significant shifts in technologies of global communication and transportation, resulting in an important new round of "time-space compression" or the accelerated "shrinking" of the world.[149] By "time-space compression," Harvey means "processes that so revolutionize the objective qualities of space and time that we are forced to alter, sometimes in quite radical ways, how we represent the world to ourselves."[150] Processes refer to shifts in technologies of global communications and transportation that began radically to transform people's lives beginning in the middle of the nineteenth century and accelerating thereafter. These shifts led to a shrinking or "compression" of both time and space, thus making the world smaller, time shorter, and life faster. Harvey explains, "The expansion of the railway network, accompanied by the advent of the telegraph, the growth of steam shipping, and the building of the Suez Canal, the beginnings of radio communication and bicycle and automobile travel at the end of the century, all changed the sense of time and space in radical ways. This period also saw the coming on stream of a whole series of technical innovations . . . new technologies of printing and mechanical reproduction allowed a dissemination of news, information, and cultural artefacts throughout ever broader swathes of the population."[151]

Focusing on space and mobility, Tim Cresswell notes that as people began to travel by train, the space they perceived was shaped by seeing it through a train window moving at relatively high speed. He writes, "For the first time it was possible to see the world as a continuous blur."[152] In his recent study of the telegraph and globalization in the nineteenth century, Roland Wenzlhuemer agrees that something unique had taken place that altered the relationship between time and space; however, he cautions against contemporary views of those who interpreted their own period—whether in reference to the telegraph or capital—as one of "annihilation of time and space" or "space with time."[153] For Wenzlhuemer, time and space must be treated as separate units and not collapsed into one time-space.[154] He emphasizes the point that space "cannot be annihilated—neither together with time nor by time itself," that instead what has happened is that advances in technologies and capital have shaped a new space "that is entangled with other spaces through its actors and objects."[155] Wenzlhuemer explains that communication and transport technologies like railways and telegraph did indeed reduce communication time within geographic space; however, this reduction, rather than having the effect of annihilating time, actually made time essential: "The shorter communication times became, the more important even minor differences could be," thus making "the standardization of time a necessity."[156]

Such time accelerations in communication affected some spaces but not all, thus excluding peripheral areas and even increasing communication times between them and hubs.[157] According to Wenzlhuemer, time-space compression applied only to certain parts of the globe and affected those people who were touched by the new technologies of the railway and the telegraph, as well as by the resulting increase in mobility and dissemination of print and ideas. Although not as advanced in communication and transportation as Europe, the regions that underwent revolution, especially the South Caucasus, Ottoman Anatolia, and Iran, and those in urban centers inhabited and traversed by activists and intellectuals did experience some form and varying degrees of "time-space" compression, as their worlds simultaneously shrank and expanded. Revolutions certainly had their local and regional causes, as we saw in the previous section on the particularities and similarities of the Russian, Iranian, and Young Turk Revolutions. They were also touched—often struck—by wider developments, such as global depression or silver devaluation, as we noted earlier. Global causal mechanisms, however, need not be catastrophic; turn-of-the-century technological advances in transportation and communication led to faster and therefore more frequent travel (by railway and steamship) and communication (by telegraph) across wider distances, thus shrinking the time it took to get to places near and far and giving the impression that the world had become smaller because it had become more easily accessible. At the same time, the world seemed to expand because these same technologies made available a range of ideas, encounters, and exchanges, thus magnifying the available and reachable horizons. This two-pronged consequence of time-space compression, shrinking and expanding, was instrumental in connecting our revolutions because it made possible the circulation of revolutionary operatives and intellectuals as well as the ideas and ideologies that fueled those revolutions.

ORGANIZATION

This book is divided into five chapters. It has begun with an introduction to the themes, argument, and conceptual framework of the study. Through a discussion of comparative, world, and related histories and of comparative revolutions specifically, it has made a case for a connected histories and connected revolutions approach and the appropriateness of its application to the study of the early twentieth-century Russian, Ottoman, and Iranian Revolutions. It then explored these revolutions in comparison and ended with a discussion of the turn-of-the-century global transformations that smoothed the road toward revolution. Chapter 2 focuses on the prevalent crisscrossing of revolutionaries, arms, and print through the South Caucasus, Anatolia, and Iran, as well as Europe, within the context of transformations in transportation and communication. It delves more deeply into the South Caucasus as an axis of cultural and revolutionary diffusion. Chapters 3 and 4 demonstrate the weight of ideas—like constitutionalism and federalism in chapter 3 and socialism in chapter 4—that filtered through the frontiers via revolutionaries and workers, as well as circulars and newspapers and the forms they took under local conditions. I conclude the study with some reflections on the incongruity of revolutionary ideals and struggles, on the one hand, and postrevolutionary aftershocks, on the other.

SOURCES

My study relies on the almost untapped Armenian-language unpublished and published documentation of the ARF, the dominant Armenian political party crossing the figurative and literal frontiers of the Russian, Ottoman, and Iranian states and revolutionary movements. The papers, which contain a much smaller number of documents in other languages (French, Persian, Russian, and Ottoman Turkish), include correspondence, minutes of meetings and congresses, circulars, details of debates and decisions, and other material. The archives have been in the midst of a rather slow process of digitization by the ARF Archives Institute. In the meantime, twelve volumes of documents have already been published.[158] Recently, the ARF Archives has taken the welcome step of opening its doors more widely to scholars in order to facilitate their work. The archives are housed in a seemingly unlikely place, Watertown, some six miles northwest of Boston, a town that once was—for a short period of time, from April 1775 to November 1776—the seat of government in Massachusetts. Watertown boasts one of the most important and oldest Armenian communities in the United States. The archival documents (and the published volumes) cover a wide global network from anywhere that the ARF has had a presence, including such seemingly unlikely places as Cuba and Central Asia, and contain documents not only by or about the ARF but also anyone or any other party/organization whose paths crossed with those of the ARF. They offer an immensely rich and wide-ranging wealth of archival sources for scholars on countless subjects of scholarly inquiry for local, regional, and global history. They are, as one of the former directors of the ARF Archives, Tatoul Sonentz-Papazian, phrased it, not a museum or a cemetery but a "living entity."[159] I wish such a "living entity" existed for the SDHP.

I also utilize for the first time in a systematic way more than two dozen contemporary Armenian-language periodicals from major cities and centers of political activity in the South Caucasus, the Ottoman Empire, Iran, and Europe. Many of these newspapers had short lives; often they were forced to shut down but reappeared under different names. For example, one paper in revolutionary Tiflis seems to have had more lives than a cat, appearing in fifteen reincarnations from 1906 to 1909.[160] These newspapers are available primarily through the National Library of Armenia, the Armenian Digital Library at the American University of Armenia, Bibliothèque Nubar (Nubarian Library) in Paris, and the Mkhitarist Congregation in Vienna. Furthermore, I take advantage of a number of important documents from the revolutionary period in archives in the British Library and the National Archives at Kew in England and the National Archives and the Archives of the Catholicosate at the Mashtots' Matenadaran in Armenia. A few select documents from Foreign Office correspondence at the British Library and War Office records at the National Archives (Kew) have been most useful. The National Archives of Armenia and the Catholicosate Archives in the Matenadaran, the latter perhaps not surprisingly, have not been as fruitful as the ARF Archives but nevertheless have supplemented the sources in important ways. Although the bulk of documentary evidence and newspapers are by or about the ARF, a significant percentage of the newspapers are by the SDHP as well as other Armenian Social Democrats and Socialist Revolutionaries. Party newspapers and official organs in Tiflis, Baku, Istanbul, Tabriz, Geneva, and Paris provide rich material on the ideas with which Armenian revolutionaries engaged and that they shared with their readers. They were also a site of contention among various political factions with differing visions, all competing to inculcate readers with their own views and vying for leadership and representation of the Armenian communities in the South Caucasus, Anatolia, and Iran.

Newspapers were important throughout much of the world in this period, which saw a flourishing of print culture in many forms. Among them were revolutionary periodicals that spanned the globe, both figuratively and literally, in terms of the subjects and news they published as well as the long distances they traveled and the numbers of literate and even illiterate readers they reached. Illiterate readers benefited from literate family members and friends, acquaintances, and neighbors reading out loud in both public and private spaces. As the study makes clear, although we do not have direct evidence of their reach or subscription numbers, their dissemination beyond their origins and the energy and resources that went into their circulation throughout Eurasia provide us with indirect evidence of their impact on activists and readers. The archival documents, too, in the form of correspondence and meeting minutes, testify to an increasing demand for existing newspapers and a growing interest in publishing new ones.

My use of the archives of a party whose members were expert circulators and cosmopolitan revolutionaries lays the foundation, along with contemporary Armenian-language periodicals and other sources, for a much-needed contribution to multiple fields of inquiry, including world history, the history of revolutions, Middle Eastern history, and Armenian history. With its global and connected histories approach and its focus on roving Armenian revolutionaries and their ideological and physical boundary crossings through the Russian, Ottoman, and Iranian revolutionary worlds, this study provides insight into how the revolutions are more than similar—how they are, at the core, connected.

CHAPTER 2

"Active and Moving Spirits of Disturbance"

Circulation of Men, Arms, and Print

Վերքերով լի ջան ֆիտայ եմ / Թափառական, տուն չունեմ,
Եարիս փոխան զէնքս եմ գրկել / Մի տեղ հանգիստ քուն չունեմ

[Full of wounds I am a fedayi / Wanderer, I have no home /
Instead of my love I carry my gun / I have no place for restful sleep]

The image of the wandering *fedayi,* constantly moving from place to place, sacrificing love, life, and home in the service of the people's homeland, is a common one in Armenian national history and memory.[1] However, Armenian historiography has almost exclusively represented the *fedayi* as a creature of national history, restricting his movements to the national stage and thereby foreclosing the possibility of seeing in the figure a border-crossing revolutionary who played a vital role in the constitutional struggles of the early twentieth century.

In this chapter, I discuss the turn-of-the-twentieth-century circulation of Armenian activists, arms, and print, especially periodicals, on three levels, which may loosely be termed global, regional, and local. On the global or macro level, circulation was facilitated by and took advantage of new and speedier modes of communication and transportation (e.g., telegraph, steamship, and railways) as well as advances in longer-standing forms of communication and transport (e.g., postal system, roads/highways). Here, my goal is to explore the ways in which the triangulated Russian, Ottoman, and Iranian region experienced these global innovations. On the regional or meso level, circulation depended on and was enabled by Armenian revolutionary and activist cells and party organizational structure, activities, and operations that spun a network throughout the South Caucasian, Ottoman, and Iranian territories and beyond. ARF, the dominant Armenian political party in this period, had cells of varying size and strength on almost all continents: Africa, Asia, Europe, and North America. Circulation accelerated during the revolutionary period but existed prior to the revolutions and was only possible because of preexisting networks and global communication and transportation advances. In this chapter, I further connect circulation in the South Caucasus, Ottoman Anatolia, and Iran to each other and to the wider network to show the way in which these networks functioned and facilitated the mobility of revolutionaries. The third level, local or micro (as in *particular*), is more accurately defined as individual. By focusing on individual activists who circulated for political and sometimes personal or professional reasons, I provide a closer look at the characters themselves: their journeys, their activities, and, when possible, their thoughts. I pay particularly close attention to the South Caucasus because of its integral role as a point of intersection and circulation.

Before moving forward to the three scales of investigation, it is necessary to comment briefly at the start on who and what circulated and, through their circulation, connected revolutionary places and periods. The crisscrossing of people, mostly men, through the South Caucasus, Anatolia, and Iran and also often the Balkans and Western Europe in the late nineteenth and early twentieth centuries was not only prevalent but also, at times, astonishing in its frequency and the number of sites it affected—for example, Tiflis, Baku, Istanbul, Erzurum, Tabriz, Tehran, Sofia, Filibe/Plovdiv, Paris, and Geneva. Although women in both the ARF and the SDHP took part in propagation of ideas, transfer of arms, distribution of bullets during fighting, and even actual fighting, they do not seem to have circulated with frequency or liberty. Women activists' homes, however, served the larger circulatory network, as they sometimes became safe houses for roving activists, weapons, and print.[2] Thus, the sundry sites through which revolutionaries passed, where they visited, or where they lived for longer periods of time are all part of a wider network that connected activists, operations, and—through them—revolutions. A good percentage of these revolutionaries and activists stand out not only because of their travels but also because of their activism in at least two, if not three, of the regions and/or revolutions under discussion. In addition to men, weapons, ammunition, and print also traveled within the same circles, facilitated by revolutionary networks and advances in transportation methods, old and new. I return to this later in the chapter. In addition to the circulation of men and arms, and equally important, was the circulation of ideas and ideologies, as we see in the next two chapters.

"THE WEB OF STEEL SPREAD THROUGHOUT THE WORLD": TRANSPORT AND COMMUNICATION

In chapter 1, I discussed the significance of time-space compression and briefly alluded to the transformative advances in transportation and communication that drove it. In this section, I explore developments in the South Caucasus, Ottoman Anatolia, and Iran to demonstrate the way in which "the web of steel spread" and how new technological advances stimulated and supported time-space compression and its close companion, circulation.[3] Armenian revolutionaries used all available modes of transportation and communication, from conventional roads and mail to the relatively new and much more rapid steamship, railways, and telegraphy, to mobilize themselves as well as to circulate arms, print, and information across the three imperial frontiers of the region and beyond—to and from the Balkans, Western Europe, and even North America—all within the revolutionary period, from 1904 to 1912. Steamship, railway, and telegraphy technologies developed unequally in these regions; for example, it may not come as a surprise that it was far more developed in Europe and North America and less so in our region, more advanced in the Russian Empire (the South Caucasus, specifically) than in the Ottoman Empire (Anatolia, particularly), and palpably more developed in the Russian Empire than in Qajar Iran. For that reason, although I begin with the Ottoman and Iranian cases and bring up the Russian case in comparison, I end this chapter with a more thorough exploration of the vital South Caucasian nexus.

Technological advances in the form of steamships, railways, and telegraphy made greater inroads in the South Caucasus than in Anatolia and Iran and became part of everyday life, as reflected partly by railroad and steamship schedules and telegrams printed in local newspapers. In fact, as Charles Issawi asserts, "There were, to all intents and purposes, no railways in Iran" until the second decade of the twentieth century. At first, opposition came from Iranian subjects and the Russian state to the granting of the seventy-year Reuters concession of 1872 to a British subject to build railways from the Caspian Sea to the Persian Gulf. Naser al-Din Shah (r. 1848–1896) was forced to cancel the concession that, in effect, would have handed over control of Iran's resources to a foreigner. Later in the nineteenth century, railway schemes were thwarted by conflicting interests among European states and Russian concerns, in particular, by anxieties that railways in Iran would challenge and even weaken Russia's foothold in the Iranian market, even threatening its position in the Russian provinces by exposing them to British and German economic competition. With these reservations in mind, Russia procured an agreement from Iran that it would neither construct itself nor grant a concession to construct railways for the next ten years—an agreement that was renewed in 1900, thus preventing the realization of any railway plans, whether by the British, Germans, Iranians, or Russians themselves, for at least twenty years. In the absence of speedy railways, roads, rivers, and steamships dominated.[4] By the late nineteenth century, steamships (mostly British, Russian, and German but also Ottoman and Iranian) operated in both the Persian Gulf and the Caspian Sea, traffic in the former being spiked by the opening of the Suez Canal.[5] Although Iran itself had no railways, it likely benefited from the Russian railways' extension in 1884 southward to Baku, only about a couple of hundred kilometers from the border with Iran, as well as Black Sea steam navigation; it also benefited from Russian investment in building roads in the north, connecting a number of important cities like Tehran, Tabriz, Julfa, and others and improving Iranian ports like Anzali.[6]

European steamers also became the first to enter Ottoman waters in the second decade of the nineteenth century.[7] They carried not only goods and passengers but also mail, as in the Russian case. In fact, steamships—foreign and domestic—occupied a central place in the transportation of mail in the late nineteenth and early twentieth centuries.[8] Russian, Italian, Egyptian, French, and Austrian steamships, operating from Gallipoli and the Dardanelles to the north (Salonika) and south (Izmir, Chios, Mersin, Iskenderun, Tripoli, Beirut, and Jaffa) as well as on the Black Sea, provided international postal service.[9] An 1892 Ottoman postal guide that exclaims, "Roads are the arteries of a country and transportation vehicles are the blood," ranked steamers along with trains as the "most important" of transportation vehicles.[10] By the end of the nineteenth century, Russian steamers, like the Russian Steam Navigation and Trading Company, frequently passed between Odessa and Batumi, navigating and carrying goods, passengers, and mail on most European and Asiatic Russian rivers and lakes as well as seas, "connecting Russian harbors with the major ports of the Old and New Worlds."[11] A number of large and small navigation companies operated steamships to and from Europe and the Caucasus quite frequently, thus providing plenty of opportunities for transportation of various items and individuals.[12]

The combination of steamships, railways, and new road construction multiplied postal correspondence as well as, presumably, passengers and goods.[13] K. V. Bazilevich's table of postal transportation methods and distances traveled from 1880 to 1900 clearly demonstrates the exponential increase in those twenty years of railroad and steamer use (with the exception of transportation on lakes, which shows a dip) and distance covered; however, it also indicates a rise in the use of dirt roads.[14] Roads crossed the Caucasus Mountains from the north to or along the Black Sea coast, to or toward the Batumi-Baku railway, and to or along the Caspian coast. They ran laterally, to the east and the west, north of the Batumi-Baku railway, and south from the railway toward or over the Ottoman-Russian and Russo-Persian frontiers.[15] These roads became vital for clandestine arms transport from the late nineteenth century to the early twentieth century, transport that peaked in the revolutionary years. Bazilevich concludes, "Construction of new dirt roads and railways plus mail transportation on steamships plying rivers and lakes increased postal communications between [various] places several times over."[16] Although Russian building and improvement of roads far exceeded the efforts and results in the Ottoman and Iranian cases, in both cases, roads improved to some extent.[17] I will return to the development of the postal system when I discuss the much speedier new mode of communication, telegraphy.

Steamships

Correspondence between comrades during the revolutionary period of approximately 1904 to 1912—and in some cases earlier—confirms the key role that steamers played in enabling the circulation of individuals to and from the Balkans, Western Europe, and the Middle East, as well as the circulation of arms, munitions, and print, specifically newspapers. For example, a letter from 1 June 1905 housed in the ARF Archives reveals how, taking advantage of their ties with three French steamships, *Anatolie, Imerethie,* and *Circassie*—all of which belonged to the Compagnie de Navigation Arménienne et Marocaine and linked Marseille to Istanbul, Batumi, and Poti—the party's comrades stationed at Batumi, a vital harbor, port, and railway terminus, saw to the transport of guns, pistols, binoculars, and "close to 1/2 million bullet capsules."[18] According to the Russian intelligence service Okhrana, which kept a close eye on revolutionary activity, Batumi and Alexandropol (Leninakan in the Soviet period and today's Gyumri, Armenia) "play an important role in routing weapons through the Caucasus."[19] Revolutionaries also used Greek and

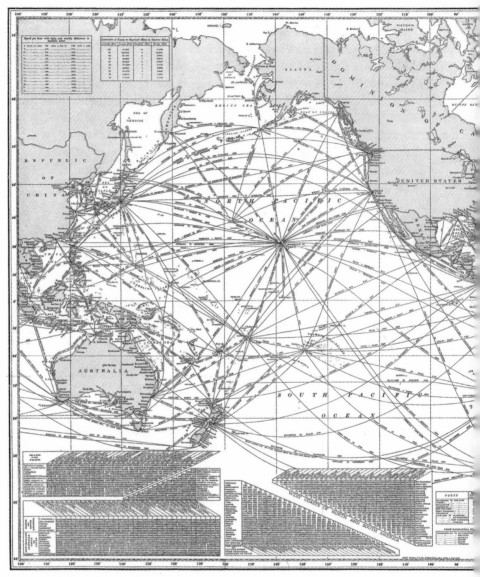

MAP 2. Global steamship routes, 1914.

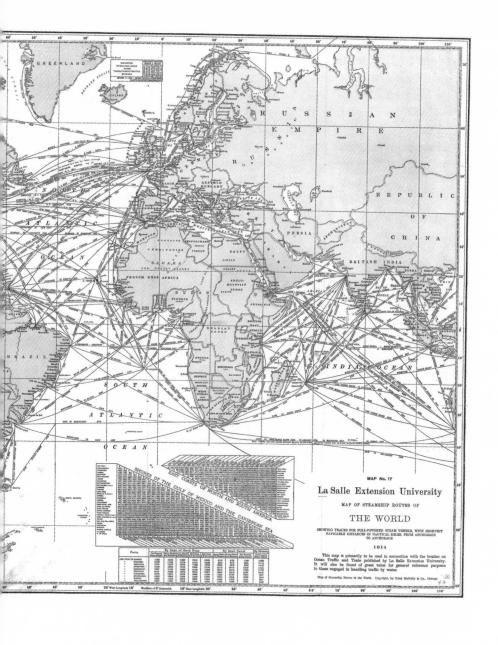

MAP No. 17

La Salle Extension University

MAP OF STEAMSHIP ROUTES OF

THE WORLD

SHOWING TRACKS FOR FULL-POWERED STEAM VESSELS, WITH SHORTEST
NAVIGABLE DISTANCES IN NAUTICAL MILES, FROM ANCHORAGE
TO ANCHORAGE

1914

This map is primarily to be used in connection with the treatise on
Ocean Traffic and Trade published by La Salle Extension University.
It will also be found of great value for general reference purposes
to those engaged in handling traffic by water.

Map of Steamship Routes of the World. Copyright, by Rand McNally & Co., Chicago

Austrian steamships.[20] Authorities, in particular Okhrana, kept abreast of efforts to procure steamships for the transfer of explosives from Switzerland, England, and Germany to Bulgaria and from there to Anatolia and the South Caucasus.[21] An Okhrana circular reveals the collaboration of the ARF and Bulgarian revolutionaries, such as anarchist Naum Tiufekchiev, with whose assistance they had obtained "a significant supply of ammunition in Sofia" along with Austrian-made rifles and pistols.[22] They did not, however, limit themselves to steamships, even considering acquiring a sailboat to transport "items in large quantities" to Batumi, an important site of strikes during the early years of the Russian Revolution.[23] Only a few months before reaching an agreement with Iranian revolutionaries for collaboration in the Iranian Constitutional Revolution, Rostom (Stepan Zorian, 1867–1919), cofounder of the ARF and one of the most itinerant of our circulating revolutionaries, even pursued the possibility of motorboats to be used in Iran. In a letter dated 21 August 1907, Rostom apprised his comrades of a meeting with Felix Badel et Cie., the Geneva representative of boat-engine vendor Gasmotoren Fabrik (which was headquartered in Cologne, Germany, with offices in Geneva and Baku), and proposed that the party purchase an engine and metal parts and assemble a boat in Iran.[24] It is unclear how frequently sailboats or motorboats came to be employed for transporting arms or newspapers, but likely it was not as often as steamships, which seem to be even more important for carrying revolutionary passengers as well as newspapers. However, steamships were more often engaged in port or near-port cities like Batumi that already had an active operative network, and, like every other method of transportation, they did not guarantee consistency of delivery. Many letters contain complaints about not receiving a sufficient number of newspapers or not receiving them at all. As one Batumi activist proclaims, for many people, newspapers—in this case, the ARF organ published in Geneva, *Drōshak* (Banner)—were "our only source from which we can reap information about Armenian revolutionary activity."[25]

Steamships, not always named, appear intermittently in our revolutionaries' correspondence; in fact, some activists are writing from the ships themselves. For example, Simon Zavarian, cofounder of the ARF (with Rostom and Kristapor Mikayelian), writes—while on a ship in the Mediterranean, bound for Beirut and Cilicia—about the "dangerous" and costly transfer of newspapers by ship from Marseille for distribution abroad (1,500–2,000 copies) and in the South Caucasus, Ottoman Anatolia, and Iran (2,000–3,000 copies), providing details of how to bundle them and specifying kilos and tighter knots.[26] Zavarian worked with comrades like Vrtanes (Varderes Ghazarian), who, according to ARF authority Hrach Dasnabedian, was very important in transporting *Drōshak* and arms by steamship from Marseille to Piraeus, Istanbul, Trabizon/Trabzon, Batum/Batumi, Cyprus, and Alexandria—all port cities or regions.[27] Armenian revolutionaries were always on the lookout for safer passages and easier ways to transfer newspapers and other items.[28] Rostom, too, wrote some of his letters from steamships—traveling, for instance, from Silistra to Ruschuk/Ruse (both on the banks of the Danube in northeastern Bulgaria) and from Vienna to Sofia (now the capital of Bulgaria) via Danube-bisected Budapest, and while awaiting a steamship in an unnamed port in Bulgaria.[29] Traveling by steamship was less expensive and more convenient than some trains.[30]

Steamships, while certainly faster than earlier modes of transportation, still involved long journeys. Zavarian, displeased about the length of a journey on the Mediterranean, writes acerbically, "Naples, Pire [Piraeus], Izmir, Istanbul, again Izmir, Beirut, Larnaka, Mersin, Iskenderun, Tripoli, Beirut, Izmir, Pire . . . you would think I was a new wine that they want to make old quickly."[31] But steamships, however imperfect, might have offered more than speed and ease of travel. They also presented their passengers with opportunities to interact, and for our revolutionaries traversing Eurasia, they became vital conduits for operatives and for tools to be employed in revolutionary struggle against autocratic regimes (whether Russian, Ottoman, or Iranian), as well as for print ,with news and propaganda that would be read (or in the case of the illiterate, heard), digested, and in some cases acted upon. Thus, steamships were instrumental in hastening the tools of revolution.

Railways

Equally important as the steamship, as a mode of transportation for passengers, goods, and post, and critical to understanding circulation of revolutionaries, arms, and literature are the railways. Steamships, railways, and the telegraph went hand in hand in contributing to a revolution in speed, both of transport and of communication, and by extension in contributing to our three revolutions.[32] Their concurrent emergence was no accident; as Daniel Headrick points out, they "grew simultaneously and interdependently" and were helped along by the improvement of canals and roads.[33] In fact, it is important to stress that old forms of transport and mail did not disappear, nor did they necessarily diminish in importance. The building or renovation of canals and roads are two

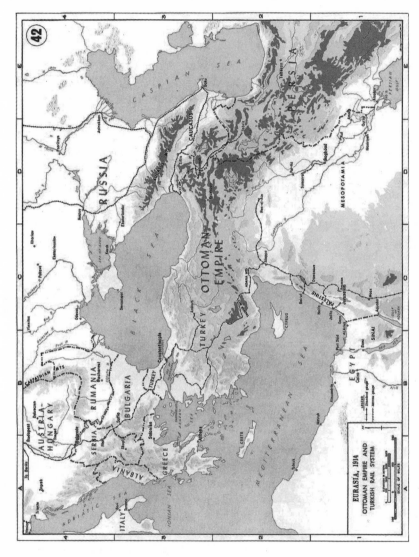

MAP 3. Ottoman and Caucasian rail, 1914. Map courtesy of the USMA, Department of History.

examples; the increase of mail is another.[34] Steamships, railways, and the telegraph had tremendous economic, social, and political consequence as they facilitated not only the transfer of goods and people but also information, news, and ideas across water, land, and air (that is, by means of telegraph wires) and altered urban and rural landscapes.[35] The second half of the nineteenth century saw the intensification of urbanization.[36] Cities became hubs of movement of "people, animals, vehicles, and goods within" the cities themselves and between them as well.[37] Railroads made a huge impact on cities. As Osterhammel contends, "No other infrastructural innovation has ever cut so deeply into the social organism of the city . . . . Railroad stations altered cityscapes: they could sometimes revolutionize the whole character of a city."[38]

Revolutionaries traveled much more easily than before, thanks in large part to the thousands of kilometers of railways built in the region. Some eight million people, for example, traveled on the Ottoman railways in 1910.[39] Moreover, the railways were built by border-crossing Kurds, Turks, Armenians, Greeks, Iranians, Slavs, and others who themselves took part in worker protests starting in the late nineteenth century and continuing through the Young Turk revolutionary period.[40] Railways had similar effects in the South Caucasus, where a "well-developed and comprehensive railway system [had] been established" since the end of the nineteenth century, with lines connecting to northern Iran.[41] Iran's railway development, however, was complicated and was halted by power plays and disagreements between major powers like Britain, Germany, Russia, and to a lesser degree France. By 1914 Iran's railroads ran merely twenty kilometers, or twelve miles.[42] As Mansour Bonakdarian explains, " . . . the trans-Iranian railway project was indefinitely postponed because of London's and St. Petersburg's failure to resolve their differences. The next time the idea of a trans-Iranian railroad was seriously entertained would be in 1925, when Reza Shah, the autocratic founder of the new Pahlavi dynasty in Iran (1925–1979), initiated his own [Iranian] scheme for constructing a line linking the Caspian littoral in the north with the Persian Gulf in the south."[43] The dismal state of speedy transportation in Iran itself, however, did not stop our roving revolutionaries from making it down to Iran from the South Caucasus and the Ottoman Empire, even if it might have slowed their journeys somewhat once in Iran.

The first railways in the Russian Empire date from the 1860s. By 1890 railroads extended from the northeastern corner of the Baltic Sea all the way south to Baku, from Odessa on the northwestern shore of the Black Sea all the way to Zlatoust on the Ay River in Russia, north of today's border with Kazakhstan.[44] By 1900 the Russian Empire had 53,234 kilometers of railroad tracks, more than Britain and India but significantly less than the United States. Ten years later, that number had increased to 66,581 and, despite carrying some 116.6 million passengers between 1900 and 1904, 148.8 million between 1905 and 1909, and 214.4 million between 1910 and 1914, its passenger numbers remained far lower than those in places like India, Britain, and Germany.[45] In 1905 alone, the Russian railways had a workforce of over three-quarters of a million, a union, and labor unrest, with, as Walter Sablinsky argues, the "highest rate of participation in strikes (100 percent) of any category of workers."[46] While the length of railroad tracks and the number of passengers did not match the numbers for other countries, they far exceeded the same numbers for the Ottoman Empire and, of course, Iran. Moreover, Russian funding and engineers enabled linkages between Russian railways and lines in the Ottoman Empire; Russia even extended some of its own railway lines into northwestern Iran.[47]

The first railroads in the Ottoman Empire, in Anatolia, appeared in the second half of the nineteenth century, with the backing of Austrian, German, and British capital, and expanded considerably in the 1890s, reaching 7,500 kilometers of track.[48] Much like the case of telegraphy, the Crimean War served as the impetus to the construction of railways, first in the Balkans, then in Anatolia, and in the late nineteenth century and early twentieth century in Syria, Iraq, and the Arabian Peninsula.[49] As Donald Quataert points out, "The railroads opened up interior regions to political control and economic development and they helped the state to shuttle troops quickly within the empire."[50] Railways also increased the circulation of people, as they carried millions of passengers. In 1908 alone, for example, the Anatolian Railway transported 1.9 million passengers; the Izmir-Kasaba line, 2.4 million; and the Izmir-Aydın line, 1.4 million. In 1911, of the 14 million passengers using the Oriental Railway, half traveled in the Balkans.[51] Not only passengers but also railway employees came into contact with Europe and, as Quataert contends, "were powerfully influenced by developments in Europe. The direct physical links between the Ottoman and European rail systems promoted the easy flow of ideas among the engineers who ran and cared for the locomotives. Also, many of the engineers and more highly skilled employees were Europeans familiar with labor syndicates or unions."[52] Therefore, although one of the primary reasons for the Ottoman government's construction of railways was to extend control over its subjects, it had the opposite effect, fomenting protest as much as railways did in the Russian

Empire. In the Ottoman Empire, strikes by railroad workers occurred as early as the 1870s and then again in 1908, weeks after the revolution. Those strikes were abetted by the creation of the first railway union in 1907, whose leadership was more than four-fifths foreign or Ottoman Christian, "certainly a reflection of actual union membership."[53]

The significance of railways did not go unnoticed by our revolutionaries. The subject peppers Simon Zavarian's correspondence of 1909 and 1910 and resulted in a contribution to *Drōshak* with the self-explanatory title, "Turkey: The Importance of Railroads."[54] In the article, Zavarian, who was very familiar with the railway systems in Europe and the United States (having personal experience with the former), links the existence of railways with economic progress and the "real rebirth" of a nation, pointing to positive developments in Rumeli (Balkans), Bursa and Aydın (in western Anatolia), and Beirut as a consequence of railroads coursing through them. He places railways at the same level as freedom of conscience and speech and other liberties, security, and justice, and believes them to be more vital for landlocked Ottoman provinces than for those near waterways.[55] For Zavarian, every whistle of a train is "equal to the beautiful speech recited about liberation and justice" and "every kilometer of every steel line is worth a school, a school that serves all . . . without distinction of language, religion, class, sex . . . " As such, his concern extended to the Ottoman state, whose union and defense, he writes, would only be strengthened by railways.[56] The key, for Zavarian, was to build railways without accruing a large debt to foreign companies and governments. Writing from Mush/Muş, in the heart of Anatolia, to a comrade a little over a year after the publication of his article, Zavarian becomes even more emphatic about the critical contribution of railways to the progress of Asia Minor. He explains that in the past, "I very much praised the role of roads and communication in terms of general progress. Now I am even more convinced that this region, *because of its being outside the roads,* is the most backward in all of Asia Minor; and it will remain that way as long as the railroad does not pass through [it]. Understand this fact well and exert all effort so that it is realized here, [and] that Tabriz-Tehran are connected to the Persian Gulf."[57] Very much like Zavarian, his comrade Rupen Zartarian, too, saw in the railways "one of civilization's life veins." Connecting economic reform and railways with progress, he adds that without railways, "our country is condemned to remain a desert where creative and free life has no place."[58]

While Zavarian and Zartarian called for more railroads linking Anatolia and Iran and were likely quite fully aware of the railroads' speed
and operational value, their comrades exploited their full capacity,
transporting arms and newspapers and also themselves, except when the
railroads were affected by strikes and track destruction. During the revolutionary struggle in the Russian Empire, when work stoppages halted
railroad transportation, no items could get through. Alexander Ter
Hakobian, an activist using the pseudonym Japonats'i (Japanese), writing in December 1905, explained that he had already received copies of
Drōshak in Saint Petersburg but could not send them to the famine-
stricken Caucasus until the end of the monthlong railway strike, adding
that communication by post or telegraph between Saint Petersburg and
the South Caucasus had also been cut for a month.[59] I will return to the
revolutionary character of the South Caucasus and the exploitation of
railways and telegraph by our revolutionaries in the service of the Russian opposition to autocracy at the end of this chapter. Suffice it to say
for now that the reach of the railways in the South Caucasus expanded
beyond it, to Ottoman Anatolia and even to Iran, connecting the three
areas and expediting and amplifying the circulation of Armenian and
other revolutionary passengers, arms, and print. The importance of the
railways, as noted earlier, was not lost on Zavarian, who saw them as a
symbol of progress; the significance also lay in the practical and tangible
impact on the flow of men and material that supported revolution.

Telegraphy

Just as the railroad vastly accelerated speed of transport, telegraphy
boosted speed of communication. The decades-long challenge of manufacturing, laying, and operating telegraph cables had been overcome by
the 1880s, and in the late nineteenth and early twentieth centuries, telegraphy experienced a rise in both speed and traffic, as "all major world
regions were brought into the network."[60] Roland Wenzlhuemer notes
that this development had a distinct impact: "It is safe to say that by 1900
global communication space had been almost completely detached from
geographic or navigational space."[61] This is a crucial revolutionary
change. As Wenzlhuemer explains, telegraphy made possible the "dema-
terialization" of information. No longer was the dissemination of information tied to objects or people: "This was what made telegraphy so
attractive to its users and what let them accept the various disadvantages
that non-material communication entailed."[62] For the time being, the

appeal was too strong and manifest to even consider drawbacks. As the telegraph linked the world in unprecedented ways, it allowed, as Bayly points out, "governments, interest groups, and radicals to concert their action at a world level. Between 1900 and 1909 the volume of press traffic on the telegraphs trebled."[63] This turn is evidenced by the number of telegrams that were exchanged between revolutionaries and their comrades within the Russian, Ottoman, and Iranian borders as well as beyond those borders in Europe. Charles Kurzman drives home the importance of the telegraph when he calls the Russian Revolution "the first revolution covered 'live' by international telegraph. . . . "[64] In the same vein, Roderic Davison calls the Young Turk Revolution a "revolution by telegraph."[65] One could apply the same labels to the Iranian Revolution.

Telegraphy was closely bound to railways, as wires followed the same tracks (with the exception, of course, of submarine cables), and much like the railways, telegraphy was, for a time, an effective instrument of government control—but ultimately, as Roderic Davison notes, "the telegraph proved to be an instrument for curbing and then for ending the six-hundred-year rule of the Ottoman dynasty."[66] Ottoman subjects could and did use the telegraph to make their grievances known to the central government, to each other, and, in the case of nondominant communities, to foreign powers.[67] Moreover, telegraphy served to disseminate news in the empire in many forms, especially stories in newspapers, and even telegraph operators became important conduits of such news.[68] Again, very much like the employees of Ottoman railways, telegraphy workers, mechanics, and operators, including station chiefs and directors at times, seem to have come largely and perhaps even disproportionately from non-Muslim subjects (Greeks, Armenians, Jews, and Levantines) of the empire—that is, those who spoke the predominant language of telegraphy at the time, French.[69]

As Daniel Headrick contends, "various parts of the transportation and communications network—shipping, railways, telegraphs, canals, port cities, and so on—grew simultaneously and interdependently"; however, telegraphy—which required less time, resources, and cost and thus was easier to construct—spread more quickly and reached some places, like Iran, much earlier than railways.[70] Like the railways, telegraphy in the Ottoman Empire and Iran owed its construction and expansion to European private funding.[71] Just as it had spurred the construction of railways, the Crimean War (1853–56), a war Russia lost to the Ottoman Empire (as well as Britain, France, and Sardinia-Piedmont), acted as the immediate stimulus of telegraphy in the Ottoman

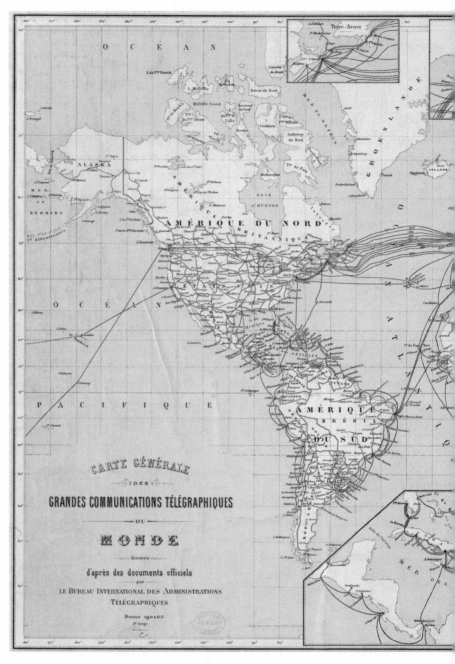

MAP 4. Global telegraphic communications, 1901/1903. Map reproduction courtesy of the Norman B. Leventhal Map Center at the Boston Public Library.

Empire. The telegraph started with an underwater cable in the Black Sea connecting Crimea with the Black Sea coastal city of Varna (in Bulgaria), followed by another cable connecting Varna to Istanbul; what ensued was what Davison calls "an orgy of extended telegraph construction" throughout the empire, not only connecting the empire's territories to each other but also connecting Ottoman lands to non-Ottoman European lands.[72] More than five million telegrams per year went out from the empire by 1914.[73]

Ayşegül Okan notes an increase of 30 percent in the number of telegraph offices from 1884 to 1892 alone throughout the empire. Although almost all vilayets (provinces) show a growth in the number of telegraph offices, the lion's share was found in cities and towns like Istanbul and Aydın (in southwestern Turkey), followed by Manastır (in southern Bulgaria), Kosovo (in southeastern Europe), Sivas (in central Anatolia), and others. The regions of Rumelia and Anatolia each had sixty telegraph offices by 1892, and presumably that number continued to increase.[74] Anyone with access to a telegraph office could send a telegram as long as the message was not deemed a threat to imperial security or to morality and was in Latin, Ottoman, or one of thirty-one other languages, including a number of Western and Eastern European languages as well as Japanese, Arabic, and Armenian.[75]

Iranian telegraphy had much in common with Ottoman telegraphy and began about the same time. In 1851 European-educated Mirza Malkom Khan, an Armenian convert to Islam, brought the idea to Naser al-Din Shah, and within six years, Iran had an intercity telegraph system.[76] The telegraph's ubiquitous lines dominated the skyline in Iran by the late nineteenth century. Iranian telegraphy also employed foreigners, particularly British, and minorities, especially Armenians, who, according to Michael Rubin, were "often fluent in both English and Persian, and invaluable staff-members and partners on the telegraph."[77] The offices of the Indo-European Telegraph Department and Indo-European Telegraph Company became a point of cultural contact between Europeans and Iranians, leading in some cases even to intermarriage with Armenians. This is not to imply that the offices were not also sites of tension, as Europeans received much higher wages than Iranians.[78] Much like Ottoman telegraphy, the multilingual Iranian telegraph experienced a two-way exchange: "Just as the telegraph allowed European officials to learn more about events in Iran, the same wires carried news of Europe to Iranian authorities."[79] Britain and later Russia recognized the importance of telegraphy in Iran. Starting in the 1860s, they enmeshed themselves in its construction, with the blessing of the Iranian government, and in expansion of the telegraph in their spheres of influence in the south and the north, respectively, made official with the Anglo-Russian agreement of 1907.[80]

In Iran, too, the telegraph became both an instrument of government control (and Iranian, British, and Russian intelligence gathering) and opposition, from the 1890s protests against the tobacco concession through the Constitutional Revolution. It is no wonder that Tabriz, the nucleus of opposition in the revolution, was also the center of telegraphy in the late nineteenth and early twentieth centuries.[81] Telegraphy became a target of strikes, and offices became places of refuge *(bast)*.[82] Iranians, too, placed restrictions on ciphered messages, although because the restrictions "proved too burdensome to honor," they might have had less impact on encrypted telegrams than similar restrictions did in the Ottoman Empire.[83] Our Armenian revolutionaries were among many telegraph users—including merchants, the Iranian state, the British, and others—who used codes of letters and numerals to send telegrams. News from within and outside Iran (for example, about the Russian Revolution and the Japanese victory over Russia) spread quickly because of telegraphy, providing much fodder for newspapers and inspiration to regime opponents and anti-imperialists. Thus, telegraphy also afforded the means by which to organize and coordinate actions. Telegrams from Iranian subjects also reached European powers, similar to the case for subjects in the Ottoman Empire.[84]

Telegraphy in all three empires became significantly more connected starting in the 1860s, with lines constructed in Iran and the Russian Empire to connect Britain to India, largely as a consequence of the 1857 Indian Mutiny, of which the British remained ignorant until it was almost too late. The Indo-European Telegraph Department took on new construction and operation, frequently making use of preexisting Iranian lines. In early 1865, the Ottoman lines joined the Indo-European line, "allowing the first uninterrupted telegraphic communication between India and Europe."[85] Another telegraphy entity, the Indo-European Telegraph Company, saw to the building of a line from Tehran to Tabriz and then across the South Caucasus to Europe. As Rubin contends, "there were more than 120 telegraph stations in Iran open to international traffic at the end of 1911."[86] These stations connected the South Caucasus to Iran and the Ottoman Empire.[87] Therefore, the Indo-European line built to link Britain and India contributed to connecting the South Caucasus, the Ottoman Empire, and Iran.[88]

Telegrams flew between Armenian revolutionary leaders and operatives. Telegrams abound in the ARF Archives; they cover a wide variety of topics, from immediately required information, items, or instructions to urgent news or reports on activities and the comings and goings of organizational members.[89] In addition to the telegrams themselves, correspondence often points to evidence of the use of telegrams, whether sent or received.[90] Money orders could be sent by telegraphy (as well as by post).[91] Rostom's letters from Filibe/Plovdiv, Geneva, possibly the South Caucasus, and Istanbul or Karin (Erzurum) to one of ARF's highest bodies, the Western Bureau, and to Kristapor Mikayelian and Simon Zavarian point to money transfers by telegraph.[92] Moreover, "friends" or "comrades" at the telegraph office could be conduits of news.[93] Telegrams themselves could divulge quick news of possible conspiracies or treacheries that would need immediate handling, as in the case of an operative, concerned about confidential information being leaked, who stated that days after being informed by ARF's Rasht branch on the Caspian coast that 320 bombs were ready in Tiflis, they found out from telegrams that 319 of the bombs had been discovered by authorities and several people had been arrested.[94]

The advent of telegraphy raised, to some degree, the expectations of speedy communication, and despite telegraphy's advantage over other modes like post, it remained an imperfect system.[95] Nevertheless, telegraphy, as the swiftest and most immediate form of communication available in the early twentieth century and as a means by which to share or disseminate news, to transmit instructions, or to communicate with greater confidence of confidentiality, had, by the early twentieth century, become—perhaps more so than the steamship, railways, and postal system—so familiar and pervasive that not only urban dwellers and, of course, our revolutionaries but also rural populations resorted to it.

Post

The telegraph, of course, did not do away with the post, despite its speed, as post continued and continues to serve a different purpose and satisfy a different market, even in the age of cyberspace. Although in the case of our revolutionaries, both were used to inform, propagate, instruct, and organize, the telegraph had an immediacy that post did not—yet one could not send books, newspapers, and long letters by telegraph. The telegraph served a complementary role to post, which expanded and became more efficient starting in the mid- to late nineteenth century in the Ottoman,

Russian, and Iranian states, all of which joined a connected global postal network, signing onto the General Postal Union within a few years after the Bern Postal Congress (1874) in order to coordinate postal policies and standards and to ensure that all post operated efficiently.[96]

The close relationship between telegraphy and post is reflected in the merging of their administration in 1871 in the Ottoman Empire as well as in the Russian Empire in 1884.[97] Ottoman postal services faced competition from European post offices—first Austrian, then Russian and French, Greek, Egyptian and Italian in the 1860s, and German in 1870. Starting in 1876, the Ottoman Empire took on delivery of international mail, which until then had been carried out by European post offices throughout the empire.[98] While Ottoman post offices were scattered throughout the Ottoman Empire, most of them in Anatolia, half of the Austrian offices were in Rumelia, on the European side of the empire.[99] Port cities housed the greatest number of European post offices. For example, in the late nineteenth century, Austria, which possessed the dominant foreign postal service, ran 42 post offices, of which 28 were in port cities, compared to 829 Ottoman post offices in the interior and 204 in port cities.[100] These numbers come as no surprise, given European steamer traffic in ports and the critical role of steamships in transporting international and Ottoman mail quickly. According to Okan, Greek and Armenian merchants prized the European steamships' speed of transport.[101] Of course, as noted earlier, so did revolutionaries. In Russia as well, steamships took on the bulk of postal transport starting in the late nineteenth century, supplemented by local post offices that sprang up.[102] The introduction of new modes of transportation like the railways, starting in the mid-nineteenth century, also greatly facilitated transport of mail as they began to be used along with steamships, cutting delivery time steeply; the reduction had to do with not only the speed of railways compared to horse-drawn carriages but also the creation of mail cars in which postal workers sorted mail while "en route, further reducing the time it took to process items."[103] These developments had a tremendous impact on the number of letters and packages sent, increasing postal communication 537.8 percent between 1875 and 1900, but they did not completely replace postal relays, which depended on postal/relay stations located across vast areas and riders who would often hand over their mail to other riders at the stations until the mail reached its final destination.[104]

Fearing sedition of any kind, the Ottoman postal administration routinely opened envelopes and packages and inspected documents to prevent entry of "*evrak-ı muzzırra* (harmful papers), i.e., newspapers and documents from Europe in opposition to the reign of Abdülhamid II."[105] An Armenian-language newspaper in Tiflis declared that the Ottoman "post is a trap," cautioning readers that all letters coming from Erzurum to Russia were being opened and read.[106] Foreign postal services, however, may have "contributed much to [the] distribution of these journals secretly"; they were also often under suspicion and "raided incessantly and their post baggage was investigated rigorously," as Ottoman employees were arrested and exiled. Okan emphasizes, however, that Ottoman post offices, too, especially in the cosmopolitan and commercial center of Galata (today's Karaköy in Istanbul) let in "harmful papers."[107] Nevertheless, the relatively limited censorship compared to Ottoman post (at least until its lifting in 1908) most probably explains why Armenian activists exclusively used European postal services to circulate letters, bundles of newspapers, and even arms. As most of the Ottoman postal service's employees were minority subjects of the empire, they came under suspicion—sometimes for valid reasons, other times not.[108] To some degree, from the late nineteenth century on, suspicion, along with reporting on suspicious activity (i.e., espionage), had become "an important part of Ottoman daily life" under Sultan Abdülhamid. This was in good part because of the advancements in communication and transportation and the subsequent increase in movement of activists, arms, and print and in dissemination of ideas deemed threatening to the sultan's unchecked rule. Intelligence reports *(jurnal)* created by official, professional, and more commonly "amateur" reporters *(jurnalcı),* who often received some material benefit for the information they provided, informed on those believed to be conspiring against the state and were so numerous and wide-reaching that they "inform[ed] and interfere[d] with everything . . . the roots penetrat[ing] the remotest parts of society."[109] Armenian activists and the Young Turks seemed to be a central concern of such surveillance and reporting.[110] According to the contemporary writer and critic of the Ottoman state, Ibrahim al-Muwaylihi, the Armenian community had been a special target of surveillance and spying. He writes:

> The restriction and supervision of their activities were so awful as to beggar description. If a spy discovered a drawing on a cigarette carton or box of matches that looked like a sail, oar, rudder, or any other part of a ship, he would immediately take the item away. He would then write a report in which the Armenians would be accused of demanding independence. After all, they were employed in that type of trade, and the drawing in question portrayed a ship, which is a symbol of authority in their culture. Anything with a picture on it would be thrown on the fire. The Minister of Police would set to work, investigating, cross-examining, and searching diligently

for the society created with the purpose of demanding independence. Spies used to spread out far and wide to uncover members of this 'society.' Some were put in prison, others were exiled, all via official decrees that were referred to his attention. The government imposed travel restrictions on Armenians which blocked their escape routes. Every ship leaving Istanbul is watched by no less than ten spies until the moment of departure.[111]

The Armenian activists' experience in transporting materials, including newspapers, even led to the solicitation of assistance from the anti-Hamidian Prince Sabaheddin, who requested that the ARF see to the transfer of his League of Private Initiative and Decentralization's organ, *Terakki* (Progress), from Europe through the South Caucasus and into the Ottoman Empire.[112] *Terakki* first appeared in Paris in April 1906 and served to transmit the league's views of decentralization. The agreement between the league and the ARF to help transport and circulate the organ soon after it first appeared reflected a rather close and mutually beneficial relationship that went far beyond print circulation, as I discuss in the next chapter. It extended to collaboration in the Eastern Anatolian revolts, including "smuggl[ing] a member of the League," Hüseyin Tosun, who was also at the Ottoman Congress of 1902 in Paris, into Eastern Anatolia "to organize joint revolutionary activities."[113] Hüseyin Tosun's travels from Paris to Tiflis and then across the Ottoman border, his access to passports to cross frontiers, and his subsequent appointment as the Russian consulate's mail carrier, "an assignment that must have helped him distribute banned publications and proclamations," were all made possible by the ARF, which by this point had become one of the master circulators in the region, smuggling men and print across frontiers.[114]

In Iran, censorship was further limited during times of upheaval or political crisis, in particular during the Constitutional Revolution, and with the intent to prevent the spread of information perhaps deemed threatening to the Qajar government, postal authorities tried to control all mail, opening items from particular senders or addresses. The Constitutional Revolution prompted the first attempt at "systematic control" of all post in the most important cities in the western part of Iran.[115] In some cases, this led to the banning of certain newspapers' entry into Iran. For example, on 3 July 1906, for the first time the Iranian Postal and Customs Ministry prohibited the import of the ARF organ, *Drōshak*, along with "other revolutionary brochures," and ordered the immediate confiscation and destruction of all copies of the paper as well as revolutionary pamphlets.[116] *Drōshak* believed the Qajar government had given in to Russian pressure, while a high-ranking member of the party, Stepan

Stepanian, claimed that Ottoman, Caucasian Azeri, and rival SDHP intrigue were responsible.[117] In July 1906 Iranian authorities destroyed 2,500 copies of *Drōshak* in Tabriz and 1,170 in Anzali.[118] Protest letters and telegrams were sent to the foreign affairs minister in Tehran as well as to the Iranian embassies in Berlin and Paris.[119] Moreover, comrades in the Azerbaijan province of Iran and the Qajar capital, Tehran, simultaneously attempted to have the order rescinded and to find ways to elude it. For example, in Anzali, an ARF member who was on good terms with the assistant to the local postal director received advice on how to continue to import *Drōshak* undetected and conveyed that information to the paper's staff in Geneva. Thus, while the organ no longer reached certain areas, by December 1906 *Drōshak* reentered Anzali.[120]

Revolutionary movements and wars—the Russo-Japanese War, for instance—also propelled censorship in the Russian Empire. However, as Alison Rowley explains, Russian censorship was a cut above that practiced by the Iranian government and was perhaps more similar to the Ottoman case, as it targeted specific groups and individuals deemed revolutionary or already "under arrest, in prison or in exile . . . By law, those in exile were required to use postcards to correspond with relatives," a practice that also made an appearance under Sultan Abdülhamid II.[121] The Russian state's reach went beyond the empire, with undercover agents in foreign post offices in places such as Romania, Bulgaria, Serbia, Austria, Germany, and France. In response, revolutionaries created "a network of couriers . . . to smuggle mail. The repeal of censorship laws at the time of the 1905 Revolution allowed revolutionary organizations to become more public in their activities, particularly in the publishing sphere."[122] In all cases, despite or because of censorship, activists found ways to circumvent it and find ways to carry on with circulation of newspapers and books and even arms. In addition to the example of *Drōshak* in Iran, Armenian activists operating in Odessa tried to elude Russian censors by taking advantage of a loophole: while all other print entering the Russian Empire had to pass through censors, Armenian books could go through Odessa's Armenian priest, who apparently had agreed to assist activists.[123]

A few words about the relationship between Armenian revolutionaries and the Armenian Church are necessary in order to contextualize the role of this particular Odessa priest in helping activists. It is now commonplace to assume that the Armenian Apostolic Church as a national church has historically been the preserver of Armenian national identity, and it is indeed true that the church has played an important role in national leadership; however, the relationship of revolutionaries and the church is rather complex. On the whole, turn-of-the-century revolutionaries saw the church as a conservative institution more concerned about maintaining the status quo and its interests than about getting actively involved in political developments. While the church itself did not promote an official position on any political party, some priests did assist activists and operations, including providing sanctuaries for roving revolutionaries and arsenals or transfer points, like the Saint Thadeus Monastery in northwestern Iran, for their weapons.[124]

The postal system served yet another purpose. Like telegraphy, it facilitated money transfers throughout the revolutionary network, whether from Istanbul to Geneva (by Austrian post) or from the United States to Alexandria (by French post).[125] Although not a perfect system, judging by complaints especially about Iran's postal system, parcel post even became the preferred method by which to collect the ARF's documents.[126] Not all things could be handled by post, steamship, or railways; some items needed to travel with their carriers and be delivered personally, whether they were letters smuggled by couriers across imperial frontiers or delicacies like *pastırma* handled by operatives in Anatolia itself.[127]

On the whole, all the Russian, Ottoman, and Qajar domains underwent profound changes in technologies of communication and transportation. The late nineteenth and early twentieth centuries experienced the growth of post offices as well as the improvement of postal roads and transportation vehicles, especially railways after 1890, which were also important for mail transport.[128] A parallel development occurred in Iran with the improvement or construction of roads under Russian initiation and post offices along these roads, which were also linked to the telegraph network in 1905.[129] The upgrading of roads facilitated the growth of the modern postal system, which began to be organized under Naser al-Din Shah with the help of Austrian postal experts.[130] Turn-of-the-century time-space compression may have affected Iran differently and unequally, but no doubt without the increased ease and speed of communication (whether by telegraph or post) and of transportation (whether by steamship, railway, or improved roads), the extent in distance and frequency of circulation of revolutionaries, weapons, print, and even money would have been significantly hampered if not, in some cases, made impossible. Contemporaries like Zavarian recognized the global impact of these new technologies: "That human relations are facilitated day to day because of telegraph lines, railways, steamships and that all countries get closer to each other—about this there is no doubt. It is possible today to pass from Istanbul to Paris in four days, while before four months was needed for that trip. Everywhere now provisions are used that are not local and are received from the globe's various corners."[131] However vital and potent, though, technological advances proved to be an additional and essential element that worked best in unison with an already rich and multifarious network of revolutionaries or operatives reaching as far east as Iran and as far west as North America.

THE PARTY NETWORK AND CIRCULATING COMRADES

During its first two years, from 1890 to 1892, the center of the ARF remained in Tiflis, the city where it was founded. It already had cells in the North and South Caucasus (in Baku, Batumi, and Yerevan) as well as to the east in Asia Minor (in Kars, Karin/Erzurum, Taron, Sasun, Van, and Trabzon), to the south in Iran (in Tabriz, in the Azerbaijan province), and to the west in the Balkans (in Romania and Bulgaria) and in Istanbul.[132] By the beginning of the twentieth century, cells sprouted in more areas, expanding further in the South Caucasus (in Alexandropol/Gyumri, New Nakhijevan, and Gandzak/Ganja), Russia (in Moscow and Saint Petersburg), and the Crimean Peninsula and Odessa (in Ukraine), as well as Asia Minor (in Dersim, Akhlat, Izmir, Sebastia/Sivas, Samson/Samsun, Marzvan/Marsovan/Merzifon, Kessaria/Kayseri, Kharpert/Harput, Tikranakert/Diyarbakır, and Cilicia), Egypt, Cyprus, Western Europe (e.g., in Geneva and Paris), and North America.[133]

According to Hrach Dasnabedian, a member and historian of the party, the ARF from its foundation remained organizationally decentralized and committed to decentralization not only as a political ideology (which I will discuss in the next chapter) but in practice.[134] This decentralized structure is lucidly reflected in Rostom's letter to the leading ARF figure in Iran, Samson Tadeosian, in which Rostom, frustrated by the constant appeals to the Bureau, exclaims, "you [pl.] again with the Bureau." Rostom emphatically reminds Tadeosian that members need not continually appeal to the party's highest-ranking body, the Bureau, before making a move, and he insists on acting independently according to local conditions and needs.[135]

Two bureaus existed: the Western Bureau was headquartered in Geneva (with a Turkish section in Istanbul after 1909) and the Eastern Bureau in Tiflis (with a section in Erzurum after 1909). Their jurisdiction corresponded roughly, with some exceptions, to the historic division of eastern and western Armenian populations in the Russian Empire and Iran (Eastern Bureau) and the Ottoman Empire, Europe, and North America (Western Bureau).[136] Most of the cells in the network named above had at least 1,000 active members each, and some had far more, as each had an elected central committee, which required at least 1,000 members.[137] By 1907 the number of central committees had reached twenty-one. They were responsible for the daily decisions and operations governing local cells and committees and for relations with other central committees, whereas the Eastern and Western Bureaus maintained responsibility for implementing decisions reached in party congresses. The ARF reported 165,000 members in over three thousand groups throughout the Ottoman Empire, the Caucasus, Iran, the Balkans, and the United States.[138] This number seems rather exaggerated and unsupported by evidence. Since the ARF had by 1907 twenty-one central committees, and each central committee required at least 1,000 members, we may conclude that the party probably had at least 21,000 members and, of course, possibly more. This number included women members, who, for example, formed about 30 percent of the total ARF membership in all of Iran.[139]

After the 1907 change to the party program, the ARF divided membership into active members (that is, those who took part in the organization and paid a fee of 2 percent of their income) and auxiliary members (that is, those who accepted the party program and helped out financially but did not follow the regulations and tactics of the organization).[140] Active members had an operational role and served the organization by going wherever the party's needs and local circumstances directed them.[141] ARF cofounders Rostom, Zavarian, and Mikayelian, about whom we have the most information, thus circulated throughout this network. Not all active members circulated or took part in the more revolutionary activities and operations of arms transfer, military collaboration, and other similar undertakings, but many in addition to the top leadership did. Reminiscent of the fourteenth-century traveler Ibn Battuta, whose travels were facilitated by a wide network of Muslim communities from Africa to East Asia, the Armenian operatives/revolutionaries took advantage of a network of ARF cells, with members who assisted circulation by providing a community with similar political vision and goals and the paraphernalia of travel, including passports. Correspondence between revolutionaries indicates that whenever possible or necessary, operatives made use of passports (*ants'agir*, or document of passage) to move across regional and state frontiers. Although Russia and Iran had an agreement in place by 1844 that required that subjects possess "explicit written permission of their administrations" in order to cross the border and that "passport rules for Transcaucasia were stricter than for the rest of the empire," Moritz

Deutschmann questions the extent to which such policies were carried out. As for the Ottoman case, according to David Gutman, control over mobility remained "largely ineffective" during the Hamidian period, only to be replaced after the Young Turk Revolution of 1908 with "freedom of mobility . . . both within and outside the empire's borders." The Young Turk government did not require documents of passage, although it did require identification documents for steamer travel.[142]

Several letters mention passports being offered and procured by activists. For example, Rostom writes about the availability of Dutch, Belgian, American, Cypriot, and Iranian passports for party members making their way across the Russian, Iranian, and Ottoman frontiers.[143] In a letter to his comrade Kristapor Mikayelian, Rostom encloses a French passport and lists several other passports in his possession. "Please be aware that we have ready: 1) one Persian passport . . . 2) [one] American . . . 3) [and one] Cypriot."[144] In another letter, he maintains, "It is possible to find as many Belgian and Dutch passports as you want."[145] And in yet another, he encloses a passport for a man and a woman, adding that he will be sending a second "Jewish" passport to Athens, and that if another Jewish passport is needed, to ask by telegram and not post.[146] "Jewish" passports may refer to Ottoman passports for Jewish subjects of the empire. Unlike Qajar passports, which did not indicate religion, Ottoman passports identified the religion of the holder (e.g., "Israelite") in both Ottoman and French. Another possibility could be that they sought European passports with Jewish names. Given that Rostom's letter was most likely written in July 1904, the latter speculation might be closer to the truth at least in one case. Kristapor Mikayelian makes at least two references, in July and September 1904, to traveling as a "Jewish merchant" named Shmuel Faïn as he made his way from Athens to Izmir on his way to Istanbul.[147]

Imperial borders were much easier to cross in the early twentieth century, when control over land remained more important than control over people. This changed later in the century, when nation-states began to "monopol[ize] . . . legitimate means of movement."[148] For instance, as Richard Schofield and more recently Sabri Ateş point out, despite British-led efforts to establish an internationally recognized Iranian-Ottoman frontier in the mid-nineteenth century (1843–1876), as Ateş writes, "control of this ill-defined and highly porous expanse and the peoples inhabiting it shifted frequently, as it continued to be a place of perpetual motion, of separation as well as crossing and mixing." It was not until 1914 that an Iranian-Ottoman land boundary was established.[149] Even across this "porous expanse," passports—legally obtained or not—nevertheless assisted and expedited frontier crossings and circulation, especially because "every empire had its open flanks," as the Russian Empire did in the Caucasus.[150] The frequency with which activists traveled between cities and across frontiers illustrates and reinforces the larger argument about the significance of time-space compression in enabling circulation and encounters, as well as the vital role of preexisting networks of party cells and members in making participation and collaboration in revolution feasible.

Who were these historical actors on the move?

I have alluded to some of them already, but a more detailed examination of the rich details of their peripatetic lives will help further elucidate their crossings and the impact of technologies of communication and transportation and will help us gain an appreciation of the polyglot and radical world in which they operated. The crisscrossing of intellectuals and revolutionaries within the South Caucasus, Anatolia, and Iran was quite ubiquitous in the late nineteenth and early twentieth centuries. Several individuals are conspicuous not only because of their numerous travels across and beyond the Russian, Ottoman, and Iranian frontiers but also because of their political activism in at least two, if not three, of these regions, in preparation for revolution or in actual collaboration with fellow revolutionaries during revolution. Rostom shows up in all three regions during revolution.[151]

Rostom was born into an overlapping cultural zone that unambiguously reflected the time and space of the nineteenth-century South Caucasus, in the village of Tsghna, in Goghtan, Nakhijevan, in Russian-ruled South Caucasus (today an exclave of Azerbaijan), bordering Armenia to the east and north, Iran to the south and west, and Turkey to the northwest. His first years of schooling were in his hometown and in Tiflis, where his parents enrolled him in an Armenian school. In his mid- to late teens, Rostom attended a state school and later the Novo-Alexandria Institute of Agriculture and Forestry in Warsaw, from which he was expelled for taking part in student protests, banned from attending other schools, and exiled to his hometown in Nakhijevan by the tsarist government. These obstacles, however, did not impede Rostom: he obtained a passport under a different surname, Abrahamian; traveled to Tiflis, where he met up with his friend Kristapor Mikayelian and attempted to set up a secret press; then traveled to Baku, and having passed the entrance exams as Abrahamian, entered Moscow's Petrovskaya Agricultural Academy, where Simon Zavarian was studying as well.[152]

Rostom's case is particularly interesting. He traveled to meetings and congresses, and he lived and worked in Bulgaria (especially Filibe/Plovdiv and Sofia but also Varna, on the Black Sea coast), Vienna, Geneva, Tiflis, Baku, Tabriz, Tehran, Istanbul, Erzurum/Karin, Van, and other sites. Rostom's surviving letters testify to his circulation. As early as 1893, Rostom was in Romania, trying to set up the ARF's organ, *Drōshak*. He found the political environment there suffocating, exclaiming, "I am drowning here; there is no air." He moved Mikayelian's Armenian typeface to Geneva and made the Swiss city *Drōshak's* home. Three years later, using an Iranian passport and passing himself off as a samovar merchant, he traveled through Karin to Trabzon.[153] In 1898 Rostom lived in Geneva and worked on *Drōshak;* from 1899 to 1902 he supervised ARF activities in Bulgaria, including collaboration with Macedonians; in 1903 he was in the South Caucasus as a leading figure in the struggle against Russian confiscation of Armenian church properties; from 1904 to 1905 he traveled between the South Caucasus (especially Tiflis) and Geneva; from 1905 to 1906, at the height of clashes between Armenians and Azeris and the Russian Revolution, he was in the South Caucasus, and he even met with Father Gapon, whose leadership of a peaceful protest in Saint Petersburg to present Tsar Nicholas II with a petition led to the infamous Bloody Sunday on January 22, 1905, one of the most significant events of the Russian Revolution. According to Rostom, Gapon proposed collaboration in early 1905.[154] In 1907 Rostom was in Bulgaria and visited Stuttgart, Germany, to attend a meeting of the Second Socialist International; in 1908 and part of 1909 he was in Tabriz and Tehran, collaborating with Iranian constitutionalists and revolutionaries; in 1909 he was in Tabriz, taking part in some military maneuvers against royalists, and in Istanbul, strengthening bonds with Young Turks who had carried out a revolution against the Ottoman sultan in July 1908. In 1910 Rostom lived in Istanbul and Erzurum/Karin, continuing his political and educational work. From 1911 until his death in 1918, Rostom worked in and traveled to several places in the Ottoman Empire (Erzurum, Kars, and Van), the South Caucasus (Baku), Iran (Qazvin), and Europe (London and Stockholm). Rostom's comrades recognized that "he lived a wandering life, completely devoted to his 'work.'" An anecdote narrated by a comrade is telling and reflective of his migratory existence. Hovsep Tadeosian recounts, "one day in Tiflis, on the street, Rostom meets his wife." Rostom's wife, Yeghsapet (Liza) Melik-Shahnazarian, surprised to run into him, asks, "When did you arrive?" Rostom responds, "It's been seven days . . . but I was very busy; I wasn't able to pass by the house." His wife replies, "Fine . . . when you have time, drop by the house, too."[155] It is worth noting that in addition, or in between visits to or stays in these cities, Rostom moved from city to city within days, weeks, or months of each other, and often traveled back and forth—for example, from Filibe/Plovdiv and Sofia, Geneva and Vienna, or Tiflis and Tabriz. Rostom may have been an exception in the number of sites and the frequency of travel, yet his journeys across frontiers, during tumultuous political moments and struggles, were also much more widespread than one might assume. His comrades Kristapor Mikayelian (1859–1905) and Simon Zavarian (1866–1913) paved a similar path.

Mikayelian was born near Rostom's birthplace in the town of Agulis in Goghtan, Nakhijevan, where he received his early education at an Armenian school; he went on to a teacher-training college in Tiflis at the age of seventeen and began his involvement in the People's Will (Narodnaya Volya) movement, a nineteenth-century Russian populist movement centered on the peasantry that remained one of the most important influences on the development of socialism in the region. After graduation he returned to his hometown as a teacher and continued to travel to Tiflis. In 1885 he audited courses at the Petrovskaya Agricultural Academy for about a year and a half and then returned to Tiflis, where his efforts to set up a secret press with Rostom, whom he already knew, failed because of the absence of funds. By 1890 both Rostom and Zavarian had returned to Tiflis and had committed to launching the Federation of Armenian Revolutionaries, as the Armenian Revolutionary Federation was first called.[156] Mikayelian spent the last few years of the nineteenth century and the first few years of the twentieth century (1896–1904) in Tiflis and Baku as well as in Geneva, Paris, Sofia, and Berlin. In the last year of his life, 1904, in preparation for the attempted assassination of Sultan Abdülhamid II, Mikayelian made his way through Sofia, Geneva, Paris, Athens, Izmir, Istanbul, and Filibe/Plovdiv.[157] Assassinations and terror tactics were not the sole recourse of Armenian revolutionaries. In fact, starting in the 1880s, a spate of attacks—first by Russian radicals of the People's Will, followed by others in Western Europe, anarchists and nationalists alike—indicated a new era in which terrorists (ահաբեկիչ/ahabekich‘, a self-ascribed term)[158] were "acting for a world audience of news agencies, newspapers . . . " and so forth.[159]

Mikayelian's trip to Paris in July 1904 was particularly productive in this regard. In addition to meetings with comrades and European Armenophiles like James Bryce, Pierre Quillard, and others, Mikayelian mentions going "shopping" in a few of his letters.[160] Unlike most shoppers in Paris, however, Mikayelian was not in the market for the latest high fashions, although, as he explains in one of his letters, he did shop for other cutting-edge material:

MAP 5. Rostom on the move, 1893–1918. Map created by Bill Nelson.

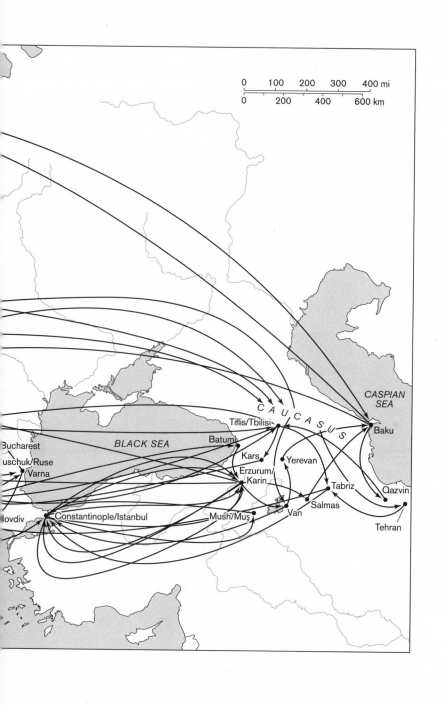

CASPIAN
SEA

Tiflis/Tbilisi
Batumi
BLACK SEA
Bucharest
uschuk/Ruse
Varna
Kars
Yerevan
Erzurum/
Karin
Tabriz
Baku
Qazvin
Salmas
Tehran
lovdiv
Constantinople/Istanbul
Mush/Muş
Van

C A U C A S U S

FIGURE 1. Kristapor Mikayelian, Rostom (Stepan Zorian), Simon Zavarian. Image reproduced courtesy of the ARF Central Committee. Source: *Hushamatean Hay Heghap'okhakan Dashnakts'ut'ean albom-atlas*, vol. 1, *Diwts'aznamart* [Commemorative album-atlas of the Armenian Revolutionary Federation, vol. 1, Heroic combat] (Glendale, CA: ARF Central Committee, 1992).

> I completed the most important and major part of my shopping yesterday. A novelty that will have great significance for us . . . I found here a gentleman, a known manufacturer, who advised me to pick up a completely new explosive; its convenience is that the important part may be sent to every free country as an innocent commodity, and the other part being found in those countries you may prepare as much as you want. Last night I was with him and learned the preparation method, which is very easy and simple; trying out its strength was the only thing left and giving in to my pleas, he promised to take me tomorrow to a village and carry out experiments. Let's see.[161]

This new explosive material, which Rostom called "Ellen's discovery" (Ellen was one of Mikayelian's pseudonyms) ended Mikayelian's life during experiments in Bulgaria in preparation for the attack on Sultan Abdülhamid II. His comrades took up the attempt to assassinate the sultan in 1905 but failed.[162] Although Mikayelian's death came before the fervent revolutionary period and his circulation predates the revolutions, his itinerant lifestyle and his activities across empires in preparation for revolutionary work were largely emblematic of those who came immediately after him and his own contemporaries, like Rostom and Simon Zavarian.

Zavarian, too, hailed from the Russian-ruled South Caucasus, the village of Igahat/ Aygehat in Lori in today's northern Armenia, bordering Georgia. He also attended Petrovskaya Agricultural Academy, where he met Rostom and Mikayelian. After graduating in 1889, he went to Tiflis, where the initial meetings regarding the establishment of the ARF took place. He traveled to Trabzon in 1890, where he was arrested by Ottoman authorities, accused of revolutionary activity, and exiled.[163] He spent

FIGURE 2. Rostom with his wife, Yeghsapet, and daughter, Taguhi. Image reproduced courtesy of the ARF Central Committee. Source: *Hushamatean Hay Heghap'okhakan Dashnakts'ut'ean albom-atlas*, vol. 1, *Diwts'aznamart* [Commemorative album-atlas of the Armenian Revolutionary Federation, vol. 1, Heroic combat] (Glendale, CA: ARF Central Committee, 1992).

about a year of his exile in Kishinev (Russian-ruled Bessarabia; now Chişinău, capital of Moldova), after which he returned to Tiflis, where he lived and worked until 1902.[164] His letters indicate that Zavarian spent that year in Europe dividing his time between Berlin, Paris, and Geneva. In Geneva he joined the editorial board of the ARF organ *Drōshak*. From 1903 to 1904 he traveled on organizational missions to Sofia and Vienna, followed in 1904 and 1905, during the height of the Russian Revolution, by time in Odessa, Alexandropol/Gyumri, Tiflis, Lausanne, and Beirut. He spent part of 1905 in Egypt, especially Alexandria, and returned to Tiflis, where he worked in collaboration with antitsarist forces and on the ARF's local paper, *Haṛaj* (Forward).[165] The record of Zavarian's correspondence for the years from 1906 to 1908 is sketchy: no letters have survived from 1906 and 1907, when he was most likely in the South Caucasus, and very few have survived from the year of the Young Turk Revolution, 1908, when he began residing in Istanbul, after fleeing the Stolypin crackdown on political activity and the persecution of all revolutionaries in the South Caucasus.[166] The reinstitution of constitution, new freedoms, and cooperation between Young Turks and the ARF propelled Zavarian to spend the bulk of his time from 1909 until his death in 1913 in Istanbul and eastern Anatolia (Izmir, Erzurum, and Muş), trying to maintain amicable relations with the ruling Young Turks, despite his increasing pessimism, as well as teaching and collecting data on the Armenian peasantry.[167] He also wrote for the local *Azatamart* (Battle for freedom), founded in July 1909 in Istanbul by the ARF.

The number of sites these three comrades visited and in which they lived and operated reflects the extent of the network of the party cells and members and also the advances in transportation—that is, steamships and railways—which accelerated and eased their travels. Despite the expanses covered, this list of places is not comprehensive; for example, the list does not necessarily include the numerous general congresses of the ARF that they attended (1898 in Tiflis, 1904 in Sofia, 1907 in Vienna, 1909 in Varna, 1911 in Istanbul, and others). However, the places should serve to provide an accurate impression of the extent and frequency with which the men crossed imperial boundaries as they propagated, organized, and collaborated in revolutionary activity. They are obviously not the only ones who circulated, but the records—mainly, several hundred letters—of their itinerant practices are much more abundant and reveal, if not fully, at least in some measure, the larger reality of the period's revolutionaries. For example, Nikol Duman (Nikoghayos Ter Hovhannesian), who was educated in the South Caucasus, traveled as a teacher and activist to northern Iran, returned to the South Caucasus in 1905, escaped arrest in 1909, and took part in the Iranian Constitutional Revolution near its end in 1911.[168] The trajectories of revolutionary leader and later chief of police Yeprem Khan Davitian, Keri (Arshak Gavafian), Martiros Charukhchian, and Dashnakts'akan Khecho (Khachatur Amirian) from activism and militancy in the South Caucasus to the Iranian Constitutional Revolution are very similar.[169] Vaso Khachaturian, a member of the Russian Social Democratic Workers' Party in Baku and activist in the Russian Revolution, also served with the *mojahedin* in Tabriz starting in 1908.[170] Others, like Sebuh (Arshag Nersesian), got their start in Ottoman Anatolia and ended up in revolutionary Iran and the Caucasus.[171] Matsun Khecho (Grigor Mirzabegian) took a different route, starting in Iran, joining militants in the South Caucasus in 1905, working in the Minerva oil fields (owned by Hambartsum Melikian) in Baku, organizing workers there during the Russian Revolution, and returning to Iran in time to defend Tehran against royalist forces.[172] Still others took a path less traveled. Khachatur Malumian (pseudonym Aknuni) left the South Caucasus for Europe, working for the party's organ, *Drōshak,* and helping establish the party's student union in Europe. His most important mission, however, was taking part in talks and negotiations with the Young Turks Prince Sabaheddin and Ahmet Rıza in Paris in 1907. Writing from Istanbul in August 1908, soon after the victory of the Young Turks in July, Malumian expressed his enthusiasm at seeing the opposition succeed: "you cannot imagine how happy I am that I can write to you from this city . . . I am shouting 'freedom' . . . after 30 years of silence, it is possible to roar . . . for 30 days."[173] After brief stints in Izmir and Egypt for organizational activity, Malumian went to America in 1910 for a year; there he wrote *Depi Yerkir* (To the land or country) and *Boghok'i Dzayn* (Voice of protest). The latter appeared in English as *Political Persecution: Armenian Prisoners in the Caucasus* to draw attention to the plight of Armenian prisoners and raise funds on their behalf. His efforts did not meet with great success.[174]

Many activists took advantage, of course, of the network of party members and allies within and across frontiers and were sometimes arrested or detained as they tried to make their way.[175] They mobilized for revolutionary activity from one region in the triangulated zone to another, yet what remains particularly striking is the dominant position and function of the South Caucasus as a pivotal site—whether as a place of origin, a destination, or a layover for revolutionaries and revolution itself. How and why is the South Caucasus key to connecting revolutions?

THE SOUTH CAUCASUS "IN THE HANDS OF REVOLUTIONARIES"

On 17 November 1905 Alexander Ter Hakobian (Japonats'i), writing in Armenian from Saint Petersburg to comrades in Geneva, remarked on the disruption of railway service from Saint Petersburg to the South Caucasus because of strikes. He exclaimed, "Purportedly, the Caucasus is in the hands of revolutionaries ... The time of strikes has passed, armed uprising has emerged."[176]

The Caucasus in the hands of revolutionaries is an image deeply bound with the region's rich and multifaceted history. The Caucasus's geographic in-betweenness as a land bridge between the Black Sea and the Caspian Sea and the Eastern Mediterranean region is reflected in its history as a crossroads between empires and between East and West. The Caucasus has been incorporated into the Persian, Arab, Mongol, Ottoman, Russian, and Soviet empires at different points in its history, yet it has remained peripheral to these empires. A long history of multiethnic, multireligious, and multilingual existence has disposed the region both to peace and conflict, division and unity—seemingly paradoxical trends. As early as 1860, Archbishop Makar Barkhutariants, recognizing the plurality of the region, writes, "No country has ever been so crammed with such a wide variety of tribes and dialects as Aghuank'. . . . [I]t is the only short and convenient transit place for movement from the south northward and vice-versa, as well as from Europe to Asia and from Asia to Europe."[177]

The Caucasus has been referred to as a "hybrid society" and a "bi- or even tri-cultural world" by scholars like Nina Garsoian.[178] More recently, Stephen Rapp has argued for a prenational view of the region that recognizes "the cosmopolitan and multicultural condition which has characterized a shared Caucasian experience since antiquity."[179] The idea of the Caucasus as representing "a shared civilizational structure of its own," a place of pluralities and mobilities, is perhaps as common as its representation as a focal point of multiethnic and multicultural conflicts and often as sealed off from the rest of the world by its mountainous topography.[180] The interplay of unity and plurality that equally reflects the reality of the Caucasus is perhaps best expressed by the unintentional use of the Caucasus as a term denoting both singular and plural. Bruce Grant and Lale Yalçın-Heckmann, in their preface to *Caucasus Paradigms,* write:

> What does it mean to think ethnographically in a world region where peoples have for so long been so closely connected yet so consciously divided? . . . For centuries, the Caucasus *have* been home to a dense conglomeration of religions, languages and communities imperfectly drawn together around changing allegiances of empire, Silk Road trade and state socialism. A long line of conquerors—Greek, Roman, Turk, Arab, Mongol, Persian, Ottoman, Russian and Soviet—changed the rules of Caucasus life in multiple ways. Yet despite such evident histories of diaspora, migration, conquest, and cohabitation, the Caucasus *is* renowned for images of closure.[181]

In this section, I argue that as a center of both cultural reception and transmission, especially in the late nineteenth and early twentieth centuries, and within a context of revolutionary transformations in transportation and communication, the South Caucasus served as the playground and battleground of revolutionary ideas that permeated both Iran and Ottoman Anatolia.[182] This section seeks to provide a clearer picture of how and why the South Caucasus was such a dynamic and important axis for revolutionaries. To this end, it will begin with a discussion of the manifestation of time-space compression in South Caucasian urban centers, with a particular focus on the role of railways and telegraph in facilitating revolutionary activity, including dissemination of literature and circulation of arms and men. This will then be followed by further exploration of the very tangible ways in which time-space compression made an impact on and was employed by activists and workers themselves who navigated the South Caucasian-Ottoman-Iranian frontiers and brought with them revolutionary expertise and ideas, which had a profound impact on imperial subjects and revolutionary struggles.

Before proceeding any further, though, it is important to provide a brief and general demographic view of the South Caucasus, also known as Transcaucasia. In 1906 over six million people populated the South Caucasus: more than 25 percent were Azeris, about 20 percent Georgians, 20 percent Armenians, less than 5 percent Russians, and the rest representatives of a variety of peoples.[183] Armenians lived in a number of areas, including Yerevan, Kars, Elisavetpol, and Batumi. They made up a large portion of residents in the capital, Tiflis—about 40 percent, or seventy-six thousand people, in a city that was 25 percent Georgian and 20 percent Russian. Tiflis was a hub of activity and central in the network of roads that led from Tiflis to Poti, Batumi, Akhalkalaki, Alexandropol, Vladikavkaz, and Tioneti; telegraph lines; and railways that connected the city with the Black and Caspian Seas at Batumi and Baku, respectively, and with Kars and the Iranian frontiers via Yerevan.[184] Baku had a smaller number of Armenians, about half of the Muslim population in 1902 out of a population of more than two hundred thousand. Russians numbered about sixty-five thousand.[185] According to Stepanyan, based on the investigation of a variety of sources, the number of Armenians in late nineteenth-century Baku province, the majority of whom were in the city of Baku, stands much higher than the number reported by Russian records at over seventy-eight thousand.[186] Of course, the South Caucasus embraced within its mountainous environs more than a dozen different ethnic and religious groups that contributed to its dynamic multiplicity.

Time-Space Compression and the South Caucasus

In the context of the historically connected world of the South Caucasus, access to easier and faster transportation technologies and to such global telecommunication technologies as the telegraph and steam-operated presses enabled and accelerated the movement and circulation of information and news from different parts of the world; it also facilitated the movement of revolutionaries and literature, especially periodicals. These encounters simultaneously gave rise to commonalities in ways of thinking as well as awareness of difference.[187] We see this phenomenon reflected in the collaboration among Armenians, Georgians, Azeris, and Russians in revolutionary activity against tsarist autocracy (and later in the Iranian Constitutional Revolution) and in the fierce intolerance and violence, especially between Armenians and Azeris in the South Caucasus.

Time-space compression did not take place in a vacuum but was part and parcel of rapid urban growth, demographic mobility, and migration.

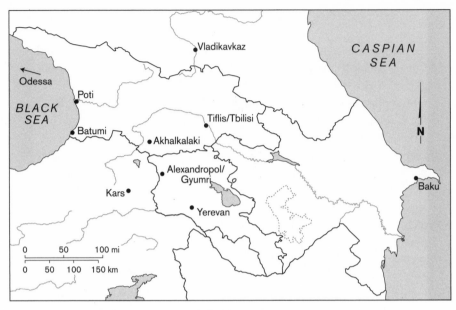

MAP 6. South Caucasus. Map created by Bill Nelson.

Starting in the second half of the nineteenth century, urbanization intensified, and cities became centers of exchange and circulation of not only commodities but also people, within and between cities, thus facilitating the exchange of information and knowledge.[188] The rapid growth of cities like Tiflis and Baku, which "expanded their populations more than ten times," and industrialization and migration all led to a particular environment in the South Caucasus that was particular to the area and yet very much part of global transformations.[189] At the turn of the twentieth century, almost three-fourths of the population of these cities was migrant.[190] According to Daniel Brower, most migrants were "young, single, male peasant[s]" without family ties in the urban centers where they searched for work as unskilled or semiskilled laborers.[191] Overcrowding due to migration led to "demands [not only] on the urban facilities" but also strains on already fragmented relationships among ethnically and linguistically diverse urban Caucasian communities in Baku, Tiflis, and Odessa, verging at times on communal violence.[192] Both Baku and Tiflis were in a turbulent and transformative stage. Ronald Suny's assessment of Tiflis as "a city in turmoil, riven by the rivalries and conflicting interests of Armenians and Georgians, the Russian state and Caucasian society, workers and the propertied middle class" as well as a sizable immigrant population also applies to Baku.[193] In the nineteenth century, Baku experienced an oil boom that, as Timothy Mitchell points out, "produced more than half the world's petroleum for a brief period at the start of the twentieth century."[194] Consequently, the city and the oil industry became magnets not only for local and foreign investors and refiners but also for migrant workers from the South Caucasus and neighboring areas, thus contributing to its already diverse and increasingly complicated urban milieu.

From 1905 to 1906, Baku was shattered by communal tensions between Armenians and Azeris, competing claims, and economic competition, all compounded by increasing numbers of immigrants from areas in the South Caucasus as well as Iran and the Ottoman Empire.[195] Brower paints a similar picture. In Baku and Tiflis, Brower writes, "ethnic and class divisions tended to reinforce one another. . . . " For Georgian and Azerbaijani workers, Armenian capitalists became both class and national foes.[196] Brower explains these social conflicts not only in terms of cultural and ethnic tensions—rather as a reflection, he attests, of a struggle "over labor conditions and inequalities of wealth."[197] The same factors that led to the potential for development and improvement also led to antipathy as the revolution took its course.[198] Both Brower and Suny agree, however, that in the first few months of 1905, different ethnic groups came together, at least temporarily, as a result of their shared enmity toward the Russian state.[199] That kind of solidarity explains, for example, the crumbling of Russian power in Tiflis.[200]

The geography of the Caucasus and its position as a crossroads have facilitated access to diverse knowledge and new ideas and ideologies. Particularly significant for the period under examination here has been the "technological component" in the dissemination and circulation of ideas and individuals: advancements in communication and information, in the form of the telegraph as well as increased and easier access to revolutionary literature, whether in the form of periodicals, pamphlets, or books; and advancements in transportation—namely, a railway system that by the early twentieth century linked Poti, Batumi, Vladikavkaz, Tiflis, and Baku.[201] Much more railway construction took place in the late nineteenth century, which saw a 75 percent increase in mileage, than in the early twentieth century, which saw only a 25 percent increase in mileage.[202] The first railway that went to the South Caucasus was that of Vladikavkaz, connecting Rostov and Vladikavkaz, just north of Tiflis, in 1875 and then going to Petrovsk (in the northern part of Lower Volga) and along the Caspian shore to Baku, with branches to Novorossiysk (a port on the Black Sea), Stavropol (in the northern Caucasus), and elsewhere. By 1906 the Vladikavkaz Railway had over 1,500 miles of rail.[203] By 1905 a second line of over 1,000 miles, the Transcaucasian Railway, connected Baku with Batumi, operating almost parallel to the Vladikavkaz Railway but to the south of the main Caucasus range, with branches from Tiflis to Alexandropol/ Gyumri (north of Yerevan) and then to Kars, Yerevan, Julfa, and on to the Iranian-Russian frontier.[204] As Westwood points out, "Russian engineers and capital also built lines in Turkey and Persia connecting with the Russian railways."[205] The dramatic changes in technologies of transportation and communication (i.e., time-space compression) are crucial for understanding the South Caucasus as a densely connected, compressed space where revolutionary ideas and elite would be expected to flow and circulate into neighboring regions.

The value of the railways in the Russian Empire, and certainly in the South Caucasus, is perhaps best expressed by Frithjof Benjamin Schenk's discussion of the way in which rail transport made an impact on the development of geographical mobility in nineteenth-century Russia. As the Russian state began to see the benefits of railways—as an "opportunity to ease the transport of goods, and as a strategic device that would enable the quick mobilization of troops in peace and war"—more energy was placed on railroad construction despite concerns about potential unwelcome consequences, mainly the mobility of people.[206] While some perceived the mobility resulting from railways as a positive and significant contributing factor to the Russian Empire's wealth, both Georg von Kankrin (finance minister) and Lev Alekseevich Perovskii (interior minister) also warned Nicholas I in the mid-nineteenth century that "the construction of railroads in Russia might cause a dangerous rise in geographical mobility."[207] As Schenk explains, conservative authors cautioned that "passengers traveling the 'iron horse' *(chugunka)* in large numbers might devastate the country as 'hordes of Arabs and Bashkirs' had done previously."[208] In Schenk's account, Von Kankrin expressed apprehension that the new system would "stimulate 'communicability' among the empire's population" and thus "make 'unstable people even more unstable.'"[209] The railway system did increase people's movements and their encounters with one another and with new ideas, and ultimately it did help "stimulate 'communicability,'" an environment more conducive to collaboration in resistance. For example, the British War Office reported "four wagon loads of revolutionaries" crossing by rail from the South Caucasus to Rasht in Gilan, Iran, as well as traveling by steamer and conventional routes.[210] These crossings concerned Russian authorities, as reported by the British ambassador in Saint Petersburg, Sir Arthur Nicolson, who assured Sir Edward Grey—the British foreign secretary from 1905 to 1916 who saw to the final agreement with Russia in 1907, dividing Iran into spheres of influence—that if Russia could cut off communication between the South Caucasus and Iran, it would. Moreover, Nicolson claimed on reportedly good Russian authority that if the struggle in Tabriz was solely about seeking a constitution, the Russian government would not be concerned with "the active and moving spirits of the disturbance" of "some hundreds of desperate Russian [read Caucasian] revolutionaries, who aim at something far beyond Constitutions. . . ."[211] Russian authorities were indeed quite concerned, as evidenced by an Okhrana report, which read, "Every day, volunteer detachments from the Caucasus arrive in Tabriz, which then make common cause with the Persian revolutionary detachments. Tabriz is waiting for the arrival of new detachments. The majority of the volunteers are Armenians from Yelizavetpol [Elisavetpol] Province. There are also Tatars and Georgians among the ranks."[212] This rather long report also assesses—in somewhat exaggerated fashion—the ARF's role in the Iranian Constitutional Revolution starting in 1908, concluding:

> Only the Dashnaks and some Georgians take part in military activities. Armenian Dashnaks display their courage in instances where 40–50 of them are able to repel the advance of more than a thousand men. As can be seen, the leadership from Tabriz is controlled from outside. That is demonstrated by the constant influx of volunteers arriving from Turkey and the Caucasus. The volunteers found in Tabriz are without exception either from the Elizavetpol Province or Baku . . . In Tabriz, the Dashnaks rule the day. The Muslim population in Tabriz currently numbers at 200,000, who have among them 500 volunteers who are armed with the latest rifles and pistols. However, these volunteers make for poor infantrymen and, as can be seen, they carry the weapons as mere decorations. With the Dashnak fedayee, it is the opposite—they are experienced and battle-hardened fighters. For that very reason, despite their numerical inferiority, they occupy the high ground.[213]

Further denigrating Muslim fighters, the report also alleges, "The distinguished defender of Tabriz, 'Sattar Khan' was nothing but a submissive tool in the hands of the 'Dashnaks.' He was brought to the fore by the Dashnaks so that he could obscure the Armenians' role in the Persian Revolution . . . 'SATTAR KHAN's' and 'Yeprem's' attack and capture of the city of Tehran was masterminded by the 'Dashnaktsutiun' party." The report then provides further details on a number of key figures like Nikol Duman, Yeprem Khan, and others and portrays Armenian and

Georgian fighters as "brigands" who "loot, kill, and prepare bombs" with the collaboration of some Muslims.[214]

The British ambassador's active and moving spirits of disturbance were among the millions of passengers benefiting from the empire's railways. From 1894 to 1911, the number of railroad passengers in the Russian Empire increased 285.7 percent.[215] In 1903 alone, 93.5 million third-class and 7.8 million fourth-class tickets were sold.[216] Although there was a slowing down in 1904 and 1905 because of the Russo-Japanese War and the Russian Revolution, as articulated by Japonats'i, with whom I began this section, numbers only increased thereafter.[217] As Schenk concludes, "the railroad contributed undoubtedly to an enlargement of the geographical radius of mobility of large parts of the society."[218] It is no surprise then that in the late nineteenth century, finance minister Sergei Witte "stressed the urgent need for geographical mobility to enhance 'the economic and moral bonds *(nravstvenye sviazi)* between the various geographical regions of the country"—a far cry from Kankrin's and others' cautionary notices about the impending threat of unstable hordes to the empire.[219]

The significance of railways should not overshadow the important role of the telegraph. In fact, in the Russian, Ottoman, and Iranian states, telegraph systems preceded the construction of railways.[220] As Marsha Siefert explains, the telegraph, along with telephony, accelerated global interconnectivity, as for the "first time . . . symbols were able to move through space without requiring physical transportation of paper or people."[221] According to Siefert, "By the end of 1864 there were five lines operating in the Caucasus," including in Poti and Yerevan, with Tiflis as a vital "node of the telegraph connection to Persia."[222] With the Russian government's grant to the Siemens brothers to construct a telegraph line from Europe to India through the South Caucasus and concessions from the Prussian and Iranian governments, in 1870 the Indo-European telegraph line ran for 8,300 kilometers and remained operational until 1930. In 1880 alone, 63 percent of telegraphic dispatches—that is, 42,719 telegrams—went through the South Caucasus via the Indo-European telegraph.[223] By 1907 at least forty-eight telegraph lines ran along railway lines.[224]

The Russian Empire's interest lay in not only securing communications and control over the Caucasus in the south but also rivaling the British farther south in Iran. Siefert concludes, "Overall, by the early twentieth century, all the provincial capitals, sea ports, industrial centres and most of the small towns of the Russian Empire were connected by the telegraph network," with the intention of more closely connecting the periphery to the center and thus establishing greater control over the vast expanse of the empire.[225] Although the telegraph, much like the railways, was established to assist imperial rule, these two technologies could be and were used to defy the states that initiated and carried out their construction, as the many telegrams between revolutionaries and the transport of arms and literature through the railways confirm.[226] The farther away from the center, the more difficult it was to control telegraph communication.[227] The telegraph often became a target of strikers and revolutionaries, as telegraph workers went on strike in the South Caucasus, the Ottoman Empire, and Iran during revolutionary struggle.[228] After all, these "more politically minded strategists understood how to use the telegraph system to challenge the very empires that supported their construction," as the many telegrams between Armenian activists in all three revolutions verify.[229]

The railways as well as the telegraph became centers of labor unrest and strikes during the Russian Revolution. Railway strikes in 1905 and 1906 caused much havoc, disrupting communication and transportation, including oil shipments from Batumi.[230] Armenian revolutionaries consciously sought to cut railway, post, and telegraph communication and to organize or take part in strikes to help the antitsarist revolutionary struggle.[231] They also, however, considered the consequences of such moves. In a notice printed in October 1905 and directed toward Batumi, the ARF Central Committee urged serious thought regarding strikes to ensure that they did good rather than harm, that they were targeted against government institutions or railways but did not close down shops and pharmacies and deprive workers. For that reason, it called an end to ARF participation in a strike but vowed not to interfere in the spirit of continued cooperation.[232] This did not mean a permanent end to strikes, however, as the ARF pondered large strikes of railway, post, and telegraph workers among a number of operations to put into action targeting the tsarist state. They included mutinies, terror against highly placed government officials, the occupation of government institutions, and the takeover of state weapons and funds, as well as military incursions. The ARF believed that some of these operations could be carried out in Baku but confessed that the dangers were "great and grave" and that failure would deal a hard blow to the revolutionary struggle.[233]

Revolutionaries also exploited the telegraph the way they exploited other forms of print. They used telegrams to incite workers to action, to spread vital news and instructions, and to communicate with each other across great distances. Therefore, much like the railways, telegraphy in the South Caucasus accelerated revolutionary communication and movement. Workers, intellectuals, and revolutionary activists all took advantage of the more rapid and far-reaching methods of transportation and communication already radically transforming the social fabric of the region, and the intellectuals and activists were remarkably adept at exploiting the telegraph, the railways, and the steamship to disseminate a variety of revolutionary literature in the form of books, periodicals, and pamphlets.[234] In the South Caucasus, Tiflis and especially Baku became hubs of circulation, along with other centers like Odessa and Batumi.[235] Abraham Giwlkhandanian, an activist and member of the ARF, who wrote his impressions of his revolutionary days in Baku sometime before his death in the 1930s, remembered the many teachers working in the oil fields of Baku after losing their jobs because of tsarist closures of village schools.[236] According to the British War Office, the majority of workers in oil fields were Azeris and Armenians, with a significant number of Iranians (about 22 percent in 1903).[237]

Oil fields in the South Caucasus served as important places of mobilization and propaganda. The Russian Empire became the first in the nineteenth century to convert "oil into a significant source of mechanical power to drive industry and transportation," thus creating, as Timothy Mitchell demonstrates, the potential for oil workers to become a political force, much like coal workers earlier on.[238] Oil fields in Baku were directly linked by railways and waterways to the rest of the empire, and they, along with the Black Sea port of Batumi, were the site of strikes and protests as early as 1901. As Mitchell explains, Baku oil workers launched the Russian Revolution with two general strikes, in 1903 and 1904, which spread "along the railway line to the marshalling yards and work-shops at Tiflis (now Tbilisi), the midpoint of the Transcaucasus Railway, then to Batumi, and then 'like a brushfire across southern Russia.'"[239]

Oil workers successfully negotiated the first labor contract in the history of the Russian Empire that included not only a nine-hour workday but also political wins like the right to elected representatives. What strengthened the hand of these oil workers was how closely and physically connected the fields, refineries, workshops, and large workforces were in the South Caucasus and how well the relatively new technologies of the railways and steamship connected them to other refineries on the Caspian Sea. Oil in the Russian Empire took on the role that coal played in other regions.[240] Thus, it makes sense that "The oil strikes that launched the 1905 Revolution were able to paralyse transportation networks and industrial activity across the Empire, much as coal strikes could in north-western Europe."[241] Oil workers' successes were limited and bound, however, by ethnic divisions that often demarcated the organization of oil production and labor mobilization and were effectively exploited by Russian authorities to thwart the progress of worker demands and the revolution itself.[242] Oil workers' ability to carry out long-term and sustained action well, compared to coal workers, was also shaped by some key differences, such as the use of oil pipelines, which were invented in Pennsylvania in the 1860s and were employed starting in the 1870s in Baku "as a means of reducing the ability of humans to interrupt the flow of energy." Revolutionaries' attempts to damage pipelines had limited and short-lived effect.[243] The moving of oil by sea rather than rail also limited sabotage and consequently the mobilization potential of oil fields; however, oil workers did have limited victories.[244] Giwlkhandanian's account speaks to the key role that oil fields played in radicalizing workers. He writes that Armenian workers set up reading rooms in the oil fields and obtained periodicals and books, which they then made available.[245] In certain cases, they formed groups and read revolutionary literature, including Marx's *Das Kapital* in Russian, until an unspecified dissension brought the reading to a halt after a few months.[246] Sometimes, workers like those of the oil fields of Arafelov formed "self-enlightenment and self-help" societies, contributing 1 to 10 percent of their salaries to the purchase of newspapers and books, thus creating a sizeable library, which workers at Pitoev and Mantashev oil fields also utilized.[247]

Newspapers, books, pamphlets, and brochures made their way to the South Caucasus and the Ottoman Empire from Europe, often through Iran, or originated in the South Caucasus and traveled west and south; after 1908 they originated in the Ottoman Empire and may have moved east and south. For example, until the banning of the ARF's official party organ, *Drōshak,* in Iran in July 1906, 1,500 to 1,700 copies arrived from Geneva, where it was published, and were passed on to the South Caucasus, along with other published material.[248] In 1905 most of 7,000 copies of *Drōshak* were carried into Ottoman Armenian provinces; a smaller number went to the South Caucasus.[249] Other regions in Iran, specifically Ardabil and Astara, reported transporting 12,000 to 15,000 copies of *Drōshak;* 500 of *Hayrenik'* (Fatherland); a small, unspecified number of *Revolutsyonnaya Rossiya* (Revolutionary Russia), the organ

of the Socialist Revolutionary Party, and Armenian and Russian brochures; and Russian Social Democratic Labor Party newspapers *Vpered*
(Forward), *Iskra* (Spark), *Proletarii,* and bourgeois-liberal *Osvobozhdenie* (Liberation).[250] The Russian periodical *Vpered* most likely traveled
from the South Caucasus to Iran while *Drōshak* (published in Geneva
and Paris), *Iskra* (published in Stuttgart, Munich, Geneva, and London),
Osvobozhdenie (published in Stuttgart and Paris), *Proletarii* (published
in Vyborg, Geneva, and Paris), *Revolutsyonnaya Rossiya* (published in
Geneva), and *Hayrenikʻ* (published in Boston) most probably took the
opposite route: once they reached Iran from Europe and the United
States, they moved up to the South Caucasus.[251] The evidence also points
to what ARF cofounder Simon Zavarian, writing from Istanbul, refers to
as a "book famine."[252] He pleads for books and photos, citing "an inex-
haustible demand."[253] In many letters, Zavarian requests that books in
general be sent to Istanbul, specifically mentioning the demand for works
by Karl Marx and Pyotr Kropotkin (a prominent Russian anarchist),
with the intent of having them translated and published in Istanbul.[254]
Zavarian notes that the majority of translations were of European writings, with added prefaces and notes "to turn the reader's attention to our
life."[255] Advertisements, announcements, or lists of publications, most of
them translations, peppered the pages of the contemporary press, as did
translations themselves.[256] Karl Kautsky's works were the most popular,
especially but not exclusively among the nonaffiliated press.[257] The ARF
press (Drōshak, Haṛaj, and Azatutʻean Matenadaran) published the largest number of translations and original works, totaling more than 140,
followed much further behind by the SDHP press at more than 30.[258]
Although according to a British War Office report published in 1907, the
South Caucasus, Tiflis especially, as well as Istanbul, were the sites of
many Armenian-language publications and "Relatively to their numbers,
the Armenians in Russia print more books than any other nationality,"
the demand and need for reading material remained high.[259] For one revolutionary, writing from Batumi, people's need was "for revolutionary
writings more than anything else," in particular Armenian revolutionary
history.[260] Others' opinions on the subject of the importance of literature
to their compatriots differed. A. Atanasian, writing in the Armenian
Socialist Revolutionary paper *Aniv* (Wheel), for example, bemoans the
state of writers in poverty, pointing to the mostly illiterate Armenians and
the "pitiful condition" of language instruction in Armenian schools. He
concludes that as long as this situation persists, "the Armenian writer, the
Armenian author, the Armenian book and press is and will remain pitiful,

mendicant, and insecure."[261] Another Armenian Socialist Revolutionary, identified as Shanturian, is also rather pessimistic in his analysis of what Armenian workers read, finding that their reading habits revolved around books with nationalist sentiment while other "scientific" books in translation did not sell. He also points out that books changed hands more often than they were bought.[262] Still others sought to "revise the corpse" of the "disdained book."[263] Despite these rather sullen expressions, the increase in the traffic of print points to its appeal.

The routes and modes of transportation by which these periodicals and other publications in the original language or in translation crossed borders point to the vital role of railroads and steamships or even sailboats, and the expressed demand for such reading material. In addition to regular mail, all modes were used to transport periodicals, books, and pamphlets or brochures with regularity across the Caucasian, Ottoman, and Iranian worlds, thus further fostering time-space compression. Bazilevich draws attention to the growth of periodicals and the number of printed copies, a phenomenon that had only increased in the nineteenth century, putting a strain—along with securities and money orders—on the postal system in the Russian Empire.[264] Its poorly paid workers, who worked under harsh conditions, became the first to be targeted by revolutionary propaganda and secret societies. The increasing number of post offices and mailboxes, provided our revolutionaries an additional avenue by which to circulate printed material.[265]

In mainly Tiflis and Baku, between 1904 and 1912, 104 Armenian-language newspapers appeared (76 in Tiflis and 28 in Baku), of which at least 32 and possibly more were revolutionary. Of these, the ARF published 14 newspapers (13 in Tiflis and 1 in Baku); the SDHP, an important social democratic Armenian party, published 4 (3 in Tiflis and 1 in Baku); and other Armenian socialists, mostly social democrats, published 14, the majority in Baku.[266] After 1908 the number of periodicals published in the South Caucasus decreased substantially as the focus of publications, as well as the individuals behind them, moved from the South Caucasus to Istanbul (and Izmir) and, to a lesser degree, Iran, in large part because of the Stolypin crackdown on revolutionaries and their activities in the South Caucasus and the legalization of political activity and lifting of censorship in the wake of the Young Turk Revolution. The number of papers published in Istanbul—at least 116—exceeded that of the South Caucasus.[267]

The print boom was in many ways a by-product of technological innovations in the nineteenth century. That century witnessed the mechanization, automation, and therefore acceleration of the printing process, which had not fundamentally changed since the invention of Gutenberg's printing press in the mid-fifteenth century, thus resulting in immense growth in quantity and diversity of printed material.[268] The demand and distribution of printed material was further assisted by railway transport, road improvements, urbanization, and a rise in literacy. The spread of news through telegraphy also contributed to the production and expansion of newspapers and their consequent distribution.[269] News and reporting arrived frequently via telegraph, and newspapers often printed the telegrams themselves, as well as news stories from sister periodicals all over Eurasia, in a number of Romance and Slavic languages as well as Ottoman and Persian. Bayly remarks on the significance of the "massive expansion of book printing worldwide" as well as "[t]he almost geometrical progression in the expansion of standardized information across the world [which] can be appreciated if we remember that people begged, borrowed, and stole copies of the newspapers."[270] Thus, the seemingly "remarkable diffusion of the printed word" was certainly not unique to the Armenians but common among all city dwellers.[271] Brower remarks on the "explosion of popular culture through books, brochures, pamphlets, and papers . . . [and] public readings and literacy schools, as well as through informal contacts (such as those facilitated by the ubiquitous tavern)."[272] Periodicals were often read aloud by the literate and discussed by both literate and illiterate audiences, for much of the time unhindered by tsarist censorship.[273] Therefore, while subscription numbers might be considered low, they do not provide the whole picture. For example, by October 1904 the literary and political monthly *Murch* (Hammer), which competed with multiple newspapers (judging merely by the ads appearing in *Murch*'s own pages), had nine hundred subscribers, largely in the Russian Empire, as well as those in Iran and elsewhere.[274] What François Georgeon has shown in his discussion of the Ottoman case also resonates for the South Caucasus and Iran: "The access to the written word is not exclusively reserved to those who know how to read and write. There exist, between the oral and written worlds, passages, mediations. . . . Very often reading is collective (in particular, reading of a newspaper, which is done aloud by somebody who knows how to read (the imam, the school teachers, the officer, . . .) in coffee houses, and especially in these kiraathane, which literally mean 'reading houses', which are halfway between European reading rooms and Eastern coffeehouses, and which began appearing in the 1860s."[275]

The private home, too, served as "an intimate locus of group reading," as Ami Ayalon shows in his study on literacy and printing in Ottoman Palestine.[276] As access to education and literacy grew, especially but not exclusively among city dwellers, men, and Christians, people sought "to quench their growing thirst for information, obtainable from written sources of many kinds. This craving for knowledge and the expanding ability to access it evolved in tandem with an unprecedented proliferation of written texts in the country—a development that at once enhanced and was boosted by the growing thirst and spreading skills."[277] Similar to Georgeon, Ayalon points to the way in which public spaces—"cafés and markets, the village madafah and grocery shops" became "places of vocal group reading, where the skills of one individual served to enlighten" and contribute to "circulating the contents of written information."[278] This phenomenon expanded into rural areas; thus, "[p]eople did not have to wait for the full elimination of illiteracy to be enlightened."[279] This development certainly applied to the region as a whole.

The impact of newspapers circulating by whatever means in many directions, originating in the South Caucasus and Europe and traversing through Iran and the Ottoman Empire, should not be underestimated. Newspapers and their readers/listeners kept abreast of news, ideas, and movements around the world, reporting on workers' demands, conditions, strikes, and unions locally and globally. Therefore, ideas disseminated not only through "connectors"—that is, individuals who spread ideas through their circulation and thus connected regions near and far—but also through print, especially the bulging and expanding world of newspapers.[280] Newspapers served to inform, enlighten, and propagate, and as Khuri-Makdisi has pointed out in the case of the Eastern Mediterranean, "One of the main lessons radicals drew from world news was 'how to "do" revolution.'"[281] Our Armenian revolutionaries were very much aware of the motivational and propagandistic effect of newspapers as well as circulars, brochures, and books, as they invested much energy and time in seeing to their publication, circulation, and dissemination. Furthermore, the spread of literacy and print had the power to bring people together. Although differences and divisions among communities intensified and ethnic bonds deepened, Michael Hamm points, in his study on Kiev, to how "[t]he printed word could break down class and national barriers, promote sensitivity and understanding, contribute to an urban environment more tolerant of diversity and more amenable to change, and stimulate new ways of thinking about equity, justice, and authority" and therefore create some form of social solidarity.[282] Print, thus, had profound consequences and multiple functions and became part of a larger process that in the long nineteenth century led, according to T. N. Harper, to:

> a world where events far afield—be it in Egypt, Japan, the Philippines or Ireland—were a common currency for all . . . In this way, in different locales, a wider range of predicaments was being discussed in similar terms; in adjacent locales, similar debates were being played out in similar ways, in similar language, translations or symbolism. At this point the local and the global converged. Often local communities did not need a direct external prompting to frame their actions in broader terms. Theirs was a response to a more general sense of proximity to others. This was not merely, or primarily, formed by a relation to those within an incipient 'nation', but to others far distant, and very unlike themselves.[283]

It is no wonder, then, that cities, including in the South Caucasus, where time-space compression was active and print thrived and contributed further to the shrinking of the world, "were at the center of the revolutionary conflict of the early twentieth century. They became both the crucible in which these movements took on real life and the spark igniting opposition in other parts of the country."[284]

Contemporary correspondence and newspapers as well as Giwlkhandanian speak to this revolutionary disposition of South Caucasian cities. Giwlkhandanian emphasizes the activist environment of the oil fields, even referring to the Tumayev oil fields as the place where "revolutionary activists were formed" and Baku as the city with the most *hayduk*s (a term borrowed from the Bulgarian romanticized heroes to refer to revolutionaries) and the center through which all *hayduks* at one point or another passed.[285] Some of these men even came from the Ottoman Empire and passed through or stayed in Iran before stopping in the South Caucasus.[286] With them (and students from Geneva too)[287] passed arms and ammunition. For example, the "Khariskh" (Anchor) arms workshop in Tabriz, which was established in 1891 by ARF members, had as many as thirty-six workers in a fifteen-year period, many of whom came from the Tula arms factory in Russia. By 1896 alone, the workshop had produced six hundred firearms. Military equipment like guns and munitions was transported to Tabriz after being bought from Russian armory workers in Tula and Tiflis and stored in different Caucasian cities. After they were assembled in Tabriz, they were delivered to various points near the Ottoman border and later across that border into Ottoman territory.[288]

In a rough several-page draft by Kristapor Mikayelian that might have been meant for publication—apparently as a response to an article

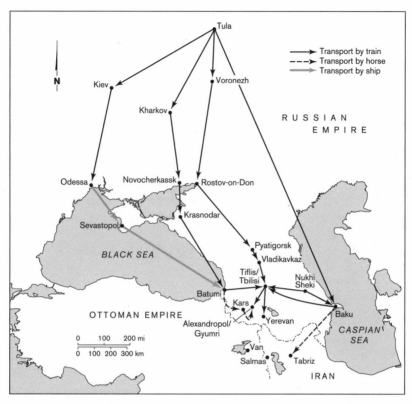

MAP 7. Arms transfer, 1890–1914. Map modified by Bill Nelson. Source: *Hushamatean Hay Heghap'okhakan Dashnakts'ut'ean albom-atlas*, vol. 1, *Diwts'aznamart* [Commemorative album-atlas of the Armenian Revolutionary Federation, vol. 1, Heroic combat] (Glendale, CA: ARF Central Committee, 1992).

written by a German Assyriologist, identified as Mr. Belck [Waldemar Belck], "the Assyriologist gentleman who so loves to occupy himself with contemporary political issues"—we find a number of interesting details about arms transfer.[289] According to Mikayelian, Belck claimed that the Russian government was supplying Armenian revolutionaries with arms. Mikayelian goes through some important detail to explain the process of arms purchase. First, he contends that Armenian revolutionaries bought weapons parts from factory workers who sold only those parts deemed to be of suspect quality after inspection and disposal by the factory. These defective parts were stamped with a *B* for *brak*, meaning "refuse." He emphasizes that all the revolutionaries' arms had a *B* on them, whereas those used by Russian soldiers did not. Also, their

MAP 8. Arms workshops, 1890–1914. Map modified by Bill Nelson. Source: *Husha-matean Hay Heghap'okhakan Dashnakts'ut'ean albom-atlas,* vol. 1, *Diwts'aznamart* [Commemorative album-atlas of the Armenian Revolutionary Federation, vol. 1, Heroic combat] (Glendale, CA: ARF Central Committee, 1992).

weapons did not bear the official state coat of arms, whereas those of the Russian soldiers did.[290] Second, Mikayelian maintains that Armenian revolutionaries also purchased weapons from "Turkish contraband arms dealers" who thrived in the Caucasus and also sold to "mountain-dwelling Turks, to Kurds, and to Turkish bandits, and those in the hundreds."[291] He adds, "not a year goes by in the Caucasus without those Turks who occupy themselves with that profession being caught on the railways."[292] Third, Mikayelian takes issue with Belck's assertion that the guardhouses on the border between the Russian and Ottoman Empires were one kilometer apart from each other, irrefutable evidence for Belck that arms were crossing the border with Russian agreement. Mikayelian points out that, contrary to Belck's claim, guardhouses were no less than five and usually eight to ten versts—that is, from five to over ten kilometers—apart from each other, making for a much more fluid and penetrable frontier for all.[293]

Materials for explosives were also transported across porous frontiers. For example, Rostom, writing to Samson Tadeosian, an ARF activist in Salmas and participant in the Iranian Constitutional Revolution, promises to bring with him samples of potassium chlorate in crystal and powder form, to use with other compounds to make explosives.[294] Rostom writes:

> I want to write a few things about explosive elements, for which there will be great need soon. Your grounds are suitable for those kinds of experiments. We always place our hope on dynamite, but that is difficult to find. It is possible to use a few compounds, which although do not have the force of dynamite, nevertheless are strong enough, which you will see from the experiments. Today, I write about two of them; henceforth, I will also communicate about others. The essential part of all these compounds is potassium chlorate [chlorate de potasse],[295] with which they [treat] the throat. It is necessary to get a hold of it in great quantity, in haste. If it cannot be found in Persia in great quantity, telegram or write, we will send it immediately; you may have it brought from Russia . . . That salt combined with other elements, brings forth good explosives.[296]

He adds that it is indeed easy to acquire and transport, and he provides instructions on storage and use and also asks that a young man from Baku be secured who knows how to make bombs.[297]

Giwlkhandanian attests to Baku's large role in transferring arms, ammunition, and explosive material for bombs.[298] Baku, however, was not alone. As the archival documents suggest, Tiflis, too, was such a site.[299] Giwlkhandanian asserts, "Baku was such a place that large numbers of workers and intellectuals were gathered from all corners of the Caucasus. True, at that time it was impossible to carry out any activity in a legal manner; however, that same living bond that existed between Baku and its environs markedly facilitated every kind of activity."[300] Both the regime and the revolutionary parties were very conscious of Baku's significance to the Caucasus, which they considered "Russia's most vulnerable spot."[301] All this demonstrates the significance of the revolutionary environment of the South Caucasus in circulation and in connecting a number of other regions from West to East.

The developments in the transportation and communication infrastructure that brought about time-space compression in the South Caucasus radically transformed the lives and activities of revolutionary subjects residing in the region's central urban hubs. The impact of these changes becomes discernible upon further exploration of the ways in which Armenian activists exploited and were moved, literally and figuratively, by turn-of-the-century time-space compression, as they spread and disseminated revolutionary activity into the neighboring empires.

Caucasian Armenians' historical impact on the Ottoman and especially on Iranian communities is significant. Starting in the late nineteenth and early twentieth centuries, teachers and activists, who were often one and the same, moved from the South Caucasus into the Ottoman Empire and especially into Iran. Their presence and activities vastly influenced and at times transformed Armenian intellectual and political life as well as political action in the Ottoman Empire and more so in Iran. Most Armenian teachers in Iran came from the South Caucasus, especially Tiflis, and some came from the Ottoman Empire. They included nationalist writers, academics, and revolutionary activists.[302] Armenian political parties began activities in the South Caucasus and Eastern Anatolia, and soon after spread to northern Iran in the late nineteenth century.[303] Many sources, some of whose authors were political activists themselves, testify to the significance and number of Armenian revolutionaries who came down to Iran from Tiflis, Baku, and other cities and towns in the South Caucasus in the late nineteenth and early twentieth centuries.[304]

Workers, too, became important conduits of ideas and experiences as they crossed the South Caucasian and Iranian frontiers. While we have no exact figures for Iranian Armenian migrant workers crossing from Iran, especially from the Azerbaijan province, to the South Caucasus, we may assume that they were part of the hundreds of thousands of Iranian migrant workers making their way to the South Caucasus in the late nineteenth and early twentieth centuries, some from heavily Armenian regions.[305] Tsarist authorities began collecting information on Iranian migration to the Caucasus and Central Asia in the late nineteenth century, even issuing visas in Mashhad, Rasht, and Azerbaijan, although workers did not always possess official documentation.[306] Most were manual workers; some worked in Baku's oil industry, and they comprised about 22 percent of the workforce in 1903 alone.[307] The numbers, which range from more than 67,000 in 1900 to more than 191,000 in 1911, reflect only legal migration and, therefore, only a portion of the actual numbers, which may have been as high as 300,000 by 1905.[308] What is equally interesting and key to our discussion of circulation is that a large number of these migrants returned to Iran. In 1900 more than 57,000 returned, and in 1911 more than 157,000 went back home.[309] This is a critical detail because it demonstrates that migrant workers returned to their communities influenced or affected by worker movements and strikes, socialist ideas, and revolutionary fervor in general.[310] As Iago Gocheleishvili demonstrates, these workers were a "live and mobile link that connected the Tbilisi, Baku, Tabriz, and Rasht revolutionary groups."[311] Workers and revolutionaries themselves, therefore, helped create and contribute to deepening bonds between urban centers, diverse political and economic groups, and revolutionary movements.

Although Iranian workers proved difficult to organize in Baku, some did take part in strikes there in 1903, 1904, and 1906, as well as in Iran in 1906.[312] Cosroe Chaqueri emphasizes the influence of the South Caucasian milieu on these workers and the development of social democratic organizations in Iran:

> Their participation in industrial strikes and political events gave them the experience that they could never have acquired at home, where both the economic and political conditions for such actions were lacking. Yet their seasonal return to northern Iran was bound to spread the word that a different kind of life, one improved through political struggle, was possible. By the time the Constitutional Revolution took place, the notion of workers striking as a means of pressuring those who hired and pitilessly exploited wage earners had been implanted inside the country and acquired sufficient credibility to be acted upon. It was against this background that various Social-Democratic organizations were born and took an active part in the struggle for political change in Iran. . . .[313]

The Azeri social democratic Hümmat/Himmat (Endeavor) Party, which collaborated closely with the Russian Social Democratic Workers Party (RSDWP) and the Armenian SDHP, played an important part in galvanizing Iranian migrant workers and assisting in the formation of the Ferqeh-ye Ejtima'iyun 'Ammiyun (Social Democratic Party).[314] Chaqueri goes further by emphasizing the essential role of Armenian social democrats like Grigor Yeghikian, Tigran Ter-Hakobian, and Vram Pilosian in shaping and even initiating Iranian social democracy, including the Democrat Party and *Iran-e Now* (New Iran).[315] He concludes, "In short, Armenian Social Democrats and their Caucasian comrades, seeking a radical political change and all round development in Iran, introduced into Iran's political life new ideas, institutions, and political methods and procedures . . . They also demonstrated profound knowledge of socio-economic issues and dedication to, and love for, their country's future."[316] Gocheleishvili, too, remarks on the significant role South Caucasians played and the close collaboration of Georgians, Azeris, and Armenians in Iran.[317] He argues:

> With years of experience in conducting revolutionary activities and with invaluable experience gained in the anti-Tsarist revolt in western Georgia

and the 1905 Russian Revolution, the Transcaucasian revolutionary groups perhaps believed that they had a lot to share with the Iranian resisters. For this to be implanted, first, the Transcaucasians needed to have in Iran not simply experienced fighters, but politically and theoretically well-prepared leaders who would work in Iran in accordance with the party programme. Secondly, it required effective coordination among those Transcaucasian volunteers in Tabriz and Rasht who were affiliated with the Transcaucasian political organizations. It did not take the Transcaucasian revolutionary organizations long to take measures towards achieving the goal of establishing control over their corps in Iran, make sure that their activities in Iran were conducted according to the directives from the Caucasus.[318]

Similar views were expressed by Iranian social democrats Mirza Abdullah and Satijik Rahimzade in Paris in 1909. In the interview, translated into Armenian and printed in the pages of the Marxist *Nor Hosank'* (New Current) in Tiflis, both men viewed the Iranian Revolution as "the daughter of the Russian revolution. It is the marvelous revolt of hearts and consciences in the expansive country of tsars that has served as a grand inspirational force for our country." When asked what factors led to the formation of the socialist party during the Iranian Revolution, the activists explained that it developed, on the one hand, under the influence of young Russian intellectuals who were following the "grand socialist city's" (Tiflis's) university courses and, on the other, through Iranian workers who had worked in Baku, where a whole "giant labor population" was "aroused by the contemporary socialist ideal."[319]

In an original departure and contribution, Scott Ury, in his study of Warsaw Jews during the 1905 Russian Revolution, argues that what drove young Jews to political organizations and revolutionary parties was very much informed by the "crisis of urbanization and community in the heart of early-twentieth-century eastern Europe, Warsaw, and the new forms of Jewish politics and community." Particularly in the third chapter, Ury convincingly demonstrates that more than ideology, at the heart of Jewish urban migrants' involvement in revolutionary activity lay their search for community, family, and networks of support. He explains, "new revolutionary groups were able to fill the gaping social and communal void by providing alienated and confused Jews in Warsaw with much of what they needed: a sense of belonging, a larger purpose, and ways to make sense of their radically transformed, quintessentially modern lives."[320] Although it is not the focus of this study, it is just as likely that similar factors attracted young Armenian migrants to the urban areas in the South Caucasus, the Ottoman Empire, and Iran to revolutionary networks.[321] Perhaps one could argue that Armenians in Caucasian cities followed a parallel path: "all three ideologies [socialism, liberalism, and nationalism] and various political movements that they spawned should be seen as attempts to wield intellectual and social order over a particularly chaotic world . . . the widespread turn to modern political ideologies and movements should be seen as a part of a larger attempt to render the fundamentally new experience of life in the urban metropolis more understandable, more digestible, and ultimately, more manageable.'"[322]

The meaningful and profound impact of the South Caucasus on its surroundings, as a pivot of revolution connecting revolutionaries and revolutionary struggles, is deeply intertwined with larger turn-of-the-century global developments and revolutions in transportation, communication, and economy. The increasing connections between and entanglements of regions, near and far, had enduring consequences for the way groups began to think of their place in the world and their social, political, and economic interests. The next two chapters explore the ideas and ideologies that inspired these groups and that the groups adopted, adapted, and circulated across imperial frontiers through print and personal interactions. The circulation of men, arms, print, news, and information made revolutionary connections feasible as new technologies of transportation seemingly shrank time and geographical distance and as communication advances (that is, the telegraph) dematerialized information; at the same time, the circulation of ideas—popular sovereignty/representation, resistance against oppression, socialism, and others—connected revolutions and revolutionaries through a common language and common concerns and activities, making possible greater uniformity and collaboration in revolutionary struggle as well as competition over degrees of radicalism and appropriate action.

CHAPTER 3

The Circulation of Ideas and Ideologies

Constitutionalism and Federalism

In October 1908 a full-page illustration appeared on the last page of the Armenian-language satirical weekly, *Khat'abala* (Trouble), in Tiflis. It features a simplified depiction of the Ottoman Empire arched by a banner-like rainbow that reads "CONSTITUTION" (see Figure 3). The backdrop is a cloudy, stormy sky. The seas are dark and tempestuous. Below the rainbow, in the center of the empire, stands a man identified as a Turk, with his back to the reader/viewer, facing the rainbow of constitution and holding a banner that proclaims "Unity, Equal[ity]." On his right, from the top, with expressions and postures that vary from attentiveness to ennui, are men identified as Kurd, Armenian (in red), Bedouin, Arab, and Jew. They hold banners that say "Autonomy," but only the Armenian's banner is upright. The others brush the ground. All except the Arab (depicted as black) and the Bedouin, both of whom are armed, are on their knees in submission or supplication. The Armenian's posture, however, appears somewhat different than that of the other kneeling Ottoman subjects. His outstretched arms, along with his gaze, seem to be directed across Anatolia toward the Balkans, perhaps with respect or in support. In the Balkans, from right to left, are those identified as Albanian, Macedonian, and Greek. Between the Albanian and the Macedonian, standing slightly in the background, is an older, white-bearded, and rather meek man, who is not identified. These figures all hold banners of autonomy and are standing; the Macedonian and the Greek, however, hold rather agitated poses, with their banners unfurled in the air. The caption to the illustration is a poem:

Թող շողշողուն ծիածան   Այս «նշանով հաշտութեան»
Ձեզ շաղկապէ, հէք ազգեր   Թող դարման են ձեր վէրքեր . . .

May the resplendent rainbow   With this "sign of conciliation"
Conjoin you, poor nations   May they remedy your wounds . . .[1]

How are we to interpret this illustration? How could this satirical portrayal of constitution and the relationship of the empire's ethnicities to it reflect a real and complicated relationship with constitutionalism in the Ottoman Empire? Could it also perhaps even help us understand the contrasting Armenian views toward constitutionalism, in general, and toward specific constitutions in the Russian and Iranian states, as well as views on autonomy, unity, and equality? The Armenians' complex relationship with constitutionalism is not unique to that concept; rather, it reflects a wider and equally multifaceted affiliation with other prevalent, global ideas and ideologies such as socialism, nationalism, and anarchism, particularly anarchist interpretations of federation, autonomy, and decentralization. Our frontier-crossing revolutionaries who traversed Eurasia in pursuit or in support of revolutionary transformation in the Russian, Iranian, and Ottoman Empires were also boundary crossers—that is, they navigated not only geographical expanses but also the world of global ideas and ideologies. They experimented, adopted, adapted, and even synthesized concepts and world visions according to the actual circumstances in which they lived and their own particular interests and aspirations. Their disagreements and debates over constitutionalism, federation and decentralization, and socialism and the national question in many ways mirror the disputes taking place contemporaneously among European (understood in its broadest and most extensive sense) leftists. They also reflect or are part of larger trends in the region, as the discussion in this and the following chapter demonstrate by drawing parallels when germane, especially with Georgians, Bulgarians, and Macedonians. This chapter and the next rely heavily on revolutionary Armenian-language periodicals and a number of books published in the revolutionary period by intellectuals and activists in the Russian, Ottoman, and Iranian Empires and in Europe. They represent the vibrant array of ideological and political leanings.

The previous chapter explored the mobility and circulation of operatives, weapons, and print. In this chapter, the focus is on the ways *in* which and the paths *through* which ideas moved as well as the ways revolutionaries accommodated and applied them. The chapter returns to the illustration with which it began to discuss constitutionalism's place

FIGURE 3. The rainbow of constitution. Image reproduced courtesy of Bibliothèque Nubar (Nubar Library), Paris. Source: *Khat'abala* (Tiflis) 43 (18 October 1908).

Իթիկէ

Քուրդ։

Հայ։

Թուրք։

Արաբ։

ROTTER.

Այս հպատակ ազգութեանը
Թող զարմանա՜ն են ձեր վերբերը...

in the Armenian revolutionary discourse and then moves to federation, decentralization, and autonomy. Chapter 4 tackles different aspects of socialism, including its relationship with its rival sibling, nationalism—for the Armenians as well as many of their fellow Russian and Ottoman subjects, specifically Georgian and Balkan peoples. This chapter seeks to answer the following questions, which are key to understanding how the circulation of global ideas contributed to connecting triangulated revolutions: How did ideas such as constitutionalism and federation motivate and inspire our revolutionaries? How did the revolutionaries understand these ideas? Which ideologues and theoreticians did they find appealing? In other words, what did they read, with what concepts did they engage, and whom did they reference and translate? How did their personal encounters and exchanges with thinkers in and from Western and Central Europe and Russia, as well as their keen awareness and deep familiarity with international leftist views, movements, publications, and world events, contribute to the mobility of ideas and revolutionaries' ideological boundary crossings? How did they adapt ideas or mental constructs to their own reality, link them to their own objectives, and accommodate them to the revolutions for which they fought?

CONSTITUTION: A "CURTAIN . . . UNDER WHICH HIDES A MURDEROUS REALITY" OR THE "SECRET OF STRENGTH"?

The illustration with which I began this chapter certainly gives us an idea of the perceptions of different ethnicities in relation to the Ottoman Empire. Even though they are all shown holding the banner of autonomy in response to or to accompany the banner of unity and equality, some seem to be more vehement advocates of autonomy than others. The Armenian is portrayed as somewhere between the aggressive Balkan peoples on one side and the rather apathetic or dispirited Kurd, Bedouin, and Jew on the other. His banner is held high, although he himself is kneeling. The Turk takes center stage, representing his dominance in the empire's power structure. Constitution is represented by the rainbow, symbolizing peace, rebirth, and promise. The illustration may be drawing from the story in Genesis, in which a great flood brought on by God to rid the world of humans who have corrupted the world and filled it with violence—an ancient form of man's inhumanity to man (Gen. 6:11)—is followed by a rainbow signifying God's covenant with man. In Genesis, God vows, "I establish my covenant with you, that never again shall all flesh be cut off by the waters of a flood, and never again shall there be a flood to destroy the earth (Gen. 9:11). . . . I have set my bow in the clouds, and it shall be a sign of the covenant between me and the earth. When I bring clouds over the earth and the bow is seen in the clouds, I will remember my covenant that is between me and you and every living creature of all flesh (Gen. 9:13–15)." Following Genesis, if we understand the rainbow of constitution as a symbol of that covenant and covenant as "a formal agreement . . . between a superior and inferior party, the former 'making' or 'establishing' (vv. 9, 11) the bond with the latter," then we can make sense of all the illustration's symbolism, including the stormy clouds menacingly looming behind the rainbow.[2] The constitution represents a covenant and a promise between the "superior" Ottoman state and its subjects not to rain violence upon them and instead to usher in a new period of unity and equality. The response of the "inferior" parties seems demoralized, hopeful, skeptical, or indignant. The poem, too, rings a note of promise and expresses a wish to "conjoin" with "conciliation" and to "remedy" past injuries. However, it does so in the context of and perhaps in contrast to competing visions or understandings of constitution.

The illustration no doubt represents a complex, newly constitutional Ottoman world. It also, however, opens a way for us to comprehend the rather nuanced relationship of Armenians to the period's global craze of constitutionalism in three empires and revolutionary movements. Much has been written about the impact of the concept of constitutionalism on Russians, Iranians, and Ottomans. I myself, in previous publications, have followed the general interpretation that constitution was believed to be a solution not only for the troubled relationship between state and citizenry of the region but a panacea for all economic, political, and social ills and injustices. Moreover, as Nikki Keddie so aptly put it more than twenty-five years ago, its adherents saw it as the "secret of strength."[3] More recently, in his comparative study of the Ottoman and Iranian Revolutions, Nader Sohrabi reasons, "Constitutionalism was understood as a tool for self-strengthening and regeneration, features that took precedence over all the other aspects of this discourse. The Russo-Japanese war served as a magical confirmation of their arguments: a Great Power that had failed to implement the political framework of the other European powers—even against the wishes of its public—was decisively and embarrassingly defeated by a small Asian nation that had made this transformation. With this spectacular event, constitutionalism's reputation as a purveyor of strength was confirmed beyond doubt."[4] Young Turk constitutionalists held similar views about constitutionalism in Europe as "Constitutionalism was taken as reason for political, economic, and 'civilizational' advances in Europe."[5] The overwhelmingly positive view, not only throughout this region but also around the world, dominated the discourse on constitution and the aspirations of people worldwide.

Constitutionalism as an idea, a goal, and an actualized model had wide reach. News of constitutional struggles as well as pamphlets and books about constitutionalism circulated not only through telegraphy and print but also frontier-crossing revolutionaries who benefitted from the other turn-of-the-century marvels, the steamship and railroad. Thus, the idea of constitutionalism and its devotees connected revolutions at home and afar. Armenians pursued and sought constitution in all three empires: Russian, Ottoman, and Iranian. Some activists and thinkers, however, had mixed feelings about the reality or practical application of constitution, even if they espoused its principle and promise. This should not be construed as a rejection or ambivalence about the significance of constitution; on the contrary, they attached so much importance to it and the multiple problems it could resolve that they worried about the kind of constitution being supported or established.

While the two main political parties, the ARF and the SDHP, joined the bandwagon of constitutionalism, they differed in degree of advocacy, depending on their own approach and the constitution in question.[6] For example, the SDHP—which, unlike the ARF, did not ally itself with the Young Turks before or during the 1908 revolution—consistently criticized and warned against the reinstatement of the Ottoman constitution of 1876, not because the party was anticonstitutionalist but because it did not want a constitution that only bore the "mocking" (ծաղրական/tsaghrakan) label of "constitution," or, as the Armenian Socialist Revolutionary *Aniv* put it, a constitution that served as a "curtain" (վարագոյր/varagoyr) hiding a "murderous reality" (սպանիչ իրականութիւն/spanich' irakanut'iwn).[7] The SDHP's criticism of the Ottoman constitution must be understood within the context of the reason it opted for nonalliance with the Ottoman opposition from the first days of talks, which had their official start in Paris in 1902, at the Ottoman Congress of Liberals. The SDHP clarified its antagonistic position by drawing attention to what it perceived as the Young Turks' limited goal of reinstituting a "pitiful" constitution and thus conceding to absolutism.[8] Despite continued efforts throughout 1905 and 1906 in preparation for the second congress in 1907, and even after the revolution in July 1908, and also despite meetings between

FIGURE 4. Stepan Sapah-Giwlian
(1861–1928). Image reproduced
courtesy of the SDHP Central
Committee. Source: Beruz Sapah-
Giwlian, *Kensagrut'iwn Step'an
Sapah-Giwleani* [Biography of Stepan
Sapah-Giwlean] (Union City, NJ:
Elmas-Satin, 1936).

a number of prominent Young Turks like Bahaeddin Şakir, Ahmed Rıza, Nazım Bey, and Diran Kelekian and SDHP leaders Murad (Hampartsum Boyajian) and Stepan Sapah-Giwlian (Stepanos Ter Danielian), the two sides could not reach an agreement.[9] The Young Turks appealed again to the SDHP and even its divorced nonsocialist split faction (Verakazmeal) before the 1907 congress but were rebuffed yet again.[10] For the SDHP, the divide was too great.[11] Much like the Macedonian and Bulgarian socialists—the Narrow Socialists, led by Dimităr/Dimitŭr Blagoev, and even the Broad Socialists, led by Yanko Sakazov (Janko Sakŭzov) after their own 1903 split—the SDHP perceived the Young Turks as nationalists. As Ibrahim Yalimov explains, Bulgarian (and Serbian) socialists "stressed that the Young Turks were neither progressive nor revolutionary, but persisted with the chauvinism and despotism of Abdülhamid."[12]

The SDHP believed that the first and elemental wish of the Young Turks was to choke the Armenian cause as they pursued a purely nationalist goal.[13] For the SDHP, the Armenian and Young Turk advocates of the reinstatement of the so-called "Midhatean constitution" of

1876—a reference to Midhat Paşa (1822–83), an Ottoman statesman of the Tanzimat period who played an important role in the promulgation of the constitution—were delusional dreamers. Stepan Sapah-Giwlian, the most vocal SDHP member on this topic and a prominent leader and intellectual who had many conversations and encounters with Young Turks in exile such as Ahmed Rıza and Prince Sabaheddin, penned several articles in SDHP papers like *Apagay* (Future), published in Tiflis; *Zang* (Bell), published in Tabriz; and *Hnch'ak* (Bell), published in Paris.[14] In several articles, Sapah-Giwlian laments that Armenians tended to become giddy (գլխու պտույտ/glkhu ptoyt) upon hearing the word *constitution,* considering it a "cure-all potion" (ամենաբուժիչ դեղ/amenabuzhich' degh).[15] He charges them with fantasizing about achieving and enjoying freedom "cheaply" by concentrating their energies on helping to restore the 1876 constitution. Sapah-Giwlian sends a stern warning: "'the Midhatean Constitution' will not bring anything *constitutional* for us, even if it is executed; therefore, we will be committing an unforgiveable weakness of mind, by forgetting everything, if we tear up, fold, and put aside our twenty-year history [as a revolutionary movement], and pursue a shadow." Sapah-Giwlian goes further by depicting the Young Turk appeal to Armenians to unite as "children of the Fatherland," "compatriots," and "victims of Hamidian despotism" as nefarious, having an "explicit purpose: first, to bury the Armenian Issue, and second, to remove that reason for Europe's intervention . . . and third, to turn the Armenian people into a footstool to the impatient Turkish *nationalism* and . . . to condemn us to immobility. . . . "[16]

Sapah-Giwlian takes great pains to go through relevant articles in the Ottoman constitution (Kanun-i Esasi), drawing from classic sources from Aristotle to Montesquieu on despotism to lay bare the constitution's "nakedness" (մերկություն/merkut'iwn). He levels his criticism against a number of constitutional articles, which, as Raymond Kévorkian sums it up, "spelled out the sultan's political-religious prerogatives, were purely theocratic in nature, . . . absolved the sovereign of all responsibility for his actions," and "also gave him the power to appoint and dismiss ministers."[17] Sapah-Giwlian argues that contrary to its promise and recognition of some freedoms, constitution in this case would only confirm and strengthen the theocratic, despotic, and unlimited government already in place. Only through solidarity and collaboration of all ethnicities, recognition of the principle of self-government, and a democratic constitution will the country join the ranks of modern states.[18] Only then will it become a "New Turkey," for which Sapah-

Giwlian expresses his willingness to shed blood in order to see to it that, like constitutional America, "Turkey's sun is the rising sun."[19]

Calling for a bottom-up approach, Sapah-Giwlian concludes that the constitution "can never be considered sufficient because it does not correspond and does not give satisfaction to the country and people's real demands ... It is time that the people themselves take control of their fates."[20] Further on the left, the internationalist Marxist Tigran Zaven (Zugasēzian) agreed, pointing out that the reinstatement of constitution was "simply the result of coup d'état" and that the sultan was merely forced to accept it. Thus, instead of being the "child of the stubborn and conscious battle of progressive bourgeoisie," it was "the fruit of the machinations of a group of individuals" and, as such, an "incomplete constitution" and not the expression of the "popular will."[21] The Armenian Social Democratic paper, *Nor Hosank'*, also joined the choir. Its editor, Garegin Kozikian, writing under the pseudonym Yesalem, mocked the military nature of the revolution and the absence of popular participation and pronounced that no clergy, landowner, agha, bey, or Kurdish tribe would accept the constitution. He saw the solution in the coalescing of all constitutional elements around the same political interests and the removal of ethnic conflicts and inequality.[22] Like fellow international socialist Zaven, Kozikian also brought up the absence of popular participation. Zaven and Kozikian were no different than itinerant Balkan Marxist Krastyo (Krŭstiu/Christian) Rakovsky, who wrote almost immediately after the Young Turk Revolution that the constitution "leaves a lot to be desired. It leaves the autocratic power of the Sultan almost intact."[23] Therefore, the SDHP and those further on the left did not object to constitution but to the particular Ottoman constitution of 1876. They recognized the significance of constitution but sought a democratic one, not only in the Ottoman Empire but also in Iran and the Russian Empire, without losing sight of their socialist ideal.[24]

Armenian constitutionalist revolutionaries, like the SDHP, distinguished between the Ottoman constitution of 1876, which was abrogated in 1878 and reinstated with the revolution of July 1908, and a "democratic" constitution. Moreover, while they remained very cautious about the existing Ottoman constitution, they were much more enthusiastic about newly created ones (for example, the one in Iran). Perhaps they recognized the divergence of constitutionalisms in places like the Ottoman Empire and Iran. As Sohrabi explains, for the Young Turks, "constitutionalism was only a means to rescue the empire ... The distaste of the major constitutionalists for popular participation ended public

FIGURE 5. Let us give the constitution a new salute. Image reproduced courtesy of Bibliothèque Nubar (Nubar Library), Paris. Source: *Khat'abala* (Tiflis) 31 (26 July 1908).

activism." Iranian constitutionalists, however, "actively sought, and received, increased popular backing as it [the constitutional movement] went along."[25] It is not altogether unfathomable that distance between constitutionalism and Armenian populations may also have had something to do with the varying degrees of advocacy. Of the three states that are our focus, Iran had the smallest population of Armenians at about seventy thousand, and although Armenians had a long history in Iran, they made no claims to reforms or autonomy, as was the case in the Ottoman and Russian Empires, where a few million Armenians resided. For Iran's Armenians, the constitution that emerged in 1906 and that they fought to preserve became a way to rise above what they considered to be their "shameful rank of visitor."[26] The Iranian constitution, like the Ottoman one, while recognizing the equality of all subjects, still retained Islam as the official religion of the country. As a constitutionally affirmed religious minority, Armenians in Iran struggled to achieve the same rights and responsibilities as Muslims, declaring unequivocally, "we are Persian citizens."[27] As such, they objected to having separate parliamentary representatives, which they viewed as only perpetuating further divisions, and they called for full political participation.[28] I will return to the question of belonging in the Iranian and Ottoman cases in the next chapter, during the discussion of socialism and the national question, but it is appropriate to mention here that for Iran's Armenians, the constitution—despite its flaws—as well as the movement behind it was inspiring and an opportunity to join the Iranian nation. Moreover, the promise of Iran's movement for constitution transcended the country and the region. A front-page article in the ARF paper *Zang* (Bell), titled "The Freedom Mob," placed especially high hopes on Iran, which it believed would have an effect on its Ottoman neighbor, and (much farther east) on China. It referred to a connected revolutionary wave sweeping Asia and credited the Russian Revolution for having an "inevitable" impact on the Ottoman Empire, Iran, and China. The SDHP paper in Tiflis, *Apagay,* even underscored how news of Iran's "flames of revolution" was spreading to transatlantic borders by telegraph.[29]

Thus, for a variety of political, pragmatic, and ideological reasons—both local and global—ranging from developments in the Ottoman and Russian Empires to commitment to socialist struggle to concern about the security of Iran's Armenian subjects, Armenians, especially the ARF, committed energy and forces to the Iranian Constitutional Revolution.[30] ARF's role in the revolution began in 1907 and received a stamp of approval after the decision in favor of participation at the party's general congress and, moreover, after Rostom reached agreement with six Majles (parliament) members led by Seyyed Hasan Taqizadeh.[31] Meetings between the Armenian and Iranian delegates took place between 30 December 1907 and 4 January 1908. Collaboration centered around protecting the newly established constitution in order to ensure its survival, strengthening constitutionalism, and influencing the direction of the movement toward greater democracy. The agreement and collaborative efforts, both military and ideological (in the case of the SDHP), indicate Iranian constitutionalists' appreciation and recognition of Armenian knowledge and practice, gained in the South Caucasus, especially since 1903, in defense of the Armenian Church during Russian confiscation of its properties and additionally in 1905–6 during the violent intercommunal fighting between Armenians and Azeris in the South Caucasus. In addition to these particular elements, Iranian revolutionaries in general respected their Caucasian neighbors' revolutionary proficiency during the Russian revolutionary movement.

The secret agreement, which neither side signed, citing Iranian concerns over a public agreement between parliamentary representatives and a revolutionary party and ARF consideration of the position held by some ARF members against participation, kept them "morally bound" nevertheless.[32] Opposition to Armenian participation in the Iranian Revolution was not limited to a few ARF members who felt that a struggle on the Iranian front would take away from more important campaigns against the Ottoman and for some Russian states. For example, the anonymous writer of a journal written in Armenian in Tabriz during May and June 1905 and again from June 1908 to the end of July 1908, despite a general support for constitutionalism and the constitutional movement in Iran, maintains a cautious and even pessimistic stance toward the revolution, which he believes has been "infected by the Russian revolution" but instigated by exploitative clerics while the "real people" of Iran remain completely ignorant, "very unripe," and "unprepared to defend its [Iran's] own rights and interests." Although the journal writer praises the Tabriz resistance against royalist forces trying to wrest control from the constitutional elements and is generally quite praiseworthy of one of the resistance leaders, Sattar Khan, he finds the South Caucasian revolutionaries to be "vampires" and "thieves and Tatar bashibozuks out to fool the Persian masses."[33] The writer seems utterly baffled by "rumors" that Armenians have been assisting constitutionalists with bombs and explosive material, considering it a "fantastical opinion" because Armenians have always held a neutral position and adding cynically that Armenians do not have the ability to think and consult among themselves, much less work with others.[34] The anonymous writer, although aware of Sattar Khan's crucial role in the Tabriz resistance, seems unaware of the Armenian Yeprem Khan, a comrade-in-arms of Sattar Khan in Tabriz, a successful military leader in his own right, and later chief of police.[35]

With the agreement with Iranian constitutionalists, the ARF promised to undertake a number of actions, including but not limited to carrying out European propaganda, pursuing good relations between Iran and Bulgaria especially vis-à-vis their position against the Ottoman sultan, organizing active resistance to bring forth revolution in the Ottoman Empire, establishing wireless telegraph in regions of military operations, providing one or two competent officers to the staff of the general of the Iranian army, placing at the disposal of the army some specialists to handle devices of explosive material, and organizing detachments for guerilla warfare. In return, Iranians promised to provide to the Armenian activists safe passage to Iran, particularly Azerbaijan, and free transport of men, arms, munitions, and print; to fund a cartridge factory in Azerbaijan; to sell at cost to the ARF arms, cartridges, cannon powder, and the like from the arsenals of the government; and to insist in all opportune circumstances on the necessity of the establishment of a constitutional regime in the Ottoman Empire, in general, and the realization of autonomy in the Armenian provinces, in particular.[36] This agreement led to many collaborative activities between the ARF and Iranian revolutionaries, which, in addition to the ideological collaboration of the SDHP discussed in the next chapter, included the Tabriz resistance (July 1908 to April 1909); the takeover of Rasht, Qazvin, and Tehran (February to July 1909); the battles to defeat the returning Mohammed 'Ali Shah and his brother, Salar al-Dowleh (June to August 1911 and mid-1912); and other battles against the anticonstitutionalist forces of Rahim Khan and the Shahsevans.

Unlike its stance in Iran, the SDHP was unwilling to enter "the bloody fray" of the Ottoman constitutional movement. Despite or because of its adherence to constitutionalism, the ARF joined in, albeit with reservations and caution, as it did the Iranian Revolution. The party took part in the first Congress of Ottoman Liberals in Paris in 1902 with a delegation headed by Avetis Aharonian.[37] Despite disagreements from the onset regarding foreign intervention and decentralization, with the ARF and Prince Sabaheddin in support and Ahmed Rıza and his faction in opposition, the ARF remained committed to efforts at cooperation and solidarity. Meetings continued to take place between a number of Young Turk players, namely Sabaheddin and Rıza, the ARF in Geneva and Paris, and ARF's Khachatur Malumian and SDHP's Sapah-Giwlian.[38] In the second Ottoman Congress in 1907, also in Paris, the participants disagreed on a number of issues, from revolutionary character to socialism and populism, but agreed to force Sultan Abdülhamid to step down, to transform the administration, and to establish constitutional government through several means, including armed and unarmed resistance, nonpayment of taxes, propaganda, and other necessary means.[39] The ARF continued to support the constitutional government for several years after the 1908 reinstatement of constitution, the 1909 Adana massacres of Armenians, the absence of real progress on the issue of land restitution and land reform, the continued insecurity of rural Armenian populations, and general disappointment in the slow, sometimes halting pace of change.[40] Land reform and security persisted as the most thorny issues in the relations between the ARF and the Committee of Union and Progress and preoccupied the ARF, especially after the 1909 massacres.[41]

Some segments of the ARF expressed doubts about the Young Turks, including Prince Sabaheddin, who was most closely allied with the Armenian opposition to the Ottoman sultan, even in 1906.[42] They called the Young Turks "colorless," "lazy," "immobile," as "inert" as the Turkish masses, "political children," and "careerists" without "revolutionary temperament."[43] The party remained cooperative until about 1912, the same time that it withdrew from the Iranian scene. It did so knowing full well that the Ottoman constitution would not and could not ameliorate the situation for all. Even only a few months after the Adana bloodshed, the ARF reaffirmed its decision to defend the Ottoman constitution by every means available.[44] The party had been particularly enthusiastic about tax revolts in places like Erzurum, Bitlis, and other eastern Anatolian vilayets, in which it saw "serious and eminently consoling" signs of an "awakening" influenced perhaps by the "Russian people's example."[45] Its support of the Young Turk movement garnered the acknowledgment of many Young Turks, including Ahmed Rıza, who, writing in French, on behalf of the CUP, to ARF "comrades," expressed his delight in their "fraternal encouragement for our movement in Macedonia." Rıza also notes the necessity to spread the revolutionary forces into Anatolia, where he believed the ARF to "have sufficient forces," asking "why not place them into the movement? Why not, at the same time, especially act in Constantinople . . . ?" He ends by underscoring and perhaps warning about the importance of a united front: "your movement should have the same patriotic character, same goal as ours; to reduce to a complete impotence the established enemies of the Ottoman Nation."[46] Good relations, of course, wavered and deteriorated, especially with Rıza and other more conservative CUP members, and the ARF's intervention or "interference" after the victory of the revolution was not welcome.[47]

The ARF consistently sought the full implementation of the constitution, demonstrating its pragmatism and continued faith that constitution remained the only acceptable alternative under the prevailing circumstances. The party press reminded its readers that Armenians had no demand different than the "complete application of the Constitution" and "all their effort is for life, dignity, the guarantee of property to be established in their beloved country."[48] The ARF found itself in a precarious situation between having to justify its alliance with the Young Turks to an Armenian audience, among them followers and detractors (both of whom were impatient with the pace of reforms), and continuing to maintain pressure for meaningful change. The party linked its constitutionalism with two key interrelated concepts: real equality and its prerequisite, peaceful coexistence. For example, Ottoman-Armenian intellectual and activist Rupen Zartarian directed readers to the contradiction between constitutionalism in a multiethnic state and the dominance of one ethnicity, exclaiming, "No, in a constitutional country there is not one dominant ethnicity/nation." As every citizen is equal before the law, he asserted, so is every ethnicity equal to the other, "no more, no less"; without this principle, a country cannot "profess itself constitutional and commit to peaceful work."[49] Furthermore, as we shall see shortly, constitutionally granted equality and peaceful coexistence were achievable, for the ARF, only through decentralization and autonomy in federation, which in ARF's view was inseparable from socialism. These are the very elements represented in the *Khat'abala* illustration: the rainbow of constitution, the central banner of unity and equality, and the encircling banners of autonomy. Thus, they may be seen not as competing components but rather as linked and aggregate segments of a greater whole.

FEDERATION: "FETISH, AN IDOL, AN EXCEPTIONAL IDEAL" OR HUMANITY'S HAPPINESS

The reception and contrasting views of constitutionalism were part of a larger engagement with contemporary ideas and ideologies fueling our revolutionaries' aspirations. Much of ARF's discourse on constitutionalism was formulated within the context of the organization's advocacy of federation, with its requisite components of decentralization and self-government. The ARF in line with most other socialist parties viewed federation, not as a "fetish," "idol," or "exceptional ideal" but "a *political form*" that will result in the happiness of the majority of humanity.[50] The periodical press active during the Ottoman and Russian Revolutions, mainly in Tiflis and in Istanbul (after 1908), took up the task of explaining and advocating federation, which, contrary to unitary systems, means that sovereignty "is non-centralized, often constitutionally, between at least two levels so that units at each level have final authority and can be self governing [sic] in some issue area."[51] Armenian federalists most commonly used the Russian term федерация/federatsiya and the Armenian term դաշնակցութիւն/dashnakts'ut'iwn to refer to federation.[52] As Robert Watts clarifies and as Armenian, Russian, Balkan, Ottoman, and other proponents of federation understood, federation "is a compound polity combining constituent units and a general government, each possessing powers delegated to it by the people through a constitution, each empowered to deal directly with the citizens in the exercise of a significant portion of its legislative, administrative, and taxing powers, and each directly elected by its citizens."[53] Beyond this basic meaning, various Armenian thinkers or parties as well as some Macedonian, Bulgarian, Georgian, Russian, and Ottoman Muslim counterparts sought federation because they believed it offered the best scenario for a multiethnic, multireligious, pluralistic society such as the Russian and Ottoman Empires and the Balkan Peninsula.[54]

Armenian-language newspapers, lectures, and three key books propagated Russian and Ottoman federation, emphasizing—among other things—the vital role of constitution in the establishment and proper functioning of a federative state. All three books were written by Armenian intellectuals and members of the ARF, which had, by the time of the publication of these books, adopted the principle of a decentralized federative state for the Caucasus and the Russian Empire and later for the Ottoman Empire. The ARF had become the main Armenian proponent of federation in both empires, working closely with counterparts, such as Prince Sabaheddin and his League of Private Initiative and Decentralization in the Ottoman Empire and Socialist Revolutionaries in the Russian Empire, to promote federalism. These works, therefore, occupy an important place in the history of the federalist approach in the two empires, especially as they come from a nondominant group's point of view, a group whose populations straddled three empires. While we do not have distribution numbers for these books, the public lectures or prepublication book talks the authors held in major political and cultural hubs within the Ottoman and Russian frontiers and the lively discussions that followed those talks at the venues and later in print certainly provide us with an impression of the impact they had on contemporaries.

Contemporary leftist periodicals reported on public lectures in major cities like Tiflis and Istanbul and carried articles about the merits and problems of federation. Lectures were often followed by vigorous debates, in which proponents of a federative republic and critics, both in the audience and in pages of periodicals, exchanged intellectual and sometimes personal barbs. For example, ARF leader Garegin Khazhak, who also authored a book on the subject of federation, faced considerably heated argumentation after his lecture on self-government, autonomy, and federalism in Tiflis. That same summer in 1906, also in Tiflis, Armenian Social Democrat Stepan Shahumian's lecture, too, faced opposition; however, in this case, Shahumian was arguing against federalism.[55] Debates were often uncivil and spilled onto the pages of the papers. In one letter to *Alik'* (Wave), Khazhak complains that both liberal and leftist Tiflis-based periodicals such as the liberal *Mshak* (Cultivator—edited by Grigor Artstruni), the Russian Social Democratic Workers Party *Kayts* (Spark—edited by Aramayis Yezkian), and Armenian social-democratic organ *Keank'* (Life—edited by Bakhshi Ishkhanian) were "throwing curses" at him.[56] The Armenian Social Democrat paper *Dzayn* (Voice), published in Tiflis from 1906 to 1907, was quite relentless and virulent in its attacks on the ARF.[57] *Drōshak* implored ARF papers to cease taking part or responding to attacks in the pages of the revolutionary press because they did not believe it served revolutionary or socialist knowledge but fed "wretched and passionate" tendencies. Instead, *Drōshak* advised remaining strong and "magnanimous toward opponents."[58] Similar articles in the ARF press counseled what one paper termed "silent contempt" as a response.[59]

Public lectures may have given orators a venue to test their ideas and address critiques before presenting more thoroughly supported and strongly argued concepts in their books. At least two of the three books that appeared roughly around the same time were based on lectures. The three books were Avetik Shakhatunian's *Fēdēralizm ew demōkratizm* (Federalism and democratism), published in Tiflis in 1907 (the author was also known as Shahkhatunian, pseudonym Artur); Garegin Khazhak's *Depi fēdērats'ia* (Toward federation), also published in Tiflis in 1907 after several public lectures; and Simon Zavarian's *Apakedronats'umě*

(Decentralization), first given as a speech in Eastern Armenian and then expanded and published as a booklet in Western Armenian in Istanbul in 1908.[60] In all three cases, constitution as an integral part of a federation appears as the superior method by which to protect the rights of minorities and obviate ethnic antagonisms.[61] This point is important for two reasons. First, it further connects at least two revolutions (Ottoman and Russian), which, for our supporters of revolution and federation, had similar goals—that is, equality and peaceful coexistence. Second, it underscores, as we shall see, the parallel concerns and aims of those Ottoman and Russian revolutionaries who advocated for federation in both empires. For Zavarian, whom we may remember from the previous chapter as one of our roving revolutionaries and cofounder of the ARF, it was a mistake to believe that constitution alone could eradicate the problems, particularly the ethnic one, facing the Ottoman Empire, and it was perhaps a bigger error to be lulled by hope that cordial relations and time would be sufficient to solve deeply entrenched problems. Zavarian locates the solution to the national question in an expanded, improved constitution within a decentralized, federative state.[62] Federation could be thought of as an extension or a close relative of ethnic solidarity and collaboration, especially between Armenians and their Muslim neighbors—that is, according to the ARF press, their "land brother[s]" (հողի եղբայր/hoghi yeghbayr), Turks and Kurds.[63] The ARF idealized the potential power of federation and believed strongly in its actualization. As *Drōshak* exclaimed, "Yesterday it was a reverie, today it is a comforting possibility, tomorrow it will become an actual, living reality."[64]

In the late nineteenth and early twentieth centuries, federation seemed to many around the world as a possible and desirable way to deal with the national or nationalities question. As legal scholar Nicholas Aroney states in his study of the Australian conception of federation, "'federation' was widely considered to be the best means by which separate peoples inhabiting extended territories could be united by a lasting political bond."[65] For federalists, whether Australian, European, Caucasian, or Armenian, the United States and Switzerland served as models of successful federations. After all, as Watts points out, the United States (1789) and Switzerland (1848), as well as Canada (1867) and Australia (1901), "continue to be remarkably effective" and "still operat[e] under their original constitutions."[66] What appealed to Armenian federalists about the American and Swiss federal systems was twofold. First, decentralization and retention of autonomy for states and cantons, respectively, lay at the core of both classic models of federation. States and cantons preserved their political autonomy as reflected, for example, in their own constitutions and rights of taxation. Moreover, they participated in the affairs of the central (i.e., federal) government, legislation, and other decisions through representatives. As they focused on states' rights, federalists like Shakhatunian referred to both countries' constitutions, in particular Article 10 of the US Constitution and Article 3 of the Swiss Constitution outlining states/cantons' powers.[67] Second and equally important, the US and Swiss federations were considered exemplars of states able to balance or combine both diversity and political unity of their citizens. Khazhak underscores the two nations' simultaneous preservation of "democracy and people's freedoms," claiming rather confidently that "neither in Switzerland nor in the American federations, does the national issue exist. The nationalities' language, their spirit, [and] their distinct culture are left absolutely free, without any oppression."[68] While their exemplary federal models were limited, their sources and references to buttress their promotion of federation were wide-ranging.

Although Rosa Luxemburg attributed an "anarchic hue" going back to Bakunin to federalists, Armenian federalists found their inspiration and evidence in a wider array of sources.[69] They often drew from the same toolkit of legal scholars, jurists, philosophers, and theoreticians, ranging from Baron de Montesquieu, Johannes Althusius, and Pierre-Joseph Proudhon to Mikhail Bakunin, Pyotr Kropotkin, James Bryce, and A. V. Dicey, to name only the authors most commonly referenced and directly engaged by the Armenian advocates of federation.[70] A closer look at the works of Khazhak, Shakhatunian, and Zavarian helps show how they engaged with an eclectic group of thinkers and their sundry ideas and also how they understood federation, how they appropriated and harnessed these thinkers for their own purposes, according to their own circumstances, and in the service of two out of three revolutionary struggles, the Russian and the Ottoman.

Khazhak's *Toward Federation* is a lengthy and serious study of centralization, decentralization, self-government, autonomy, and federation/federalism that references the key works in Russian, French, and German on these and related topics. Khazhak makes extensive use of major works by German Social Democrat theoretician Karl Kautsky, Austrian Social Democrat and statesman Karl Renner (pen name R. Springer), and professor of law Georg Jellinek, as well as Russian anarchocommunist Pyotr Kropotkin, Polish Social Democrat intellectual Rosa Luxemburg, Russian anarchist Mikhail Bakunin, French philosopher of the Enlightenment Baron de la Montesquieu, British historian and statesman

James Bryce, and British jurist and constitutional theorist A. V. Dicey, among others. The study is very much reflective of the author's educational background as well as the circulation common to his circle. Khazhak (born Garegin Chakalian in Alexandropol/Gyumri) had a degree in sociology from the University of Geneva. As a member of the ARF, he worked for the party organ, *Drōshak,* in Geneva, wrote for the left-leaning *Murch* in Tiflis, was on the editorial board of ARF's *Haṟaj,* also in Tiflis, and traveled to Baku (1894), Izmir and Egypt (1897–98), and Istanbul (1898–1903). After spending some time between 1903 and 1912 as a teacher in the South Caucasus as well as serving two stints as a political prisoner, he returned to Istanbul. Only a few years later, he was one of the first Armenian intellectuals and leaders killed at the start of the Armenian Genocide in 1915. His other works, both published in 1912, are *Inch'ē dasakargĕ?* (What is class?) and *Inch' ē azgut'iwnĕ? Gitakan hetazōtut'iwnĕ* (What is nationality? The scientific research).[71]

Khazhak's book strongly advocates for a federation through a discussion of the advantages and disadvantages of different political forms and presents a comparison of New and Old World countries—for example, France, England, Russia, Belgium, United States, Switzerland, Australia, New Zealand, and, to lesser extent, Spain and Italy.[72] Khazhak's work is a perfect example, along with the contemporary periodical press and writings on socialism to be discussed in the next section, of Bayly's contention that movements were connected because "activists and working-class intellectuals across the world now read translations of Marx, Lenin, Bakunin, Proudhon, and other radical thinkers. . . . "[73] In this case, they were not merely connected through reading these texts in translation as well as in the original but also through direct engagement with the texts. As we saw in the previous chapter, their readings and engagement were also enabled and expedited by the greater availability of philosophical and social scientific works through the turn-of-the-century wonders of steam-operated presses, steamships, and railroads. These technological transformations brought different worlds closer together and made ideas more accessible in print.

Khazhak's and others' federation (and socialism, as we shall see later) drew from diverse and not so obviously congruent sources that nevertheless were part of the intellectual and revolutionary history of Western and Central Europe and Russia, whether those sources had anarchist, socialist, or liberal leanings. It did not seem at all contradictory to Khazhak and his contemporaries to appreciate or draw, for example, from Enlightenment philosophe Montesquieu's *De l'esprit des lois,* in which he argued for a federal form of government, as well as anarchist Bakunin's *Federation, Socialism, Antitheologism* or from the "true father" of anarchism—and, as Bakunin himself said, "the master of us all"—Proudhon and his *Du Principe fédératif.*[74] Although these early proponents of federation certainly received a hearty nod from profederalist Armenian intellectuals, those to whom Khazhak and, to a lesser extent, Shakhatunian resorted most often were contemporary theoreticians or academics, including but not limited to the following: from Germany and Austria, Kautsky, Renner (pseudonym Springer), Jellinek, and Maximilian (Max) Anton von Seydel; from Britain, Bryce and Dicey, for their historical studies of American, Canadian, and Swiss federation; and others on autonomy and federation, including Kropotkin on the decentralization of industry; Z. Avalov on decentralization and self-government in France; Vladimir Matveevich Gessen on autonomy, federation, and the national question; and Nikolaĭ Ivanovich Lazarevskiĭ on autonomy.[75] These sources informed the way in which the Armenian intellectuals approached federation, understood its history, grasped its theoretical value and practical application, and employed the sources—whether to concur or to counter—in order to build a case for federation in both the Ottoman and Russian Empires.

As these Armenian thinkers saw it, the revolutionary period that saw constitutional movements unfold in three empires, one taking inspiration from the other, promised equality, liberty, and fraternity; however, as we saw earlier, constitution was not the panacea its adherents may have envisioned, nor could it bring forth the realization of the great French Revolution's pledge. For them, the path to complete equality, real liberty, and meaningful fraternity lay in federation and socialism—that is, a decentralized, democratic/constitutional, federative, and socialist state that respected the rights of all peoples to govern themselves, as reflected in the illustration of unfurled banners. I will return to socialism and the important place it occupied in the writings and vision of Armenian revolutionaries in the next chapter, but a more explicit elaboration on federation for the Armenians will help further unfurl those banners.

For Zavarian, as for Khazhak, federation and its essential components of decentralization and local autonomy or self-government were the solution to the national question and problems of inequality and ethnic conflict. Zavarian's discussion of decentralization was also a way to introduce and propagate for a federalist Ottoman Empire. Zavarian begins with the example of Greek city-states, clearly drawing from Montesquieu's *De l'esprit des lois,* which presents the Greek city-states as federative, although he does not directly refer to Montesquieu's work in this case.[76] Zavarian attributes Greece's progress and achievements in the sciences and philosophy to the "natural" consequence of its decentralization and its subsequent decline to centralizing forces.[77] His main focus, though, is the Ottoman Empire, which, according to Zavarian, had been in decline for some 450 years, having become a pawn in the hands of foreigners and decreasing in territorial expanse and population. It is time, he says, to place the empire in the wake of revolution on new foundations. He clarifies, "Those new foundations—with my deep conviction—can only be decentralization . . . " because, given the vast empire's markedly different regions, from cold, mountainous Armenia to hot, desert Yemen, "Turkey is able to remain independent, have a healthy life and progress" solely under a decentralized system.[78] To attempt to meet the needs of the empire's disparate elements while disregarding the particularities would mean to "trample the demands of reality."[79] The solution lies in local government, through which people "master their own fate."[80] In order to illustrate, rather comically, the practical problem of relying on the center to deal with all issues that have secondary or even "denary" value, Zavarian brings up the Russian duma, whose important work had recently been obstructed by such mundane issues as the construction of Dorpat University's washroom. He concludes, "Parliament will drown under the weight of examining 'regulations.' That is how it is today in Russia."[81] Although Zavarian does not explicitly call for a Russian federation as he was speaking to an Ottoman audience, his reference to the undesirability of the Russian dilemma as well as his party's stance makes it clear that he was indeed also a proponent of federation in the Russian Empire.

Drawing from Montesquieu's comparisons of the French and British systems and Ukrainian-born sociologist (and acquaintance of Zavarian) Maksim Kovalevsky's treatment of autonomous communities, Zavarian concludes, "Everywhere *the level of a country's freedom is tied to the level of local autonomy.*"[82] In oppressive regimes, autonomy does not exist; in moderately constitutional countries, autonomy is limited; and in countries where there is "complete freedom," local autonomy is also comprehensive.[83] For Zavarian, as for his federalist comrades, two countries stood out as models of the last case: Switzerland and the United States.[84] Even in centralized countries, Zavarian sees aspects of local autonomy at work, presuming the principle of centralization realized only in China and Iran.[85] To come out of "our centuries-old stupor," he writes, requires the establishment of a "reborn country" on decentralized foundations with the examples of others in mind but, most of all, according to the country's "internal conditions."[86] Therefore, despite the US and Swiss exemplars of federal systems, based on the Ottoman Empire's political, economic, and educational level, Austrian decentralization grounded on national regional autonomy would be the most appropriate model.[87] In praising the Austrians and Americans by pointing to education, artisanal talents, and the spirit of taking initiative, Zavarian facetiously or perhaps seriously comes to a problematic classification: that an Austrian is worth two Armenians but an American is worth two Austrians and four Armenians. He surmises that "private initiative" is stimulated by autonomy. His short discussion of private initiative may have been inspired by Edmond Demolins's *A quoi tient la supériorité des Anglo-Saxons* (To what is the superiority of Anglo-Saxons due?) (1897). As Stefano Taglia explains, Demolins was a favorite of Prince Mehmet Sabaheddin, a proponent of federalism himself, who based his own views on Demolins's concept of private initiative as one of the key bases of an ideal society.[88]

Zavarian then proposes the reconfiguring of boundaries according to ethnographic and geographic differences with the right of local self-government while guaranteeing the state's union.[89] The critical (and, of course, ideal) result of such a configuration that ensures real equality would be the forgetting of the separatist tendencies of the past and the conviction by rulers that the privileges they were enjoying were unjust. The natural progression, Zavarian adds, will then inspire the increased broadening of local self-government, resulting ultimately in a "general Ottoman federation," an ARF revolutionary goal supported by federalists like Prince Sabaheddin and the League of Private Initiative and Decentralization and opposed by more nationalist, procentralization Young Turk figures like Ahmed Rıza.[90] ARF's Istanbul paper *Zhamanak* (Time) joined the call against separatism, asserting that the only obstacle against it is decentralization and that despite the "stain" of separatism placed on the ARF, the party stands firmly against it, concluding, "Eternally we reject *separatism*. . . ."[91] In this regard at least, the ARF and the internationalist Tigran Zaven seemed to agree. Railing against recurrent rumors that Armenians were demanding independence, Zaven denies it unequivocally, arguing that it is not only unrealizable but undesirable. He writes, "Armenians, separatist?. . . . No! we the unshaken defenders of fraternity, real equality, [and] real freedom do not desire independence because for us equally precious, equally sacrosanct are the rights of Turkish labor, that labor which has for centuries on mixed its sweat with the sweat of Armenian labor to irrigate the same soil that for centuries on has carried the same burden of tears and blood. . . . " Zaven then chastises those talking about separatism, considering it a betrayal of the interests of the fatherland.[92]

The ARF's appeals for an Ottoman Federation had begun as early as 1901, or possibly earlier, during preparations for revolution and in meetings with Young Turks.[93] Around the same time, the ARF began to work closely with Prince Sabaheddin, who was among a smaller contingent of Young Turks who advocated decentralization as a way to solve the Eastern Question and "secure political unity alongside social diversity in the Ottoman Empire"—a position that garnered much opposition from other Young Turks who viewed decentralization as a "cure [that] would cause a worse disease."[94] For such critics as Bahaeddin Şakir (member of the Committee of Union and Progress Central Committee, 1907–18), decentralization would only serve its main proponents, Europeans and Armenians, to the detriment of "Ottomanness."[95]

Armenians, however, were not the only Ottoman subjects who made appeals for a federal form of government for the Ottoman Empire. In early 1903 the Albanian nationalist leader, Derviş Hima, sought autonomy for Albania and called for Ottoman federation in the pages of İttihad-ı Osmanî—La Fédération Ottomane (Ottoman Union—The Ottoman Federation). Albanians were one of the Ottoman subjects, including Armenians, who gathered in Paris in 1902 at the Congress of Ottoman Opposition.[96] Even as early as 1885, Bulgarian Marxist and founder of the first Bulgarian social-democratic party (in 1891) Dimitûr Blagoev called for a Balkan federation, believing it to be the only path to the independence of all peoples in Macedonia.[97] According to Blagovest Njagulov, Blagoev "declared himself in favor of its [Macedonian] liberation from Ottoman rule . . . [and] asserted that the national problems in the Balkans would be solved by the implementation of the 'socialist ideal' in the form of a Balkan 'United States' or a 'Balkan republic.'"[98] However, while Blagoev insisted on autonomy for Ottoman subjects, he refrained from advocating secession. As Andreja Živković contends, "Blagoev opposed the right to secession, as it would unleash a process of endless fragmentation in the Balkans [and] internecine war, leaving the door open to the Great Powers to divide and rule the region. Instead, a revolutionary, federal Turkey provided the model and basic unit for the construction of a Balkan-Turkish federation that could defend the national independence of all the peoples against the imperialist powers and enable modern, capitalist development to flourish."[99]

Romanian socialist Rakovsky, too, adamantly proclaimed that it is "only in a federation of all the peoples of the [Ottoman] Empire that they [Young Turks] can find their salvation," and, like Blagoev, he rejected secession.[100] However, unlike Blagoev, who believed Balkan independence and federation would come only through revolutionary overthrow of the Ottoman Empire, leading to a "truly democratic solution to the national question," Rakovsky instead supported a stagist and reformist approach, beginning with a bourgeois revolution.[101] Indeed, after the 1908 revolution, as Živković argues, Rakovsky "defended the integrity of the oppressive Ottoman Empire as the only barrier to further fragmentation and war in the Balkans, as the only barrier to imperialism . . . "[102] Rakovsky seemed convinced that the postrevolutionary Ottoman Empire "had removed much of the cause for conflict between the Balkan states and Turkey."[103]

The First Balkan Socialist conference, held in Belgrade in 1910 and attended by Serbian, Croatian, Slovenian, Bosnia-Herzegovinian, and Macedonian socialists, Bulgarian Narrow Socialists (Broad Socialists and the Workers' Federation of Thessaloniki/Salonika were not invited), and the SDHP, further ratified a Balkan federative republic as a sought-after goal.[104] Macedonian social democrat and the first editor of *Rabotnicheska Iskra* (Workers' Spark, 1909–11), Vasil Glavinov, supported the "creation of an independent 'federative' Macedonian republic,' conceived as a kind of 'Balkan Switzerland.'" Therefore, like Switzerland, it would have a "cantonal organization of all local 'national elements' that would have the possibility to choose the official language in the cantons where they constituted the ethnic majority."[105] The federative Macedonian republic would then be the basis of a broader Balkan federation.[106] Njagulov concludes that all socialists who advocated Balkan unification believed that a federation was possible, whether from above or within the framework of the Ottoman Empire, or whether a process from below carried out by workers or from above carried out by states.[107] What they shared with each other and with Armenian and other federalists like the Workers' Federation of Thessaloniki/Salonika (established 1909), which collaborated with both the ARF and the SDHP, was the belief that federation would resolve ethnic and national antagonism and quarrels.[108] The Internal Macedonian Revolutionary Organization (IMRO), under the leadership of the Bulgarian-Macedonian Narrow Socialist and revolutionary Dimo Hadzi Dimov, sought a Balkan federation with "other 'nationalities' of Macedonia" outside Bulgaria for the same reason: "because only a federation could create the necessary conditions for a reconciliation of conflicting national interests."[109] As was the case for the ARF, for Dimov the answer lay not in the dissolution of the Ottoman Empire but in "regional self-government within the empire" as well as "self-government for *districts* within regions; and *for local communities within districts.*"[110] The IMRO and the ARF worked jointly in opposition to the Ottoman state, starting in the late nineteenth century and formally after the ARF's 1904 decision to collaborate with Macedonian elements at the Third General Congress, which was confirmed in 1907.[111] In 1906, after a meeting of unity against the Ottoman Empire, the ARF along with Macedonians, Bulgarians, Serbians, Greeks, Bosnians, and Herzegovinians called for good relations among the participants, solidarity against the Ottoman state, constitutional rule, autonomy for Macedonians, Armenians, and Bosnia-Herzegovinians, and a federation of all small Balkan states.[112] Thus, Balkan peoples and Armenians unambiguously linked constitution, autonomy, and federation.

Despite their endorsement of a Balkan federative republic at the First Balkan Socialist conference in 1910, the SDHP had serious doubts about decentralized Ottoman federation. Sapah-Giwlian insisted that federation could not develop in "Turkey" (in reference to Anatolia) for several reasons: (1) for a federation to work, Turkey must recognize the idea of nationality, which it did not; (2) federative systems in the United States, Switzerland, and Germany had emerged through a long historical process and thus could not be established hastily; (3) Turkey lacked the essential elements for federation; and (4) it had no minimum internal sovereignty. The only solution, therefore, for Sapah-Giwlian was separatism and self-government—not as principle but as a matter of fact and reality. He qualified that while for the nationalists they are principles, for the socialists they are merely the consequence of a historical process that has already taken place, a "fait accompli," which socialists merely accept.[113]

The SDHP's approach stood in stark contrast to that of the ARF, which concluded at its Fourth General Congress in Vienna in 1907 that "in order to put an end to baseless misunderstandings widespread among the Turks, the Congress deems it necessary to declare that the [Armenian Revolutionary] Federation has never had and does not now have any secessionist aspirations in Turkey, rather its objective has been complete equality among nations and, in accordance with the principle of broad local autonomy, the establishment of administrative autonomy in the six Armenian vilayets, which is not contrary to the rights of the other nations."[114] Within a couple of months following the Young Turk Revolution and after a meeting with the CUP in Istanbul, however, even Sapah-Giwlian and his party, the SDHP, had a public change of mind. Sapah-Giwlian admitted that although he found the constitution problematic, he did believe that it had advantages over despotism. He added that under the current regime, the SDHP rejects any "desire of separation" and that "it accepted and defended Turkey's integrity." Furthermore, he affirmed that the SDHP was always willing to collaborate for the betterment and progress of the country, making available "to the current regime all its forces for defense." In response, Sabaheddin, who had been key in trying—unsuccessfully—to get the SDHP on board since the Ottoman congresses, expressed his joy about the party's "precious" solidarity, assuring it that for the CUP, "national, racial, and religious distinctions have absolutely no existence." This may have been the case for Sabaheddin, who by this point had been marginalized by more conservative factions of the Young Turks. At any rate, this meeting did not lead to a volte-face regarding federation.[115]

Zavarian, on the other hand, insisted that federation "is neither a dream nor vain delirium . . . This is *life's path,* the consequence of Humanity's progress that not one obstacle may stop."[116] Zavarian, like other contemporary Armenian and other federalists, saw a federal political system "combining shared rule and self-rule" as "a practical way of linking the benefits of unity and diversity through representative institutions, but they are no panacea for humanity's political ills."[117] Whether Zavarian and others truly believed in its panacean quality, they certainly often presented it as such, and thus they may have agreed with Watts, who wrote almost a century later, "Although no panacea, federal arrangements and the idea of federalism have shown that they can provide a means for reconciliation in the world."[118] What they saw in federation was a system that was superior to mere popular sovereignty. Zavarian points out that this method of political organization does not necessarily guarantee the rights of small groups—for example, Muslims, Armenians, and Protestants in the Russian Empire, whose voices are drowned out by the majority's "scream."[119] A decentralized federative order and the principle of proportional representation whereby every nation, sect, or party will have a voice according to its size is the only means to resolve the rule of the majority.[120]

Zavarian then moves to the national question and, perhaps influenced by Kautsky's emphasis on language as "the most powerful of the threads uniting the nation," underlines the critical role of language for a nation.[121] He writes that language "is our contemporary generation's most precious heritage left by our forebears. That is the most important part of our spirit, our blood which we should preserve with all our might . . . As religions in the past, one's own language for nationalities is kind of sacred today, every nation's inviolable right that should be free from any oppression."[122] Zavarian sees particularistic linguistic and national preservation in a decentralized federative system the way Catholicos Khrimian viewed the multiplicity of churches—as a bouquet of flowers whose "great diversity presents a singular beauty."[123] Therefore, so too the variety of nationalities should not be feared: "let us put aside the desire of one diminishing the other . . . Let us benefit mutually from the positive characteristics of each nationality" through a federation, not independence.[124] He recalls French anarchist Élisée Reclus's words on the Near East's civilizational role as being the consequence of "its favorable geographical and ethnographic position."[125] Much like the "richness" produced by the variety of produce and minerals, so too *"Diversity, singular free progress in exchange with intimate relations* is an imperative condition for the progress of each country" and will lead only to the advancement of the Ottoman Empire, the East, and all of humanity.[126] Zavarian concludes by returning to advocating for and propagating decentralization and federation as the superior way to rebuild the Ottoman Empire, "our fatherland," on the revolution's foundations of "Liberty, Fraternity, and Justice."[127]

Shakhatunian, the representative of the ARF's Russian student union and later the author of a Russian-language study of the South Caucasus, is in agreement with Zavarian, on the whole. He provides, however, a much more systematic analysis—although still not as detailed and methodical as Khazhak—of a number of aspects of decentralization and federalism, including but not limited to the structure of a federative state; the differences among unitary states, federative states, and federation of states; federation's internal legislative ways; the historical, sociological, and social origins of a federative state; appraisal of decentralization in relation to democracy and socialism; and a discussion of the two models of federation, the United States and Switzerland. Shakhatunian draws and quotes from some of the same sources as Khazhak, especially Jellinek on a federal system generally and Bryce and Dicey on the United States and England particularly (all in Russian translation), as well as the US, Swiss, and Austrian constitutions.[128] For Shakhatunian, "The structure of the federative state is not only more perfect compared to the centralized, but it is also higher than the decentralized state composed of autonomous provinces." There, "local legislation is indispensable" and "one of the conditions of democracy [ժողովրդապետութիւն u/zhoghovrdapetut'iwn]."[129] Quoting Jellinek, Shakhatunian writes, "the only healthy and normal method is the federative state."[130] He, like Khazhak, remains dissatisfied with mere nonterritorial national-cultural autonomy as advocated, for example, by the socialist Bund (General Jewish Labor Bund in Lithuania, Poland, and Russia, founded in 1897). Not surprisingly, it reminds Shakhatunian of the principle of national personal autonomy expounded by Austrian Social Democrats Karl Renner and Otto Bauer, which organized nations according to associations of persons rather than territorially.[131]

Shakhatunian objects to Renner's understanding of nation in purely cultural terms and nonterritorial autonomy focused solely on cultural issues. As Alexander Osipov aptly sums up, "The leading Austro-Marxist ideologists, Karl Renner and Otto Bauer, proposed the organization of ethnic groups as corporate entities with mandatory membership independent of individual residence, and the granting to these corporations of certain legislative and executive powers with respect to education and culture. These measures were expected to put an end to ethnic conflicts over territory and access to state power."[132] Shakhatunian argues that nationality was not merely cultural but also political and legal, and therefore it needed to be addressed not merely by cultural autonomy but also by political autonomy.[133] Territorial autonomy in a federative system would not only satisfy cultural demands but also lessen national antagonisms.

Khazhak, too, challenges Renner's national-cultural autonomy, writing, "for us it is impossible to imagine an *incorporeal* [անմարմին/ anmarmin] *federation,* a federation without territory."[134] To explain what he views as the unbreakable bond of nation, territory, and federation, Khazhak reminds his readers that despite Renner's cultural and nonterritorial approach to national association, he did not necessarily reject the territorial principle as artificial. Khazhak also raises Kautsky's emphasis of language along with his support of the establishment of an autonomous union of Czech states, to stress his point. He contends that a federation that does not take into account the real boundaries of a nation's distribution will be like a *"body* without spirit"—that is, without nationality—and a federation of nationalities without the territorial principle will be like a "spirit without a body."[135] Although a proponent of national-territorial autonomy, Khazhak does allow for the possibility of organization on nonterritorial national-cultural grounds for those living outside the designated territory.[136] Ultimately, though, Khazhak believes that territory is critical to the preservation of national identity: "Nations without home [բնակավայր/bnakavayr, in the sense of "territory"] are nations, it is true, but they are condemned finally . . . to assimilate with local peoples."[137] Therefore, the implication here is that diversity and coexistence would be welcome and that assimilation would be an undesirable loss. For diversity to cohabit with equality and cooperation, one's own territory—self-determined, autonomous, and in federation—was paramount.[138] Moreover, for Shakhatunian and others, democracy and decentralization were closely linked, and a democratic federation divided along ethnic and cultural lines and with broad self-government, whether in the form of an Ottoman or South Caucasian Federation, was as close to a panacea as they could achieve.[139] Just as the ARF, with the support of Sabaheddin and his League of Private Initiative and Decentralization, had earlier proposed an Ottoman federal system to the Young Turks, the party's instructions to duma delegates called on them to work toward replacing centralization with decentralization on the principles of federation and toward solving the issue of ethnic equality through general, equal, secret, direct, and proportional vote, redistribution of land, and meeting the demands of the working class. While the Caucasian Socialist Revolutionaries agreed, the Social Democrats rejected their appeal.[140] This development was reflective of one of the basic differences between the two sides, as the Social Democrats unequivocally dismissed federation.

Khazhak objected to the Caucasian Social Democratic view that a Caucasian federation was unrealizable, stating that if federation is in principle imperative and beneficial, then it is indeed "feasible" for the Caucasus and Russia as a whole.[141] He provides population statistics for the whole of the Caucasus, noting the diversity of peoples, as well as specifically for Armenians in the South Caucasus.[142] He proposes that the Caucasus be divided into three regions: northern, mountainous, and southern. The southern area would encompass Baku, Gandzak/Ganja, Yerevan, Tiflis, and Kutais provinces, Kars and Batumi regions, and Zakatala/Zakatali *okrug* (district) and would be made up of a population of largely (Azeri) Turks, Georgians, and Armenians. The Caucasus, in addition to entering into "indivisible federative bonds" with "Mother-Russia" in a future federation of Russian United States, will have its own "internal federation."[143] Khazhak stresses the critical need for studies on the region and populations but asserts that a democratic Caucasian federation made up of three parts, on territorial and national foundations, is a matter of principle and probability.[144] Khazhak even employs Social Democrat Rosa Luxemburg's words from a 1906 article on Polish local self-government and autonomy to make his own case for Caucasian autonomy, although Luxemburg herself saw both self-determination and autonomy as "untenable" in the Caucasus, where "intractable ethnic problems" existed. As Michael Forman explains, "Luxemburg's data suggested that not even the largest ethno-national groups (Russians and Georgians) were a significant majority in any jurisdiction. There was simply no acceptable way to establish territorially based local self-rule for any nationality."[145] Although Luxemburg did not equate cultural freedoms and equal rights with political autonomy, Khazhak draws on her advocacy of Polish autonomy to make his own case. He translates Luxemburg: "Local self-government or Polish autonomy means that those issues that are particularly related to our country must be decided by the population of our country through the *sejm* [lower house of parliament] . . . Polish schools, Polish classes and other indispensable institutions, which in their operation must be subject to the Polish *sejm*, must be introduced."[146] There is no question that Luxemburg was sympathetic to Polish cultural autonomy; as Andrzej Walicki points out, she saw "'nationality' not as a fiction but as a distinct cultural reality, manifesting itself in language, art and literature." However, "acknowledging nationalities' right to existence does not involve recognizing the territorial delimitations and political sovereignty of each one. In this respect the SDKPiL [Social Democracy of the Kingdom of Poland and Lithuania] theorists readily agreed with the leading Austro-Marxists, Karl Renner and Otto Bauer, who wanted to de-politicize the nationalities question by giving each nationality the right to extraterritorial cultural autonomy—the right to its own cultural institutions, such as schools, journals, publishing houses, theatres, and so forth."[147] Khazhak also marshals a number of other prominent figures (e.g., anarchist Bakunin, Russian populists Alexander Herzen and Pyotr Lavrov, and others) in favor of federalism.[148]

It is not surprising that our Armenian revolutionaries and intellectuals were knowledgeable about the individuals and ideas making an impact in the global revolutionary and intellectual milieu. As we saw, they were clearly familiar with them, engaged with them, and appropriated them for their own purposes, which included a future vision for the Russian and Ottoman Empires. That engagement and adoption also meant that they had to respond to critiques of their views and their particular appropriation or, for their critics, misappropriation of certain concepts. The harshest ideologically based criticism came from the Russian and Caucasian Social Democratic corner, and a debate ensued— sometimes in quite bitter and abrasive tones—in the pages of newspapers and books on federalism and even more so on socialism. As we shall see in the next chapter, they resorted to the same tactics when discussing socialism, drawing, as did Khazhak and his comrades, from Social Democratic tracts in an attempt to support their arguments for a federal system and galvanizing support from a number of corners. In particular, they pointed to Russian Socialist Revolutionaries and also the Jewish Bund, which called for national cultural self-determination (and extraterritorial national federation), Polish and Lithuanian Social Democrats who demanded Polish self-government, the Polish Socialist Party, Ukrainian and Latvian socialists, and Georgian Socialist Federalists, as well as certain Austrian Social Democrats like Victor Adler, Engelbert Pernerstorfer, and others.[149] In their quest for a federative system, they also had common cause with Georgian and Ottoman federalists, and especially Bulgarians and Macedonians. Furthermore, they argued for a federative system through a refutation of Russian Social Democratic objections to federation and decentralization by pitting either some prominent Western European and Russian Social Democrat theoreticians against each other or a select group of often Austrian and German Social Democrats against Russian and Caucasian Social Democrats. For example, Khazhak often relies on Kautsky, in particular his *Nationalities Question in Russia* (which Khazhak had translated into Armenian), as a way to counter Social Democratic objections to federation. ARF authors like Khazhak and the ARF papers often employed Social Democratic theoreticians, especially Kautsky, against Social Democrats themselves, citing, for example, Kautsky's acceptance of "a federal state, the 'United States of Russia.'"[150]

One of the main arguments Social Democrats made against federation was that it was a bourgeois form of political organization that offered nothing to the proletariat and that furthermore weakened their power.[151] The Armenian federalists insisted that contrary to Social Democratic claims that federalism harmed the proletariat, the ones who suffered most from contemporary national antagonisms were the working class because they were the ones spilling their blood; it was their "class struggle that was being disrupted because of that cursed reason."[152] Quoting from Kautsky on the positive relationship between federalism and workers, Khazhak explains that the proletariat desired to work in the country in which he lived and to transform it according to the interests of the masses, and for that reason, he had "the need to resolve the national question" via federation "because only then when the state of *kingdoms and countries* is replaced by national states, those nationalities which live side by side autonomously, only then can the proletariat's class struggle come into the open in its proper way."[153] Khazhak finds federation unambiguously beneficial to the working class.[154] He allows that the "sweat-drenched" proletariat may not currently appreciate or understand the benefits of autonomy and federation, but that tomorrow, "under the influence of the class struggle's merciless attacks, it will be forced to engage with it, to become aware and demand the only form corresponding to its interests—Federation."[155]

Khazhak devotes a whole chapter to centralization and decentralization, with a greater focus on the latter, which he defines as that government whose authority, in whole or in part, goes to provincial, state, or communal authorities. What differentiates federalists like himself and the ARF is that they insisted on administrative decentralization, not just legislative, as most other parties, from bourgeois liberal to revolutionary, did. Khazhak defines legislative decentralization as self-government and both legislative and administrative decentralization as autonomy or federation.[156] Drawing from Dicey and Lazarevskii, Jellinek, and Springer, Khazhak points to another distinction, one between autonomy and federation, whereby a federation would be made up of several independent parts with complete authority over all affairs except custom duties, external/foreign policies, military, and post-telegraph, all of which would be under federal authority.[157] The center would have no veto power or supervision. As in the case of Switzerland's cantons or the states of the United States, each state within a federation would have final and only say in all internal matters, their own constitution, judicial system, and legislation. Therefore, they would differ from autonomy, which would have an internal self-governing system with some legislative and administrative authority, but ultimately the central government would remain the authority over all of it.[158] Khazhak finds autonomy on its own an insufficient and inferior order to federation, which has internal sovereignty and which is united with other federative states with its own sovereignty; thus, two sovereignties "complete" each other.[159]

The advantages of federalism over autonomy seemed to occupy the satirical *Khat'abala* as well. In an article entitled "Philological: Autonomy or Federation," the author, Stora-Kēt (Comma), confesses that the question of which system is better for Armenians has been on his mind for six months. Despite having read Khazhak, Topchian, and others as well as having listened to forums on the subject, his insight came after attending a meeting of Armenian teachers. He adds that in all the meetings where only Armenians were present, there has been "noise, disorder, fighting." In fact, the president presiding over one of those meetings had to undergo a week of "electric therapy" because of "nerve fatigue."

He labels these kinds of assemblies with only Armenians or Georgians "autonomy" and "find[s] . . . it the most dangerous thing" for a nation's progress. In contrast, multiethnic meetings with Armenians, Georgians, Russians, and Turks have always been "organized, calmer, and more anti-nervous [հակա-նեարդային/haka-neardayin]." This, he contends, is federation, attributing the difference in behavior to the wish of all nationalities to conduct themselves in such a way that others do not get a bad impression of them. Therefore, he concludes, federation is preferable to autonomy. It seems that Khazhak and Stora-Kēt had reached the same conclusion, admittedly with contrasting approaches.[160]

As a means to strengthen their own position and through reference to the programs of the Russian SDs (Social Democrats) and SRs (Socialist Revolutionaries), both Khazhak and other ARF sources point to what they view as a contradiction in the SD stance on federalism and autonomy.[161] While the Russian and Caucasian SDs balked at the federative system, the Russian and Caucasian SRs and other socialist and federalist parties favored it. Khazhak's *Dēpi fēdērats'ia*, however, still received criticism from some SR corners. For example, an article appeared in *Aniv* accusing Khazhak of expressing purely democratic views. The author asserted that Khazhak's nationalism dwarfed his socialism, his book (which did not show how socialism would be reached through decentralization) had no value from a socialist perspective, and Khazhak himself was "far from being socialist."[162]

Khazhak and his comrades charged the SDs of simultaneously announcing their objection to federalism and autonomy in the pages of *Iskra* and backing the right of self-determination in their program: *"all nationalities forming the state have the right to self-determination"* (point 9 of the RSDLP program) and ethnic groups have a right to schools in their own national languages at state expense and a right to use their languages at assemblies and on an equal level with state language in all state and public functions (point 8). Even Rosa Luxemburg found fault with RSDLP's upholding of the right of self-determination, but she did so for different reasons.[163] Luxemburg did not consider self-determination a right; moreover, when she spoke of it, as Horace Davis explains, she and her followers meant the right of self-determination of the proletariat.[164] For Luxemburg, the duty of the proletariat to protest and resist national oppression did not arise out of the right of nations but because of general opposition to oppression and domination.[165] In agreement with Kautsky, she argues that solving all nationality questions with self-determination was tantamount to "complete utopia."[166]

While the ARF believed federation and the self-determination it implied was realizable, Armenian SDs like Stepan Shahumian and Bakhshi Ishkhanian felt they were regressive, bourgeois, and improbable for Russia and especially the Caucasus.[167] Moreover, even if it were possible, they questioned its desirability, as it weakened the proletariat and contributed to further antagonism between ethnicities. The SD conviction that federation would harm the proletariat and the advancement of class struggle was one that the ARF tried hard to refute, as they considered themselves and presented themselves as a socialist party with the interests of urban and rural workers (i.e., peasants) in mind. Yervant Topchian, a prominent ARF member and editor of ARF's *Haṛaj* in Tiflis (1906) and Erzurum (1909–10), declares centralism—that is, the opposite of decentralized federation—more harmful to proletarian interests in a country as wide as Russia than federation. He argues that centralization means "to choke one's freedom" and cultural progress in the name of homogeneity, and to "sacrifice one's interests because of the others"—reminiscent of the "majority principle." Such a system, he continues, would only lead to enmity and conflict, which the federative system of the ARF and the SRs aimed to avoid. The only means by which to realize the self-determination the SDs claim to back is through federation: "To give satisfaction to vast Russia's multiethnic and multilingual elements, imbibed with different economic-cultural demands and to contribute to the solidarity of different ethnicities/nations and class consciousness the most favorable way is federation not centralism, decentralization and not centralization, whose bitter fruits our country especially has tasted far too much."[168]

Khazhak went so far as to characterize Russian and especially Caucasian SDs as "Talmudist," meaning fundamentalists who have as their Talmud Marx and Engels, adding that if there is nothing in the works of Marx and Engels on a particular issue, then they declare that issue backward, bourgeois, and against the interests of the proletariat.[169] While Khazhak labels them Talmudists, Yervant Topchian[170] likens SD views to "Catholic fanaticism" because they believe themselves to be "infallible, like Rome's pope."[171] Topchian brings in the example of Austria-Hungary, where SDs believed federation to be the only way to solve the national issue, as well as the usual list of names, and calls Social Democrats Adler and Kautsky "warm defenders" of federation. He accuses Russian and Caucasian SDs of ignoring the Kautskys, Bebels, Vanderveldes, Jaurèses, and Adlers when it does not suit their purpose.[172] Khazhak exhorts Caucasian and Russian SDs to hear

Kautsky's "golden words and thoughts" that internationalism means "not the denial or the contempt of nationality, but the liberation and equality of nations."[173] For Khazhak and his comrades, federation had a bright future, even entering the "darkness and violence" of Asia and Africa and creating an Asian United States and an African United States and moving toward a "Universal Federation" or "Universal United-States."[174]

Although utopian claims were made about universal federation, the Ottoman and Russian Empires emerged as not only the main targets of propagation for federation but also as ideal regions for a federative system. I have not come across similar discussions or advocacy for Iran, most probably because of the minuscule Armenian population and relative absence of ethnic conflict there, compared to the Russian Caucasus and Ottoman Anatolia. In Iran, demands were limited to cultural and linguistic rights, and federation was never actively sought.[175] For Iranian Armenians, federation must have seemed impracticable and unnecessary, whereas for Caucasian and Ottoman Armenians, it appeared imperative. For the ARF, which was heavily invested in federation in principle and in practice in the Caucasus and the Ottoman Empire, federation remained indivisible from the national question.

To a great degree, the commitment to federation and its promise to bring equality, respect diversity, and wipe out ethnic and religious animus—a commitment embraced by not only the Armenian subjects of the Russian and Ottoman Empires but also by many other subjects—seemed to be a way to realize the gains the revolutions promised. As unrealistic as it may seem in hindsight, especially given the fleeting post-world-war Transcaucasian Federative Republic (22 April to 28 May 1918), the idea of federation along with constitutionalism not only seemed to their multiethnic adherents like an obvious solution to the problems debilitating the three empires, but it also serves as another way to approach the revolutions as connected. Therefore, with its supporters, the ARF, which was itself a decentralized federation, sought federation along with other Ottoman and Russian subjects because it deemed it to be the consummate and sole method to solve national antagonisms, achieve minority rights, and protect workers' interests. Therefore, federation, the national question, and socialism were closely linked and, in fact, inseparable from each other as well as from the revolutionary struggles. Alongside the rainbow proclaiming constitution and the banners pronouncing unity, equality, and autonomy, an additional banner—that of socialism—arose for our revolutionaries and the revolutions they connected through their struggles, their mobility, and the circulation of global ideologies. As Mikayel Varandian summed it up, "Universal fraternity—in a federation of free, autonomous, equal nationalities—it is in the name of that ideal that the banner of contemporary socialism is unfurled."[176]

CHAPTER 4

Connected through and beyond Reading

Socialism across Imperial Frontiers

. . . Դաշնակցությունը անվերադարձ կերպով գնում է
դէպի սոցիալիզմը. ուստի փոխել այդ ուղին
աննպատակ է եւ անoգուտ

. . . the Federation is progressing without retreat toward
socialism;
thus, to change that path is without purpose and useless.

All the signs, activities, and workers' mood that Abraham Giwlkhandanian witnessed in Baku in the early years of the Russian Revolution and
his own endeavors to organize workers there undoubtedly color his
assessment of the ARF's path toward socialism.[1] In a national(ist) historiography that has dominated the approach to Armenian revolutionary
movements and actors, Giwlkhandanian's words reflect a minor and
inconsequential blip in the forceful growth of a national movement
with a fully formed nationalist ideology. One should be cautious of
such facile conclusions made in hindsight from a postgenocidal perspective that does not recognize or acknowledge the multiplicity of identities, ideas, and ideologies with which Armenian and other revolutionaries experimented, adapted, and helped circulate in a transforming world
that read and engaged with the same standard radical—socialist and
anarchist—texts as well as news of world events.[2] Instead, in this chapter, I follow a path similar to that adopted by Ilham Khuri-Makdisi in
her study on radicalism in the Eastern Mediterranean, in which she
challenges national(ist) historiography's hegemonic grip on the past.
She aptly maintains, "Leftist and generally radical ideas were not

incompatible with emerging nationalist ideas at the time, whether in the Arab world or elsewhere. But the discussions about leftist concepts and the various radical experiments that took place during the period in Beirut, Cairo, and Alexandria have been either obliterated by a nationalist historiographical framework or forcibly incorporated into the nationalist narrative."[3] Khuri-Makdisi's study demonstrates that multiple ideas and practices made their way through the Eastern Mediterranean and that, in particular, "nationalism coexisted, competed, and grew symbiotically with its relationship to other forms of political and social contestations."[4] Benedict Anderson makes a similar point regarding movements on the other side of the globe, deeming nationalism in the Spanish American independence movements to be developing in combination with other currents, including but not limited to Marxism and anarchism.[5] Closer to our revolutionary movements, in the South Caucasus, Stephen Jones demonstrates the complementarity rather than contradiction of socialism and nationalism.[6] In this way, too, instead of viewing Armenian nationalism as determined, homogeneous, singular, and exclusive, it is much more fitting to see it within a larger, contentious ideological and practical, local and global context that takes into account a revolutionary and intellectual network crossing the vast expanse of Eurasia and gives proper due to the role that socialist ideas played. Therefore, my purpose here is, as Khuri-Makdisi writes, "not to dismiss the strength of nationalist ideas"; it is, rather, to illustrate how deeply enmeshed they were with socialist ideas, especially but not exclusively for the ARF.[7] Therefore, the focus in this section is not on the liberal, nationalist tendencies represented, for instance, by the periodical *Mshak* but instead on the radical and socialist milieu represented by the more leftist press burgeoning in the early twentieth century, especially in the revolutionary period of 1905 to 1911, in the major revolutionary hubs of Tiflis, Baku, and (after 1908) Istanbul. By focusing on socialism, rather than on nationalism (as is more conventionally done), in this chapter, I explore the hold that socialist ideas and the socialist ideal had on our revolutionaries and intellectuals and how they understood and appropriated those ideas in large part but certainly not exclusively as it related to the national question. Many of the questions raised in the previous chapter regarding constitutionalism and federalism apply to socialism as well. For example, how did socialism on its own and along with the national question impassion and galvanize our revolutionaries? How were they shaped by the repertoire of socialist and radical ideas, ideologues, and theoreticians? How did they engage with and, in turn, give form to ideas informed by their own local environment and accommodated to revolutionary struggles? What does multiplicity or synthesis of ideas signify, both locally and globally? What role did face-to-face exchanges with revolutionaries and intellectuals in Eurasia and an enthused mindfulness of their worlds play in boundary-crossing mobility—both ideological and geographical?

By the time of the revolutionary struggles of the early twentieth century, socialism had become a powerful revolutionary ideology, even prompting one observer in the Tiflis ARF paper *Alik'* to note that it had captivated "the imagination of the masses like Muhammad's supernatural paradise."[8] According to its adherents, socialism would transform the world, bringing forth social and economic justice as well as harmonious coexistence, especially important for our Armenian revolutionaries, who were justly concerned about ethnic rivalries and antagonisms. They believed that socialism was the path to victory and that already socialist groups stood behind successes all over Europe, particularly in France, Germany, England, and Russia.[9] Socialism, whether it came directly from Central and Western Europe or via Russia, was, as Bayly surmises, "dramatically recast as [it] passed from continent to continent."[10] In many ways, however, local debates and disagreements surrounding different aspects of socialism emulated those taking place in Europe. As Bayly demonstrates, intellectuals (and revolutionaries) who wrote and talked about these ideas, as well as their reading and listening audiences, "rapidly transformed their meanings into a variety of doctrines, often very different from their exemplars. The diffusion, reception, or rejection of these ideas depended on many different circumstances."[11] It is to those circumstances and the forms that these ideas took that this chapter will now turn, gleaning from the contemporary revolutionary press and placing the discussion of Armenian socialism within the local and wider global context of socialist ideas and proponents and connected revolutions in bordering areas.

A commitment to socialism, whether eclectic or diluted—by orthodox Marxist standards—was especially meaningful for Caucasian Armenians facing growing ethnic antagonism, culminating especially in the violence between Armenians and Azeris in the South Caucasus in the years 1905–6. This on-the-ground practical experience may have been strengthened by decreasing international interest in the Armenian question after the 1880s and the subsequent weariness of some Armenian revolutionaries and intellectuals with moderate liberal nationalism, thus leading them to consider the need for a more radical socialist ideology that held the potential of deliverance for Armenians and their neighbors from unjust and despotic Ottoman, Russian, and Iranian rule. The violent conflict between Armenians and Azeris (referred to by some contemporary accounts as the Armeno-Tatar War) and the Russian Revolution made a strong impact on the socialist leanings of both the SDHP and the ARF as well as other Armenian socialists, some of whom were Social Democrats, and led to a strengthened commitment to socialist ideas and to closer collaboration with Caucasian, Ottoman, and Iranian revolutionaries. The ARF 1905 Caucasian Project formally declared tsarism the enemy of the Armenian people, putting the Russian state on equal footing with the Ottoman state. The inclusion of Russia as a target had also very much to do with the intensifying Russification policies throughout the empire as well as the change in the relationship among Russian authorities in Saint Petersburg, Russian officials in the South Caucasus, Armenian subjects, and in particular the ARF. Concerns had been growing among some Russian government circles that the Armenian Church was supporting revolutionaries "and promoting Armenian nationalism with its privileged status in cultural matters," as Stephen Riegg demonstrates.[12] Although the focus of the revolutionaries remained, at least until 1905, the Ottoman Empire and its Armenian population, Russian authorities presumed that their goal was independence in the South Caucasus. In 1903 the high commissioner in the Caucasus, Prince Grigorii Golitsyn, carried out a tsarist decree ordering the confiscation of Armenian Church properties despite the apprehensions of some Russian officials who warned that such action would only alienate the Armenian population.[13] As they had foreseen, the confiscation operation backfired; the church resisted, and so did the populace and even anticlerical ARF revolutionaries. As Onur Önol reveals, although relations between the Armenian Church and the Russian state improved, starting with Viceroy Illarion Vorontsov-Dashkov's return of confiscated properties in 1905 and reaching excellent relations between 1912 and 1914, relations between revolutionaries, especially the ARF, and the Russian authorities worsened, resulting in persecution and climaxing in the trials of hundreds of ARF members as well as those considered to be affiliated with them. The trials started at the height of the Stolypin crackdown in 1908 and ended in 1912, crushing the ARF in the South Caucasus.[14]

In addition to including the Russian state in its plan of action, the 1905 Caucasian Project also emphasized collaboration with Russian revolutionary parties, especially Socialist Revolutionaries, and committed the ARF more openly to the socialist cause and the working classes. It reinforced these elements in 1907 by linking socialism to collaboration with radical forces.[15] These developments in the ARF's program, recommitment to and promotion of socialism and solidarity, led directly to collaboration with Ottoman and Iranian constitutionalists and participation in the Ottoman and Iranian revolutionary movements. The SDHP collaborated closely with the Russian Social Democratic Workers Party in the worker strikes and uprisings of the Russian Revolution of 1905.[16] In 1905 the SDHP Congress resolved "[t]o struggle and obtain political democracy based on Marxist principles" in the Ottoman Empire and "proletarian revolutionary activity in the Caucasus."[17] The SDHP also joined the Iranian struggle, collaborating with Caucasian and Iranian Social Democrats, and even forming an Iranian branch of the party with fellow Iranian constitutionalists.[18] Some Caucasian SDHP members considered this move insufficient, committed themselves to a purely class struggle in the Caucasus, renounced the new program, and seceded from the party to join the Russian Social Democratic Workers Party (RSDWP).[19] Others who leaned toward the right and renounced socialism had already formed their own rather ineffective faction, the Reformed (Verakazmeal) Hnchakian Party, in 1896. Despite attempts at reunification, resignations from the left and right had a negative impact on the party's efficacy.[20] Similar factional disputes took place in the ARF; they centered around the figure of Mihran (Gabriel Keshishian), who objected to socialism as articulated in the 1905 Caucasian Project. He and his followers, Mihranakans, split off from the party, but the split itself did not lead to a decline in party power as a similar split did with the SDHP. However, Mihran's involvement as an informant for Russian intelligence during the ARF trials in the South Caucasus certainly harmed the ARF.[21]

These party splits indicate the inherent relationship or, as some might argue, the tension between nationalist and socialist goals and approaches. Just as the pursuit of federation for many contemporary revolutionaries was closely tied to the national question, so too was socialism, promising along with constitution and federation to resolve all that ailed the region—from oppressive and unjust rule to ethnic conflict and economic exploitation. Like the Armenians, fellow imperial subjects and socialists of the period, such as Balkan peoples and Georgians, often mingled socialism with and within national movements. Contemporary socialist parties even faced similar factional splits (into Broad and Narrow socialists). According to Augusta Dimou, "The history of the Bulgarian socialist movement is a tormented story of fierce ideological debates, power struggles and multiple schisms (at least four occurred—1892, 1903, 1905, 1907—before the establishment of the Third International)."[22] In a sense, they suffered from the same dilemma as they tried to reconcile their socialist ideas with their national reality or as they attempted to reconcile competing socialist and nationalist ideals. For example, some Bulgarian socialists, particularly those who came to be identified as Broad Socialists, led by Yanko Sakazov (Janko Sakŭzov), even participated in the workings of the national Internal Macedonian Revolutionary Organization. As Augusta Dimou argues, the Broads' intermingling of socialism and nationalism was "an attempt at a local adaptation of Marxism" in "a society where socialism's true protagonist, the working class, was still at an embryonic stage."[23] To a great degree, as Fikret Adanır explains, "political autonomy was understood as only a first step to the further economic and social development of Macedonia."[24] For many Armenian advocates, such as the ARF, socialism was a future ideal of a federation composed of the Ottoman or Russian Empire's diverse ethnicities.[25] For others, like the SDHP, socialism also remained a long-term objective after the short-term aim of an independent democratic Turkish Armenia had been realized; and for a smaller minority faction, as in those Social Democratic groups not affiliated with the SDHP, the national question had no place in a socialist struggle.[26] Whatever their differences, however, they all believed that contemporary reality and historical development acted as the driving forces behind their position, and they all fiercely contested in the press the label of *nationalist,* which they associated with chauvinism.[27]

The National Question

How did they understand nationalism? Why and how did Armenian revolutionaries try to shake off the label of nationalism at every turn? Part of the reason lies in their leftist rivals' interchangeable characterization of the ARF and even the SDHP at times as nationalist and chauvinist. The parties objected to both terms, as nationalism and chauvinism were equated in the minds of their accusers and thus in their own minds as well. They were rather sensitive to the label of nationalist/chauvinist not only because they did not believe it to be an accurate assessment, but also because the connotation was so negative that it threatened to delegitimize their place and their coveted leadership in a socialist environment. Moreover, they perceived the socialism ambit as an inherently empowering constellation or network; membership would bring certain privileges.

How many times, they exclaimed, had the Polish socialists, the Jewish Bund, the ARF, the Georgian, and other non-Marxist parties been labeled in the SD press with "that contemptuous title—nationalism?" With that word, "they baptized even the just, legal desire of nations toward political autonomy, even their desire to preserve the most elemental and trampled national rights."[28] For the Armenian socialists, nationalism/chauvinism implied regression and conservatism, whereas socialism denoted an avant-garde, or at least current, ideology for the present and the future. They did not believe that they were nationalist and by extension chauvinist because they argued that they did not espouse a nationalism that assumed or propagated dominance of one nation or ethnicity and subjugation over another. Instead, as they saw it, they promoted an understanding of nation in socialist terms—that is, as upholding the rights of nationalities, persevering against political oppression and economic exploitation, and maintaining alliance and solidarity with workers of other countries—for them, a far cry from chauvinism.

For many Armenian revolutionaries, like those in the ARF, Armenian liberation also did not necessarily imply separation and independence. For others, like those in the SDHP, it did. However, time and time again during the revolutionary years that rocked Russia, the Ottoman Empire, and Iran, there were appeals for inclusion—whether in the form of being part of a Caucasian whole, Ottomanism/Ottoman identity, or inclusive Iranian nationalism. Some contemporaries critical of any kind of consideration of the national question argued that this was a front and that the revolutionaries' real intention was exclusively or primarily nationalist. This insistence defied context and reality. Logically, it is that very context and reality that Armenian populations in all three empires faced and that intellectuals and revolutionaries expressed in print and action, that shaped their adoption of socialism, decentralized federation, and inclusion. Their ideologies and ideas did not exist or develop outside reality. The frequent application of the words "our country" to all three states by their respective Armenian populations as well as their emphasis on encompassing part of a wider society and identity signified an acute consciousness of their realities and a path that promised their own welfare and progress unambiguously in line with the well-being and development of their host societies and states.[29] Solidarity, in particular—whether between Armenians and Turks or Armenians and Iranians—recurred as a common refrain in print.[30] The ARF's call for solidarity was even often expressed and encapsulated in the dictum, "All for one and one for all."[31]

The expressed relationship of Armenians to the states in which they lived was very similar to that of other Ottoman non-Muslim subjects. As Alexander Vezenkov argues in his study on the importance of Tanzimat reforms (1836–76) for the development of Ottomanism and universal values, "one could detect . . . the presence of 'Ottomanist' rhetoric in the Bulgarian, Macedonian and Albanian national discourses, such as insistence on equality, justice and tolerance and different nations and faiths living like brothers." Vezenkov points out that some of the same phrases and "catchwords like 'brotherhood,' 'equality' and 'justice' . . . . appear in the 'Ottomanist' and the national discourses, the former most likely serving as a source for the latter." He brings in the Bulgarian and Macedonian examples, showing the use of identical expressions and discourse similar to that which appeared in the Turkish-language official press.[32] As we shall see below, Armenians, too, engaged with the same ideas and vocabulary as "'the children of the same father' and of 'the same fatherland.'"[33]

Whenever Armenians explained their participation in the three revolutions, they positioned themselves not apart from but as part of an inclusive society to be transformed by connected revolutionary struggles. Thus, their adoption and adaptation of ideas and, by extension, identities strongly linked their present and their future with those of their fellow subjects. Their campaign to serve in the Ottoman and Qajar military serves as an excellent example of the application of an inclusive identity. They often used similar language; for example, in Iran, the ARF paper *Aṛawōt* (Morning) pursued military service and other modes of inclusion in larger Iranian society as self-identified children of the same fatherland. The pages of both the SDHP and ARF periodicals published in Tabriz—*Zang* and *Aṛawōt*, respectively—pushed for military service and government positions, seeking "to be not the illegitimate but real child of a free fatherland and to enjoy the fatherland's beneficence and bitterness with 10 million Iranians."[34] As I have argued elsewhere, Iranian Armenians began to take part in a broader Iranian nationalism that at the time of the constitutional revolution was fairly inclusive and embraced linguistically, ethnically, and religiously diverse Iranian citizenry. This approach was represented most noticeably by the Democrat Party, which espoused a larger encompassing Iranian citizenship over an exclusive ethnicity or religious-based nationalism. For instance, an editorial of the organ of the Democrat Party, *Iran-e Now*, maintained, "Iranians are of one millat [i.e., nation], a millat that speaks in different dialects and worships God in various ways."

This kind of reconfiguration of Iranian nationhood expressly appealed to Iranian Armenians as an ethnically and religiously distinct minority that sought incorporation into the Iranian nation in place of "otherness."[35]

Similarly, in the Ottoman Empire, Istanbul's *Zhamanak* demanded that "as children of the Ottoman fatherland, we too must participate in the work of our country's defense."[36] Although in principle, non-Muslims could serve in the military starting in 1856 with the promulgation of the Hatt-ı Hümayun (Imperial Edict), in practice they did not do so until 1909.[37] *Zhamanak* also reported on a meeting of the ARF and Armenian parliament delegates that insisted on the conscription of Armenians according to the Ottoman constitutional principle of equality and the right of the Armenian man "to serve his Fatherland with his own person and blood and not with the unjust and unconstitutional financial compensation, a right that will simultaneously serve Muslim and Christian elements' honest and fruitful intimacy."[38] Moreover, it objected to Turkish nationalist rhetoric that portrayed Armenians as "foreign," with contrary interests and an ambiguous relationship to the Ottoman homeland, as if the homeland for Armenians is "a temporary residence whence, like tent-dwelling races, by untying our tents we can one day move elsewhere." It argued that despite chauvinist claims that Turks are the only "children of the land" and that Armenians are "illegitimate/step children," Armenians remain "inseparable from the Ottoman fatherland where they have released roots in every way and from where not one force can distance them."[39] The "happiness" of the country is also their happiness, and its "misfortune" their misfortune.[40] The ARF clearly distinguished between an Ottoman fatherland and an Ottoman nation. Turks, Arabs, Armenians, Greeks, Kurds, and others with their own past and particularities in language are all "Ottomans [osmanlı], the children of the fatherland without ceasing to be Turks, Armenians, Greeks, Arabs, etc." Therefore, they deduced, "To defend the general fatherland's interests, to extend its well-being does not signify eliminating those different nationalities' particularity or to subject all to the authority of the majority-forming nation."[41] Armenians were not alone in adopting two loyalties. Vezenkov explains how for non-Muslims, belonging to the same fatherland did not mean waiving one's ethnic and/or religious identity. He explains, "Non-Muslims who accepted the idea of preserving and even strengthening the Ottoman Empire identified themselves as Greeks, Bulgarians, Armenians, Jews and so on . . . [thus] the supranational character of official Ottoman patriotism left space for the development not only of non-Muslim nationalisms but also of a more 'identity-oriented' Ottomanism."[42] This was the case at least for a time, but even from its onset, Bedross Der Matossian contends that the perceptions of Young Turks and non-Turkish subjects of the Ottoman Empire differed in important ways from each other. He points out, "While the Young Turks' version of Ottomanism entailed the assimilation of ethnic difference, Ottoman Turkish as the main language, a centralized administrative system, and the abandonment of ethno-religious privileges, the ethnic groups perceived Ottomanism as a framework for promoting their identities, languages, and ethno-religious privileges, as well as an empire based on administrative decentralization."[43] Therefore, Ottomanism as envisioned by ethnoreligiously nondominant groups became more difficult to sustain after disappointment in the 1908 revolution, various growing nationalisms (including Turkish), the Ottoman loss of most of its European territory in the Balkan wars of 1912–13, and other developments, including European intervention.[44]

References to the Ottoman Empire and Iran dominate the fatherland discourse, leaving one to wonder why the Russian Empire does not receive the same attention. It may be that while Russian autocracy had increasingly in the early twentieth century become concerned about Armenian revolutionary activity in its South Caucasian backyard and presumed that Armenian revolutionaries sought independence there, Armenian revolutionaries did not seem to see the need to tout as vociferously their loyalty or belonging to a Russian or Caucasian fatherland.[45] Perhaps the difference was due to latent or even explicit assumptions of coreligionist amity in the Russian case. Whatever the reasons, our revolutionaries could not imagine separating their cause from those of their neighbors within and outside frontiers. As Tigran Zaven reiterated in at least two issues of the Tiflis-based socialist *Yerkri Dzaynĕ* (The voice of country), "Just as the Armenian people in Russia and Persia has not severed its fortune [and] does not think to sever from the fortune of other peoples living in the same countries, in that way the Turkish-Armenian will not separate his cause of freedom from the cause of those peoples, with whom inextricably tied, he bears the same yoke of despotism."[46] Zaven's comrade and *Nor Hosank'* editor Garegin Kozikian bluntly pointed out the absurdity of separatism for the Armenians divided for centuries among three states: "that which is possible to sing in poems or novels with beautifully colored pen and mighty breath and to inspire men, that thing cannot be obtained in reality ... Complex political problems are not resolved by constructing castles in the sky [օդային պալատներ/odayin palatner] or by wandering in the world of imagination." He cautions readers that to recreate historical Armenia means to wage war against three states, to eliminate existing borders, and to take back by force—an impossibility "even if the whole of the Armenian people, starting from the cradle [օրօրոց/ ōrōrots'] infant to the old man who has reached the tomb's door [at death's door], turned into heroes armed from head to toe." The only solution for Kozikian lies in a socialist order; only then will "the chains of human inequality" be pulverized, and only then will "true freedom, fraternity and equality" be realized.[47]

The issues of belonging to a larger whole and the concept of fatherland while grounded in the reality of Armenian populations dispersed among three empires were also part of the discourse of socialism's challenging relationship with the national question and, therefore, issues that the Armenian press, both the ARF and the SDHP, took up. They were prompted not only by their uncertain situation in emergent or newly constitutional empires facing counterrevolutionary threats and the criticism of "fatherlandless" (that is, antipatriotic) internationalism by bourgeois elements but also by the need they saw to defend their right to a national home against some Marxists' inflexible adherence to *The Communist Manifesto*'s "The working men have no country."[48] For example, both the ARF and SDHP press took issue with Gustave Hervé's interpretation of Marx and Engels's declaration. Hervé was at the time an ardent French socialist opposed to the idea of fatherland/motherland. It was only years later, in 1912, that he reversed himself and joined the ranks of the ultranationalists after his release from imprisonment for antimilitarist activities. In a speech to the jury at his trial in 1905, Hervé proclaimed, "For you, the country is a mother; for us, it is a cruel stepmother, a shrew whom we detest."[49] Picking up on this theme of fatherland as stepmother, party organs *Hnch'ak* and *Drōshak* criticized Hervé and appealed to August Bebel's position that every people had the right to defend the fatherland, that this was a sign not of nationalism but of the "demand of the socialist mind."[50] Kautsky, Pernerstorfer, Jaurès, Bernstein, Ferri, and others also made their appearance as evidence of the evolution of Marxism since *The Communist Manifesto*'s first publication in 1848.[51] The SDHP paper in Istanbul, *Apagay*, took a somewhat different approach; it accepted that "today's fatherlands are stepmothers" for subjugated peoples because as oppressed peoples in these "fatherlands," they do not reap any benefit. The fatherland does not give them bread; instead, it robs them, so that only a few are satiated. In lieu of this kind of fatherland (that is, fatherland as stepmother), socialists provide "bread, light and happiness" (that is, a legitimate mother or a real fatherland for the majority, not the exploitative few).[52]

The Armenian revolutionary press's discussion of fatherland was a reflection of a larger concern and engagement with the national question and socialism. It was imperative for Armenian activists and intellectuals to reconcile socialism, on the one hand, and cultural and political autonomy for nationalities, on the other, and to demonstrate that the two were not incompatible and, in fact, were supported by the "most brilliant" socialist minds.[53] They struggled against the extremism of both nationalism and internationalism; quoting revisionist German Social Democrat Georg von Vollmar, the Tiflis ARF paper, Kovkasi Aṛawōt (Caucasus's morning), printed, "it is not correct that we do not have a fatherland. We have a fatherland, I say . . . We deride the chauvinists' caricature of nationalism, but at the same time we do not want to give our opponents' hand a worse caricature of internationalism."[54] In response to the question of how to reconcile the class cause with the national cause, leading member and historian of the ARF Mikayel Varandian, writing under the pen name Mik. Hovhannisian, pointed out, "All European socialists reconcile it but ours only shout continuously: it is irreconcilable. . . . "[55] By appealing to European socialists, Armenian activists not only joined the larger debate taking place among socialists on the national question but also tried to silence their own critics, especially but not exclusively those further on the left who accused them—rather colorfully—at every turn of only bearing a "socialist mask," of operating "in the claws of nationalism," of "decorat[ing] themselves with socialism's feathers," and of spreading their "chauvinist venom."[56] While SDs charged the ARF and even SDHP sometimes with nationalism and chauvinism, the ARF in turn talked about the chauvinism (as in dogmatism) of the SDs, and both the ARF and the SDs pointed to the nationalist chauvinism of the Turks and defended their own stance.[57]

Armenian thinkers and propagandists extracted the most salient arguments from the most agreeable thinkers to explain and justify their own position as socialists on the national question, just as they had done when advocating federation. Their arguments revolved around three issues: first, that reality—local, regional, and global—dictated their position on the national question; second, that every socialist party in any given country was national; and third, that the national question was not going away and in actuality had become even more relevant in the twentieth century. Little did they know that it would remain relevant in the twenty-first century.

The ARF remained, above all, a practical party quite conscious of the contemporary reality, even though it retained a rather optimistic—and some might argue idealistic—vision of future harmony. Its pragmatism, however, was key to how it viewed the national question and the Armenian situation in the revolutionary period and the three empires. Its appraisal of the plight of Armenian populations, especially in the Ottoman Empire and the South Caucasus, highlighted "the historical moment," which did not allow limiting the party's activities to class struggle alone and forced the national cause to center stage. Varandian writes that because Armenians still lived in the "current hellish situation in Turkey and in Transcaucasia surrounded on all sides by cannibals," it is a "categorical imperative" to oppose oppression, to defend trampled rights, and "to that degree, yes, our organization is 'national,' but to that degree every country's, every nation's socialist party is national."[58] He adds that the party had an obligation to defend both the working class and the bourgeoisie because it was their Armenianness that brought on persecution. Varandian reminds his readers that while the interests of the working class must be the party's "leitmotif," as he writes, there are moments—according to Kautsky, as he reminds his readers—when the general public's progress must be elevated above the narrower interests of the working class.[59] In that sense, the party appealed both to the practical Armenian conditions as well as to the situation of socialist parties in Europe, which acted within a national framework.

Through a survey that began with Hegelian dialectics, reviewed the ideas of Marx and Engels, and ended with the revisionism of German Social Democrats Eduard Bernstein and Wilhelm Liebnecht, *Drōshak* contended that the dawn of socialism and the end of capitalism proved to be no more imminent than the assimilation of peoples into a union of humankind and the disappearance of national antagonism.[60] After all, it pointed out, the nineteenth century was said to be the century of the national question and the twentieth century that of socialism, but national antagonisms had not evaporated, and socialism was left to deal with the national question, which persisted in Europe as well as in the Ottoman Empire.[61] In an effort to enlighten its readers and emphasize the long history that led to the formation of nations and national feeling, *Drōshak*, in a series of articles, explored the evolution from families, clans, and tribes to nations through encounters and with references to the contributions of Immanuel Kant, Charles Darwin, Adam Smith,

August Comte, and Herbert Spencer. It demonstrated the different approaches, from the Darwinist "struggle of all against all," meaning survival of the fittest, to its diametric opposite, the more positively rendered concept of the role of solidarity in evolution expounded by anarcho-communist Pyotr Kropotkin.[62]

Much like the ARF, the SDHP, too, had to explain itself. Both parties faced challenges not only from those further on the left or right but also from their own members, who questioned their advocacy of a struggle on socialist grounds and their activities on three fronts, but especially the Ottoman and the Russian. The ARF successfully avoided a split and committed the party as a whole to socialism, of course with a special place accorded to national problems, by stressing the complexity of the class struggle in countries where the dominant ethnicity and the non-dominant oppressed shared the same territory.[63] As discussed earlier, despite threats of a split because of its commitment to socialism and struggle on the South Caucasian front, the ARF managed to maintain its unity. The SDHP, however, faced with similar challenges, did not fare as well and suffered multiple splits that weakened it. Therefore, *Hnch'ak* was quite persistent in defending its position on various levels, best exemplified by Sapah-Giwlian's numerous articles. Sapah-Giwlian underscored that local conditions, circumstances, and developments dictated the position that one took and that it was not a simple matter of nationalist or nonnationalist, socialist or nonsocialist.[64] Writing before the 1908 revolution, he referred to the Ottoman Empire in particular and explained that the SDHP's desire to separate from the empire did not rise out of nationalism: "it is not because we are nationalists, but because that direction, that current, the history, the course of affairs, the situation of a dying state has made it imperative and indispensable . . . We do that which every socialist would have done if he wanted to stand on the path of historical materialism and civilization."[65] Sapah-Giwlian insisted that specific conditions—not ideology—dictated the party's position.

Appealing to European examples in order to further SDHP's stance and to respond to criticisms of pan-Armenianism, an author with the pen name Endizhen (*indigène*, or native) compares SDHP action to the actions of any Russian, Polish, French, or English Social Democratic organizations, concluding that just as they do not contradict the principle of class struggle and are considered socialist, the same criteria should be applied to the SDHP. He asks, does not the socialist, therefore, have the right to defend the fatherland? While Endizhen admits that for

Hervé the answer was emphatically no, he believes his view to be bolstered by a greater number of socialists for whom the answer was yes.[66] Endizhen then states that the Armenian socialist's activity is a realization of Marx's call for all workers of the world to unite because the Armenian socialist does not accept the boundaries drawn by despots and provides "socialist help" to his brother. He concludes, "If the Turkish-Armenian Cause was purely national, purely nationalist, we would have no place there; we consider that Cause one of the faces of the general socialist Cause, and it is for that reason that we are there."[67] Turning to the critiques by conservative nationalists, Sapah-Giwlian explains that socialism does not stipulate or necessitate the loss of one's ethnicity or nationality; it does not aim to eliminate, denationalize, and assimilate.[68] He reminds them that Marx stood for the right of nations to defend themselves in the face of Napoleon III's preparations toward Austria and Russia's toward the Ottoman Empire.[69] He then invites his readers to familiarize themselves with the writings of Karl Marx from the 1840s and 1850s as well as the writings of French socialist and academic Georges Renard. In an effort to back up his point further, he quotes (translating into Armenian) from Renard's *Le socialisme à l'oeuvre: ce qu'on a fait, ce qu'on peut faire:*

> The end which Socialists are seeking to attain is not the disappearance of national unities; it is the grouping of nations in great peaceful federations, which shall gradually draw closer so as to embrace the whole civilized world; it is the gradual elaboration of international laws which shall organize humanity, as state laws have organized nations. But that great structure which we wish to build vast enough to contain the whole human race will have nations as its pillars: it will rest upon their strong foundations, which have been cemented by the labors of ages, and whose destruction would bring about its own ruin.[70]

Here and elsewhere, Sapah-Giwlian, like his ARF counterparts, refers to European socialist thinkers—in particular Emile Vandervelde, Jean Jaurès, August Bebel, and Karl Kautsky. He, like leading ARF activist Harutiwn Shahrigian, embraced these thinkers as well as others from the 1907 Stuttgart Second International and supported the International's decision on the inviolability of a nation's independence and liberation and the right of workers to defend national independence against violence and aggression. After a detailed discussion of their views, Sapah-Giwlian concludes that in socialist terms, every nation must have its own right to exist, rule itself, control its own fate, and live in equality in a universal alliance of nations without one subjugating the other. As for Shahrigian, he found in the speeches of the "Bernsteins" and "Vanderveldes" the justification that nationalities are the "substance of Humanity."[71]

"THIS WAY OR THAT WAY": SOCIALISM WITH AN ARMENIAN FACE

There is no doubt that the approach of most Armenian revolutionaries or thinkers to socialism was tainted or, to use a more neutral term, influenced by the looming national problem that existed in at least two of the three empires—Russian and Ottoman—before their respective revolutions, but it may equally be the case that their relationship with socialism was accentuated by the promise of revolutionary change. Does this necessarily mean, then, as their contemporary critics often insisted, that their socialism was a dodge or a deception at its worst or a hodgepodge at its best? Was their socialism a ruse for a purely or primarily nationalist agenda? Could it have been a sincere albeit eclectic (or as their critics would say, confused) synthesis? Or was it merely a developing (or according to their critics, immature and naive) position? By extension, therefore, was their role as mobile connectors in the three revolutions solely driven by a national agenda?

Before addressing these questions directly, it would be useful to look at somewhat analogous cases in the South Caucasus and the Ottoman Empire. In the case of Georgian national socialism, Stephen Jones points out that Georgian Social Democrats "were among the first socialists to show that nationalism and socialism were not contradictory but complementary."[72] In his study, aptly titled *Socialism in Georgian Colors,* Jones demonstrates that Georgian socialists adopted an "eclectic approach to doctrine" and borrowed and adapted revolutionary and socialist ideas from a number of sources "from Russian populism, European Marxism, or Georgia's own brand of national liberation," engaging with thinkers like Karl Kautsky, Rosa Luxemburg, August Bebel, Jean Jaurès, Jules Guesde, Emile Vandervelde, Karl Renner, and Otto Bauer, much like our Armenian socialists.[73] Their viewpoint was "filtered through Georgians' own culture" and their particular situation, much like that of the Armenians, as a land in a multiethnic region, under Russian imperial rule, and in a precapitalist society with a majority peasant population.[74] As such, they were forced "to adapt practically, to innovate tactically, and to reinterpret theoretically" and thus produce a socialism with a "Georgian face" or in "Georgian colors."[75] In similar fashion, Dimou emphasizes the Bulgarian (Broad) socialists' "rethinking of 'tactics' more adapted to the concrete problems of Bulgarian society." She explains that although their critics singled out their "'aberration' from Marxism," their position "was more about what Janko Sakŭzov called the 'Scylla and Charybdis' of Marxism, the tension between theoretical prescriptions and their practical application." Dimou's contention that the "dilemmas" Bulgarian socialists faced "were neither exceptional nor unique" and that "similar preoccupations, such as the relationship to the peasantry, the tension between theory and practice, and politics in the intersection between long-term and short-term goals" were shared by other contemporary socialists certainly rings true as well for the Armenians. Moreover, her qualifying remark that due to particular local circumstances, the "preoccupations" of Bulgarian socialists "took on a more incisive and existential character" serves to connect these cases further.[76] Both Georgian and Bulgarian experiences and relationship to socialist thought as well as Jones's and Dimou's lines of argument quite easily apply to the Armenian case, as we witness comparable as well as distinctive developments in the Armenian example.

There is no question that Armenian revolutionaries used any approach, thought, or concept within their reach from the large arsenal of Eurasian socialist and sociological sources in order to understand the world around them and to explain their stance; they were, however, partial to certain ideas because those concepts helped explain their perception of the present reality and the promise of the future. Their participation, especially in the case of the ARF, in three revolutionary movements—Russian, Ottoman, and Iranian—simultaneously affected the development of their socialist ideological bent and was motivated by their adherence to socialism, with all its promise of social, political, and economic justice, equality, and multiethnic unity. In other words, circulation and connection or transrevolutionary mobility were not necessarily factors that transformed the revolutionary struggles, although there is no doubt that they had an effect on the struggles, especially in the Iranian case, but certainly they acted as dynamics that shaped Armenian revolutionary thought itself.

Social Democrats believed that the ARF would dissolve under the weight of its multiple and, for them, mutually irreconcilable ideological commitments, conflicting socialist and nationalist visions, and outright chauvinism. Perhaps they had in mind the earlier SDHP rift. Referring to the ARF presence in the South Caucasus, the leftist *Hosank'* (Current) anticipated that the party "will dissolve completely and disappear from the Caucasian reality. That hour is not far."[77] In another article in the same paper, the author draws readers' attention to a clever proverb about a pike, which—having become bored with hunting for fish—one day decides to hunt mice like a cat, but instead of filling its belly with mice, it loses its tail to the mice that gnaw at it. In this way, the author reminds the ARF of the perils of venturing into the area of conscious workers because like the pike out of water, the ARF can only live in its own environment: "Advice for you, little pike, not to try to hunt for mice next time."[78] Yet perhaps because the party's perspective more accurately represented the reality of the Armenian mosaic and its own practicality, which Social Democrats labeled with the motto "this way or that way," the ARF did not meet the same demise as the pike that lost its tail; instead, it survived and often dominated the Armenian political scene.[79] How was the criticism of an Armenian brand of socialism by the ARF's main rivals on the left, however, in many ways a reflection of the larger disagreements taking place in Europe (and to some degree among fellow imperial subjects)? And how was socialism with an Armenian face or in Armenian colors that different from the non–orthodox Marxist positions of Jean Jaurès, Eduard Bernstein, and other socialist reformers or that of Caucasian socialist revolutionaries?[80]

The ARF was quite cognizant of leftist criticisms of the "fantastical weaving" of socialist views, contradictions, and nationalist approaches that were in opposition to the class issue, which the party saw as dividing instead of uniting Armenians.[81] These criticisms began to increase in 1905 and after the ARF committed itself to a struggle on two fronts, in the Ottoman and Russian Empires, joined the Iranian constitutional movement, and more openly espoused socialism in 1907.[82] Because the ARF presented itself as the protector of workers, urban and rural, it sought to fight against economic exploitation and to teach the masses socialist ideals in preparation for the great struggle.[83] As ARF's *Haṛaj* expressed, one of its "essential purposes" was as "a defender of Armenian workers' interests, to bring forth consciousness in them . . . "[84] Much of the ARF's teaching, as well as that of the SDHP and other Armenian Social Democrats, about class struggle, the history of socialism, unions, and other related issues was done through print—that is, newspapers, pamphlets, and books in translation and in the original—as well as through public lectures.[85] Despite or because of the criticism leveled against it, the ARF insisted on its version of socialism and explained its position first through a Marxist, class-based analysis and second by reference to the particularity of the mostly Ottoman and Russian environment, with occasional references to Iran. Its approach in many ways resembled, as we shall see in the next section, that of the middle path between orthodox Marxism and the Bernsteinian revisionism proposed by Jaurès as well as by Russian and Caucasian Socialist Revolutionaries, especially in relation to the agrarian question and populist influences.

As Varandian explains, as a response to accusations of not being a homogeneous, revolutionary party, of having a nationalist program, and of defending bourgeois interests, the ARF, like the SDHP and every other party, had a program composed of both practical and theoretical aspects, the former (minimum) more immediate and the latter (maximum) "a distant ideal." Varandian defines the minimum program as the consequence of reality on the ground and the maximum as the evolution of universal life and thought. Although the ARF, he continues, espoused socialist principles in the 1890s, even before the existence of the Social Democrats, having been influenced by the Russian populist Narodnaya Volya movement, socialism remained a distant ideal because of the reality of Ottoman economic life—no industry and no capital production—as well as because of Ottoman persecution of Armenians. Others, with less faith in the people's understanding of reality, articulated a deep pessimism about the place of socialism in the Ottoman Empire in general and among Armenians in particular. An article titled "Is It Possible to Be Socialist in Haste?" exclaims, "imbibing our people's mind with socialist ideas" is like "forcing the seven-year-old child to throw a stone ten times his weight far, which is of course an impossibility . . . " The article asks how it was possible to defend the rights of workers in a country where working life does not exist, adding (in Eurocentric fashion) that defending workers' rights among Ottoman Armenians is like setting up a Parisian fashion boutique among the Hottentots.[86]

Varandian was not as cynical and made connections between socialism and the national question, asserting that the ARF had no interest in separatism and sought the freedom of all nationalities through socialism, that "universal movement which wants to shatter all the chains weighing heavy on the working classes, all the class privileges and seeks humanity's sincere equality and fraternity."[87] The ARF's maximum program, its long-term objective, sought a socialist state that would put an end to exploitation by the few capitalists of the many workers. It would do so by bringing all modes of production under the control of working people and by putting an end to the capitalist economy, thus bringing about equality and political liberation. To that end, working masses must carry out a steady and fierce struggle. In the meantime, the minimum program of socialist parties and the ARF, in particular, is to do whatever possible to minimize capitalist rule and improve the situations of the working masses, turning them into strong and enlightened citizens in charge of their rights.[88]

The minimum program sought the actualization of reforms necessary on the path to socialism, including the eight-hour workday, a minimum legal wage, equal pay to women and foreign workers for equal work, no labor for school-aged children (under sixteen), measures to improve the working conditions and health of workers, and so forth.[89] In a discussion of the ARF 1907 program and socialism, *Drōshak* reminded its readers that "the class struggle is particularly complex in those countries where the representatives of the ruling ethnicities, having taken in hand all state and popular institutions, oppress the weak nations . . . " Therefore, the workers of oppressed ethnic groups suffer doubly—economically and culturally—and this situation stalls the workers' social liberation because it hinders the advancement of class antagonism, on the one hand, and solidarity among working classes of oppressed nations, on the other. The only solution lies, the article concludes, in the elimination of boundaries and distinctions among nations and the creation of a harmonious socialist humanity in federation to supersede the divided, exploitative, and antagonistic world. As we saw earlier, like the SDHP and non–orthodox Marxist socialists, the ARF organ contends that the realization of socialism does not demand the assimilation of all national unions.[90] This view coincided with the view of the Georgian Social Democrats, too, who believed that socialism would ensure their survival.[91]

The SDHP, too, worked toward socialism as a long-term objective and not necessarily an immediately achievable aim because it realized, like the ARF, that conditions did not allow for the speedy triumph of socialism. To reach the desired socialist system, it was first necessary to create democracy, political freedom, and national independence.[92] However, as Sapah-Giwlian explained, the party and the working class would struggle toward that goal with the aim of shortening the period of "pregnancy" and lessening the "pains of childbirth"—that is, the passing from capitalism to socialism, when the proletariat would take full control over the political and economic reins and bring forth political and economic liberation.[93] As another *Hnch'ak* author wrote, the party had two fields of action, Ottoman Anatolia and the Caucasus, and while it was preparing for a general revolt in the former, it had already been working under the Social Democratic proletarian banner, collaborating with other socialists in strikes, for example.[94] The SDHP differed from the ARF, however, in seeing the existence and development of capitalism not only in the Russian Empire but also in the Ottoman Empire. Responding to Armenian nationalists who criticized the SDHP for mixing socialism with the Armenian cause in the Ottoman Empire, Sapah-Giwlian asserts that socialism is *a part of* and not *apart from* the struggle in the empire. He argues that the Ottoman Empire is as capitalist as the Russian or any other capitalist state and that the only difference is that other countries' centers of capitalist production are located internally, whereas those of the Ottoman Empire profit in Manchester, London, Hamburg, Berlin, and other European cities, thus killing the small artisan and landholder and creating an army of unemployed. The product or victim of the capitalist economy, although located externally, nevertheless leaves an internal impact.[95]

While Armenian socialists observed in the Ottoman Empire and certainly in the Russian Empire aspects of their stage of economic development that they believed helped make their case for a socialist struggle in these two states, they found it difficult to do so in the Iranian case. Nevertheless, they worked around this difficulty. In a series of articles exploring Iran and its revolutionary movement, Social Democrat Arshavir Chilinkirian considered Iran to be in a precapitalist stage. Chilinkirian writes that since the 1890s, foreign capital had been spreading in Iran, but one could not speak of capital production or manufacturing; therefore, the current movement in Iran was not the result of the advancement of the country's production. Foreign capital entering through industry, railways, and other methods would ultimately quicken the destruction of the economy and hasten the entry of capitalism into Iran. The current movements, thus, were directed against foreign capital and foreign culture and therefore "reactionary."[96] Chilinkirian's and other Armenian Social Democrats' perception was the result of much reflection and discussion about where Iran stood in Marxist economic development. For some socialists, the Iranian Constitutional Revolution was the first stage in the struggle that would ultimately end in socialism.

Armenian Social Democrats, especially those like Chilinkirian as well as Vram Pilosian, Vasso Khachaturian, and others in Tabriz, maintained close ties with the RSDWP, and some even came down from the Caucasus, especially from Baku. They also sought the counsel of Karl Kautsky and Georgi Plekhanov, founder of the Russian social democratic movement, regarding two issues: first, the character of the revolution—that is, was it regressive or progressive, and what role, if any, should Social Democrats play in each of those two scenarios?; second (and closely linked to

the first), what was Iran's stage of capitalist production?[97] Kautsky
encouraged participation because of the movement's primarily democratic character and considered Iran to be experiencing the first condition
of industrial development, foreign capitalism and exploitation, much like
the Ottoman Empire, according to Sapah-Giwlian's interpretation discussed earlier and that of Tigran Zaven.[98] The triumph of democracy,
which the revolution would bring about, would then usher in the final
class struggle and thus social democracy. In the absence of Plekhanov's
response to Khachaturian, his letter to Plekhanov may be used to indicate
the Tabriz Social Democrats' concerns. Referring to Kautsky's assessment
that if the country had no modern proletariat then social democrats must
take part in the revolution as democrats rather than as social democrats,
Khachaturian inquired whether Plekhanov agreed. He also sought
answers to questions regarding the role of social democrats in the struggle
against foreign capital and in favor of free trade and the appropriateness
of forming a popular militia, which he feared the bourgeoisie would ultimately transform into a permanent army.[99]

It seems that the SDHP in Tabriz agreed with Kautsky's overall
assessment in response to Chilinkirian. In an attempt to explain and
justify its limited participation in Iran's revolutionary movement, it concluded that the state of the working class, mostly in manufacturing production, demanded that the party work on two levels in Iran: first, as
democrats, to work in defense of democracy and in the service of free-
ing the country from any foreign encroachment; second, to continue to
pursue socialist activity among progressive workers. Kautsky's response
also inspired the majority of Tabriz Social Democrats to accept a proposal presented by Khachaturian and Chilinkirian in October 1908.
Despite minority objection that Iran had not entered the stage of industrial production and had no modern proletariat and therefore no basis
for social democratic agitation, the proposal accepted—in agreement
with Kautsky—that because Iran had entered the stage of manufacturing and industrial production and had developed a small class of workers alongside a larger class of small artisans, a foundation for socialist
agitation already existed. They rejected Kautsky's recommendation,
however, to participate in the revolution merely as democrats and "to
collaborate with the bourgeoisie." They insisted on continuing a struggle as social democrats whose worldview significantly departed from
that of mere democrats. They contended that their role at all times was
to mobilize and agitate among workers and intellectuals and to arouse
a "class consciousness for the socialist struggle."[100] As such, their view

more closely resembled that of Rosa Luxemburg.[101] While there is no direct evidence that they had contact or corresponded with Luxemburg, the position that they ultimately took and what we have learned about revolutionaries' familiarity with the contemporary revolutionary press and intellectual currents indicates that they were keenly aware of and quite conversant with contemporary socialist thought. The Tabrizi Armenian Social Democrats were no different than their ethnic or ideological counterparts in seeing in the Iranian Constitutional Revolution a path to socialism and accompanying promise for dramatic change in the country and the region.

Chilinkirian, along with two former SDHP members, Vram Pilosian and Sedrak Banvorian, took his ideological proficiency to the Iranian Constitutional Revolution by helping to found the Tabriz Social Democratic Party in 1905 and the Democrat Party in 1909 with Seyyed Hasan Taqizadeh, Tabriz delegate to the Majles (assembly). Chilinkirian, along with Tigran Ter Hakobian, became the intellectual leader of the Tabriz Social Democratic Party.[102] Ter Hakobian, like Pilosian, formed Democrat groups and also organized workers in Tabriz.[103] When he moved to Tehran in 1910, he became a regular contributor to the Democrat Party organ, *Iran-e Now*.[104] According to Janet Afary, Ter Hakobian wrote many of his "more substantial" theoretical essays in French; they appeared in Persian translation.[105] In January 1910 SDHP members and Iranian social democrats created an Iranian branch of the SDHP.[106] Moreover, as *Hnch'ak* theoretician Grigor Yeghikian (pen name Astghuni) writes, close relations between SDHP member Simon Simonian and his student in the Russian language Key Ostovan (Hosein Mo'tamed)—subsequently a Majles delegate—led to the translation of the SDHP program into Persian.[107] Yeghikian was yet another roving activist who started out in the Ottoman Empire, went to the South Caucasus, and ended up in Iran in 1902, a few years before the Russian and Iranian Revolutions.[108]

South Caucasian Armenian social democrats, whether affiliated with the SDHP or not, acted as a mobile link between the Caucasus and Iran and between the Russian and Iranian revolutions. In all three revolutions—the Russian, the Ottoman, and the Iranian—Armenian activists with various ideological and pragmatic commitments circulated and mobilized across imperial frontiers in collaborative struggle for the promise of a socialist future. Their ideas, whatever form they took, also crossed frontiers—Western and Central European, Russian, Ottoman, and Iranian—not only through individuals but also through print in the form of philosophical, intellectual, and ideological tracts. What enabled and accelerated these developments were advances in both communication and transportation. As revolutionaries and ideas flowed across national and imperial entities and movements, their physical and ideological boundary crossings connected revolutions. Such ideological boundary crossings involved, on some level, negotiation, compromise, or balancing of often divergent positions within socialism itself.

A BALANCING ACT: BETWEEN ORTHODOXY AND REFORMISM

A close look at Mikayel Varandian's *Hosank'ner* (Currents), published in 1910 in Geneva, gives us a good idea of the array of intellectual currents and debates with which Armenian socialists familiarized themselves and helps us understand how and why they settled on their syncretic brand of socialism. In many ways, Varandian's book captures the contemporary intellectual environment and underscores the significance of socialism in the period not only for Armenians but also for fellow subjects in the Russian, Ottoman, and Iranian states. Although it is difficult, if not impossible, to come by quantitative data about the number of copies printed, circulated, and/or read, we can ascertain the study's importance from the author's own presence as a prolific author of books and articles in the contemporary press (e.g., in *Mshak, Murch,* and other periodicals), sometimes using the pseudonym Ego or Mikayel Hovhannisian, and as a member of the editorial boards of *Drōshak* and *Haṛaj.* Varandian was also an ARF leader, serving on the Western Bureau and representing the party at the Second International Congress in Stuttgart in 1907. He is probably best known for his two-volume history of the ARF.[109]

Varandian divides *Hosank'ner* into three sections: orthodox Marxism (with subsections on the Amsterdam Congress of 1904 and orthodox Marxism in Russia and the Caucasus), anarchism (on the two periods before and after the 1860s), and revolutionary syndicalism. Before moving to his presentation of socialism, it is valuable to see how Varandian portrays other European movements of the time.

Varandian traces revolutionary syndicalism's history and development by focusing on the movement's major figures of Georges Sorel, Arturo Labriola, and Enrico Leone. His assessment of the movement is very critical. He finds fault particularly in its complete reliance on what he views as the "direct action" of workers, "contempt" for intellectuals, and denial

FIGURE 6. Mikayel Varandian (1870–1934). Image reproduced courtesy of the ARF Central Committee. Source: *Hushamatean Hay Heghap'okhakan Dashnakts'ut'ean albom-atlas,* vol. 1, *Diwts'aznamart* [Commemorative album-atlas of the Armenian Revolutionary Federation, vol. 1, Heroic combat] (Glendale, CA: ARF Central Committee, 1992).

of any role for the intelligentsia, asserting that the focus on deed is insufficient without its ally, theory. He likens the movement to a sailor thrown into an unfamiliar ocean "without map and compass."[110] Varandian also objects to its critical stance on nations, stating that its "declared cosmopolitanism seems completely metaphysical delirium. . . . "[111] Anarchism fares better, perhaps because Varandian recognizes some similarities with socialism. Varandian seems to respect the "brilliant theoreticians" of this "rich and original" ideology: Pierre-Joseph Proudhon, Max Stirner, Mikhail Bakunin, Pyotr Kropotkin, Élisée Reclus, and Louise Michel of Paris Commune fame. He critiques, nevertheless, anarchism's support of "absolute freedom" in contrast to socialism's "relative freedom," finding that anarchism exaggerates human solidarity and harmony, expecting men to "turn into angels," and he disparages it as utopian, "a splendid dream, but . . . a dream."[112]

Varandian considers socialism, on the other hand, as it had evolved in the sixty years since the intervention of Marx and Engels, as very much a realizable reality, especially in close association with the national question. In the first three hundred pages or so, Varandian surveys the evolution of socialism and Marxism from an unyielding position of *Alles oder Nichts!* (all or nothing) to "a tenacious and resolute struggle that will advance us [to our position] gradually."[113] He begins with Hegel; goes through Marx and Engels, the first and second Socialist Internationals, social democracy, Eduard Bernstein and revisionism, the significance of the agrarian issue, the dispute between Guesde and Jaurès, and the socialist stance on the Dreyfus affair; and ends with orthodox Marxism in Russia and the Caucasus. Varandian's views reflect those found in the ARF press. First and foremost, Varandian emphasizes the positive development of socialist views on the national question, reminding his readers (and referencing Kautsky) that "any intelligent Marxist, after 60 years of evolution, is forced to confess that the national question is intimately tied to the class question, that for the working masses its national freedom is equally important as its general electoral 'right'" and "only in that kind of freedom can it ... carry forward its class struggle in an unhindered way until the victory of the grand ideal, that finally even in the future, in the universal socialist family, nations will probably preserve ... their particularity [ինքնուրոյնութիւն/ink'nuroynut'iwn] and variation [այլազանութիւն/aylazanut'iwn]."[114]

Varandian is just as critical of Russian social democracy as his ARF colleagues, finding them uncompromising and stuck in the past. He supports the rejection of the principle of the catastrophic collapse of capitalism as well as the theory of pauperization and sharpening of class struggle. Instead, he believes that it is clear that working conditions will improve under socialist pressure and that only then will the proletariat achieve its goals. Although appreciative of Bernstein's much-needed reform of social democracy, which laid bare the contradiction between (revolutionary) word and (reformist) deed, he believes it took a turn toward extremism, thus muddling socialism. He asserts that Bernstein "almost forgot socialism's final purpose and, raptured by democracy's progress, he assimilated socialism with democratism, the working class with other classes."[115] He praises the darling of Armenian socialists, Jean Jaurès, whom he considers far more revolutionary in character and deed than Bernstein and social democracy "dogmatists."[116] Varandian points to Jaurès's pragmatic yet principled stance, never giving up class conflict but acknowledging that reforms may be the path toward the ultimate socialist goal.[117] He goes into great detail about the assault by Kautsky, Plekhanov, Guesde, and others on Jaurès and Bernstein, who were at first confused and were thought to hold the same views.[118] Varandian writes approvingly of Jaurès's ardent antimilitarist resolution and role in the Second International Congress in Stuttgart in 1907 and appreciatively of Adler's and Vandervelde's amended resolution, which declared it the duty of workers "to exert every effort in order to prevent the outbreak of war by the means they consider most effective" and, in case of war, "to intervene in favor of its speedy termination and with all their powers to utilize the economic and political crisis created by the war to rouse the masses and thereby to hasten the downfall of capitalist class rule."[119]

In addition to his antimilitarism and more favorable view of the national question, what appealed most to Varandian and the ARF in general about Jaurès were four interrelated aspects of his approach: first, as Irving Howe submits, his "clear vision of the indissoluble link between democracy and socialism"; second, his nondeterminist conception of history; third, his advocacy of working across classes with the nonsocialist, liberal bourgeoisie; and fourth, his amalgamation of the ideal and the real.[120] Jaurès's approach straddled the middle path between Kautsky and Bernstein. While he supported Bernstein's push for reforms, he disagreed with Bernstein's critique of orthodox Marxism. He was quite careful to strike a balance between offering an alternative to orthodox Marxism that took into account liberal principles and maintaining the fundamentals of class conflict and class struggle.[121] As Geoffrey Kurtz explains, Jaurès rejected the historical determinism of orthodox Marxists like Kautsky and Guesde; "Instead, he borrowed from Marx precisely those ideas that he found useful in constructing a theory of radical reform."[122] Therefore, while accepting the very basics of Marxian analysis of economic development, he "insisted that Marx's 'materialist conception of history' be understood in a flexible and nuanced way," thus accepting that economic conflict was not the only driving force of history and giving greater importance to ideas and politics.[123] By inserting ideas and politics into a Marxist conception of history, then, Kurtz contends that he helped explain the importance of reforms as well as participation in democratic government and cross-class alliances with liberal bourgeoisie in the service of the interests of the working class.[124] As Kurtz concludes, "Jaurès's involvement in the reformism debates merged a non-determinist version of Marxist social theory with a liberal insistence on universal norms of justice, by way of a conception of working-class political action as the force that brings the socialist ideal into contact with political reality."[125]

These aspects of Jaurès's thinking closely aligned with the ARF's own merger of ideal and real, its criticism of economic determinism at the expense of other elements, its openness to working with liberal nonsocialist forces, and a general commitment to democratic liberal principles along with socialist goals. These elements were the same points of criticism that orthodox Marxists hurled at the ARF about its brand of socialism and the same points that the ARF found so appealing about Jaurès's approach. The ARF's democratic liberal principles found expression particularly in its activity in the postrevolutionary Ottoman Empire after the ARF had become a legal party. This development coincided with renewed and fierce tsarist persecution that targeted the ARF and revolutionary parties in the South Caucasus in 1908 in what became known as the Stolypin crackdown.

In the Ottoman Empire, the ARF, the SDHP, and others faced a much more entrenched antisocialist position among the dominant Young Turks. They did, however, try (largely unsuccessfully) to insert or infuse socialist ideals through the press into Armenian readers and, through their encounters and exchanges, influence the CUP and postrevolutionary policies.[126] As Anahide Ter Minassian explains, "From 1909 to 1911, a great many articles in the Dashnak [ARF] and Henchak [SDHP] press were dedicated to the labour question . . . Socialism was constantly presented as the only remedy for the misery and the exploitation of the workers and farmers."[127] Although the ARF and the SDHP dominated the Armenian socialist press in the Ottoman Empire, other leftist papers made their mark on the socialist scene. One example, of course, is Istanbul's *Surhandak* (Messenger), after its turn further to the left under the editorship of Tigran Zaven, who likened workers to slaves. According to Zaven, the slaves of the past had been replaced by "free-slave[s]," who are in a worse position, as the "new slave"—the worker, the landless peasant—does not have the luxury of eating daily because work is not guaranteed every day. Thus, the bourgeoisie understands "freedom of work" to mean "freedom of exploitation." This article was picked up and reprinted in Turkish translation in the literary journal *Servet-i Fünun* (Wealth of knowledge) and the CUP organ, *Şûra-yı Ümmet* (The council of the community).[128] Another nonaffiliated Marxist paper, *Nor Hosank'*, had a very short but noteworthy run from March to June 1909. Its motto, straight out of *The Communist Manifesto*, "Proletarians of all countries, unite," reflected the social democratic tendencies of its Caucasian and Ottoman Armenian contributors, including the former Narodnik Gevorg Gharajian (pseudonym Arkomed), one of the founders of the SDHP and one of three translators "who were the first to translate the Manifesto of the Communist Party into the Armenian language."[129] *Nor Hosank'* appeared on behalf of the "abandoned and derided, exploited and harassed worker class to protect its interests, to advance in it class consciousness and to help its sound organizing" in order to rescue "Turkey's political existence as an independent state" and liberate it from foreign intervention.[130]

In ARF's case, Ter Minassian believes, however, that "liberalism and socialism were in development and the border between the two was not yet clear . . . [In] the Ottoman Empire, the ARF . . . suffered from growing pains . . . It had a socialist viewpoint, but at the same time it played the part of a liberal party that recruited representatives from the liberal bourgeoisie. . . . "[131] In a series of articles in the ARF paper, *Azatamart* (Battle for freedom), Rupen Tarpinian (the pen name of Ardashes Chilinkarian) both explained and advocated for the ARF's liberal activity.[132] Tarpinian acknowledges that the ARF was socialist, its "optic is socialist, the *tendency* of the party press; the mentality of the leading individuals is socialist, the party's program, world view, its literature, are socialist." However, its major political steps have had "only a *liberal* nature/character," and thus it could accomplish no more than a "democratic-liberal party" in "our reality."[133] For this reason and because socialist activity in the empire was only "preparatory," liberal bourgeois elements had entered the ranks and would naturally have more influence. Tarpinian insists that the ARF must embrace both socialists and liberals in its ranks.[134] Writing under the pen name Adom, Shahrigian, the author of *Mer Havatamkě* (Our credo), admits the necessity to carry out liberal politics and to collaborate with liberal-bourgeois elements in the political reality of the Ottoman Empire, but he contends that this allowance did not in any way "signify that it has folded and put to one side its socialist aim and ideal." He adds that liberal activity was not unique to the ARF, but "Life's inexorable indispensability has obliged that tactic in all countries and on all socialist parties."[135] Although Shahrigian does not provide specific examples, one of the many examples closer to home was Yanko Sakazov and the Broad Socialists, who, like the ARF, were open to cooperation with liberal, bourgeois, and petty bourgeois tendencies.[136] For Shahrigian, these were necessary steps that would ultimately lead toward socialism; however, disagreeing fiercely with Tarpinian, Shahrigian opposed the "participation and influence" of liberal-bourgeois elements in the party, cautioning that it would "neutralize the socialist aim and ideals" of the ARF.[137]

PEOPLE, CLASS, AND THE LABORING PEASANTRY

The members of ARF and other Armenian socialists drew from the Western European socialists Jaurès, Kautsky, and others, as we have noted, to shape their socialism and their revolutionary positions within and across the Russian, Ottoman, and Iranian frontiers. The ARF, in particular, as the one party involved in all three revolutions, also found ideological and revolutionary comrades among Russian and Caucasian Socialist Revolutionaries regarding their shared populist influences and rivalries with social democrats, especially when it came to their positions on federation (addressed in the previous chapter), as well as the agrarian question. According to Manfred Hildermeier, the ARF and the Georgian Socialist Revolutionaries were some of the Russian Socialist Revolutionaries' "influential helpers," providing them with "periodic financial support" and personnel help.[138] Moreover, they were often allied not only because of their shared vision but also because they both competed with social democratic advancement among the workers and faced similar social democratic attacks.

In his study on the Russian Socialist Revolutionaries, some of whom previously belonged to the Russian populist movement (Narodnichestvo), Hildermeier demonstrates their populist influence, especially in their approach to the peasantry and terror, asserting, "The SR understanding of class was thus revealed to be a new version of the populist concept of the *people*."[139] Varandian noted this as well at the time, stating that the Socialist Revolutionaries had replaced "narod" (people) with proletariat.[140] A few Armenians, like ARF cofounder Kristapor Mikayelian, were involved in Narodnichestvo and shared its emphasis on the peasantry over the urban proletariat, its agrarian socialism, its adoption of terror as a necessary tactic, and the important role it ascribed to the intelligentsia in the workers' struggle, all of which most Social Democrats opposed or did not privilege.[141] The Georgian Social Democrats differed in this regard from other Social Democrats. As Jones demonstrates, they had both a "peasant orientation" and "support for terror."[142] In fact, he argues that Georgian Social Democrats fused "workers, artisans, traders, and peasants into the 'working people.'"[143] Thus, in this regard they resembled the Socialist Revolutionaries and the ARF, for whom the revolutionary struggle against autocracy and capitalism involved workers, peasants, and intellectuals, with the last group leading the movement because of their special position or calling in society. In the Balkans, they were joined by the Broad Socialists, who acknowledged the important contribution of all classes in addition to the workers, including peasants, artisans, intellectuals, and others. Even though the Broad Socialists "made no attempt to attract the peasants," this issue acted as the catalyst that formally separated them from the Narrow Socialists in 1903.[144]

The ARF championed the positive and necessary role of the intelligentsia in raising workers' consciousness and joining as well as leading the socialist struggle.[145] Moreover, most young Armenian activists and intellectuals emulated the populist call to serve the "people" and maintained populist leanings even as socialists. The tsarist secret police, Okhrana, which surveilled the ARF's activities as it did those of other revolutionary parties, also corroborated these connections in a report on the ARF. According to the report, the ARF was very much swayed by the populist Narodnaya Volya (People's Will) party and had economic demands no different than other Russian revolutionary parties.[146] Okhrana maintained that the ARF came "under the influence of the Caucasus's socialist workers movement and as a consequence of the spread of Armenian intelligentsia's socialist ideas," it quickly adopted the views of the Socialist Revolutionaries, moving increasingly closer to their party.[147] However, Okhrana also referred to ARF members as "anarchist-communists" and considered its terror operations especially threatening to the Russian state.[148] Reporting on an interparty meeting of representatives of the Georgian Social Democratic Party, the Russian Social-Democratic Labor Party (probably the RSDWP), Socialist Revolutionaries, the SDHP, and the ARF held in Baku or Tiflis, the Tiflis provincial gendarmerie chief (through Okhrana) purports that a "decision was made to execute immediately terror." He provides specific details: "all the political parties must seek, jointly and individually, to murder at least five officials of the Security Divisions who arrived with me from Russia to the Caucasus since they consider all of us guilty of having a different disposition toward revolutionary groups in the Caucasus. For that reason permission is granted to every political party to carry out terrorism against all those whom they consider harmful to them."[149] The ARF was no different than the Party of Socialist Revolutionaries in viewing terror as a "*legitimate* and *essential* weapon" that "show[ed] the people the means and the objectives of the revolutionary struggle 'with the *fewest possible victims* and in *the shortest possible time*.'"[150] It is very likely that just as the Party of Socialist Revolutionaries' theoretical justification for terror came from Narodnaya Volya, as Hildermeier explains, so did that of the ARF, and in the same way that the Party of Socialist Revolutionaries viewed terror as honorable and holy, so did the ARF.[151] It was no coincidence that Victor Chernov, one of the key figures in shaping the Party of Socialist

Revolutionaries' approach to terror and the architect of its minimal and maximal programs and land socialization policy, was also read and translated by the ARF.[152]

Land socialization was intimately linked with the agrarian policy of the Party of Socialist Revolutionaries and the ARF, both of which, like Georgian Social Democrats, extended the definition of *worker* to correspond more closely to reality as they perceived it and include the majority of the Russian peasantry, and, in the case of ARF and the Bulgarian Social Democrats, also the Ottoman Empire.[153] Land socialization or, as the ARF often called it, land communalization provided an alternative to social democracy's nationalization of land and all means of production. It maintained a "very strong decentralized character" whereby local, self-administrative institutions held land.[154] The ARF advocated land socialization in the Ottoman Empire without much success and professed to be the party that had brought the concept into the Ottoman Empire.[155] It explained and defended land socialization in its press in some detail, although it had detractors even within its own ranks. Writing in ARF's Istanbul paper, *Azatamart,* Rupen Tarpinian characterizes ARF's support for land communalization as a consequence of *narodnik* influence on the "Armenian revolutionary mind." Referring to an absence of studies on Turkish land relations when compared to Russia and the need for a systematic census, he contends that land communalization in Turkey (i.e., Anatolia) "will for a long time be devoid of any practical value." Moreover, it will "barely be able to carry out the role of leading principle in the resolution of the land question in its present phase."[156] For the ARF as for the Party of Socialist Revolutionaries, land communalization or socialization was directly linked to peasant deprivation—a direct consequence of land scarcity and unequal partition of land. The only solution lay, according to V. Araratski, in the elimination of property right over land, giving peasants the right to work and benefit from a freed land, reminding readers of the laboring peasantry's saying: "the land is God's; the land is no one's."[157] He sees in land socialization the path to socialism for the village in the same way that the communalization of labor and modes of production opened up the city's path to socialism, contending that land communalization is the "indispensable ring, the inevitable terminus in the evolution of the 'village'—toward socialism."[158] The ARF recognized that it had much in common with the much more developed agrarian program of the Party of Socialist Revolutionaries and nothing with the Social Democrat view of the peasantry as a backward bourgeois element. It considered the land issue the Party

FIGURE 7. The Armenian peasant—Where should I go? There are three paths [the Armenian Revolutionary Federation, the Social Democratic Hnchakian Party, or the Social Democrats]. Image reproduced courtesy of Bibliothèque Nubar (Nubar Library), Paris. Source: *Khat'abala* (Tiflis) 17 (7 October 1906).

of Socialist Revolutionaries' most significant demand and accurately pointed out that the Socialist Revolutionaries pursued a struggle on three fronts—popular liberation, labor and liberation, land and liberation—all conspicuously similar to the struggle of the ARF.[159] To some degree, the ARF also concurred with the Georgian Social Democrats. Although they opposed land socialization, the Georgian Social Democrats, having recognized that the majority of the country's population was peasant and having been deeply influenced by the agrarian movements in Georgia between 1902 and 1905, equated peasant and worker "conditions of poverty and powerlessness," much as the ARF did.[160]

As we have seen, the connections between Armenian revolutionaries and socialists and their European counterparts extended to Russian and Caucasian comrades and coconspirators, especially when it came to federation, land, and peasantry. What set the Armenians, particularly the ARF, apart, however, was that because of their reality of dispersion across three empires and their conviction that they belonged to three societies, their socialist ideas and operations traveled beyond the South Caucasus, connecting three revolutionary struggles.

CONNECTING THROUGH AND BEYOND READING

Clearly, Armenian revolutionaries and thinkers were keenly aware of and deeply familiar with the current debates and events taking place in Europe and with leftist movements and views; they read and engaged with much of the same philosophical, intellectual, and social scientific material as their counterparts. As Khuri-Makdisi shows in the case of Eastern Mediterranean radicals, "They wrote, translated, indigenized, and published" on a number of socialist and other relevant concepts, which simultaneously exposes their influences and the ideas they deemed critical to comprehend and circulate.[161] In an effort to "elevat[e] our people's revolutionary knowledge/consciousness," the ARF and other revolutionaries committed themselves and a fraction of their annual budget—20 percent in ARF's case—to "propaganda and literature."[162]

Revolutionaries in this period learned from each other within and beyond their local and regional frontiers and from the widely available print resources. Along the way, they appropriated social and political ideas in vogue in relation to their own conditions and modified their own views and tactics according to the ideas they acquired—but always within their own reality. Thus, they were connected intimately to a new, expansive world brought closer by all the developments in transportation and communication, including print, that marked turn-of-the-century time-space compression. In turn, they connected their own smaller world within the Russian, Ottoman, and Iranian frontiers through crossings—physical and ideological—during a tumultuous revolutionary period and milieu, which they embraced passionately. These physical and ideological boundary crossings merged in their encounters and exchanges with intellectuals and revolutionaries beyond their immediate frontiers in Europe.

Revolutionaries also had contact and collaborated with their contemporaries in all three empires as well as in Europe. High-ranking ARF members who resided in Europe's urban centers or who traveled there on party business often met with European statesmen, intellectuals, and socialists. This was the case especially for those who were on the editorial boards of the SDHP's *Hnch'ak*, in Paris at this time, and of the ARF's *Drōshak,* in Geneva, periodicals that were clandestinely or sometimes openly brought into Russian, Ottoman, and Iranian territories, and of *Pro Armenia* (1900–14), an ARF paper edited by Pierre Quillard and published in Paris for the purpose of garnering European support for the Armenian cause.[163] *Pro Armenia*'s editors also included key European statesman Georges

Clemenceau, literary figure and socialist Anatole France, and socialists Jean Jaurès and Francis de Pressensé.[164] Based on the correspondence of ARF cofounders Rostom, Mikayelian, and Zavarian, as well as party newspapers published in Tiflis and Geneva, professional and personal relationships between key ARF leaders and European socialists and public figures were rather frequent as they encountered each other in socialist circles and congresses and also met one-on-one.[165] Similar encounters took place between key SDHP figures and European socialists, as attested by Sapah-Giwlian. As we saw earlier in the chapter, meetings also included those between ARF, SDHP, and Ottoman and Russian oppositional elements in major European cities like Paris.[166] In addition to or as part of the working relationship focused around *Pro Armenia* and European propaganda on behalf of Armenians, writer, revolutionary, and later politician Avetis Aharonian met with Quillard, de Pressensé, France, and Victor Berard and received their support for the Armenian appeal to the Hague peace conference in 1907 to resolve the Armenian issue peacefully. They were apprehensive at first about approaching de Pressensé and France—who, as socialists, might reject backing a national appeal—but were relieved when both agreed and de Pressensé exclaimed, "C'est une stupidité de combattre l'idée de la nation" (It is stupidity to fight the idea of the nation).[167] The Armenian attempt to obtain the support of European nations to resolve the Armenian issue through the "splendid comedy" of the Hague peace conference failed.[168]

The year 1907 seemed to be one of encounters and cooperation between Armenians and Europeans and between Armenians and Ottomans (the 1907 Ottoman congress) and between Armenians and Iranians (the collaboration agreement between the ARF and Iranian constitutionalists). According to Rostom, Austrian Social Democrat Victor Adler, the founder of the Social Democratic Workers' Party, met with Rostom and helped to secure a hall for the ARF's Fourth General Congress, scheduled to take place in Vienna starting in late February—this despite a disagreement over the national question they had had at one of their meetings.[169] Later in 1907 and then again in 1910, the ARF sent its delegates to the Socialist International Congresses in Stuttgart and Copenhagen. The Armenian revolutionary press of the ARF filled many of its pages with reports of the congresses, including the debates, resolutions, and speeches by European representatives and socialist leaders like the favored Jaurès (France), Bebel (Germany), Plekhanov (Germany), Vandervelde (Belgium), Adler (Austria), Ferri (Italy), and Ignacy Daszyński (Poland), among others.[170] The press spoke glowingly of internationalism and harmony as imagined by "humanity's better children," named above, and of being "accepted [despite its opponents] into the lap of the International . . . as a legitimate member of the universal socialist family."[171] Having been able to convince the International Socialist Bureau's plenary meeting in Brussels in 1908, ARF representative Mikayel Varandian took an active role in the Copenhagen congress as part of a four-member ARF delegation—split equally between Ottoman and Russian Armenians—despite the continued efforts and protests of Russian and Armenian Social Democrats who viewed the ARF as tainted by nationalist "poison."[172] After his speech highlighting the party's participation in all three revolutionary movements in the South Caucasus, Iran, and the Ottoman Empire and its efforts to organize workers, Varandian reported being invited to Prague by Czech representative Anton Nemetz because Varandian expressed interest in forming a small International in the Caucasus and Iran inspired by the Austrian one.[173]

Immediately following the Socialist International Congress in Copenhagen, Varandian and his comrades joined the meeting of Russian socialist parties in the same city and took part in discussions with the likes of then seventy-five-year-old Polish socialist Bolesław Limanowski (who lived to be ninety-nine); Aleksandr Vronski (pseudonym of Witold Tomasz Jodko-Narkiewicz), from the Polish Socialist Party; Russian Socialist Revolutionaries Mark Natanson (a former member of Narodnaya Volya and one of the founders of the Socialist Revolutionary Party), Victor Chernov (cofounder of the Russian Socialist Revolutionary Party and proponent of land socialization), Nikolai Avksentiev, I. A. Rubanovich, and I. Bunakov (pen name of Isidorovich Fondaminskii); and other Socialist Revolutionaries and representatives from the Polish Socialist Party, the Latvian Social Democrats, and the Jewish SERP (Jewish Socialist Workers Party). The purpose of the meeting, according to Varandian, was to keep each other abreast of their parties' activities and discuss organizational issues and the situation on the ground. The meeting between Russian Empire socialists and Caucasian Armenians was one of many, official and unofficial, that took place throughout the Russian revolutionary period with the goal of strengthening bonds of solidarity and coordination, with participants fully aware that "The Russian liberation question . . . is simultaneously a Turkish and Iranian question."[174] Similar meetings had been held much earlier. For example, a multiparty conference in November 1904 in Paris attracted Russian, Polish, Finnish, and Georgian non–orthodox Marxist socialist parties and the ARF. Social

Democrats were conspicuously absent, having declined an invitation. The participants emphasized collaboration against tsarist autocracy and reaffirmed their support of democracy, national self-determination, and the elimination of oppressive measures on individual nationalities.[175] Another meeting several months later, in 1905, brought together various socialists including the Party of Socialist Revolutionaries, Polish Socialist Party, and the ARF, as well as Finnish, Georgian, Latvian, and Belarus/Byelorussian socialists. Their resolution demanded the restructuring of the Russian Empire on democratic foundations, calling on people to choose either "monarchy" or the "born-again" people going toward a "new life" and adding, "Whoever is not with us is against us." The resolution listed fourteen demands, which may be summarized by the following slogans: (1) "Work to the unemployed, bread to the hungry!"; (2) "Land and its products for all workers!"; (3) "Long live the revolution, long live socialism!"[176] As discussed earlier in the chapter, similar meetings took place between Armenian and Young Turk revolutionaries in Paris in preparation for revolution in the Ottoman Empire.[177] The picture that emerges is one of private and public encounters and exchanges that ultimately led to the 1907 congress in Paris, on which the ARF placed great hopes, concluding, "We are soldiers of internationalism and the unreserved partisan of solidarity."[178]

The illustration that introduced the previous chapter reflected the wider world of ideas—constitution and autonomy (i.e., federation)—that occupied most of our revolutionaries and connected them to counterparts in the region. The representation of the promise of constitution in the rainbow and its relationship to the various ethnicities and their vision of their present circumstances and of the future gives us a glimpse of the multiplicity and heterogeneity of global ideas our revolutionaries espoused. They experimented with and adapted, in varying degrees, different aspects of constitutionalism, socialism, nationalism, and anarchism (through federalism) to meet their own conditions and their related revolutionary aspirations. They learned and circulated these ideas by traversing intellectual and geographic frontiers through reading and translation as well as personal and professional encounters and exchanges. Solidarity and collaboration in revolutionary movements in the Russian, Ottoman, and Iranian Revolutions and their adoption and adaptation of global ideas remained an important part of their agenda, but they continued to maintain a distinct identity as a movement of Armenians for Armenians *and* a movement of imperial subjects for fellow imperial subjects. They did not believe that they could achieve their goals by complete and whole absorption into an internationalist movement or by giving up completely on the national question, although one wonders if either was even possible given their environment. However, at the same time that they dedicated themselves to advancing the interests of Armenians in three empires, they advanced the interests of their neighbors, not necessarily out of some self-sacrificing altruism but because they saw the concerns and gains linked by an unbreakable bond. Ultimately, whatever idea and ideal they pursued, whether at the forefront or background of their vision and their activism, the ideas of averting ethnic antagonism and realizing peaceful coexistence through political and economic justice and equality endured. Global ideas and ideologies, whether federalism or socialism, molded in accordance to their circumstances, circulated through revolutionaries' various physical and intellectual crossings during and in support of revolutionary movements and served in their vision as the consummate solution for all their ills.

CHAPTER 5

"The Egoism of the Cured Patient"

(In Lieu of a) Conclusion

"A kind of egoism has enveloped all. Now they want *to live,* they are tired of suffering, of sacrificing. That is the egoism of the cured patient . . . ," writes Rostom, most likely from Erzurum, as he complains about stalled operations to his ARF comrade Mikayel Varandian.[1] There seems to be a certain note of resignation in his tone, at least based on what one could uncover from a letter. Could one really find fault with him or his comrades if they paused to take a breath after numerous years of struggle? We had not considered how exhausting and draining constant struggle on multiple fronts could be. First, before the Russian, Ottoman, and Iranian revolutions, was the decade or so of a more limited Armenian revolutionary movement against Ottoman and Russian oppression. Then came the negotiations, collaboration, and operations in the service of a larger revolutionary wave overtaking the region. They required constant crisscrossing of imperial frontiers, transporting arms and print. Alongside these political and military struggles were the unrelenting internal—that is, intra-Armenian—and external ideological disputes and debates in print and in person during lectures and meetings that required constant vigilance as well as defense and propagation of one's ideas, vision, and objectives. In another letter to the Western Bureau, Istanbul section, Rostom again makes reference to an altered atmosphere, this time pointing to weakened organizational operations, adding that no one is occupied with them. Instead, he grumbles, they seem much more interested in mundane affairs of everyday existence—"the desertion of one's wife, another's having fun [pɫʃ/kʿēf, from Arabic; Turkish *keyf*], a third's wedding et cetera"—all of which, he exclaims, "devalue the organization!"[2] By the time Rostom was writing these words, the ARF and the SDHP, along with other political organizations, had been legalized in the Ottoman Empire. Even a close reading of the contemporary press after 1908 in comparison with the period of 1905–8 leaves the impression that radical tendencies were waning. With legalization of political activity in the Ottoman Empire and persecution and trials in the Russian Empire, which destroyed the ARF there as a forceful political opposition, the only active field of struggle that remained was Iran, at least for another year or two. Perhaps it should not be surprising then that following the reinstatement of constitution in the Ottoman Empire and renewed alliance with the Committee of Union and Progress after the Adana massacres of 1909, Rostom's comrades were fatigued and wanted to come up for air after difficult years of a multipronged campaign on three revolutionary fronts.

The "cured patient," however, was not allowed to rest for long. While in partial remission for a very brief period, the prerevolutionary diseases returned with full deadly force in the form of genocide in the Ottoman Empire and world war. All that revolution promised and the general optimism that had characterized the revolutionary years in all three empires disappeared, like the short-term effects of a placebo, and were replaced by unprecedented, catastrophic destruction, loss of human life, and disillusionment. Between 1915 and 1918, somewhere between 800,000 and 1,500,000 Armenians (in addition to hundreds of thousands of Assyrians, Greeks, and others) were killed through state-ordered deportations of populations from the Armenian vilayets in eastern Anatolia to the Syrian and Iraqi deserts, organized killings, and death by deprivation, as well as peremptory massacres in some cases. The perpetrators included government forces (including gendarmes and a special paramilitary force) and some local populations of Turks and Kurds. It is important to note that there were also many Turks and Kurds, as well as Arabs, who helped hide and protect Armenians, without whose intervention they would have met certain death. Besides the obvious impact of the genocide on the Ottoman Empire, its effects reverberated throughout the rest of the Middle East, including Iran, and the South Caucasus as Armenians crossed borders again, this time as refugees. Some of the figures who appeared prominently in the previous chapters as geographic or intellectual boundary crossers, like Garegin Khazhak, Rupen Zartarian, Khachatur Malumian, and Harutiwn Shahrigian, were among the hundreds of leading Armenian intellectuals murdered at the onset of genocide.

This book has explored these crossings and circulations in order to shed light on the connectedness of three bordering—in time and space—revolutions: the Russian, the Ottoman, and the Iranian. The focus has been on Armenian revolutionaries, activists, and intellectuals, particularly those affiliated with the ARF, who collaborated with constitutionalists, federalists, socialists, and liberals in the three empires and in Europe in favor of the immediate aim of constitutional government and a future socialist state or federation. The study has analyzed the turn of the twentieth-century circulation of Armenian revolutionaries, arms, and print on three levels: global, regional, and local. It has demonstrated that circulation was reliant upon and exploited faster modes of communication and transportation (e.g., telegraph, steamship, and railways) as well as advances in longer-standing forms of communication and transport (e.g., postal system, roads/highways). Circulation also took advantage of and was made possible by Armenian revolutionary and activist cells and party organizational structure, activities, and operations that spun a network throughout the South Caucasian, Ottoman, and Iranian territories and beyond. To provide a more intimate portrait, the book has also focused on the historical actors on the move across imperial frontiers. The South Caucasus has taken central stage because of its critical role as a nodal hub of revolutionary activity and thought. Arms, print, and ideologies also had transimperial lives and journeys. Ideas and ideologies—constitutionalism, federalism, and various configurations of socialism—spread through revolutionaries, intellectuals, workers, and print, including revolutionary pamphlets, circulars, newspapers, and revolutionary party organs. Although these ideas emanated from Western and Central Europe and Russia, they were transformed by local and regional thinkers and activists as they were appropriated according to local conditions and aspirations. Therefore, they were not frozen in time; rather, they developed and were recalibrated within a moving reality. As such, they reflected and were the consequence of various entanglements of (for example) ideals, world visions, circumstances, and even personalities. To a great degree, the specific shape global ideas took was very much informed by the activists' desire to find peaceful and satisfactory solutions to the national question and problems of inequality and ethnic conflict plaguing the region. Armenian intellectuals' and revolutionaries' debates and discussions over topics such as socialism and the national question, federation and decentralization, resembled those occurring concurrently among Western and Central European and Russian leftists yet took on different form because of local circumstances. Constitutionalism, federalism, and socialism were intertwined with each other and with the national question and autonomy. They were also closely linked to the revolutionary movements; they informed those movements and were informed by them. As in the rainbow illustration that began chapter 3, banners of constitution, unity, equality, and autonomy coexisted and struggled together and sometimes against each other on the same platform. Absent from the illustration but clearly present in the revolutionary circle was the banner of socialism, which stole contemporary activists' hearts and minds. The mobility and circulation of these universally appealing ideas and their advocates connected these struggles.

Armenians' participation in three revolutions, their journeys across and within imperial frontiers, and their experimentation with global ideologies make them ideal subjects for scholarly inquiry and for grasping the connections between these early twentieth-century revolutions. I am not implying that no one else, or no other group, circulated or connected these revolutions through their circulation or that such connections do not have their historical equal. They indeed do, and that is why a connected histories approach, when applied and when sustainable through availability of documentation, is viable, meaningful, and welcome. The examples of circulating individuals, participating in multiple struggles, are numerous. In our own region of focus, Jamal al-din al-Afghani is one example of a prominent thinker and activist who traveled throughout the Middle East and Europe in the late nineteenth century, largely because of expulsions due to his anticolonial agitation. On the other side of the globe and a century earlier, we find Thomas Paine, author of *Common Sense* and *Rights of Man,* and the Marquis de Lafayette, coauthor with Thomas Jefferson of *Declaration of the Rights of Man and of the Citizen.* All three were involved in both the American and the French Revolutions. Closer to our time, Ernesto "Che" Guevara, an Argentine of Cuban Revolution fame, also attempted to foment revolution in Congo and Bolivia. Perhaps the best examples, however, come from the studies of Anderson and Khuri-Makdisi, who demonstrate the connections and coordination of late nineteenth-century networks of Cuban, Filipino, Puerto Rican, and Dominican radicals (in Anderson's case) and eastern Mediterranean radicals (in Khuri-Makdisi's study). As was common in the period, activists and intellectuals "did not merely read about each other but had crucial personal connections and, up to a point, coordinated their actions—the first time in world history that such transglobal coordination became possible."[3]

Thus, Armenians were only one of many groups that, through their mobility, acted as connectors in history; for that reason, they should be viewed as one part of a larger whole within the wider regional and global context. However, they are also a unique group for investigation because, unlike other groups, they prepared for all the movements and participated in varying degrees in all three revolutions; they constituted large minority populations in at least two regions, Anatolia and the South Caucasus; and their engagement went beyond individuals to involve primarily organizations with preexisting party cells, networks of activists, and channels for arms and print transfer. Hence, by the time the revolutions began in 1905, Armenian revolutionaries already had the experience and expertise necessary for revolutionary struggle on three fronts. Their operations were already in place because of the foundation laid down by a national struggle and the development of a culture of resistance, both of which contributed to circulation, involvement, and connection, all made feasible by the Armenians' geographic presence in three empires and ease of transportation and communication due to turn-of-the-century transformations.

This book has employed roving Armenian revolutionaries and circulating arms, print, and ideologies as a vehicle to tell a bigger story of revolutionary connections through a connected histories approach, at the same time that it has engaged with the larger global context to make sense of their mobility. A connected histories approach that is focused on accelerated circulation during revolutionary turning points at the turn of the twentieth century allows us to grasp not just the similarities and parallel developments of the three revolutions but also the ways in which they were linked to each other and to the wider world. Sometimes scholars studying in hindsight do not see eye to eye with contemporary observers or historical actors. In this case, though, the connectedness of revolutions is attributable not merely to the imaginative or interpretative powers of the scholar but to the actors themselves, who repeatedly—through words and deeds—linked revolutionary aims, processes, and outcomes and viewed them beyond their local and regional significance. They were not completely oblivious to the complications, problems, and obstacles in the way of enduring success and achievement of their goals and vision, but they fought on despite them, sometimes even against their own and others' cynicism and serious doubt, because they believed that circumstances required them to do so and because they believed that too much was at stake if they did not take the reins over intertwined futures: their own and that of their neighbors in the "East." Some may have taken a rest, as would a "cured patient," but many continued their committed struggle in different forms and wherever they could in the triangulated empires, until the world war and genocide shattered—for a time, anyway—hope and resistance.

Viewing our subjects within a global context has the benefit of expanding our local and regional lens to appreciate more fully the global transformations affecting revolutionary fervor, dissemination of print and ideologies, and the journeys of our revolutionaries while simultaneously bringing our historical actors from the margins into the center. In other words, the book inserts Armenians into global history and global historical studies. It also invites global historical studies to rethink the place of less well-represented and little-studied peoples like the Armenians. In a sense, therefore, a retelling of revolutionary history through the lens of roving Armenian revolutionaries brings Armenians out of the marginality they have at times inscribed for themselves—and others have inscribed for them—to tell a more compelling and intriguing story that spans three empires and provides a way to foreground histories often hidden by national as well as nationalist approaches. In his assessment of Ottoman Armenian history, Gerard Libaridian writes, "The problem, simply phrased, is that historians and others who have tried to tell the story of Turkish-Armenian relations toward the end of the nineteenth and early twentieth centuries have been unable to imagine a common [or shared] history, one that accounts for the complexities each found in its situation and the areas where common thought and action evolved."[4] The same applies to Russian-Armenian and Iranian-Armenian relations at the turn of the twentieth century. The postgenocidal national and nationalist narrative by Armenian and other scholars has edged out almost all other perceptions and treatments of the Armenian role in its own revolutionary movement and in regional struggles with global dimensions. This book is an invitation and a challenge to imagine complex and connected local and global transformative and revolutionary contexts, to perceive both universality and distinctiveness in the experience of imperial subjects in opposition to manifold injustices and inequalities, and to concede a transimperial existence—all of which question assumptions about the insularity of our active and mobile revolutionaries and about the inevitability of the catastrophe that followed at least one revolution.

Historical actors like the Armenian revolutionaries, whose legacies this book has brought back to life, are to some extent—despite their agency—always enveloped in fog, to borrow Milan Kundera's characterization. In his description of Leo Tolstoy's conception of history, which minimizes the role of individual will, Kundera writes:

> Knowing neither the meaning nor the future course of history, knowing not even the objective meaning of their own actions (by which they "involuntarily" participate in events whose meaning is "concealed from them"), they proceed through their lives as one proceeds *in the fog*. I say fog, not darkness. In the darkness, we see nothing, we are blind, we are defenseless, we are not free. In the fog, we are free, but it is the freedom of a person in fog: he sees fifty yards ahead of him, he can clearly make out the features of his interlocutor, can take pleasure in the beauty of the trees that line the path, and can even observe what is happening close by and react.
>
> Man proceeds in the fog. But when he looks back to judge people of the past, he sees no fog on their path. From his present, which was their faraway future, their path looks perfectly clear to him, good visibility all the way. Looking back, he sees the path, he sees the people proceeding, he sees their mistakes, but not the fog.[5]

And so our revolutionaries could see only a few steps ahead, but we look back and see a clear path into the past. We might then wonder why they did not see the Genocide around the corner or any of the other relatively smaller disappointments and barriers on that foggy yet promising revolutionary path. Was it also perhaps "the egoism of the cured patient" that accompanied the procession in the fog? With the advantage of hindsight, with far more sources at our disposal, and with a global lens that sees more deeply and more widely, we look back in time onto opaque and misty pathways in an attempt not to offer a sharp and tidy past but to shine light on a past full of nuances and complications, promise and disillusion. We do so without forgetting the fog that enveloped our roving revolutionaries as they struggled and envisioned a brighter future near and far.

Notes

1. Hugh Trevor-Roper, "The General Crisis of the Seventeenth Century," *Past & Present* 26 (1959): 32.

2. C. A. Bayly, *The Birth of the Modern World, 1780–1914* (Malden, MA: Blackwell, 2004), 323.

3. The "Armenian question" refers to a diplomatic problem that emerged after the Congress of Berlin in 1878, as European powers involved themselves, for their own interests and with varying degrees of commitment, in the protection of Armenian subjects of the Ottoman Empire and the enactment of reforms. The Armenian question was part of the larger "Eastern question" of how to apportion the Ottoman Empire among European powers without triggering a massive and intense war among them. For a discussion of Ottoman and Patriarchate censuses before and after 1895 and the Armenian demographic issue, see Raymond Kévorkian, *The Armenian Genocide: A Complete History* (2006; London: I. B. Tauris, 2011), part 4, chap. 1. For the Armenian Patriarchate census, see the table in Kévorkian, *Armenian Genocide*, 272–78.

4. Armenians made up 20 percent (1.2 million) of the South Caucasian population of 6 million. See RUSSIA: Military Report. Trans-Caucasia. (W.O.) (1907), 98–104, National Archives, Kew, United Kingdom. The city of Elisavetpol has had several appellations: Elisabethpol, Kirovabad, and Ganja.

5. The Armenian population in Iran, which was much higher before the nineteenth century, decreased because of territorial losses to Russia with the Treaty of Torkamanchay/Turkmenchai, which ended the Russo-Persian War in 1828, and because of Armenian migration to the Russian Empire. Houri Berberian, *Armenians and the Iranian Constitutional Revolution of 1905–1911: "The Love for Freedom Has No Fatherland"* (Boulder: Westview Press, 2001), 122–27.

6. For a summary of the awakening, see Razmik Panossian, *The Armenians: From Kings and Priests to Merchants and Commissars* (New York: Columbia University Press, 2006), 128–87.

7. Houri Berberian, "Armenian Women in Turn-of-the-Century Iran: Education and Activism," in *Iran and Beyond: Essays in Honor of Nikki R. Keddie,* ed. Rudi Matthee and Beth Baron (Costa Mesa, CA: Mazda, 2000), 78–79, 82–85.

8. Berberian, "Armenian Women," 91; M. L. Adanalyan, "Azganuer Hayhuyats' Ěnkerut'iwně" [Patriotic Armenian women's society], *Patma-banasirakan handes* [Historical-Philological Review] 4, no. 87 (1979): 255–59.

9. See Victoria Rowe, *A History of Armenian Women's Writing 1880–1922* (Amersham, UK: Cambridge Scholars Press, 2003), chaps. 2–4. Although Zabel Yesayan has often been portrayed as a feminist, recently scholars have pointed to her own disavowal of feminism. See Marc Nichanian, "Zabel Yesayan, Woman and Witness, or the Truth of the Mask," *New Perspectives on Turkey* 42 (2010): 31–53.

10. Houri Berberian, "Armenian Women and Women in Armenian Religion," in *Encyclopedia of Women and Islamic Cultures,* vol. 2, ed. Suad Joseph and Afsaneh Najmabadi (Leiden: Brill Academic Publishers, 2005): 13.

11. The Armenian Constitution was later revised and accepted by Sultan Abdülmecid I in March 1863. For a discussion of the constitution, see Aylin Koçunyan, "Long Live Sultan Abdulaziz, Long Live the Nation, Long Live the Constitution!," in *Constitutionalism, Legitimacy and Power: Nineteenth-Century Experiences,* ed. Kelly Grotke and Markus Prutsch (Oxford: Oxford University Press, 2014), 189–210; Vartan Artinian, *The Armenian Constitutional System in the Ottoman Empire, 1839–1863: A Study of Its Historical Development* (Istanbul, 1988). For a classic study on the *amira* class, see Hagop Barsoumian, *Armenian Amira Class of Istanbul* (1980; repr., Yerevan: American University of Armenia Press, 2007). See also Pascal Carmont, *The Amiras: Lords of Ottoman Armenia* (London: Gomidas Institute, 2012).

12. For a definitive study of the Tanzimat and the Ottoman Constitution, see Roderic Davison, *Reform in the Ottoman Empire, 1856–1876* (Princeton, NJ: Princeton University Press, 1963). For a more recent study on Armenian attitudes about the Tanzimat, see Masayuki Ueno, "'For the Fatherland and the State': Armenians Negotiate the Tanzimat Reforms," *International Journal of Middle East Studies* 45 (2013): 93–109.

13. See contributions in the issue devoted to the massacres in *Armenian Review* 47, nos. 1–2 (Spring/Summer 2001).

14. See Richard G. Hovhannisian, "The Historical Dimension of the Armenian Question, 1878–1923," in Richard G. Hovhannisian, ed., *The Armenian Genocide in Perspective* (New Brunswick, NJ: Transaction, 1987), 18–41.

15. For a thought-provoking take on the conflict, see Leslie Sargent, "The 'Armeno-Tatar War' in the South Caucasus, 1905–1906: Multiple Causes, Interpreted Meanings," *Ab Imperio* 4 (2010): 143–69.

16. For the 1903 confiscation, see Stephen B. Riegg, "Beyond the Caucasus: The Russian Empire and Armenians, 1801–1914" (unpublished manuscript, 2017), chap. 6; Onur Önol, *The Tsar's Armenians: A Minority in Late Imperial*

Russia (London: I. B. Tauris, 2017); Vartan Gregorian, "Impact of Russia on the Armenians and Armenia," in *Russia and Asia: Essays on the Influence of Russia on the Asian Peoples,* ed. Wayne S. Vucinich (Stanford: Hoover Institution Press, 1972), 167–218; Ronald Grigor Suny, *Looking toward Ararat: Armenia in Modern History* (Bloomington: Indiana University Press, 1993), chap. 1. For a focus on nineteenth-century Russian-Armenian intellectuals through an analysis of four leading Armenian-language journals, see Lisa Khachaturian, *Cultivating Nationhood in Imperial Russia: The Periodical Press and the Formation of a Modern Identity* (New Brunswick, NJ: Transaction Publishers, 2009).

17. Berberian, *Armenians and the Iranian Constitutional Revolution,* 20.

18. Bedross Der Matossian, "Ottoman Armenian Kesaria/Kayseri in the Nineteenth Century," in *Armenian Kesaria/Kayseri and Cappadocia,* ed. Richard G. Hovannisian (Costa Mesa, CA: Mazda, 2013), 203.

19. The Armenian revolutionary movement's classic sources are the following: Louise Nalbandian, *The Armenian Revolutionary Movement: The Development of Armenian Political Parties through the Nineteenth Century* (Berkeley: University of California Press, 1963); Anahide Ter Minassian, *Nationalism and Socialism in the Armenian Revolutionary Movement (1887–1912)* (Cambridge, MA: Zoryan Institute, 1984); Ronald Grigor Suny, "Marxism, Nationalism, and the Armenian Labor Movement in Transcaucasia, 1890–1903" and "Labor and Socialism among Armenians in Transcaucasia," chaps. 4 and 5 in *Looking toward Ararat.* For an important discussion on Ottoman Armenian history and political parties, see Gerard J. Libaridian, "What Was Revolutionary about Armenian Political Parties in the Ottoman Empire?," in *A Question of Genocide: Armenians and Turks at the End of the Ottoman Empire,* ed. Ronald Grigor Suny, Fatma Müge Göçek, and Norman M. Naimark (Oxford: Oxford University Press, 2011), 82–112.

20. Nalbandian, *Armenian Revolutionary Movement,* 211n73. See also Arsen Kitur, *Patmut'iwn S. D. Kusakts'ut'ean* [History of the S. D. Hnch'akean Party] (Beirut: Shirak Press, 1962), 1:290.

21. "Sots'ialistakan Mijazgayin Biwroyi namakě" [The letter of the Socialist International Bureau], *Drōshak* [Banner] (Geneva) 6 (12 May 1905); "Mer pataskhaně" [Our response], to Socialist International Bureau from *Drōshak* editorship, 17 May 1905, in *Niwt'er H. H. Dashnakts'ut'ean patmut'ean hamar* [Materials for the history of the A. R. Federation], ed. Yervant Pambukian (Beirut: Hamazgayin Vahē Sēt'ean Tparan, 2010), 7:208; "Nakhagits kovkasean gortsunēut'ean" [Protocol for Caucasian activity], June 1905, in *Niwt'er H. H. Dashnakts'ut'ean patmut'ean hamar* [Materials for the history of the A. R. Federation], ed. Hrach Dasnabedian (Beirut: Hamazgayin Vahē Sēt'ean Tparan, 1973 and 1985), 2:232; see also the council's resolution on the Caucasian issue, April 1905, in *Niwt'er,* 2:229–30.

22. The delegates were Mikayel Varandian, Martiros Harutiwnian, Armenak Barseghian, and Nikol Duman. "Voroshumner H.H. Dashnakts'ut'ean Ch'orrord Ěndhanur Zhoghovi, 1907" [Decisions of the Fourth General Congress of A.R. Federation, 1907] (Geneva: Dashnakts'ut'ean Tparan, 1907), in *Niwt'er H. H. Dashnakts'ut'ean patmut'ean hamar* [Materials for the history of

the A. R. Federation], ed. Hrach Dasnabedian (Beirut: Hamazgayin Vahē Sēt'ean Tparan, 1976 and 2007), 3:309; "H. H. D.-I pashtonakan dimumĕ" [ARF's official application], Brussels, 23 July 1907, Geneva (doc. 50–87), in *Niwt'er,* 7:210. For sections of the ARF report in Stuttgart, see *Drōshak* 9 (1907), also in *Niwt'er,* 7:211–14. Regarding the Ottoman section, see Socialist International Bureau letter to ARF, 17 August 1907, Brussels (doc. 1675–1), in *Niwt'er,* 7:215. Regarding acceptance to the Socialist International, see Mikayel [Varandian] to Hamo Ohanjanian, 29 August 1907, Stuttgart, in *Niwt'er,* 7:220. Regarding acceptance of the Ottoman branch, see Socialist International Bureau to ARF, 22 December 1908, doc 1676–79, in *Niwt'er,* 7:224; Rapport présenté au Congrès Socialiste International de Copenhague par le Parti Arménien "Daschnaktzoutioun" Turquie-Caucase-Perse [Report presented to Socialist International Congress of Copenhagen by the Armenian "Dashnakts'ut'iwn" Party—Turkey-Caucasus-Persia], Geneva 1910, in *Niwt'er,* 7:227–245.

23. *Drōshak* editorship to Socialist International Bureau, 14 September 1908, in *Niwt'er* 7:222. No Turkish socialist parties existed until the founding of *Osmanlı Sosyalist Fırkası* (Ottoman Socialist Party) in 1910. Those that existed were outside Anatolia—for example, the Jewish Socialist Workers' Federation (1909), as well as the Bulgarian and Macedonian socialist parties starting in the late nineteenth century. For a study on Ottoman socialism, see Meltem Toksöz, "'Are They Not Our Workers?': Socialist Hilmi and His Publication *İştirak:* An Appraisal of Ottoman Socialism," in *The Young Turk Revolution and the Ottoman Empire: The Aftermath of 1908,* ed. Noémi Lévy and François Georgeon (London: I. B. Tauris, 2017), 286–317. Toksöz's analysis of *İştirak*'s articles on socialism resemble in many ways some of the discussions in the Armenian newspapers on socialist issues, as discussed in chap. 4.

24. For a detailed discussion of this development, see Berberian, *Armenians and the Iranian Constitutional Revolution,* chap. 2.

25. Cited in "Leh sots'ialistnerĕ 'Dashnakts'ut'ean' masin" [The Polish socialists regarding the Federation], *Drōshak* 7–9 (July–September 1910): 94–95 (95).

26. Transnational history focuses on the flows of peoples, ideas, objects, and so forth across national or imperial borders. For a discussion on transnational history, see "*AHR* Conversation: On Transnational History," with C. A. Bayly et al., *American Historical Review* 111, no. 5 (December 2006): 1441–64. Jürgen Kocka defines an entangled history as one that is interested "in the processes of mutual influencing, in reciprocal or asymmetric perceptions, in entangled processes of constituting one another. In a way, the history of both sides is taken as one instead of being considered as two units for comparison." Kocka, "Comparison and Beyond," *History and Theory* 42 (February 2003): 42. Michael Werner and Bénédicte Zimmermann explain the intricacies of *histoire croisée:* briefly, "*Histoire croisée* focuses on empirical intercrossings consubstantial with the object of study, as well as on the operations by which researchers themselves cross scales, categories, and viewpoints." See Michael Werner and Bénédicte Zimmermann, "Beyond Comparison: *Histoire Croisée* and the Challenge of Reflexivity," *History and Theory* 45 (February 2006): 30. I will delve more deeply into connected histories later in the chapter.

27. Raymond Grew, "The Case for Comparing Histories," *American Historical Review* 85, no. 4 (October 1980): 777.

28. Grew, "Case for Comparing Histories," 763, 764.

29. Micol Seigel, "Beyond Compare: Comparative Method after the Transnational Turn," *Radical History Review* 91 (Winter 2005): 78.

30. See, for example, Heinz-Gerhard Haupt, "Comparative History—A Contested Method," *Historisk Tidskrift* 127, no. 4 (2007): 697–714.

31. Philippa Levine, "Is Comparative History Possible?," *History and Theory* 53 (October 2014): 331, 333, 334; Haupt, "Comparative History—A Contested Method," 697; Seigel, "Beyond Compare," 65.

32. Eliga H. Gould, "Entangled Histories, Entangled Worlds: The English-Speaking Atlantic as a Spanish Periphery," *American Historical Review* 112, no. 3 (June 2007): 766. See Levine's discussion of Gould in Levine, "Is Comparative History Possible?," 336.

33. Gould, "Entangled Histories, Entangled Worlds," 785, 786. See also Kocka, "Comparison and Beyond," 43.

34. Levine, "Is Comparative History Possible?" 336, 337, 343. See Sanjay Subrahmanyam, "Connected Histories: Notes towards a Reconfiguration of Early Modern Eurasia," *Modern Asian Studies* 31, no. 3 (July 1997): 735–62. See also Sanjay Subrahmanyam, "Holding the World in Balance: The Connected Histories of the Iberian Overseas Empires, 1500–1640," *American Historical Review* 112, no. 5 (December 2007): 1359–85.

35. Haupt, "Comparative History—A Contested Method," 714.

36. Kocka, "Comparison and Beyond," 43–44.

37. Levine, "Is Comparative History Possible?," 347.

38. Levine, 343.

39. Jerry H. Bentley, "Why Study World History," *World History Connected* 5, no. 1 (2013): 4. See also Jerry H. Bentley, "The New World History," in *A Companion to Western Historical Thought,* ed. Lloyd Kramer and Sarah Maza (Malden, MA: Blackwell, 2002), 393.

40. Bentley, "New World History," 394–96, 403, 409–10; Jerry H. Bentley, "The Task of World History," in *The Oxford Handbook of World History,* ed. Jerry H. Bentley (Oxford: Oxford University Press, 2011), 2–10.

41. Bentley, "New World History," 396, 405; Bentley, "Task of World History," 12.

42. Bentley, "Task of World History," 1.

43. Heinz-Gerhard Haupt and Jürgen Kocka, "Comparative History: Methods, Aims, Problems," in *Comparison and History: Europe in Cross-National Perspective,* ed. Deborah Cohen and Maura O'Connor (London: Routledge, 2004), 25.

44. Haupt and Kocka, "Comparative History," 25; Haupt, "Comparative History—A Contested Method," 698, 699.

45. Haupt, "Comparative History—A Contested Method," 714; Levine, "Is Comparative History Possible?," 337; Kocka, "Comparison and Beyond," 39; Haupt and Kocka, "Comparative History," 33; Bentley, "Task of World History," 1.

46. For an important and early collection on some of these debates, see Nikki R. Keddie, ed., *Debating Revolutions* (New York: New York University Press, 1995).

47. Influential definitions of revolutions include those of Charles Tilly, Jack Goldstone, Theda Skocpol, and others.

48. See, for example, Michael S. Kimmel, *Revolution: A Sociological Interpretation* (Philadelphia: Temple University Press, 1990), 6; Perez Zagorin, *Rebels and Rulers* (Cambridge: Cambridge University Press, 1982), 1:17.

49. Eric Selbin, *Revolution, Rebellion, Resistance: The Power of Story* (London: Zed Books, 2010), 3.

50. Jack A. Goldstone, "Comparative Historical Analysis and Knowledge Accumulation in the Study of Revolutions," in *Comparative Historical Analysis in the Social Sciences,* ed. James Mahoney and Dietrich Rueschemeyer (Cambridge: Cambridge University Press, 2003), 41–90. See also Theda Skocpol, *States and Social Revolutions: A Comparative Analysis of France, Russia, and China* (Cambridge: Cambridge University Press, 1979).

51. Goldstone, "Comparative Historical Analysis," 55–56. See Crane Brinton, *The Anatomy of Revolution* (New York: Norton, 1938); Lyford P. Edwards, *The Natural History of Revolutions* (Chicago: Chicago University Press, 1927); George S. Pettee, *The Process of Revolution* (New York: Harper & Row, 1938).

52. Goldstone, "Comparative Historical Analysis," 57–62. See Charles Tilly, "Does Modernization Breed Revolution?," *Comparative Politics* 5 (1973): 425–47; Tilly, *From Mobilization to Revolution* (Reading, MA: Addison-Wesley, 1978); Barrington Moore Jr., *Social Origins of Dictatorship and Democracy* (Boston: Beacon Press, 1966).

53. Goldstone, "Comparative Historical Analysis," 63.

54. See, for example, William Sewell Jr., "Ideologies and Social Revolutions: Reflections on the French Case," *Journal of Modern History* 57 (1985): 57–85, who begins his essay with "This article was inspired—perhaps I should say provoked—by Theda Skocpol's *States and Social Revolutions.*"

55. Goldstone, "Comparative Historical Analysis," 64. For a summary of these conditions, see the introduction to Skocpol, *States and Revolutions,* 3–43.

56. For an "anti-explanation" of the Iranian Revolution of 1978/1989, see Charles Kurzman, *The Unthinkable Revolution in Iran* (Cambridge: Harvard University Press, 2004).

57. John Foran, *Taking Power: On the Origins of Third World Revolutions* (Cambridge: Cambridge University Press, 2005), 6; Skocpol, *States and Revolutions,* 4.

58. Foran, *Taking Power,* 18.

59. Other examples include William Sewell Jr., "Ideologies and Social Revolutions: Reflections on the French Case," *Journal of Modern History* 57 (1985): 57–85; Timothy Wickham-Crowley, *Guerrillas and Revolution in Latin America: A Comparative Study of Insurgents and Regimes since 1956.* (Princeton, NJ: Princeton University Press, 1992); Jack Goldstone, "Is Revolution Individually Rational? Groups and Individuals in Revolutionary Collective Action," *Rationality and Society* 6, no. 1 (January 1994): 139–66.

60. Misagh Parsa, *States, Ideologies, and Social Revolutions: A Comparative Analysis of Iran, Nicaragua, and the Philippines* (Cambridge: Cambridge University Press, 2000), 5.

61. Selbin, *Revolution, Rebellion, Resistance,* 3, 4, 7, 9.

62. Eric Selbin, "Stories of Revolution in the Periphery," in *Revolution in the Making of the Modern World: Social Identities, Globalization, and Modernity*, ed. John Foran, David Lane, and Andreja Zivkovic (London: Routledge, 2008), 130.

63. For studies centered on why people participate in revolutions, see, for example, Ted Gurr, *Why Men Rebel* (Princeton: Princeton University Press, 1970); Will Moore, "Rational Rebels: Overcoming the Free-Rider Problem," *Political Research Quarterly* 48 (June 1995): 417–54; Edward N. Muller and Karl-Dieter Opp, "Rational Choice and Rebellious Collective Action," *American Political Science Review* 80, no. 2 (June 1986): 471–88; Timur Kuran, "Now out of Never: The Element of Surprise in the East European Revolution of 1989," *World Politics* 44, no. 1 (1991): 7–48.

64. Joseph Fletcher, "Integrative History: Parallels and Interconnections in the Early Modern Period, 1500–1800," in *Studies on Chinese and Islamic Inner Asia* (London: Variorum, 1995), 2.

65. Fletcher, 2.

66. Fletcher, 3.

67. Fletcher, 3–6.

68. Bayly, *Birth of the Modern World*, 1.

69. Fletcher, "Integrative History," 3–4.

70. Jack Goldstone, "East and West in the Seventeenth Century: Political Crises in Stuart England, Ottoman Turkey, and Ming China," *Comparative Studies in Society and History* 30, no. 1 (January 1988): 104; Goldstone, *Revolution and Rebellion in the Early Modern World* (Berkeley: University of California Press, 1993), 459.

71. Werner and Zimmermann, "Beyond Comparison," 37, 38.

72. Benedict Anderson, *Under Three Flags: Anarchism and the Anti-Colonial Imagination* (London: Verso, 2005).

73. Charles Kurzman, *Democracy Denied, 1905–1915: Intellectuals and the Fate of Democracy* (Cambridge: Harvard University Press, 2008).

74. Ilham Khuri-Makdisi, *The Eastern Mediterranean and the Making of Global Radicalism, 1860–1914* (Berkeley: University of California Press, 2010).

75. Janet Polasky, *Revolutions without Borders: The Call to Liberty in the Atlantic World* (New Haven: Yale University Press, 2015).

76. Subrahmanyam, "Connected Histories," 735–62. See also Subrahmanyam, "Holding the World in Balance," 1359–85; Serge Gruzinski, "Les mondes mêlés de la monarchie catholique et autre 'connected histories'" [The entangled worlds of the Catholic monarchy and other "connected histories"], *Annales* 56, no. 1 (January–February 2001): 85–117. For a historiographic treatment of connected histories, see Caroline Douki and Philippe Minard, "Histoire globale, histoires connectées: un changement d'échelle historiographique" [Global history, connected histories: A historiographic change of scale], *Revue d'histoire moderne and contemporaine* 54, no. 4 (2007): 7–21.

77. Subrahmanyam, "Connected Histories," 745.

78. Malcolm Gladwell, *The Tipping Point: How Little Things Can Make a Big Difference* (New York: Back Bay Books/Little, Brown, 2000), 30–32;

Geoffrey Parker, *Global Crisis: War, Climate Change and Catastrophe in the Seventeenth Century* (New Haven: Yale University Press, 2013), xxxi, 561.

79. For an important study on comparative historical analyses of revolutions, including the advantages of comparative analyses and a history of the literature on comparative revolutions, see Goldstone, "Comparative Historical Analysis."

80. Nader Sohrabi, "Historicizing Revolutions: Constitutional Revolutions in the Ottoman Empire, Iran, and Russia, 1905–1908," *American Journal of Sociology* 100, no. 6 (May 1995): 1383–1447. Mangol Bayat's study on the role of Caucasians in the Iranian Constitutional Revolution and Ivan Spector's on the impact of the Russian Revolution on Asia are important early contributions, although both treatments focus on a unidirectional flow of influence from the Caucasus and Russia rather than on a model of circulation that avoids the pitfalls of ascribing agency to one party and rendering the other passive. Mangol Bayat, *Iran's First Revolution: Shi'ism and the Constitutional Revolution of 1905–1909* (Oxford: Oxford University Press, 1991); Ivan Spector, *The First Russian Revolution: Its Impact on Asia* (Englewood Cliffs, NJ: Prentice Hall, 1962).

81. Sohrabi, "Historicizing Revolutions," 1441–42.

82. Sohrabi, 1389.

83. Sohrabi, 1441.

84. Nader Sohrabi, *Revolution and Constitutionalism in the Ottoman Empire and Iran* (Cambridge: Cambridge University Press, 2011), 1. Clifford Geertz refers to an "instructive comparison" of Morocco and Indonesia: "At once very alike and very different, they form a kind of commentary on one another's character." See Clifford Geertz, *Islam Observed: Religious Development in Morocco and Indonesia* (Chicago: University of Chicago Press, 1971), 4.

85. Levine, "Is Comparative History Possible?," 340, 341.

86. Sohrabi, *Revolution and Constitutionalism*, 1–2.

87. Sohrabi, 16.

88. Sohrabi, 21, 22–23.

89. Sohrabi, 28–29.

90. Bayly, *Birth of the Modern World*, 323.

91. For Japan as beacon of inspiration, see Rotem Kowner, ed., *The Impact of the Russo-Japanese War* (London: Routledge, 2007), in particular Kowner's introduction, "Between a Colonial Clash and World War Zero: The Impact of the Russo-Japanese War in a Global Perspective," 1–26.

92. Nikki R. Keddie, "Iranian Revolutions in Comparative Perspective," *American Historical Review* 88, no. 3 (June 1983): 586; Nikki R. Keddie, "Religion and Irreligion in Early Iranian Nationalism," in *Iran: Religion, Politics and Society*, ed. Nikki R. Keddie (London: Frank Cass, 1980), 13–14.

93. Jürgen Osterhammel, *The Transformation of the World: A Global History of the Nineteenth Century*, trans. Patrick Camiller (Princeton: Princeton University Press, 2014), 522, 561.

94. Osterhammel, 561–65. For a discussion of personalist rule—meaning the concentration of power and personalization of political interactions—see Milan W. Svolik, *The Politics of Authoritarian Rule* (Cambridge: Cambridge University Press), 30. Svolik draws from Barbara Geddes's classification of dictatorships.

Barbara Geddes, "Authoritarian Breakdown: Empirical Test of a Game Theoretic Argument" (paper presented at the Annual Meeting of the American Political Science Association, Atlanta, September 1999), http://eppam.weebly.com/uploads/5/5/6/2/5562069/authoritarianbreakdown_geddes.pdf.

95. Osterhammel also brings China into the discussion. Osterhammel, *Transformation of the World*, 568.

96. James Gelvin, *The Modern Middle East*, 4th ed. (Oxford: Oxford University Press, 2016), 161.

97. Kurzman, *Democracy Denied*, 4, 5. For a detailed discussion of the Young Turks and the global wave, see Sohrabi, chap. 2, *Revolution and Constitutionalism*.

98. Kurzman, *Democracy Denied*, 4.

99. Kurzman, 5.

100. Abraham Ascher, *The Revolution of 1905: A Short History* (Stanford, CA: Stanford University Press, 2004), 217. See also Ascher's more detailed and comprehensive two-volume work, *The Revolution of 1905*, vol. 1, *Russia in Disarray* (Stanford, CA: Stanford University Press, 1988) and *The Revolution of 1905*, vol. 2, *Authority Restored* (Stanford, CA: Stanford University Press, 1994). An earlier classic study of the revolution's causes, development, and consequences is Sidney Harcave, *The Russian Revolution of 1905*, originally published as *First Blood* (London: Collier, 1964).

101. Abraham Ascher, introduction to *The Russian Revolution of 1905: Centenary Perspectives*, ed. Jonathan D. Smele and Anthony Heywood (London: Routledge, 2005), 1. According to Ascher, the revolution began in the last quarter of 1904. See Ascher, *Revolution of 1905*, 1:58.

102. Ascher, introduction to *Russian Revolution of 1905*, 2.

103. Ascher, 3.

104. Ascher, *Revolution of 1905*, 2:375.

105. Beryl Williams, "1905: The View from the Provinces," in Smele and Heywood, *Russian Revolution*, 35.

106. Franziska Schedewie, "Peasant Protest and Peasant Violence in 1905: Voronezh Province, ostrogozhskii Uezd," in Smele and Heywood, *Russian Revolution*, 138, 139.

107. John Morison, "Russia's First Revolution," *History Today* 38 (December 2000), https://www.historytoday.com/john-morison/russias-first-revolution.

108. For a discussion of peasants, see Teodor Shanin, *Russia, 1905–07: Revolution as a Moment of Truth*, vol 2., *The Roots of Otherness: Russia's Turn of Century* (London: Macmillan, 1986), especially chaps. 3 and 4. For a regional focus on Kursk, see Burton Richard Miller, *Rural Unrest during the First Russian Revolution: Kursk Province, 1905–1906* (Budapest: Central European University Press, 2013).

109. As Beryl Williams explains, "In towns like Tbilisi or Baku or Odessa racial conflict added to class conflict, and could be antisemitic or anti-Armenian or just anti-foreign, and workers organized on national rather than on class lines. The Caucasus was particularly volatile, with the government losing control of major cities and parts of the countryside by the autumn." Beryl

Williams, "Russia 1905," *History Today* 55, no. 5 (May 2005), https://www
.historytoday.com/beryl-williams/russia-1905.

110. Williams, "Russia 1905." See also Beryl Williams, "1905: The View
from the Provinces," 50–51. For a detailed discussion on the planning of the
march by Gapon and his followers, see also Harcave, *Russian Revolution of
1905*, chap. 3.

111. Ascher, *Russian Revolution of 1905*, vol. 2, chaps. 2 and 3.

112. Ascher, chaps. 8 and 9.

113. Anthony Heywood, "Socialists, Liberals and the Union of Unions in
Kyiv during the 1905 Revolution: An Engineer's Perspective," in Smele and
Heywood, *Russian Revolution*, 177–95.

114. See, for example, Şükrü Hanioğlu, *Preparation for a Revolution: The
Young Turks, 1902–1908* (Oxford: Oxford University Press, 2001). For a different approach, see Aykut Kansu, *The Revolution of 1908 in Turkey* (Leiden:
Brill, 1997). See also Hasan Kayalı, *Arabs and Young Turks: Ottomanism, Arabism, and Islamism in the Second Constitutional Period of the Ottoman Empire,
1908–1918* (Berkeley: University of California Press, 1997). For strikes, see
Donald Quataert, "Ottoman Workers and the State, 1826–1914," in *Workers
and Working Classes in the Middle East: Struggles, Histories, Historiographies,*
ed. Zachary Lockman (Albany: SUNY Press, 1994), 21–40. For a revealing
study on the boycott movement in the late Ottoman period, see Y. Doğan
Çetinkaya, *The Young Turks and the Boycott Movement: Nationalism, Protest
and the Working Classes in the Formation of Modern Turkey* (London: I.B.
Tauris, 2013).

For a focus on minorities and interethnic relations, see Michelle Campos,
*Ottoman Brothers: Muslims, Christians, and Jews in Early Twentieth-Century
Palestine* (Stanford, CA: Stanford University Press, 2011); Bedross Der
Matossian, *Shattered Dreams of Revolution: From Liberty to Violence in the
Late Ottoman Empire* (Stanford, CA: Stanford University Press, 2014).

115. Michael A. Reynolds, *Shattering Empires: The Clash and Collapse of
the Ottoman and Russian Empires, 1908–1918* (Cambridge: Cambridge University Press, 2011), 14.

116. Erik J. Zürcher, *The Young Turk Legacy and Nation Building: From the
Ottoman Empire to Atatürk's Turkey* (London: I.B. Tauris, 2010), 34.

117. Osterhammel, *Transformation of the World*, 137.

118. Hanioğlu, *Preparation for a Revolution*, 205.

119. Hanioğlu, 296, 299.

120. For the best discussion to date on ethnic groups' relationship to the
1908 revolution, see Der Matossian, *Shattered Dreams of Revolution*.

121. Bedross Der Matossian, "From Bloodless Revolution to Bloody Counterrevolution: The Adana Massacres of 1909," *Genocide Studies and Prevention* 6, no. 2 (Summer 2011): 163.

122. Hanioğlu, *Preparation for a Revolution*, 95, 103, 123.

123. Kansu, *Revolution of 1908 in Turkey*, 33, 37. See also E. Attila Aytekin,
"Tax Revolts during the Tanzimat Period (1839–1876) and before the Young
Turk Revolution (1904–1908): Popular Protest and State Formation in the Late
Ottoman Empire," *Journal of Policy History* 25, no. 3 (2013): 308–33.

124. Kansu, *Revolution of 1908 in Turkey,* 47.

125. Hanioğlu, *Preparation for a Revolution,* 121, 123–24. See also Kansu, who argues that it was the CUP that transformed "widespread dissatisfaction" to "distinctly revolutionary activity." Kansu, chap. 2 in *Revolution of 1908 in Turkey,* 30.

126. Kansu, *Revolution of 1908 in Turkey,* 52.

127. Kansu, 29.

128. For an exploration of revolution and war in genocide, see Robert Melson, *Revolution and Genocide: On the Origins of the Armenian Genocide and the Holocaust* (Chicago: University of Chicago Press, 1996).

129. Kansu, *Revolution of 1908 in Turkey,* 3 (emphasis mine).

130. Hanioğlu, *Preparation for a Revolution,* 313, 315–17.

131. Hanioğlu, 312.

132. Janet Afary, *The Iranian Constitutional Revolution, 1906–1911: Grassroots Democracy, Social Democracy, and the Origins of Feminism* (New York: Columbia University Press, 1996); for a more recent collection that has as one of its foci the transnational aspects of the Iranian revolution, see H.E. Chehabi and Vanessa Martin, eds., *Iran's Constitutional Revolution: Popular Politics, Cultural Transformations and Transnational Connections* (London: I.B. Tauris, 2010), in particular Farzin Vejdani, "Crafting Constitutional Narratives: Iranian and Young Turk Solidarity, 1907–09," 319–40. See also Mansour Bonakdarian, "Iranian Nationalism and Global Solidarity Networks 1906–1918: Internationalism, Transnationalism, Globalization, and Nationalist Cosmopolitanism," in *Iran in the Middle East: Transnational Encounters and Social History,* ed. H.E. Chehabi, Peyman Jafari, and Maral Jefroudi (London: I.B. Tauris, 2015), 77–129. For a succinct discussion, see Ervand Abrahamian, *History of Modern Iran* (New York: Cambridge University Press, 2008), chap. 2.

133. Gelvin, *Modern Middle East,* 162.

134. Nikki R. Keddie, *Iran: Religion, Politics and Society: Collected Essays* (New York: Frank Cass, 1980), chap. 5; Hooshang Amirahmadi, *The Political Economy of Iran Under the Qajars: Society, Politics, and Foreign Relations, 1799–1921* (London: I.B. Tauris, 2012).

135. For a classic text on the tobacco protests, see Nikki Keddie, *Religion and Rebellion in Iran: The Tobacco Protest of 1891–92* (Frank Cass, 1966).

136. For a discussion of Japan in Iranian political discussion during the Constitutional Revolution, see Roxane Haag-Higuchi, "A Topos and Its Dissolution: Japan in Some 20th-Century Iranian Texts," *Iranian Studies* 29, nos. 1/2 (Winter–Spring 1996): 71–83.

137. For a detailed discussion of the development of *anjomans* and their role throughout the revolution, see Afary, *Iranian Constitutional Revolution,* chaps. 4, 6, 7.

138. Firuz Kazemzadeh, *Russia and Britain in Persia, 1864–1914: A Study in Imperialism* (New Haven: Yale University Press, 1968), chap. 7.

139. See, for example, Bayat, *Iran's First Revolution;* Iago Gocheleishvili, "Introducing Georgian Sources for the Historiography of the Iranian Constitutional Revolution (1905–1911)," in Chehabi and Martin, *Iran's Constitutional*

Revolution, 45–66; Moritz Deutschmann, "Cultures of Statehood, Cultures of Revolution: Caucasian Revolutionaries in the Iranian Constitutional Movement, 1906–1911," *Ab Imperio: Studies of New Imperial History and Nationalism in the Post-Soviet Space* 2 (2013): 165–90.

140. Keddie, *Iran: Religion, Politics and Society,* chaps. 1, 2.

141. For Shuster's own narrative, see W. Morgan Shuster, *The Strangling of Persia* (London: T. Fisher Unwin, 1913).

142. Sohrabi, *Revolution and Constitutionalism,* 3.

143. Bayly, *Birth of the Modern World,* 21.

144. Khuri-Makdisi, *Eastern Mediterranean,* 3–4. Here, Khuri-Makdisi refers to the work of Edmund Burke III and others.

145. Osterhammel, *Transformation of the World,* 63–66.

146. Quoted in Khuri-Makdisi, *Eastern Mediterranean,* 27.

147. Osterhammel, *Transformation of the World,* 63, 69, 74, 154, 244, 514, 719. Bayly, *Birth of the Modern World,* 19.

148. Osterhammel, *Transformation of the World,* 64.

149. David Harvey, *The Condition of Postmodernity: An Enquiry into the Origins of Cultural Change* (Cambridge: Blackwell, 1989), 240.

150. Harvey, 240.

151. Harvey, 264.

152. Tim Cresswell, *On the Move: Mobility in the Modern Western World* (New York: Taylor and Francis, 2006), 5.

153. Roland Wenzlhuemer, *Connecting the Nineteenth-Century World: The Telegraph and Globalization* (Cambridge: Cambridge University Press, 2015), 38, 39. See also Wolfgang Schivelbusch, *The Railway Journey: The Industrialization of Time and Space in the Nineteenth Century* (Berkeley: University of California Press, 2014), 33–44. Wenzlhuemer's reference is to Karl Marx, who writes, "Thus, while capital must on one side strive to tear down every spatial barrier to intercourse, i.e. to exchange, and conquer the whole earth for its market, it strives on the other side to annihilate this space with time, i.e. to reduce to minimum the time spent in motion from one place to another." From Karl Marx, *Grundrisse: Foundations of the Critique of Political Economy (Rough Draft)* (Harmondsworth, UK: Penguin Books, 1973), 538–39.

154. Wenzlhuemer, *Connecting the Nineteenth-Century World,* 44. See also Doreen Massey, "Politics and Space-Time," *New Left Review* 196 (1992): 80.

155. Wenzlhuemer, *Connecting the Nineteenth-Century World,* 45.

156. Wenzlhuemer, 46. See also Vanessa Ogle, *The Global Transformation of Time, 1870–1905* (Cambridge: Harvard University Press, 2015).

157. Wenzlhuemer, *Connecting the Nineteenth-Century World,* 47. See also Jeremy Stein, "Reflections on Time, Time-Space Compression and Technology in the Nineteenth Century," *TimeSpace: Geographies of Temporality* (London: Routledge, 2001), 108, 113. Regarding timekeeping systems, practices, and attitudes in the Balkans and Ottoman Empire, see the special issue of *Études balkaniques* 53, no. 2 (2017).

158. The first of twelve volumes of *Niwt'er H.H. Dashnakts'ut'ean patmut'ean hamar* [Materials for the history of the A.R. Federation] was published in 1972, the most recent in 2017.

159. ARF Archives Institute DVD, 2009.

160. One ARF paper began as *Haraj* [Forward] (1906) and went through several reincarnations as *Alik'* [Wave] (1906), *Zang* [Bell] (1906), *Yerkir* [Country] (1906), *Zhamanak* [Time] (1906–7), *Arōr* [Plough] (1907), *Paylak* [Lightning] (1907), *Kovkasi Arawōt* [Caucasus's morning] (1907), *Khariskh* [Anchor] (1907), *Nor Alik'* [New wave] (1907), *Zhayr* [Rock] (1907), *Vtak* [Brook/Stream] (1907), *Zangak* [Bell] (1908), *Gorts* [Work/Stream] (1908–9), and *Horizon* (1909).

CHAPTER 2. "ACTIVE AND MOVING SPIRITS OF DISTURBANCE"

1. "Vērk'erov li chan fiday em/T'ap'arakan, tun ch'unem/Yaris p'okhan zēnk's em grkel/Mi tegh hangist k'un chunem" is the first verse of an Armenian revolutionary song written in memory of Petros Seremjian, who was killed along with Macedonian revolutionaries in an incursion into Ottoman territory in 1901. *Azgayin hayrenasirakan heghap'okhakan yergaran* [National patriotic revolutionary songbook] (Beirut: Hamazgayin Vahē Sēt'ean Tparan, 2004), 18. For a discussion of this Armenian-Macedonian collaborative operation and others, see Garabet K. Moumdjian, "Rebels with a Cause: Armenian-Macedonian Relations and Their Bulgarian Connection, 1895–1913," in *War and Nationalism: The Balkan Wars, 1912–1913, and Their Sociopolitical Implications,* ed. Hakan Yavuz and Isa Blumi (Salt Lake City: University of Utah Press, 2013). The term *fedayi* derives from the Arabic فداء (fidā'/sacrifice) and means "the one who sacrifices himself"; in this case, the reference is to Armenian militants.

2. See discussion in Berberian, "Armenian Women in Turn-of-the-Century Iran," 89–90. See also Sona Zeitlian, *Hay knoj derě hay heghap'okhakan sharzhman mēj* [The role of the Armenian woman in the Armenian revolutionary movement] (1968; Los Angeles: Hraztan Sarkis Zeitlian Publications, 1992). For photos of revolutionary women, see *Hushamatean Hay Heghap'okhakan Dashnakts'ut'ean albom-atlas,* vol. 1, *Diwts'aznamart* [Commemorative album-atlas of the Armenian Revolutionary Federation, vol. 1, Heroic combat] (Glendale, CA: ARF Central Committee, 1992), 224–27. A notable example of a revolutionary woman is Rubina (Sofi Areshian, 1881–1971) who was instrumental in the planning of the attempted assassination of Sultan Abdülhamid II in 1905 as well as the actual assault. Areshian married Hamazasp Ohanjanian, prime minister in 1920 of the First Republic of Armenia. For more on Areshian, see Zeitlian, *Hay knoj derě,* 57–63; Gaidz Minassian, "The Armenian Revolutionary Federation and Operation 'Nejuik,'" in Houssine Alloul, Edhem Eldem, and Hank de Smaele, eds., *To Kill a Sultan: A Transnational History of the Attempt on Abdülhamid II, 1905* (London: Palgrave, 2017), 35–66. Minassian refers to Areshian as Aghechyan.

3. Daniel R. Headrick, *The Tentacles of Progress: Technology Transfer in the Age of Imperialism, 1850–1940* (New York: Oxford University Press, 1988), 49.

4. Charles Issawi, "European Economic Penetration, 1872–1921," in *The Cambridge History of Iran,* ed. Peter Avery, Gavin Hambly, and Charles Melville (Cambridge: Cambridge University Press, 1991), 590, 593, 594.

5. Issawi, 591.

6. Issawi, 592, 595.

7. Donald Quataert, "Transportation," in *An Economic and Social History of the Ottoman Empire, 1300–1914*, ed. Halil İnalcık and Donald Quataert (Cambridge: Cambridge University Press, 1994), 800.

8. Ayşegül Okan, "The Ottoman Postal and Telegraph Services in the Last Quarter of the Nineteenth Century" (MA thesis, Boğaziçi University, 2003), 56–57, 69.

9. Okan, 70, 71.

10. Cited in Okan, 71.

11. K. V. Bazilevich, *The Russian Posts in the XIX Century*, trans. David M. Skipton (Millersville, MD: Rossica Society of Russian Philately, 1987), 121, 124; RUSSIA: Military Report. Trans-Caucasia. (W.O.), 1907, National Archives of the UK. (TNA): Foreign Office (FO) 881/8999X, 180, 182.

12. For example, the Messageries Maritimes sailed to Batumi from Marseille three times a week, the Russian Steam Navigation and Trading Co. from Odessa four times a week, N. Paquet and Co. from Marseille fortnightly, the Austrian Lloyd's Steam Navigation Co. from Istanbul weekly in winter and fortnightly in summer, the Danube Steam Navigation Co. from Galatz/Galati (on the Danube River, in the historical region of Moldavia—now Romania) fortnightly, the Italiana (Navigazione Generale) from Genoa monthly, and the German Levant Steamship Co. from Hamburg, Rotterdam, and Newcastle monthly. See RUSSIA: Military Report. Trans-Caucasia. (W.O.), 1907, 186, 195.

13. Bazilevich, *Russian Posts*, 149.

14. Bazilevich, 128.

15. RUSSIA: Military Report. Trans-Caucasia. (W.O.), 1907, 223. See also Appendix A, 257–414.

16. Bazilevich, *Russian Posts*, 149.

17. Willem Floor, "The Chapar-Khāna System in Qajar Iran," *Iran* 39 (2001): 268; Quataert, "Transportation," 818; Okan, "Ottoman Postal and Telegraph Services," 69.

18. Sixth Central Committee to [Geneva] comrades, Navahangist [Batumi], 1 June 1905, Archives of the Armenian Revolutionary Federation [Dashnakts'ut'iwn], Watertown, Massachusetts, Folder/Part B, file 376, document 6; Sixth Central Committee to [Geneva comrades], Navahangist [Batumi], 17 May 1906, B 377–32; Sixth Central Committee to *Drōshak* editorship, 8 April 1906, B 377–31; for use of a Romanian steamship, see Kris [Fenerjian] to [Geneva comrades], 14 March 1906, ARF Archives B 377–1; regarding ship names and directions of travel, see *Lloyd's Register of British and Foreign Shipping*, vol. 2 (London, 1905).

19. This quotation appears in a document reporting on a meeting with an agent named Tagvorian in Varna during the ARF Congress. See Document 13, Report on ARF relations with the Young Turks and their activities during the Fifth General Congress, deputy to the Chief of the Odessa Provincial Gendarmerie Directorate, 17 September 1909, Odessa, in *The Armenians and the Okhrana, 1907–1915: Documents from the Russian Department of Police Archives*, ed. Vartkes Yeghiayan (Los Angeles: Center for Armenian Remembrance, 2016), 56.

20. Simon Zavarian to Geneva comrades, 20 July 1904, Beirut, and Simon Zavarian to Taparik (Alexandria), Beirut, 1/13 January 1905, in *Simon Zavarean,*

comp. and ed. Hrach Dasnabedian (Antʻilias: Hrat. H.H. Dashnaktsʻutʻean, 1997), 2:228.

21. Document 6, circular regarding ARF activities in Bulgaria, Ministry of Interior Department of Police Special Section, 20 February 1908, no. 125302, in Yeghiayan, *Armenians and the Okhrana*, 15.

22. Document 13, report on ARF relations with the Young Turks and their activities during the Fifth General Congress, deputy to the Chief of the Odessa Provincial Gendarmerie Directorate, 17 September 1909, Odessa, in Yeghiayan, *Armenians and the Okhrana*, 55–56. Regarding Tiufekchiev, see Anna Geifman, *Thou Shalt Kill: Revolutionary Terrorism in Russia, 1894–1917* (Princeton: Princeton University Press, 1993), 201.

23. Kris [Fenerjian] to [Geneva] comrades, 17 April 1906, B 377–4; Kris [Fenerjian] to [Geneva] comrades], 13 May 1906, Odessa, ARF Archives B 377–5; Kris [Fenerjian] to [Geneva] comrades, [17?] May 1906, ARF Archives, B 377–6. Fenerjian's letters from Odessa and Batumi and references to travel to the Galatz, Caucasus, and Bulgaria throughout file 377 are evidence of his own circulation in the Balkans and Caucasus and his role in circulating arms and print.

24. Gasmotoren Fabrik, founded in 1864, invented the four-stroke internal combustion engine. For Rostom's letter dated 21 August 1907, see *Ṛostom namakani: Mahuan utʻsunameakin artʻiw* [Rostom letters: On the occasion of the eightieth anniversary of his death], comp. and ed. Hrach Dasnabedian (Beirut: Hamazgayin Vahē Sētʻean Press, 1999), 427.

25. The reference to receipt of newspapers is most likely to *Drōshak*, as the letter is to its editorship. [Tatyos?] to Mikayel [Varandian], 28 January 1904, ARF Archives B 443–2. In another letter, an operative informs his Geneva comrades about a steamship that arrives at Galatz once a week and stands ready to transport sixty to seventy thousand gun parts as well as books and newspapers, but he wonders whether sending many newspapers—surprisingly, he does not mention weapons—at once could draw undesired attention. Kris [Fenerjian] to [Geneva] comrades, 17 April 1906, ARF Archives B 377–4. This is not to assume that precautions were not taken for weapons; for example, ARF cofounder Kristapor Mikayelian, having traveled on a steamer with comrade Hovnan Davtian from Marseille to Athens, recommends hastening an agreement with the Batumi branch for the transportation of explosives, detonators, capsules, and other items but cautions that they should be sent in the same way that *Drōshak* is—that is, no address shall be provided, and only on the day of delivery will Batumi be notified of shipment and the name of the steamship carrying supplies. Kristapor Mikayelian to Western Bureau [Geneva], 28 July 1904, in *Kʻristapʻor Mikʻayeleani namaknerě*, comp. and ed. Hrach Dasnabedian (Beirut: Hamazgayin Vahē Sētʻean Tparan, 1993), 347. (Original document in ARF Archives, 212–2.) In some cases, caution also stemmed from comrades' "inability" and "operations in disarray." Kris [Fenerjian] to Khachatur [Malumian], 22 August 1906, Odessa, ARF Archives B 377–9.

26. Simon Zavarian to Western Bureau, 8 July 1904, in *Simon Zavarean*, 2:222, 225. For travel by steamship, see also Zavarian's letters to Geneva comrades, 20 July 1904, Beirut, in *Simon Zavarean*, 2:227; to Dr. K. Pashayian, 6 August 1904, Beirut, in *Simon Zavarean*, 2:233; to Dr. K. Pashayian (Alexandria), 9 August 1904, Beirut, in *Simon Zavarean*, 2:234; to [?], 19–20 December

1904, in *Simon Zavarean,* 2:242; to Rostom, 13 April 1905, in *Simon Zavarean,* 2:269; to [Geneva?] comrades, 15/28 January 1909, in *Simon Zavarean,* 2:303.

27. *Simon Zavarean,* 2:227n13.

28. See, for example, Kris [Fenerjian] to [Geneva comrades], 7 April 1906, Odessa, ARF Archives, B 377–3. The author suggests Port Saʿīd to be a safer and more trusted port than Alexandropol/Gyumri to receive newspapers and books.

29. Rostom to Western Bureau, 7 August 1900, in *Ṛostom namakani,* 223; to *Drōshak* editorship, 5 September 1902, in *Ṛostom namakani,* 284 (original in ARF Archives, 1144–60); to Western Bureau, 5 June 1907, in *Ṛostom namakani,* 425 (original in ARF Archives, 1149–31).

30. See Rostom's complaints about not being able to afford even a second- or third-class ticket. Rostom's letters often contain references to his limited or insufficient funds. In one letter, he even pines, "How good would it be if I did not need to worry about that financial problem and could completely surrender to my work." Rostom to Western Bureau, 5 June 1907, in *Ṛostom namakani,* 425; to *Drōshak* editorship, 5 September 1902, in *Ṛostom namakani,* 284 (original in ARF Archives, 1144–60).

31. Simon Zavarian to Western Bureau, 8 July 1904, in *Simon Zavarean,* 2:223.

32. Peter J. Hugill, *Global Communications since 1844: Geopolitics and Technology* (Baltimore: Johns Hopkins University Press, 1999), 18.

33. Headrick, *Tentacles of Progress,* 19, 36. See also Osterhammel, *Transformation of the World,* 719. J.R. McNeill and William H. McNeill, *The Human Web: A Bird's-Eye View of World History* (New York: W.W. Norton, 2003), 218.

34. Osterhammel, *Transformation of the World,* 723.

35. See, for example, tables showing number of passengers and amount of goods from 1871 to 1939 in India, France, Germany, Britain, and Russia/USSR in Headrick, *Tentacles of Progress,* 56, 57.

36. Osterhammel, *Transformation of the World,* 244.

37. Osterhammel, 245.

38. Osterhammel, 300, 301.

39. Suraiya Faroqhi et al., *An Economic and Social History of the Ottoman Empire,* vol. 2 (Cambridge: Cambridge University Press, 1997), 810.

40. Faroqhi, 810, 811.

41. Frederik Coene, *The Caucasus: An Introduction* (London: Routledge, 2010), 21–22; Ronald Grigor Suny, *The Making of the Georgian Nation,* 2nd ed. (Bloomington: University of Indiana Press, 1994), 152–53. See also Ronald Grigor Suny, "Tiflis: Crucible of Ethnic Politics, 1860–1905," in *The City in Late Imperial Russia,* ed. Michael F. Hamm (Bloomington: Indiana University Press, 1986), 249–81.

42. Nikki R. Keddie, "The Economic History of Iran, 1800–1914, and Its Political Impact: An Overview," *Iranian Studies* 5, no. 2/3 (Spring–Summer 1972): 59; Ahmad Seyf, "Obstacles to the Development of Capitalism: Iran in the Nineteenth Century," *Middle Eastern Studies* 34, no. 3 (July 1998): 69.

43. Mansour Bonakdarian, *Britain and the Iranian Constitutional Revolution of 1906–1911: Foreign Policy, Imperialism, and Dissent* (Syracuse, NY: Syracuse University Press, 2006), 334. See also Oliver Bast, "'Sheer Madness' or 'Railway

Politics' Iranian Style? The Controversy over Railway Development Priorities within the Persian Government in 1919–1920 and British Railway Imperialism, Iran," *Journal of the British Institute of Persian Studies* 55, no. 1 (2017): 62–72.

44. J. N. Westwood, *A History of Russian Railways* (London: George Allen and Unwin, 1964), 100.

45. Headrick, *Tentacles of Progress*, 55, 56. See also Walter Sablinsky, "The All-Russian Railroad Union and the Beginning of the General Strike in October, 1905," in *Revolution and Politics in Russia: Essays in Memory of B. I. Nicolaevsky*, ed. Alexander and Janet Rabinowitch with Ladis K. D. Kristof (Bloomington: Indiana University Press, 1977), 115.

46. Sablinsky, "All-Russian Railroad Union," 115, 132. See also Sixth Central Committee, "Gortsadul ew k'aghak'akan ts'oyts'" [Strike and political protest], 28 January 1905, Batumi, ARF Archives, B 376–11.

47. Westwood, *History of Russian Railways*, 140.

48. Quataert, "Transportation," 804; Sena Bayraktaroğlu, "Development of Railways in the Ottoman Empire and Turkey" (MA thesis, Boğaziçi University, 1995), 22.

49. Quataert, "Transportation," 807.

50. Quataert, 812.

51. Quataert, 813. For railroads in the Ottoman Empire and the Turkish Republic by date of construction, name of line, length, and source of foreign capital for funding of construction, see Bayraktaroğlu, "Development of Railways," 76, fig. 5.

52. Quataert, "Transportation," 811.

53. Quataert, 811. Regarding control, see also Yakup Bektas, "The Sultan's Messenger: Cultural Constructions of Ottoman Telegraphy, 1847–1880," *Technology and Culture* 41, no. 4 (October 2000): 670.

54. Simon Zavarian, "T'iwrk'ia: Yerkat'ughineru kareworut'iwně" [Turkey: The importance of railroads], *Drōshak* 1 (January 1909): 8–11.

55. Zavarian, 8, 9.

56. Zavarian, 10.

57. Simon Zavarian to Hovnan Davitian, 16 February 1910, Mush/Muş, in *Simon Zavarean*, 2:330. For other references to railways, see Zavarian to *Drōshak* editorship, 24 January/6 February 1909, in *Simon Zavarean*, 3:38; to Eastern Bureau Yerkir [Country] Section, 1 June 1910, Mush/Muş, in *Simon Zavarean*, 352; to Abro, 9 June 1910, Mush/Muş, in *Simon Zavarean*, 354.

58. Rupen Zartarian, "Anapat yerkirě . . . " [The desert country . . .], *Zhamanak* (Istanbul) 69 (3/16 January 1908): 1. Zartarian was the editor of *Razmik* [Warrior] (Filibe) from 1905 to 1908 and *Azatamart* (Battle for freedom) from 1909 until 1915. He fell victim to the Genocide.

59. Japonats'i [Alexander Ter Hakobian] to comrades, 19 December 1905, ARF Archives, B 444–5.

60. Wenzlhuemer, *Connecting the Nineteenth-Century World*, 119.

61. Wenzlhuemer, *Connecting the Nineteenth-Century World*, 128, 257.

62. Wenzlhuemer, 249. See also James W. Carey, "Technology and Ideology: The Case of the Telegraph," in *Communication as Culture: Essays on Media and Society*, ed. David Thorburn (Boston: Unwin Hyman, 1989), 3.

63. Bayly, *Birth of the Modern World,* 461–62.

64. Kurzman, *Democracy Denied,* 3.

65. Roderic H. Davison, "The Advent of the Electric Telegraph in the Ottoman Empire," in *Essays in Ottoman and Turkish History, 1774–1923: The Impact of the West* (Austin: University of Texas Press, 1990), 156.

66. Davison, "Advent of the Electric Telegraph," 133; Bektas, "Sultan's Messenger," 694, 695.

67. Davison, "Advent of the Electric Telegraph," 148; Bektas, "Sultan's Messenger," 696.

68. Davison, "Advent of the Electric Telegraph," 154, 155.

69. Davison, 152; Bektas, "Sultan's Messenger," 688.

70. Headrick, *Tentacles of Progress,* 19.

71. Davison, "Advent of the Electric Telegraph," 133.

72. Davison, 134, 136; Bektas, "Sultan's Messenger," 686.

73. Davison, "Advent of the Electric Telegraph," 138.

74. Okan, "Ottoman Postal and Telegraph Services," 100–102.

75. Okan, 104.

76. Michael Rubin, "The Formation of Modern Iran, 1858–1909: Communications, Telegraph and Society" (PhD diss., Yale University, 1999), 14.

77. Rubin, "Formation of Modern Iran," 279, 280, 305–9, 321; Michael Rubin, "The Culture of Telegraph Workers in Iran," in *Iran, questions et connaissances: Actes du IVe Congres européen des études iraniennes; organisé par la Societas Iranologica Europea* [Proceedings of the 4th European Congress of Iranian Studies; organized by Societas Iranologica Europea], ed. Maria Szuppe (Leuven, Belgium: Peeters, 2002), 2:354–55, 359–60.

78. Rubin, "Formation of Modern Iran," 230.

79. Rubin, "Culture of Telegraph Workers," 361, 362, 368; Rubin, "Formation of Modern Iran," 28, 225.

80. Rubin, "Formation of Modern Iran," 32, 100.

81. Rubin, 16, 35–36, 138, 193–95, 323, 330, 333, 349, 367.

82. Rubin, 368, 374.

83. Rubin, 338, 347, 373, 374, 408; see also chaps. 11, 13.

84. Rubin, 493, 503–4, 509, 518.

85. Bektas, "Sultan's Messenger," 686.

86. *Encyclopaedia Iranica,* s.v. "Indo-European Telegraph Department," by Michael Rubin, 2012, www.iranicaonline.org/articles/indo-european-telegraph-department; Rubin, "Formation of Modern Iran," 232.

87. Steven Roberts, "The Indo-European Telegraph Company," http://atlantic-cable.com/CableCos/Indo-Eur/, last updated 11 October 2011.

88. Roberts.

89. For evidence of the variety of uses, see, for example, telegrams about the results of the 1912 Ottoman parliamentary elections and Armenian delegates: ARF Archives, C 791–6, received 18 February 1912; C 791–16, received 10 March 1912; C 791–20, received 16 March 1912. The first two telegrams are in both Ottoman and Armenian, and the third is in romanized Armenian. For telegrams sent to *Drōshak* by Yeprem Khan, in romanized Armenian, see, for example, ARF Archives, C 60a–66, 60a–67, 60a–68.

90. See *Ṛostom namakani* and *Simon Zavarean.*

91. Bazilevich, *Russian Posts,* 101, 143.

92. Rostom to Western Bureau, 3 July 1901, Filibe, in *Ṛostom namakani,* 251 (original in ARF Archives, 1143–13); to Western Bureau, received 20 July 1901, in *Ṛostom namakani,* 254 (original in ARF Archives, 1143–16); to Kristapor, late 1904/early 1905, in *Ṛostom namakani,* 362 (original in ARF Archives, 212–117); to Simon Zavarian, Mush/Muş, 14 December 1910, in *Ṛostom namakani,* 517 (original in ARF Archives, 99–76). See also Kristapor to Western Bureau, 12 July 1904, Paris, in *K'ristap'or Mik'ayeleani namaknerĕ,* 340 (original in ARF Archives, 1268–52); Simon Zavarian to Dr. Karapet Pashayian [Taparik], 29 August 1904, Beirut, in *Simon Zavarean,* 238. Zavarian specifies that the money must go through Crédit Lyonnais and not an Ottoman bank, most probably out of fear of discovery and confiscation.

93. Azerbaijan Central Committee to Western Bureau, 21 February 1905, ARF Archives, B 468–40. A. Vramian (Onnik Terdzakian), for example, was an ARF member and a postal employee in the Russian postal office in Istanbul. See Gabriel Lazian, *Heghap'okhakan dēmk'er* [Revolutionary figures] (Aleppo: Hamazgayin, 1990), 101.

94. Telegram to Western Bureau (author unknown), New Julfa, 17 June 1905, ARF Archives, B 580–15.

95. Rostom (probably writing from Geneva, on behalf of the Western Bureau, to the Azerbaijan Central Committee) complains that telegrams from Tabriz were arriving later than letters from Kars and that it would be better to send them from New Julfa, Isfahan, to Paris, London, or Geneva so that they would arrive within a day or two. Western Bureau/Rostom to Vrezh [Azerbaijan] Central Committee, 9 July 1904, in *Ṛostom namakani,* 311 (original in ARF Archives, 43–52).

96. Bazilevich, *Russian Posts,* 102; Okan, "Ottoman Postal and Telegraph Services," 40; *Encyclopaedia Iranica,* s.v. "Philately i. The Postage Stamps of Iran," by Roman Siebertz, last updated 28 January 2011, www.iranicaonline .org/articles/philately-stamps.

97. Okan, "Ottoman Postal and Telegraph Services," 28; Bazilevich, *Russian Posts,* 107; A. C. Wilson, "A Thousand Years of Postal and Telecommunications Services in Russia," *New Zealand Slavonic Journal* (1989): 142.

98. Okan, "Ottoman Postal and Telegraph Services," 32, 33–36, 46.

99. Okan, 68.

100. Okan, 67. At the end of the century, the number of Austrian post offices had decreased to thirty-three, but the total of European post offices was ninety-seven. See Okan, 80.

101. Okan, 67, 69, 80.

102. Alison Rowley, *Open Letters: Russian Popular Culture and the Picture Postcard, 1880–1922* (Toronto: University of Toronto Press, 2013), 17; Bazilevich, *Russian Posts,* 121, 124–28, 141.

103. Bazilevich, *Russian Posts,* 121, 139, 149, 155, 156; Rowley, *Open Letters,* 17.

104. Rowley, 17.

105. Okan, "Ottoman Postal and Telegraph Services," 53, 83–85.

106. "T'iwrk'ahay keank': Postĕ Tsughak' ē" [Turkish Armenian life: The post is a trap], *Alik'* [Wave] (Tiflis) 81 (5 August 1906): 3.

107. Okan, "Ottoman Postal and Telegraph Services," 36, 85, 86, 89.

108. Okan, 46, 108.

109. Yavuz Selim Karakışla, "Sultan II. Abdülhamid'in istibdat döneminde (1876–1909): Hafiyelik ve jurnalcilik" [During Sultan Abülhamid II's period of tyranny (1876–1909: Spying and reporting], *Toplumsal Tarih* [Social history] 119 (November 2003): 13, 14, 18–19. I thank Yagmur Idil Ozdemir for the translation of this article. See also François Georgeon, *Abdülhamid II: Le sultan calife (1876–1909)* (Paris: Fayard, 2003), 161.

110. Karakışla, "Sultan II. Abdülhamid'in istibdat döneminde," 17.

111. Ibrahim al-Muwaylihi, *Spies, Scandals, and Sultans: Istanbul in the Twilight of the Ottoman Empire* (translation of *Ma Hunalik*), trans. and intro. Roger Allen (London: Rowman and Littlefield, 2008), 80.

112. To Western Bureau, unsigned but in Nitra's handwriting, 1 April 1907, ARF archives, B 328–8; Nitra [Harutiwn Shahrigian] to Eastern Bureau, 17 February 1907, ARF Archives, B 328–17. ARF member and activist Vahan Papazian (whose pseudonym was Koms) also alludes to *Terakki* in the context of Armenian-Turkish relations in the Van region. He recalls that activists there had requested that *Drōshak* and other revolutionary literature be sent, including Sabaheddin's and Ahmad Rıza's publications. He notes that they were already receiving, with the help of Turkish friends, Rıza's *Meşveret* (Consultation) as well as *Inkilab* (Revolution) and other booklets, which had an "explosive" influence on the population and the government. See also Vahan Papazian, *Im husherē* [My memoirs] (Boston: Hayrenik', 1950), 2:285.

113. Hanioğlu, *Preparation for a Revolution*, 95, 97, 109–16. See Hanioğlu, chap. 5, for a detailed discussion of the ARF and the league's clandestine alliance and joint activities, including the formation of what the author calls "bogus" committees, and the publication of bilingual and trilingual journals. While Garabet Moumdjian finds Hanioğlu's claim of ARF participation completely unfounded, Raymond Kévorkian questions the characterization of one of those committees, the Liberal Turkish Action Committee or Turkish Revolutionary Federation, as bogus. Relying on a 1904 report by Vahan Papazian, "the chief of the party [ARF] in Van in this period," Kévorkian concludes:

> [A] certain Haci Idris, a Turkish landowner, contacted him with the intention of collaborating with the ARF. Idris was soon joined by the emlak müdüri (the head of the land registration office) in Van, Şeref; the assistant chief of the telegraph office, Halil; and a tax official, Hakkı, all of whom were opponents of the regime. He also notes that he had some of Sabaheddin's and Rıza's publications brought from Europe for his Turkish friends, adding that they were a distinct success and that, finally, in fall 1906, at Şeref's request, "we decided to publish a bimonthly periodical in Turkish, which we wrote, edited and printed ourselves, while they were responsible for distributing it." *Sabah ul-Hayr* (Good Day), which called for joint Armenian-Turkish action, was well received, according to Papazian. Şakir, however, was convinced that "such a committee could never be Turkish or Ottoman." Hanioğlu goes so far as to describe it as a "bogus organization of the Dashnaktsutiun" because he is unaware of the part, however modest, played in these anti-Hamidian propaganda campaigns by a handful of Turkish notables from Van.

Kévorkian, *Armenian Genocide,* 29. See also Vahan Papazian, *Im Husherě* [My memoirs] (Boston: Hayrenik', 1950), 1:282–85, 512–35; Garabet Moumdjian, "Struggling for a Constitutional Regime: Armenian-Young Turk Relations in the Era of Abdulhamid II, 1895–1909" (PhD diss., UCLA, 2012), 233–47.

114. Hanioğlu, *Preparation for a Revolution,* 116–17. See also Papazian, *Im Husherě,* 1:280–81.

115. *Encyclopaedia Iranica,* s.v. "Philately vi. Postal History," by Mano Amarloui, last updated 25 January 2012, www.iranicaonline.org/articles/philately-vi-postal-history.

116. Administration des Postes, 3 July 1906, ARF Archives, B 581–17. See also handwritten copies of order, ARF Archives, B 49–146 and B 49–147. The satirical *Molla Nasreddin,* which began publication in Tiflis in 1906, was also prohibited, confiscated, and burned. See Customs and Postal Minister J. Naus's Telegram, 1 December 1906, ARF Archives, B 581/49. For a discussion of this case, see Berberian, *Armenians and the Iranian Constitutional Revolution,* 94–96.

117. The ARF seems to have accepted or understood Ottoman and Russian censorship but not Iranian. See articles from the ARF press: "'Drōshaki' argilumě Parskastanum" ["Drōshak's" ban in Persia], *Drōshak,* 7 (July 1906): 98; "'Drōshaki' argilumě Parskastanum" ["Drōshak's" ban in Persia], *Alik'* 77 (1 August 1906): 2; S. Tseruni [Stepan Stepanian] to Eastern Bureau, 4 July 1906, in *Niwt'er,* 3:317–19.

118. Statement of Anzali Chief of Postal Service Hasan Khan and Customs Inspector Jules Duhem, July 1906, ARF Archives, B 581–50; Ministère des Postes to Dr. A.D. Stepanian, 19 July 1906, ARF Archives, B 581–22. See also Garegin to Vaspurakan (Van) Central Committee, 29 July 1906, ARF Archives, B 470–101; Gilan Postal and Customs General Director J. Monard to Customs and Postal Minister J. Naus, 1 August 1906, ARF Archives, B 581–35.

119. "'Drōshaki' argelman khndirě" [The issue of "Drōshak's" ban], *Drōshak* 8 (August 1906): 128; Western Bureau to Vrezh [Azerbaijan] Central Committee, 30 July 1906, ARF Archives, B 49–3.

120. The measures involved sending the publication in smaller batches of twenty to fifty papers, changing the color of packaging, sending the batches through another country, and other precautions. See Arsen to *Drōshak,* 9 August 1906, ARF Archives, B 581–27; B 581–45. In some areas, the prohibition continued well into 1907. See, for example, Shavarsh to *Drōshak,* 4 January 1907, ARF Archives, B 582–2; Session 25, 21 May 1907, Minutes of the Azerbaijan Central Committee, ARF Archives, B 540-b.

121. Rowley, *Open Letters,* 42, 43; Okan, "Ottoman Postal and Telegraph Services," 55. For Russian censorship, see also Wilson, "Thousand Years of Postal and Telecommunications Services," 146.

122. Rowley, *Open Letters,* 43.

123. Kris [Fenerjian] to Khachatur [Malumian?], 1 September 1906, Odessa, ARF Archives, B 377–10. Fenerjian also complained about failing new transport routes, increasing expense, and decreasing number of newspapers getting in. See Kris [Fenerjian] to Khachatur, 14 September 1906, Odessa, ARF Archives, B 377–11. However, some newspapers were entering through Galatz. See Kris [Fenerjian] to Khachatur, 2 October 1906, Odessa, ARF Archives, B

377–12. In 1907 Baku, at least one operative believed that censors were no longer a problem as copies of Montesquieu's *De l'esprit des lois* and Marx's *Das Kapital* had been returned by the government after being confiscated by censors; therefore, he requested that additional copies of two of Nietzsche's books, which they had already received, be sent. See letter to [Geneva] comrades (sender unknown), 28 February 1907, Baku, ARF Archives, B 328–2. Titles are not provided.

124. See Berberian, *Armenians and the Iranian Constitutional Revolution*, 50. For a discussion of the Russian government's changing relationship with the Armenian Church and its assumption of church culpability in the Armenian revolutionary movement, see Önol, *Tsar's Armenians*. For photos of Armenian "revolutionary clergy," see *Hushamatean*, 1:220–21. For churches assisting revolutionary activity, see *Hushamatean*, 1:222–23.

125. Simon Zavarian to *Drōshak* editorship, Istanbul, 21 November/3 December 1912, in *Simon Zavarean*, 3:120 (original in ARF Archives, 109–49); Rostom to American Central Committee, 30 August 1904, in *Rostom namakani*, 241–42; Rostom to Western Bureau, 27 June 1900, Filibe, in *Rostom namakani*, 216–17.

126. For complaints, see, for example, Rostom to Salmas comrades, 6 September 1904, in *Rostom namakani*, 333 (original in ARF archives, B 43–26]; to Azerbaijan Central Committee, 17 February 1905, in *Rostom namakani*, 377. Regarding archives, see Rostom to Azerbaijan Central Committee, 29 August 1905, in *Rostom namakani*, 394 (original in ARF Archives, 46–6).

127. Rostom, in western Anatolia, informs Zavarian, on the other side of Anatolia, in Mush/Muş, that he is sending *pastırma* with comrade Madteos with the proviso that if, for some odd reason, Zavarian is not partial to the rather malodorous cured meat, he should share it with visiting comrades, as they will "absolutely love it." Rostom to Simon Zavarian, Mush, 14 December 1910, in *Rostom namakani*, 517 (original in ARF Archives, 99–76).

128. Okan, "Ottoman Postal and Telegraph Services," 66, 70, 71.

129. Floor, "Chapar-Khāna System in Qajar Iran," 268, 270. For a history of the Iranian post, see also Firaydun Abdulifard, *Tarikh-e post dar Iran az sadarat-e Amir Kabir ta vizarat-e Amin al-Dowlah (1267–1297 h.q.* [A history of postal service in Iran: From the premiership of Amir-Kabir to the ministry of Amin al-Dowlah, 1888–1918]) (Tehran: Hirmand, 1375/1996).

130. *Encyclopaedia Iranica*, "Philately i. The Postage Stamps of Iran."

131. Simon Zavarian, *Apakedronats'umě* [Decentralization] (Istanbul: Azatut'ean Matenadaran, 1908), 36.

132. Hrach Dasnabedian, *H. H. Dashnakts'ut'ean kazmakerpakan karoyts'i holovoyt'ě* [The evolution of the Federation's organizational structure] (Beirut: Hamazgayin Vahē Sēt'ean Tparan, 1974), graph 1.

133. Dasnabedian, graphs 2 and 3.

134. Dasnabedian, 28; see also *Niwt'er*, vol. 2.

135. Rostom to Samson Tadeosian, undated, perhaps from Caucasus late 1905 or 1906 or from Geneva 1904 or 1905, in *Rostom namakani*, 363–65 (original in ARF Archives, B 15–6).

136. Dasnabedian, *H. H. Dashnakts'ut'ean kazmakerpakan karoyts'i holovoyt'ě*, 29–30.

137. Dasnabedian, 58.

138. The report presented by the ARF to the Socialist International meeting in Stuttgart also maintained organizing 110 unions with 10,990 members in Tiflis, Baku, Batumi, Gandzak, Yerevan, Alexandropol, and Shushi. See "Kusakts'ut'ean gortsunēut'enēn (mi kani p'aster)" [From the party's activity (a few proofs)], *Drōshak* 9 (September 1907): 137. Despite the high number of members, the ARF paper *Haṛaj* [Forward], published in Tiflis, complained about the absence of operatives. See "Mardu sov ē" [It is a famine of men], *Haṛaj* 53 (22 March 1906): 1. Okhrana estimated that the ARF, which it called a state within a state, maintained an "army" of 100,000. Of course, not all or even a plurality of ARF's membership was actually militant. For Okhrana's report, see Tsarist Spy Service "Okhrana's" Report about the A.R. Federation, in *Niwt'er*, 2:325, 331, 333.

139. The numbers for women ARF members in Iran are the following: 21 percent for Tabriz, 27.5 percent for Rasht, 24 percent for Anzali, and 25 percent for Qazvin. The exceptions are Khoy and Ardabil. While Khoy's female membership stands at about 13.5 percent of the total membership of that region, Ardabil's is much higher than the mean at 57 percent. The information is drawn from several sources: Report of Azerbaijan's Activities, 1904–06, in *Niwt'er H.H. Dashnakts'ut'ean patmut'ean hamar* [Materials for the history of the A.R. Federation], vol. 4, ed. Hrach Dasnabedian (Beirut: Hamazgayin, 1982), 228–37; Azerbaijan Regional Congress, Sessions 2–7, 2 February to 8 February 1906, and Session 17, 20 February 1906, in *Niwt'er*, 4:240–58; Report of Minaret [Salmas] Region, 1904–1905, in *Niwt'er*, 4:266–70; Report of Avarayr [Khoy] Region, 1 February 1906, in *Niwt'er*, 4:270–75; Report of Shahsevan [Ardabil] and Andar [Astara] Region, 1 February 1906, in *Niwt'er*, 4:295–98. For a more thorough discussion of Iranian women's activism, see Berberian, "Armenian Women in Turn-of-the-Century Iran," 70–98.

140. Dasnabedian, *H.H. Dashnakts'ut'ean kazmakerpakan kaṛoyts'i holovoyt'ē*, 56.

141. Dasnabedian, 59.

142. Moritz Deutschmann, *Iran and Russian Imperialism: The Ideal Anarchists, 1800–1914* (London: Routledge, 2016), 47. David Gutman, "Travel Documents, Mobility Control, and the Ottoman State in an Age of Global Migration, 1880–1915," *Journal of the Ottoman and Turkish Studies Association* 3, no. 2 (November 2016): 349, 363, 365.

143. See, for example, Rostom to Kristapor [Mikayelian], undated (possibly end of 1904), in *Ṛostom namakani*, 354–55 (original in ARF Archives, B 212–114); Rostom to Kristapor [Mikayelian], 4 February 1905, in *Ṛostom namakani*, 373–74 (original in ARF Archives, B 213–53). Money also circulated as indicated by the correspondence in the ARF Archives and by Rostom's letters in *Ṛostom namakani*.

144. Rostom also states that it would be possible to obtain an "Assyrian (Persian) passport." Rostom to Kristapor [Mikayelian], 4 February 1905, in *Ṛostom namakani*, 354–55 (original in ARF Archives, B 213–53).

145. Rostom to Kristapor [Mikayelian], undated (possibly end of 1904), in *Ṛostom namakani*, 373–74 (original in ARF Archives, B 212–114).

146. Rostom to unknown recipient, 26 July or December 1904, in *Ṛostom namakani*, 319 (original in ARF Archives, B 212–112).

147. Kristapor Mikayelian to Western Bureau, 6 July 1904, Paris, in K'ristap'or Mik'ayeleani namaknerě, 331 (original in ARF Archives, 1268–47); to Western Bureau, 16/29 September 1904, Izmir, in K'ristap'or Mik'ayeleani namaknerě, 367 (original in ARF Archives, B 212–22). Based on whence the letters originated, it seems Mikayelian traveled from Paris to Athens before heading to Istanbul through Izmir.

148. See John Torpey, *The Invention of the Passport: Surveillance, Citizenship and the State* (Cambridge: Cambridge University Press, 2000), 1.

149. Richard Schofield, "Narrowing the Frontier: Mid-Nineteenth Century Efforts to Delimit and Map the Perso-Ottoman Boundary," in *War and Peace in Qajar Persia: Implication Past and Present,* ed. Roxane Farmanfarmaian (London: Routledge, 2008), 149, 168; Sabri Ateş, *The Ottoman-Iranian Borderlands: Making a Boundary, 1843–1914* (Cambridge: Cambridge University Press, 2013), 1. See also Deutschmann, *Iran and Russian Imperialism.*

150. Osterhammel, *Transformation of the World,* 110–12, 113.

151. For Rostom's collaborative activities, see, for example, Hovsep Hovhannisian, *Husher* [Memoirs] (Yerevan: Abolon, 1995), 176, 196–97; Kitur, *Patmut'iwn S.D. Hnch'akean Kusakts'ut'ean,* 1:399–400. For a French translation of Kitur, see Cosroe Chaqueri, *La social-démocratie en Iran: Articles et documents annotés et presentés* [Social-democracy in Iran: Annotated and presented articles and documents] (Florence: Mazdak, 1979), 238. See also Sokrat Khan Gelofiants, *Kayts: S.D. Hnch. Kusakts'ut'ean gortsunēut'iwnits' togh p'asterě khosin* [Spark: Let the evidence from the S.D. Hnch. Party activity speak] (Providence, RI: Yeritasard Hayastan, 1915), 13–15, 24–27; Hrant Kankruni, *Hay heghap'okhut'iwně Osmanean brnatirut'ean dēm (1890–1910)* [The Armenian revolution against Ottoman despotism (1890–1910)] (Beirut: G. Doniguian et Fils, 1983), 195–96. See also Afary, *Iranian Constitutional Revolution, 1996),* 239.

152. Excerpted from *Hushapatum H.H. Dashnakts'ut'ean,* 1890–1950 (Boston: H.H. Dashnakts'ut'iwn Biwrō, 1950), in *Ṛostom: Mahuan vat'sunameakin aṛt'iw* [Rostom: On the sixtieth anniversary of his death] (Beirut: Hamazgayin Vahē Sēt'ean Tparan, 1979), 12.

153. *Ṛostom: Mahuan vat'sunameakin aṛt'iw,* 13, 14.

154. Rostom to Kristapor [Mikayelian], 24 February 1905, in *Ṛostom namakani,* 379 (original in ARF Archives, B 213–54a).

155. Hovsep Tadeosian, "T'ap'aṛumner ants'iali husheri mēj" [Strolls into the memories of the past], in *Ṛostom: Mahuan vat'sunameakin aṛt'iw,* 251. Reprinted from *Hayrenik' Amsagir* [Fatherland Monthly] 24, no. 6 (November–December 1946): 83–88. See Rostom to Azerbaijan Central Committee, 17 February 1905, in *Ṛostom namakani,* 379 (original in ARF Archives, B 46–1), and letters in *Ṛostom namakani.* The map of Rostom's circulation in this book tries to capture the breadth of his travels and to be as comprehensive as possible, based on his correspondence.

156. Lazian, *Heghap'okhakan dēmk'er,* 11–13.

157. Regarding the failed assassination attempt on Sultan Abdülhamid II and the Yıldız bombing, see Alloul et al., *To Kill a Sultan;* see, in particular,

Toygun Altıntaş, "The Ottoman War on 'Anarchism' and Revolutionary Violence," 99–128, and Gaidz Minassian, "The Armenian Revolutionary Federation and Operation 'Nejuik,'" 35–66.

158. Ահարեկիչ is a compound word formed from the root words ահ (ah/fear) and բեկել (bekel/to break), with the meaning of "one who causes fear"—that is, a terrorist.

159. Anderson, *Under Three Flags*, 4.

160. Ellen [Kristapor Mikayelian] to Martin [Muratian] and Etgar [Karapet Ayvazian], 11 April 1904, in *K'ristap'or Mik'ayeleani namaknerě*, 324 (original in ARF Archives, B 212–19); Mikayelian to Western Bureau, 6 July 1904, Paris, in *K'ristap'or Mik'ayeleani namaknerě*, 331 (original in ARF Archives, 1268–47); to Western Bureau, 12 July 1904, Paris, in *K'ristap'or Mik'ayeleani namaknerě*, 338 (original in ARF Archives, 1268–52); to Western Bureau, 28 July 1904, in *K'ristap'or Mik'ayeleani namaknerě*, 347 (original in ARF Archives, B 212–2).

161. Mikayelian to Western Bureau, 28 July 1904, in *K'ristap'or Mik'ayeleani namaknerě*, 347 (original in ARF Archives, B 212–2).

162. Mikayelian to Western Bureau, 28 July 1904, in *K'ristap'or Mik'ayeleani namaknerě*, 347. Mikayelian's pseudonym Ellen might refer to Ἕλλην/Héllēn, the son of Deucalion and Pyrrha and grandson of Prometheus in Greek mythology.

163. Lazian, *Heghap'okhakan dēmk'er*, 33.

164. Mikayel Varandian, *Simon Zavarean: Gtser ir keank'ēn* [Simon Zavarean: Sketches from his life] (Boston: Hayrenik', 1927), 15; Lazian, *Heghap'okhakan dēmk'er*, 34.

165. Zavarian to Rostom, 13 April 1905, in *Simon Zavarean*, 2:269.

166. See Dasnabedian's notes in *Simon Zavarean*, 3:12, 2:298.

167. Zavarian was hopeful in 1908 as he wrote, "We are partisans of solidarity, peace—hoping that liberty, brotherhood and justice will not remain just empty *words* but that they will be *realized* in life." Zavarian to Taron comrades, 26 November/8 December 1908, Istanbul, in *Simon Zavarean*, 3:24.

168. See Hovak Stepanian, "Nikol Duman (mahuan 15-ameaki art'iw)" [Nikol Duman (on the occasion of the 15th anniversary of his death)], *Hayrenik' Amsagir* 8, no. 12 (October 1930): 158. For Duman's limited role during Mohammad 'Ali Shah's assault in 1911, see Andre Amurian, *H.H. Dashnakts'ut'iwně Parskastanum, 1890–1918* [The A.R. Federation in Persia, 1890–1918] (Tehran: Alik', 1950), 81–85. See also Lazian, *Heghap'okhakan dēmk'er*, 323; *Hushamatean*, 1:22.

169. *Hushamatean*, 1:27, 56. For Keri, see, for example, H. Elmar [Hovsep Hovhannisian], *Yep'rem* (Tehran: Modern, 1964), 140–44, 151–64; Amurian, *Dashnakts'ut'iwně Parskastanum*, 57–59, 60–63, 66–73, 162–66; Ahmad Kasravi, *Tarikh-e mashrutah-ye Iran* [History of the constitution of Iran] (Tehran: Amir Kabir, 1984), 2:838, 842. See also "Parskastan: mi ēj parskakan heghap'[okhakan] patmut'iwnits'" [Persia: A page from Persia's revolutionary history], *Drōshak* 1 (January 1911): 13–14; Ahmad Kasravi, *Tarikh-e hijdah saleh-ye Azerbaijan* [The eighteen-year history of Azerbaijan] (Tehran: Amir

Kabir, 1978), 1:115–17; Farro [Hovsep Hovhannisian], "Grishayi husherĕ" [Grisha's memoirs], *Hayrenik' Amsagir* 3, no. 4 (February 1925): 90–92; Elmar, *Yep'rem*, 338–46, 483, 489–93, which includes extracts from Grisha's memoirs; Isma'il Ra'in, *Yeprem Khan Sardar* [Commander Yeprem Khan] (Tehran: Zarin, 1971), 321–25; "Yep'remi arshavĕ Atrpatakan" [Yeprem's march to Azerbaijan], in A. Amurian [Andre Ter Ohanian], *Dashnakts'ut'iwn, Yep'rem, parskakan sahmanadrut'iwn, H.H.D. kendronakan arkhiv* [A.R. Federation, Yeprem, Persian Constitution, A.R.F. Central Archive] (Tehran: Alik', 1976–79), 1:43–44; "Yep'remi arshavĕ Salar Dovlei dēm" [Yep'rem's march against Salar al-Dowleh], in *Dashnakts'ut'iwn, Yep'rem, parskakan sahmanadrut'iwn, H.H.D. kendronakan arkhiv*, 1:46–48; "Yep'rem ew ir gortsĕ" [Yep'rem and his activity] in *Dashnakts'ut'iwn, Yep'rem, parskakan sahmanadrut'iwn, H.H.D. kendronakan arkhiv*, 1:97–102, 105–10. Farro, "Grishayi husherĕ," *Hayrenik' Amsagir* 3, no. 5 (March 1925): 112–15; Ibrahim Fakhra'i, *Gilan dar jonbesh-e mashrutiyat* [Gilan in the constitutional movement] (Tehran: Ketabha-ye Jibi, 1974), 216–18; "Parskastan: verjin taruay chakatamartnerĕ ew 'Dashnakts'ut'ean' masnakts'ut'iwnĕ" [Persia: The battles of the last year and the "Federation's" participation], *Drōshak* 4 (April 1912): 84–87.

170. Afary, *Iranian Constitutional Revolution*, 244; see also Afary, "Armenian Social Democrats and *Iran-e Now*: A Secret Camaraderie," in *Reformers and Revolutionaries in Modern Iran: New Perspectives on the Iranian Left*, ed. Stephanie Cronin (London: Routledge/Curzon, 2004), 67–84. See also Chaqueri, *La social-démocratie en Iran*; Iraj Afshar, ed., *Owraq-e tazehyab-e mashrutiyat va naqsh-e Taqizadeh* [Newly found constitutional papers and the role of Taqizadeh] (Tehran: Bahman, 1980).

171. *Hushamatean*, 1:38, 144, 176.

172. *Hushamatean*, 56. According to Giwlkhandanian, Matsun Khecho also co-organized arms transfers from Julfa to Salmas. See A[braham] Giwlkhandanian, *Bagui derĕ mer azatagrakan sharzhman mēj* [Baku's role in our liberation movement] (Tehran: Alik', 1981), 27–28.

173. To comrades from Aknuni [according to index, but no signature], 8 August 1908, ARF Archives, C 191–6.

174. Lazian, *Heghap'okhakan dēmk'er*, 131–33.

175. An interesting example comes from a letter written from Zhytomyr (west Ukraine) prison by an ARF operative named Stepan. The letter describes being detained in Volochisk (a small town in western Ukraine located on the left bank of the Zbruch River) after leaving Geneva. Upon inspection, Russian authorities found open letters on him, realized he was Armenian, and asked if he was carrying a weapon. Assuming that he would be strip-searched, Stepan admitted to carrying a pistol and was arrested. In prison, he met a young Armenian from Tiflis who had been caught transporting arms with Georgians. Stepan to comrades, 24 February 1906, ARF Archives, B 445–6.

176. Japonats'i [Alexander Ter Hakobian] to [Geneva] comrades, Saint Petersburg, ARF Archives, B 444–5. Some of the material in this section has been previously published as "Nest of Revolution: The Caucasus, Iran, and Armenians," in *Russia and Iran: Ideology and Occupation*, ed. Rudi Matthee and Elena Andreeva (London: I.B. Tauris, 2018), 95–121.

177. Makar Barkhutariants, *Patmut'yun Aghuanits'* [History of the Albanians], vol. 1., 1860 (Ejmiatsin: Tparan Mayr At'oroy Srboy Ejmiatsni, 1902), 12, cited in Gevorg S. Stepanyan, *Armenians of Baku Province in the Second Half of the 19th Century: Historical-Demographic Study* (Yerevan: Lusakn, 2013), 250. Aghuank'/Aghvank' refers to a region, roughly the area around Gharabagh/Karabagh/Artsakh in the South Caucasus, which was once home to a Christian medieval kingdom known as Caucasian Albania. The Caucasus's multiplicity was also not lost on the British War Office, which reported in 1907 that "There is probably no country in the world which contains a greater variety of races than Trans-Caucasus." RUSSIA: Military Report. Trans-Caucasia. (W.O.), 1907, 89 [National Archives].

178. Nina Garsoian, "Iran and Caucasus," in *Transcaucasia, Nationalism, and Social Change: Essays in the History of Armenia, Azerbaijan, and Georgia,* ed. Ronald Grigor Suny, rev. ed. (Ann Arbor: University of Michigan Press, 1999), 14, 15, 16.

179. Stephen H. Rapp, "Recovering the Pre-National Caucasian Landscape," in *Mythical Landscapes Then and Now: The Mystification of Landscapes in Search for National Identity,* ed. Ruth Büttner and Judith Peltz (Yerevan: Antares, 2006), 17.

180. Bruce Grant, *The Captive and the Gift: Cultural Histories of Sovereignty in Russia and the Caucasus* (Ithaca, NY: Cornell University Press, 2009), xi. See also A. Giwlkhandanian, *Kovkas: Yerkirĕ, zhoghovurdĕ, patmut'iwnĕ* [Caucasus: The country, people, history], vol. 1 (Paris: Librairie Universitaire J. Gamber, 1943), 37; Bruce Grant and Lale Yalçın-Heckmann, introduction, in *Caucasus Paradigms: Anthropologies, Histories and the Making of a World Area,* ed. Bruce Grant and Lale Yalçın-Heckmann (Münster: Lit, 2007); Bruce Grant, "Brides, Brigands and Fire-Bringers: Notes towards a Historical Ethnography of Pluralism" and Sergei Arutiunov, "Notes on the Making of a World Area," both in Grant and Yalçın-Heckmann, *Caucasus Paradigms.* Charles King attributes the Caucasus's plurality to its varied topography and climate. See Charles King, *The Ghost of Freedom: A History of the Caucasus* (Oxford: Oxford University Press, 2008), 8–9. See also Stepanyan, *Armenians of Baku Province,* 250.

181. Grant and Yalçın-Heckmann, *Caucasus Paradigms,* xi. Emphases are mine.

182. For an earlier discussion of connecting revolutions through the circulation of revolutionaries, material, and ideas, see Houri Berberian, "Connected Revolutions: Armenians and the Russian, Ottoman, and Iranian Revolutions in the Early Twentieth Century," in *"L'ivresse de la liberté": La révolution de 1908 dans l'Empire ottoman,* ed. François Georgeon ["The intoxication of freedom": The 1908 revolution in the Ottoman Empire] (Louvain, Belgium: Peeters, 2012), 487–510; for a Russian translation, see http://hamatext.com/articles /item/71-vzaimosvyazannye-revolyutsii; http://hamatext.com/articles/item/72- vzaimosvyazannye-revolyutsii-2.

183. RUSSIA: Military Report. Trans-Caucasia. (W.O.), 1907, 98–104.

184. RUSSIA: Military Report. Trans-Caucasia. (W.O.), 1907, 86.

185. RUSSIA: Military Report. Trans-Caucasia. (W.O.), 1907, 194.

186. Stepanyan, *Armenians of Baku Province,* 258–59.

187. Bayly, *Birth of the Modern World,* 1. See also McNeill and McNeill, *Human Web.*

188. Osterhammel, *Transformation of the World,* 244–45, 249, 263.

189. Daniel R. Brower, "Urban Revolution in the Late Russian Empire," in Hamm, *City in Late Imperial Russia,* 326.

190. Brower, 327.

191. Brower, 327.

192. Brower, 326, 328, 329, 333. See also Ronald Grigor Suny, "Tiflis: Crucible of Ethnic Politics, 1860–1905," in Hamm, *City in Late Imperial Russia,* 249–81; Audrey Altstadt-Mirhadi, "Baku: The Transformation of a Muslim Town," in Hamm, *City in Late Imperial Russia,* 283–318. Such multiethnic conflict was, of course, not limited to the South Caucasus. See, for example, a discussion of multiethnic Kiev between the 1860s and 1905, by Faith Hillis, in part 2 of *Children of Rus': Right-Bank Ukraine and the Invention of a Russian Nation* (Ithaca, NY: Cornell University Press, 2003).

193. Suny, "Tiflis," 276.

194. Timothy Mitchell, *Carbon Democracy: Political Power in the Age of Oil* (London: Verso, 2011), 33.

195. Suny, "Tiflis," 254, 276; Altstadt-Mirhadi, "Baku: The Transformation of a Muslim Town," 308–9. See also Brower, "Urban Revolution in the Late Russian Empire," 328, 329, 333.

196. Brower, "Urban Revolution in the Late Russian Empire," 333.

197. Brower, 334.

198. Brower, 334.

199. Brower, 329–30, 346; Suny, "Tiflis," 275.

200. Brower, "Urban Revolution in the Late Russian Empire," 349.

201. Frederik Coene, *The Caucasus: An Introduction* (London: Routledge, 2010), 21–22; for the technological component, see also Bernhard Struck, Kate Ferris, and Jacques Revel, "Introduction: Space and Scale in Transnational History," *International History Review* 33, no. 4 (December 2011): 573–84. For telegraph advances and history, see Hugill, *Global Communications since 1844.* For Russian railways, see Westwood, *History of Russian Railways.*

202. Westwood, *History of Russian Railways,* 140.

203. RUSSIA: Military Report. Trans-Caucasia. (W.O.), 1907, 246. For railway itineraries, see also Appendix B, 414–45.

204. RUSSIA: Military Report. Trans-Caucasia. (W.O.), 1907, 247.

205. Westwood, *History of Russian Railways,* 140.

206. Frithjof Benjamin Schenk, "'This New Means of Transportation Will Make Unstable People More Unstable': Railways and Geographical Mobility in Tsarist Russia," in *Russia in Motion: Cultures of Human Mobility since 1850,* ed. John Randolph and Eugene M. Avrutin (Chicago: University of Illinois Press, 2012), 219.

207. Schenk, 220.

208. Schenk, 220.

209. Schenk, 220.

210. Sir G. Barclay to Sir Edward Grey, 16 March 1909, Tehran, Further correspondence respecting the affairs of Persia, British Library (BL): Foreign Office (FO) 26/1, no. 150; Sir A. Nicolson to Sir Edward Grey, received 3 December 1908, Further correspondence respecting the affairs of Persia, BL: FO25/4, no. 299.

211. Sir A. Nicolson to Sir Edward Grey, received 3 December 1908, Further correspondence respecting the affairs of Persia, BL: FO25/4, no. 299.

212. *Tatar* is a term used in the nineteenth century and into the twentieth century to refer to Muslim Turks in the Caucasus. Here, it refers in particular to the people of what today is Azerbaijan. Document 55, Secret police evaluation of ARF activities in Iran during the Constitutional Revolution, in *Armenians and the Okhrana,* 211–21. For the quoted excerpt, see 211. The first part of this document, including the date, is missing, but it most likely dates from 1911 or 1912.

213. Document 55, in *Armenians and the Okhrana,* 212–13.

214. Document 55, in *Armenians and the Okhrana,* 213–14.

215. Schenk, "Railways and Geographical Mobility," 226.

216. Schenk, 224 and 225.

217. Schenk, 226–27.

218. Schenk, 225.

219. Schenk, 225.

220. Marsha Siefert, "'Chingis-Khan with the Telegraph': Communications in the Russian and Ottoman Empires," in *Comparing Empires: Encounters and Transfers in the Long Nineteenth Century,* ed. Jörn Leonhard and Ulrike von Hirschhausen (Oakville, CT: Vandenhoeck & Ruprecht, 2011), 82.

221. Siefert, 80–81, 99. Although Siefert focuses on Harold Adams Innis's argument that the "bias of communication" in empire "shifted from time to space," thus "reducing signaling time" and "controlling space," one could also point to the impact of the telegraph in compressing both time and space (82). See also Harold A. Innis, *The Bias of Communication* (Toronto: University of Toronto Press, 1951) and *Empire and Communications* (Toronto: University of Toronto Press, 1972).

222. Siefert, "'Chingis-Khan with the Telegraph,'" 93.

223. Andre Karbelashvili, "Europe-India Telegraph 'Bridge' via the Caucasus," *Indian Journal of History of Science* 26, no. 3 (1991): 277–78, 281.

224. RUSSIA: Military Report. Trans-Caucasia. (W.O.), 1907, 252–53.

225. Siefert, "'Chingis-Khan with the Telegraph,'" 101. For details about telegraph locations, see RUSSIA: Military Report, 1907, 67–89, 182, 195, 252.

226. Siefert, "'Chingis-Khan with the Telegraph,'" 103–4.

227. Siefert, 102.

228. Siefert, 103. Siefert mentions only Russian and Ottoman telegraph strikes, but the same also applied to Iran. See Cosroe Chaqueri, *Origins of Social Democracy in Modern Iran* (Seattle: University of Washington Press, 2001), 93.

229. Siefert, "'Chingis-Khan with the Telegraph,'" 82, 103–4.

230. Patrick W.J. Stevens, the British Consulate, to the Marquess of Lansdowne, 24 December 1905 (received 6 January 1906), Batumi, TNA: FO

371/119/50, No. 249 [Folios 249, Russia Code 38, File 8, Paper 769]; RUSSIA: Military Report. Trans-Caucasia. (W.O.), 1907, 185. See also Sebuh to Vrezh [Azerbaijan] Central Committee comrades, 11 December 1905, ARF Archives B 293–21.

231. Havakhiants to comrades, n.d. (possibly 1907), ARF Archives, B 49–148.

232. Notice, Sixth Central Committee, 26 October 1905, ARF Archives, B 376–84.

233. Havakhiants to comrades, n.d. (possibly 1907), ARF Archives, B 49–148.

234. For Varna sailboat, see ARF Archives, B 377–4; for Romanian steamships, B 377–1, B 377–5. Regarding the transport of books and newspapers via sailboat and steamship, see B 377–31, B 377–32, B 377–34, 445–4. Folder B 580 is full of references to newspapers and arms being received in Iran but does not specify that they came from the Caucasus. An abundance of information and detail regarding transportation of arms and literature and the traffic of activists may be found in the correspondence, reports, and minutes of ARF bodies and members in the ARF Archives.

235. Kris [Fenerjian] to Khachatur [Malumian], 1 September 1906, Odessa, ARF Archives, B 377–10.

236. Giwlkhandanian, *Bagui derě mer azatagrakan sharzhman měj*, 23. Giwlkhandanian was in the South Caucasus during the Russian Revolution of 1905 and the Armeno-Azeri clashes (1905–6). In 1910 he was arrested in Tiflis and imprisoned until 1912. During the short period of independence, from 1918 to 1920, Giwlkhandanian served the Republic of Armenia as a parliamentarian and later minister. See "January 1, 1951" in *"Hamazgayini" ōrats'oyts'-tarets'oyts' 1951* [Hamazgayin's almanac-annuary 1951], comp. Gaspar Ipekian (Beirut: Hamazgayin, 1956), n.p.

237. RUSSIA: Military Report. Trans-Caucasia. (W.O.), 1907, 148. Afary, *Iranian Constitutional Revolution*, 22.

238. Mitchell, *Carbon Democracy*, 31.

239. Mitchell, 33.

240. Mitchell, 34. See also Beryl Williams, "1905: The View from the Provinces," 48.

241. Mitchell, *Carbon Democracy*, 34–35.

242. Mitchell singles out ultranationalist Black Hundreds for an important role in instigating interethnic violence, as, for example, between Armenians and Azeris. Mitchell, *Carbon Democracy*, 35.

243. Mitchell, *Carbon Democracy*, 36.

244. Mitchell, *Carbon Democracy*, 38, 43.

245. Giwlkhandanian, *Bagui derě*, 23, 25.

246. The Marx reading group had eight to ten workers. See Giwlkhandanian, 27.

247. Workers at the Caspian Co. read mostly Russian literature. See Giwlkhandanian, 24, 25.

248. Report of A.R.F. Vrezh Committee, 25 November 1906, in *Niwt'er,* 4:282. Both the Azerbaijan Central Committee report and an article appearing in *Drōshak* blamed the Russian state for exerting pressure on the Iranian government. See Rostom to Azerbaijan Central Committee, 17 February 1905,

document 46–1, in *Rostom namakani,* 379; Western Bureau to Vrezh [Azerbaijan] Central Committee, n.d., in *Rostom namakani,* 385–86 (original in ARF Archives, B 46–7).

249. Minutes of Azerbaijan Regional Congress, Session 3, 3 February 1906, in *Niwt'er,* 4:240–58. See also "Kusakts'ut'ean gortsunēut'enēn (mi kani p'aster)" [From the party's activity (a few proofs)], *Drōshak* 9 (September 1907): 137.

250. Report of Shahsevan [Ardabil] and Andar [Astara] Regions, 1 February 1906, in *Niwt'er,* 4:295–98.

251. The Social-Democratic paper, *Murch* (Hammer), certainly had subscribers in Iran, as confirmed by special subscription fees. For mention of publications and periodicals crossing the border from the South Caucasus to Iran, see Ali Miransari, "The Constitutional Revolution and Persian Dramatic Works: An Observation on Social Relations Criticism in the Plays of the Constitutional Era," in Chehabi and Martin, *Iran's Constitutional Revolution,* 242; Touraj Atabaki, "Constitutionalists *Sans Frontières:* Iranian Constitutionalism and Its Asian Connections," in Chehabi and Martin, *Iran's Constitutional Revolution,* 345.

252. Zavarian to Mikayel [Varandian] and Hovnan [Davtian], 10/23 October 1908, Geneva, in *Simon Zavarean,* 3:16.

253. Zavarian to Drōshak editorship, 9 September 1908, Istanbul, in *Simon Zavarean,* 3:12 (original in ARF Archives, C 191–38).

254. See, for example, Zavarian to Mikayel [Varandian] and Hovnan [Davtian], 10/23 October 1908, Geneva, in *Simon Zavarean,* 3:16; to Drōshak editorship, 9 September 1908, Istanbul, in *Simon Zavarean,* 3:12 (original in ARF Archives, C 191–38); to Eastern Bureau, 14/27 November 1908, Istanbul, in *Simon Zavarean,* 3:21; to Drōshak editorship, 17/30 February 1909, Istanbul, in *Simon Zavarean,* 3:42–44 (original in ARF Archives, C 193–35). The ARF Archives contain lists of books (B 580–26) and lists of ARF publications (C 96). For other translations, see Nitra [Harutiwn Shahrigian] to comrade, 1 December 1907, ARF Archives B 328–23; Nitra to comrade, 16 December 1907, ARF Archives, B 328–24.

255. Zavarian to Hovnan Davtian, 9/22 December 1908, Istanbul, in *Simon Zavarean,* 3:26–27. Zavarian takes issue with Davtian's dissatisfaction with their publications and mentions a number of already published and to-be-published translations from the Azatut'iwn (Liberty) press, including Ferdinand Lassalle's *On the Essence of Constitutions* (speech delivered in Berlin, April 16, 1862).

256. See, for example, S. Banvorian's translation of a speech by Paul Lafargue made in Paris in 1892 as part of a debate with Edmond Demolins, "Banasirakan"— "Komunizmě ew tntesakan ēvoluts'ia" [Study—Communism and economic evolution], *Hosank'* [Current] 70 (24 February 1907): 2–3; *Hosank'* 72 (27 February 1907): 2–3; *Hosank'* 73 (28 February 1907): 2–3; *Hosank'* 74 (1 March 1907): 2–3; *Hosank'* 78 (8 March 1907): 2–3; *Hosank'* 83 (14 March 1907): 2–3; translation of Eduard Bernstein, "Ěndhanur k'aghak'akan gortsadulě ew heghap'okhakan romantizm" [The general political strike and revolutionary romanticism], *Murch* 6, no. 1 (January 1906): 131–43.

257. See Ter Minassian, "Role of the Armenian Community in the Foundation and Development of the Socialist Movement in the Ottoman Empire and Turkey, 1876–1923," in *Socialism and Nationalism in the Ottoman Empire and Modern Turkey,* ed. Mete Tunçay and Erik J. Zürcher (London: I. B. Tauris, 1994), 135, 200n47. For a list of nine publications from the 1890s by the short-lived anarchist press, see Ter Minassian, 199n4. Of the hundreds of translations published in the early twentieth century, several socialist and anarchist great books or classics stand out either because their works appeared in more than one edition or because at least two if not more of their writings were published. They include but are not limited to the following: Marx and Engels, German Social Democrat Karl Kautsky, French socialist Jean Jaurès, French anarchist Élisée Reclus, German socialist F. Lasalle, French Social Democrat Paul Lafargue, and anarcho-communist Pyotr Kropotkin, as well as Bolshevik Aleksandr Bogdanov, German Social Democrat Ferdinand August Bebel, Menshevik L. (or Julius) Martov, Russian Socialist Revolutionary Victor Chernov, and Belgian socialist Emile Vandervelde. See, for example, ARF Archives B 580–26, C 96–11, C 96–12, C96–13; *Apagay* [Future] (Tiflis) 7 (11 March 1907): 1; *Dzayn* [Voice] (Tiflis) 1 (1 October 1906): 16; *Drōshak* 5 (May 1907): 69; *Vtak* [Brook/Stream] (Tiflis) 22 (15 December 1907): 1; *Vtak* 23 (16 December 1907): 1; *Yerkir* [Country] (Tiflis) 11 (13 October 1906): 4; *Zang* [Bell] (Tiflis) 12 (25 August 1906): 6. (All references to Apagay are to the paper published in Tiflis unless otherwise noted as Istanbul.)

258. For lists of publications, see Ter Minassian, "Role of the Armenian Community," 190–97, nn. 23, 24, 25, 31, 33, 34. Ter Minassian uses Western Armenian instead of classical orthography, so, for example, Italian socialist Camillo Prampolini is spelled as Brambolini and Austrian Englebert Pernerstorfer as Pernersdorfer. See Ter Minassian, 194n33.

259. RUSSIA: Military Report. Trans-Caucasia. (W.O.), 1907, 121.

260. Sixth Central Committee to [Geneva], 1 June 1905, ARF Archives, B 376–7. Russian revolutionary publications and newspapers, however, continued to be requested. See Kris [Fenerjian] to Geneva, [17?] May 1906, ARF Archives, B 377–6; see also Gilan Committee to Western Bureau, 22 January 1905, Rasht, ARF Archives, B 580–4; unknown author to compatriot, 7 February 1905, Tehran, ARF Archives, B 580–7; Rshtuni to Western Bureau, 9 April 1905, Rasht, ARF Archives, B 580–10; [Mozer?] of Shahsavan Group to Western Bureau, 1 July 1905, Ardabil, ARF Archives, B 580–19.

261. A. Atanasian, "Mamuln u girkĕ meznum" [The press and the book among us], *Aniv* [Wheel] (Baku) 5 (10 January 1908): 2.

262. See Shanturian, "Inch' ē kardum Hay banvorĕ?" [What does the Armenian laborer read?], *Aṛawōt* [Morning] (Baku) 2 (26 April 1909): 20–21.

263. "Ch'unenk glkhavorĕ" [We do not have the principal], *Horizon* (Tiflis) 40 (20 February 1910): 1; "Patcharnerits' mekĕ" [One of the reasons], *Horizon* 14 (21 January 1910): 1. Although *Horizon* sprang from an ARF paper, it was not partisan, as its editor, Leo (Arakel Grigori Babakhanian), historian and author of the multivolume *Hayots' patmut'iwn* [History of the Armenians], 1927, and many others explained in "Mi bats'atrut'iwn" [An explanation], *Horizon* 100 (11 May 1910): 1. Leo became quite critical of the ARF's politics. See his *T'iwrk'ahay heghap'okhut'ean gaghap'arabanut'yunĕ* [The ideology of the Turkish-Armenian revolution], vol. 2 (1934; Yerevan: Shaghik, 1994).

264. Bazilevich, *Russian Posts*, 91, 94.

265. Bazilevich, 120, 141.

266. Kirakosian provides the most comprehensive list of periodicals. A. Kirakosian, *Hay parberakan mamuli matenagitut'yun, 1794–1967: hamahavak' ts'ank* [Bibliography of Armenian periodical press, 1794–1967: compiled catalog] (Yerevan: Hanrapetakan Gradaran, 1970), 530–31, 544. Levonian's numbers are lower, totaling fifty-seven. However, unlike Kirakosian, Levonian's information indicates which periodicals may have been revolutionary or political. See Garegin Levonian, *Hayots' parberakan mamulě, 1794–1934* [The Armenian periodical press, 1794–1934] (Yerevan: Melkonian Foundation, 1934). See also Ter Minassian, "Role of the Armenian Community," 121–34, 190n23, 191–94n31; 194–97n33, 194–97; for Social Democratic publications, see Ter Minassian, 200–201n47.

267. Kirakosian, *Hay parberakan mamuli matenagitut'yun*, 546, 548–49. For print censorship, see Ipek K. Yosmaoğlu, "Chasing the Printed Word: Press Censorship in the Ottoman Empire, 1876–1913," *Journal of Turkish Studies* 27, no. 1/2 (2003): 15–49.

268. Nicole Howard, *The Book: The Life Story of a Technology* (Baltimore, MD: Johns Hopkins University Press, 2009), 113, cited in Sebouh D. Aslanian, "Port Cities and Printers: Reflections on Early Modern Global Armenian Print Culture," *Book History* 17, no. 1 (2014): 51–93.

269. Wenzlhuemer, *Connecting the Nineteenth-Century World*, 90; Bayly, *Birth of the Modern World*, 461–62.

270. Bayly, *Birth of the Modern World*, 19, 20.

271. Brower, "Urban Revolution in the Late Russian Empire," 342.

272. Brower, 342.

273. Brower, 342; Altstadt-Mirhadi, "Baku: The Transformation of a Muslim Town," 303. See also Bayly, *Birth of the Modern World*, 19, 20.

274. For subscription numbers, see *Murch* (Tiflis) 4, no. 10 (10 October 1904): 158. Specifists—a "political minority in a national minority," as Ter Minassian calls them—had seven newspapers in Baku and Tiflis between the years 1904 and 1912 and more than a dozen brochures and publications, including translations of Kautsky and Plekhanov, in 1906 alone, interested mostly in the national question and syndicalism, "confirm[ing] the prestige of German social democracy and the triad of Bebel-Liebknecht-Kautsky" (96). Anaïde Ter Minassian, "Aux origines du marxisme arménien: Les spécifistes" [At the origins of Armenian Marxism: The Specifists], *Cahiers du monde russe et soviétique* 19, no. 1–2 (January–June 1978): 67–117. See also Ter Minassian, "Role of the Armenian," 133, 134.

275. François Georgeon, "Lire et écrire à la fin de l'Empire ottoman: Quelques remarques introductives" [Reading and writing at the end of the Ottoman Empire: Some introductory remarks], *Revue du monde musulman et de la Méditerranée* 75–76 (1995): 169–79 (178); translated by Khuri-Makdisi in *Eastern Mediterranean*, 36–37.

276. Ami Ayalon, *Reading Palestine: Printing and Literacy, 1900–1948* (Austin: University of Texas Press, 2004), 139.

277. Ayalon, 42.

278. Ayalon, 139.

279. Ayalon, 145.

280. Parker, *Global Crisis*, xxxi, 564; Wenzlhuemer, *Connecting the Nineteenth Century*, 461–62.

281. Khuri-Makdisi, *Eastern Mediterranean*, 32. Anderson makes a similar point. See Anderson, *Under Three Flags*, 2.

282. Michael F. Hamm, "Continuity and Change in Late Imperial Kiev," in Hamm, *City in Late Imperial Russia*, 109.

283. T. N. Harper, "Empire, Diaspora and the Language of Globalism, 1850–1914," in *Globalization in World History*, ed. A. G. Hopkins (London: Pimlico, 2002), 156–57. Bayly makes a similar argument. See, for example, Bayly, *Birth of the Modern World*, 462.

284. Brower, "Urban Revolution in the Late Russian Empire," 344.

285. Giwlkhandanian, *Bagui derě*, 27–29, 64. Examples include Kristapor Mikayelian, Matsun Khecho, and Nikol Duman.

286. See, for example, Report of Avarayr [Khoy] Region, 1 February 1906, in *Niwt'er*, 4:274.

287. Report of Avarayr [Khoy] Region, in *Niwt'er*, 4:53, 56.

288. Report on central arms factory of Vrezh [Tabriz] presented to Fourth General Congress. This piece is undated, unsigned, and unsealed but was most probably prepared in 1906 by the Azerbaijan Central Committee as it was found among the committee's papers. It is a brief history of the factory from 1891 to 1906 and includes a list of gunsmiths, their apprentices, and the years they worked. "A. R. Federation Vrezh 'Khariskh' workshop," in *Niwt'er*, 4:284–87. For the arms "factory," see Malkhas [Artashes Hovsepian], *Aprumner* [Life experiences] (Boston: Hayrenik', 1931), 141, 331. Rostom writes from the Caucasus about being in negotiations with someone specializing in purchasing arms and transferring them to Iran. See Rostom/Western Bureau to Vrezh [Azerbaijan] Central Committee, 1 October 1904, in *Rostom namakani*, 339.

289. *K'ristap'or Mik'ayeleani namaknerě*, 407 (original in ARF Archives, B 43–60). Dr. Waldemar Belck (1862–1932) was a German chemist and amateur archaeologist who conducted archaeological expeditions in the Caucasus and Anatolia with Carl Lehmann-Haupt (1861–1938), a German professor and historian of the ancient Near East who published two studies of Armenia. See "Alexander Ruhe: Frankfurts Schliemann; der self-made Archäologe Belck. Okt. 2011," www.fws-ffm.de/Belck.htm; "Carl Ferdinand Friedrich Lehmann-Haupt," Universität Innsbruck, https://www.uibk.ac.at/alte-geschichte-orient/institutsgeschichte/altorientalistik/carl_ferdinand_friedrich.html.

290. *K'ristap'or Mik'ayeleani namaknerě*, 405.

291. *K'ristap'or Mik'ayeleani namaknerě*, 406.

292. *K'ristap'or Mik'ayeleani namaknerě*, 406.

293. *K'ristap'or Mik'ayeleani namaknerě*, 406, 407. A verst is a Russian measurement; one verst is the equivalent of a little over a kilometer.

294. For a comprehensive study of Armenian participation in the Iranian Constitutional Revolution, see Berberian, *Armenians and the Iranian Constitutional Revolution*.

295. Rostom, although writing in Armenian, uses the French *chlorate de potasse*.

296. Rostom to Samson Tadeosian, undated, in *Rostom namakani*, 363 (original in ARF Archives, B 15–6). Because the letter is undated, it is unclear whether Rostom was in Tiflis or Geneva at the time. In another letter, Rostom requests that comrades send him a book on pyrotechnics that he had bought while in Geneva, adding, "I have fallen in love with rockets." Rostom to Western Bureau, 14 February 1906, Kars, in *Rostom namakani*, 411 (original in ARF Archives 274–16).

297. *Rostom namakani*, 363, 364.

298. Giwlkhandanian, *Bagui derĕ*, 141. See also Rostom to Samson Tadeosian, undated, in *Rostom namakani*, 363 (original in ARF Archives, B 15–6); Sixth Central Committee to [Geneva], Batumi, 8 February 1906, ARF Archives, B 377–30; Sixth Central Committee to *Drōshak* editorship, 8 April 1906, B 377–31; Sixth Central Committee to [Geneva comrades], Navahangist [Batumi], 17 May 1906, B 377–32; Sixth Central Committee to *Drōshak* editorship, 28 June 1906, ARF Archives, B 377–34.

299. Stepan to comrades, 24 February 1906, ARF Archives, B 445–6; [author unknown] to Western Bureau, New Julfa, 17 June 1905, ARF Archives, B 580–15. Georgians played a similar role in circulating arms and ammunition. See, for example, Gocheleishvili, "Introducing Georgian Sources," 65.

300. Giwlkhandanian, *Bagui derĕ*, 148.

301. Giwlkhandanian, 153.

302. See H. G. Inchikyan, ed., *Merdzavor ew Mijin Arewelk'i yerkrner ew zhoghovurdner* [Countries and peoples of the Near and Middle East], vol. 8, *Iran* (Yerevan: Haykakan SSH Gitut'yunneri Akademia, 1975), 244. See also Dikran Mesrob Kaligian, *Armenian Organization and Ideology under Ottoman Rule, 1908–1914*, rev. ed. (Piscataway, NJ: Transaction Publishers, 2011), 130.

303. Nalbandian, *Armenian Revolutionary Movement*, 173.

304. See, for example, Malkhas, *Aprumner*. Malkhas, a member of the ARF, participated in the traffic of arms and men through Iran. See also Kitur, *Patmut'iwn* 1:203, 208, 209.

305. Hassan Hakimian, "Wage Labor and Migration: Persian Workers in Southern Russia, 1880–1914," *International Journal of Middle East Studies* 17, no. 4 (November 1985): 444, 454, 456–57.

306. Chaqueri, *Social Democracy in Iran*, 80.

307. Chaqueri, 84.

308. Chaqueri, 81, 82; Hakimian, "Wage Labor and Migration," table 2, 447.

309. Chaqueri, *Social Democracy in Iran*, 81, 82.

310. See, for example, Audrey Altstadt, *The Azerbaijani Turks: Power and Identity under Russian Rule* (Stanford, CA: Hoover Institution Press, 1992), 32, 37; Hakimian, "Wage Labor and Migration," 445–47, 449. See also Bagratuni, "Namak Bagvits'" [Letter from Baku], 16 July 1908, *Hnch'ak* [Bell] (Paris) 6–7 (June–July 1908): 61–63.

311. Iago Gocheleishvili, "Georgian Sources: Sergo Gamdlishvili's memoirs of the Gilan Resistance," in Stephanie Cronin, ed., *Iranian-Russian Encounters: Empires and Revolutions since 1800* (London: Routledge, 2013), 208.

312. Chaqueri, *Social Democracy in Iran,* 87, 90. Gocheleishvili, "Georgian Sources," 208. See also Gocheleishvili, "Introducing Georgian Sources," 45–66; Afary, *Iranian Constitutional Revolution,* 22.

313. Chaqueri, *Social Democracy in Iran,* 95–96.

314. Chaqueri, 117, 119. See also Afary, *Iranian Constitutional Revolution,* 81–82; Sohrab Yazdani, "The Question of the Iranian *Ijtima'iyun-i Amiyun* Party," in *Iranian-Russian Encounters: Empires and Revolutions since 1800,* ed. Stephanie Cronin (London: Routledge, 2013), 189–206. Unlike Chaqueri, Yazdani concludes that although the party leaders "in the Caucasus and/or in Iran, studied different types of Russian party organization and adopted those forms which they considered most suitable for Iranian conditions," the party was "an Iranian organization with its own internal dynamism. As such, it would be preferable to study this first Iranian political party, with its leftist tendencies, in accord with Iranian sociopolitical and cultural conditions, and not merely as a by-product of struggles taking place beyond the country's borders." Yazdani, 200, 203.

315. Chaqueri, *Social Democracy in Iran,* 148, 154, 173, 181, 188.

316. Chaqueri, 192.

317. Gocheleishvili, "Georgian Sources," 211.

318. Gocheleishvili, "Introducing Georgian Sources," 58.

319. "Asiayi zart'ōnk'ĕ ew Parskakan heghap'okhut'iwnĕ" [Asia's revival and the Persian revolution], *Nor Hosank'* [New Current] (Tiflis) 6 (6 June 1909): 47–48; translated from the original French and printed in *L'Humanité,* founded in 1904, by Jean Jaurès.

320. Scott Ury, *Barricades and Banners: The Revolution of 1905 and the Transformation of Warsaw Jewry* (Stanford, CA: Stanford University Press, 2012), 90, 93.

321. Florian Riedler's chapter may be a step in the right direction. See Riedler, "Armenian Labour Migration to Istanbul and the Migration Crisis of the 1890s," in *The City in the Ottoman Empire: Migration and the Making of Urban Modernity,* ed. Ulrike Freitag et al. (London: Routledge, 2011), 167.

322. Ury, *Barricades and Banners,* 3–4.

CHAPTER 3. THE CIRCULATION OF IDEAS AND IDEOLOGIES

1. "T'ogh shoghshoghun tsiatsan/Dzez shaghkapē, hēk' azger/Ays 'nshanov hashtut'ean'/T'ogh darman en dzer vērker." *Khat'abala* 43 (18 October 1908): 489. The word *khat'abala* has an interesting etymology, with origins in Arabic. *Khata'* [خطا] means error, while *bala'* [بلا] means tribulation or trouble. The cartoonist/illustrator is D. Rotter, a "descendant of ethnic Germans living in the Caucasus" and regular contributor to the influential Azeri Turkish-language satirical weekly *Molla Nasreddin.* See Fuad Pepinov, "The Role of Political Caricatures in the Cultural Development of the Meshketian (Ahiska) Turks," in *Islamic Art and Architecture in the European Periphery: Crimea, Caucasus, and the Volga-Ural Region,* ed. Barbara Kellner-Heinekele, Joachim Gierlichs, and Brigitte Heuer (Wiesbaden: Harrassowitz Verlag, 2009), 161. Regarding *Molla*

Nasreddin (Tiflis, 1906–31), see Hasan Javadi, "Molla Nasreddin ii. Political and Social Weekly," *Iranica Online,* www.iranicaonline.org/articles/molla-nasreddin-ii-political-and-social-weekly.

2. *The New Oxford Annotated Bible with the Apocrypha,* 3rd ed. (Oxford: Oxford University Press, 2001), 22nn8–17.

3. See Nikki R. Keddie, *Modern Iran: Roots and Results of Revolution* (New Haven: Yale University Press, 2003), 67.

4. Sohrabi, *Revolution and Constitutionalism,* 19–20.

5. Sohrabi, 72.

6. For a study on the perspective of the Armenian-language newspaper *Zhamanak,* in Istanbul, on the Ottoman Constitution after the Young Turk revolution of 1908, see Aylin Koçunyan, "Historicizing the 1908 Revolution: The Case of *Jamanak,*" in *The Young Turk Revolution and the Ottoman Empire: The Aftermath of 1908,* ed. Noémi Lévy and François Georgeon (London: I. B. Tauris, 2017), 236–64.

7. S. Sapah-Giwlian, "Feuilleton: Midhatean sahmanadrut'ean aṛt'iw" [Feuilleton: On the occasion of the Midhatean constitution], *Apagay* 41 (27 April 1907): 1–3. *Apagay* was an SDHP paper. "The Turkish constitution is one of those beautiful examples of a curtain only, under which hides a murderous reality generally very far from constitutions." See V., "Osmanean sahmanadrut'iwnĕ" [The Ottoman constitution], *Aniv* 21 (27 July 1908): 1–4 (4).

8. H. Kh., "Yeritasard T'iwrkia ew yeritasard Hayastan—antagonizmĕ" [Young Turkey and young Armenia: The antagonism], *Hnch'ak* 2 (1 May 1902): 11–14.

9. Kévorkian, *Armenian Genocide,* 29–33, 35. For a rich biography of Ahmed Rıza, see Erdal Kaynar, "Ahmed Rıza (1858–1930): Histoire d'un vieux Jeune Turc" [Ahmed Rıza (1858–1930): History of an old Young Turk] (PhD diss., École des Hautes Études en Sciences Sociales, Paris, 2012). Diran Kelekian was a journalist and editor-in-chief of the Istanbul daily newspaper *Sabah* (Morning) from 1908 to 1915, the year he became one of the Genocide's first victims along with Hampartsum Boyajian. Boyajian (whose pseudonym was Medzn Murad) was a high-ranking member of the SDHP who served several years in prison and in exile for his part in the Sasun rebellion of 1894 before becoming an Ottoman parliament deputy from 1908 to 1915. Sapah-Giwlian took on the pseudonym Petros Kiwreghian in Erzurum province and continued to use it in Paris, London, Ruschuk, and other places. In fact, his French university degree is in that name. See Beruz Sapah-Giwlian, *Kensagrut'iwn Step'an Sapah-Giwleani* [Biography of Stepan Sapah-Giwlean] (Union City, NJ: Elmas-Satin, 1936), 40, 45. He served as editor of many SDHP papers, including *Yeritasard Hayastan* (Young Armenia), *Hnch'ak* (Bell), *Veratsnund* (Revival), and *Nor Ashkharh* (New World), and was a prolific translator of European socialist tracts by Marx, Kautsky, Lasalle, and others. *Kensagrut'iwn Step'an Sapah-Giwleani* is an intimate biography written by his wife. The collection also includes letters between the couple, who spent many years apart because of his activism and travels throughout the Ottoman Empire, Europe, and North America, which often left her to raise their children alone. His letters portray a self-reflective man aware of his own and his partner's sacrifices, oscillating between pride and regret. For example, in a letter to Beruz, he writes (probably

in 1914), "If it were not for you, I would have died as a common teacher; but you bore your *cross* and gave me the means to fulfil my responsibility toward my *Nation, Party* and *Fatherland* . . . May you live long, my bala . . . . You have not just been a spouse to me, but friend; for that reason my burden appears light" (142, 143). And in 1925, complaining of comrades who seem to have abandoned him and his family, he writes, "I sacrificed everything for whom and for what? Why did I come and reach this condition? There is an environment that wants to choke me with poison . . . Where are those comrades?" (181). *Bala* means "child" but may be used, as here, as a term of endearment. One of the other fascinating aspects of the biography is the way in which the ideological split in the SDHP resulted in intraparty conflict and violence, including assassination attempts on Sapah-Giwlian's and others' lives, as related by Beruz Sapah-Giwlian.

10. Kévorkian, *Armenian Genocide*, 44.

11. S. Sapah-Giwlian, "Menk' ew mer k'nnadatnerě" [We and our critics], *Hnch'ak* 9–10 (September–October 1906): 91–95.

12. Ibrahim Yalimov, "The Bulgarian Community and the Development of the Socialist Movement in the Ottoman Empire during the Period 1876–1923," in Tunçay and Zürcher, *Socialism and Nationalism in the Ottoman Empire, 1876–1923*, 100.

13. "T'urk' brnapetut'iwně ew 'Yeritasard T'urk'erě'" [Turkish despotism and the 'Young Turks'"], *Hnch'ak* 1 (January 1908): 2–10. See Kévorkian, part 1, chap. 1, in *Armenian Genocide*.

14. Kévorkian also discusses Sapah-Giwlian's many encounters with Young Turks in Paris. See *Armenian Genocide*, 12.

15. S. Sapah-Giwlian, "Midhatean sahmanadrut'ean art'iw" [On the occasion of the Midhatean constitution], *Hnch'ak* 3–4 (March–April 1907): 26–36 (26); S. Sapah-Giwlian, "Feuilleton: Midhatean sahmanadrut'ean art'iw," 2–3; Stepan Sapah-Giwlian's other contributions: *Yeritasard T'urk'ia* [Young Turkey] (1908), a criticism of the Young Turks and their ideology; *Sots'ializm ew hayrenik'* [Socialism and fatherland] (1916); *Yewropayi k'aghak'akan drut'iwně Berlini dashnagrut'iwnits' hetoy* [Europe's political situation after the Berlin treaty (1898).

16. Sapah-Giwlian, "Feuilleton: Midhatean sahmanadrut'ean art'iw," 2–3. See also T. [Tigran] Zaven, "Mi khabēk zhoghovrdin" [Do not fool the people], part 2, *Yerkri Dzayně* [The voice of country] (Tiflis) 16 (11 May 1908): 1–2, which attacks Sapah-Giwlian's views as nationalist at the same time that it calls the Midhatean constitution "false." Sapah-Giwlian's "children of Fatherland" here may be a reference specifically to Sabaheddin's paper *Terakki*'s common refrain of unity with non-Muslims—for example, in 1907 *Terakki* printed, "The Muslims and Christians, who are the *children of the same fatherland*, should live in a harmony that would be appropriate for the children of the same fatherland"—although, as we shall see in the next chapter, this was part of the larger discourse on Ottomanism (emphasis mine). Cited in Hanioğlu, *Preparation for a Revolution*, 93.

17. Kévorkian, *Armenian Genocide*, 35. For a discussion of the Islamic discourse on constitutionalism and the Young Ottomans, see Sohrabi, *Revolution and Constitutionalism*, chap. 1.

18. A lead article in the *Hnch'ak* organ, "Sahmandrakan T'iwrk'ia ew hay-kakan khndirĕ" [Constitutional Turkey and the Armenian issue], declares that one cannot speak of a "true constitution" until articles 7 and 9 are completely eliminated. See *Hnch'ak* 6–7 (June–July 1908): 49–50. For Sapah-Giwlian, articles 7 and 9 leave no doubt that the constitution is a "contract" and a "top-down command" to operate according to the interests of the sultan, his supporters, and ruling forces. See "Noragoyn T'iwrk'ian," *Hnch'ak* 8–12 (August–December 1908): 65–66 (66). Sapah-Giwlian, "Feuilleton: Midhatean sahmanadrut'ean art'iw," 2–3. See also S. Sapah-Giwlian, "Feuilleton: Mid-hatean sahmanadrut'ean art'iw," *Apagay* 43 (29 April 1907): 2–4; S. Sapah-Giwlian, "Midhatean sahmanadrut'ean art'iw," *Hnch'ak* 3–4 (March–April 1907): 26–36; S. Sapah-Giwlian, "Midhatean sahmanadrut'ean art'iw," *Hnch'ak* 6–7 (June–July 1908): 49–50. The other objectionable articles for Sapah-Giwlian and SDHP more generally were articles 3, 4, 5, 11, 27, and 87.

ART. 3: The Ottoman sovereignty which is united in the person of the sovereign of the supreme Kalifat of Islam belongs to the eldest of the princes of the dynasty of Osman conformably to the rules established *ab antiquo*.

ART. 4: His majesty the Sultan is by the title of the Kalif the protector of the Mussul-man religion. He is the sovereign and the Padishah' of all the Ottomans.

ART. 5: His majesty the Sultan is irresponsible: [sic] His person is sacred.

ART. 7: His majesty the Sultan counts among the number of his sovereign rights the following prerogatives: He names and revokes the Ministers; he confers grades functions *[sic]* and the insignia of his orders; gives investiture to the chiefs of the privileged provinces in the forms determined by the privileges granted to them; he coins money; his name is pronounced in the mosques during the public prayers; he concludes treaties with the powers; he declares war; he makes peace; he commands the armies by sea and land; he orders military movements; he causes to be executed the dispositions of the Sheri (sacred law) and the laws; he makes the regulations for public administration; he remits or commutes penalties imposed by the criminal tribu-nals; he convokes or prorogues the general assembly and he dissolves, if he deem necessary, the chamber of deputies on condition of proceeding to the reelection of the deputies.

ART. 9: All the Ottomans enjoy individual liberty on condition of not attacking the liberty of other people.

ART. 11: Islamism is the religion of the State. While maintaining this principle the state protects the free exercise of all the religions recognized in the Empire and accords the religious privileges granted to the different communities on condition that no offence is committed against public order or good morals.

ART. 27: His majesty the Sultan invests with the charge of Grand Vizier and that of Sheik-ul-Islam the persons whom his high confidence thinks proper to be called. The nomination of the other Ministers takes place by imperial Irade (order).

ART. 87: Affairs concerning the *Sheri* [Şeriat] shall be judged by the tribunals of the *Sheri* [Şeriat]. The judgment of civil affairs belongs to the civil tribunals.

See "The Ottoman Constitution, Promulgated the 7th Zilbridje, 1293 (11/23 December 1876)," *American Journal of International Law* 2, no. 4, Supplement: Official Documents (October 1908): 367–87, www.jstor.org/stable/2212668?seq = 1#page_scan_tab_contents. Armenian translations of the constitution appeared in the pages of the contemporary press as well as Tigran Zaven, *T'iwrk' sahmadrut'iwně ew Yeritasard T'iwrk' kusakts'utiwnner* [The Turkish constitution and Young Turk parties] (Tiflis: Epokha, 1908), 9–38.

19. "Hnch'akean Kusakts'ut'iwn ew ir dirk'ě: B. Sapah-Giwleani hraparakakhosut'iwně" [Hnch'akean party and its position: Mr. Sapah-Giwlean's speech], *Surhandak* [Messenger] (Istanbul) 79 (2/15 September 1908): 1. The article, which is reporting on a speech given by Sapah-Giwlian, points out that he received long and enthusiastic applause after this statement. The story of George Washington's chair is slightly misrepresented in the article, but the substance is clear. The chair's name derives from "Franklin's famous 1787 observation that the gilded half sun on the chair's top was analogous to the new nation under the Constitution in that both were 'rising' to greatness." "The 'Rising Sun' Chair," Independence National Historical Park collections, accessed 23 April 2018, https://indecollections.wordpress.com/2012/09/18/the-rising-sun-chair.

20. "Hnch'akean Kusakts'ut'iwn ew ir dirk'ě," 1.

21. Tigran Zaven served as editor of *Surhandak* from October to December 1908. The paper became visibly more leftist once he took over and shut down almost immediately after his departure as editor. See Zaven's commentary in his *T'iwrk' Sahmadrut'iwně*, 39–40.

22. Yesalem, "Hakaheghap'okhut'iwně, Yeritasard T'urk'erě u gortsavor dasakargě" [The revolution, the Young Turks, and the working class], *Nor Hosank'* 2 (25 April 1909): 9.

23. Christian Rakovsky, "The Turkish Revolution," *Le Socialisme* (Paris), 37 (1 August 1908): 1–2, www.marxists.org/archive/rakovsky/1908/08/01.htm.

24. "Parskastani sharzhumnerě" [Persia's movements], *Apagay* 21 (29 March 1907): 2–3. *Apagay* ran a series of articles on different aspects of Iran, including the constitutional movement as well as letters from Iran, in the first half of 1907. Regarding the impact of the Japanese victory and the Russian Revolution in Iran, see *Apagay* 24 (1 April 1907): 6; regarding the importance of constitution to the Iranian people, see V. Vrezhuni, "Mer dirk'ě," *Hnch'ak* 12 (December 1904): 105–7. The SDHP paper *Apagay,* like many of the contemporary Armenian-language Caucasian periodicals of all sorts—ARF, Socialist Revolutionary, Social Democratic, and others—regularly covered the Iranian constitutional movement, especially during 1907 in *Apagay*'s case.

25. Sohrabi, *Revolution and Constitutionalism*, 25.

26. "Mer irakan drut'iwnits'—datarannerě" [From our real situation—the courts], *Aṟawōt* [Morning] (Tabriz) 13 (15 November 1909): 2. (All references to *Aṟawōt* are to the paper published in Tabriz unless otherwise noted as Baku.)

27. "Mer irakan drut'iwnits'—datarannerě."

28. "Mejlisě Mebhussan ew Hay patgamavorě" [The Chamber of Deputies and the Armenian delegate], *Aṟawōt* 15 (29 November 1909): 1. See also "Korstaber payk'ar: Ts'eghayin khndir" [Fatal struggle: An ethnic issue], *Aṟawōt* 23 (24 January 1910): 1; "Motenank' irar" [Let us get close], *Zang* (Tabriz) 7 (27

May 1910): 1–2; "Shabte-Shabat: 'havasarut'iwnĕ' orēnk'i araj" [From week to week: "Equality" before the law], *Aṟawōt* 27 (21 February 1910): 1; and "Usumnasirenk' mer yerkirĕ" [Let us study our country] *Aṟawōt* 45 (27 June 1910): 1.

29. From the SDHP press: "Azatut'ean grohĕ" [The freedom mob], *Zang* (Tiflis) 19 (3 September 1906): 1; untitled lead article, *Apagay* 56 (16 May 1907): 1. See also "Ch'inakan sahmanadrut'iwnĕ" [The Chinese constitution], *Gorts* (Tiflis) 61 (21 November 1908): 3. From the ARF press: "Shahnshahneri ashkharhĕ" [The world of the Shahenshahs], *Alik'* 78 (2 August 1906): 1; "Voroshumner" [Decisions (of the Fifth General Congress)], *Drōshak* 10–11 (October–November 1909): 132–39; Arevelk'ts'in [The Easterner], "Patmakan metsamets dēpk'er: Arevelk'i geragoyn kṟivĕ" [Great historical events: The East's sublime fight], *Zhamanak* (Istanbul) 223 (9/22 July 1909): 1.

30. For a thorough treatment of these reasons, see Berberian, *Armenians and the Iranian Constitutional Revolution,* chap. 3.

31. "Ch'orrord Ēndhanur Zhoghovi voroshumner: Parskastani shrjanum" [Decisions of the Fourth General Congress: Persian Region], in *Niwt'er,* 3:309–10; File 583, document 41, ARF Archives.

32. "Ch'orrord Ēndhanur Zhoghovi voroshumner," in *Niwt'er;* Rostom to Western Bureau, 10 January 1908, File 1729, Document 2, ARF Archives.

33. *Bashibozuk (başıbozuk* in Turkish) literally means "broken head" and referred to irregular troops in the Ottoman army, who were noted for their disorderly behavior.

34. "Niwt'er apagay patmut'yan" [Material for future history], 1908, Archives of the Catholicosate, Folder 237c, Document 257/1, Mesrop Mashtots Institute of Ancient Manuscripts (Matenadaran). No pagination in document; page numbers are my own. For the above references, see especially 34, 35, 76, 82, 109, 110, 125, 171, 179, 134, 139. Although the journal bears no author's name, it may be the work of someone at the Armenian Prelacy in Tabriz or at least familiar with its workings because the author seems informed about the prelacy's correspondence. See "Niwt'er apagay patmut'yan," Archives of the Catholicosate, 161.

35. For discussions of Yeprem Khan, see A[ndre] Amurian, *Dashnakts'ut'iwn, Yep'rem, parskakan sahmanadrut'iwn, H.H.D. kendronakan arkhiv* [A.R. Federation, Yep'rem, Persian constitution, A.R.F. central archive], 2 vols. (Tehran: Alik', 1976–79); Amurian, ed., *Heghap'okhakan Yep'remi vodisakanĕ* [Revolutionary Yep'rem's odyssey] (Tehran: Alik', 1972); Amurian, ed., *Hamasah-e Yeprem* [The epic of Yeprem] (Tehran: Javid, 1976); Ra'in Ism'il, *Yeprem Khan-e Sardar* [Commander Yeprem Khan] (Tehran: Zarin, 1971); Elmar, *Yep'rem*; Farro [Hovsep Hovhannisian], comp., "Yep'remi gortsunēut'iwnĕ Parskastanum (Grishayi husherĕ)" [Yep'rem's activity in Persia (Grisha's memoirs)], *Hayrenik' Amsagir,* 3 (1924–25); Hayrik, comp., "Heghap'okhakan banaki arshavĕ Tehrani vray ew Yep'remi gndi derĕ (khmbapeti husherĕ)" [March of the revolutionary army on Tehran and the role of Yep'rem's regiment (Memoirs of the commander)], *Hayrenik' Amsagir* 3 (1925): 26–38; Yeprem Khan, *Az Anzali ta Tehran: Yaddashtha-ye khususi-ye Yeprem Khan mojahed-e armani* [From Anzali to Tehran: Personal memoirs of Yeprem Khan, Armenian

mojahed], trans. Narus (Tehran: Babak, 1977); *Encyclopædia Iranica,* s.v. "Ep'rem Khan," by Aram Arkun, 8 (1998), Fasc. 5, 513–15, www.iranicaonline .org/articles/eprem-khan.

36. Rostom to Western Bureau, 10 January 1908, file 1729, document 2, ARF Archives. For the French agreement in French, see file 583, document 41, ARF Archives. See also Berberian, *Armenians and the Iranian Constitutional Revolution,* 120–27; Berberian, "Armenian and Iranian Collaboration in the Constitutional Revolution: The Agreement between Dashnakists and Majles Delegates, 1908," annotated translation with introduction, in *The Modern Middle East: A Sourcebook for History,* ed. Camron Michael Amin, Benjamin C. Fortna, and Elizabeth B. Frierson (Oxford: Oxford University Press, 2006), 339–43.

37. See the report by the Armenian delegation: "Osmants'i azatakanneri hamazhoghově" [The Congress of the Ottoman liberals], *Drōshak* 2/12 (February 1902): 23–6; "Dashnakts'ut'ean Ch'orrord Ěndhanur Zhoghovi voroshumnerě" [Decisions of the Fourth General Congress], in *Niwt'er,* 3:305. See also "H.H. Dashnakts'ut'ean Ch'orrord Ěndhanur Zhoghovi voroshumnerě" [Decisions of the ARF's Fourth General Congress], *Drōshak* 5 (May 1907): 72.

38. Kévorkian, *Armenian Genocide,* 43.

39."Haytararagir: Osmanean kaysrut'ean ěnddimatir tarreru congrein, gumaruats Yevropayi měj" [Declaration: To the congress of the Ottoman Empire's oppositional elements, convened in Europe], *Drōshak* 1 (January 1908): 2–4. For a jointly planned assassination, see "Gortsi propagandě" [The propaganda of deed], *Drōshak* 10 (October 1907): 141–43. "Ch'orrord Ěndhanur Zhoghovi voroshumner: hamerashkhut'iwn T'iwrk'ioy aylatar ts'egheru het (13)" [Decisions of the Fourth General Congress: Solidarity with Turkey's dissimilar ethnicities], in *Niwt'er,* 3:305. See also "Ch'orrord Ěndhanur Zhoghovi voroshumner" [Decisions of the ARF's Fourth General Congress], 72; Hanioğlu, *Preparation for a Revolution,* 205.

40. Sapah-Giwlian, "Feuilleton: Midhatean sahmanadrut'ean aṛt'iw," *Apagay* 41 (27 April 1907), 1–3 (2). For the Adana massacres, see Der Matossian, "From Bloodless Revolution to Bloody Counterrevolution," 1. Regarding relations between the ARF and Young Turks after the revolution, see Der Matossian, *Shattered Dreams of Revolution;* Kaligian, *Armenian Organization and Ideology;* Kévorkian, *Armenian Genocide;* Gaïdz Minassian, "Les relations entre le Comité Union et Progrès et la Fédération Révolutionnaire Arménienne à la veille de la Première Guerre mondiale d'après les sources arméniennes" [Relations between the Committee of Union and Progress and the Armenian Revolutionary Federation on the eve of the first world war according to Armenian sources], *Revue d'histoire arménienne contemporaine* 1 (1995): 45–99. For a firsthand account, see Papazian, *Im husherě,* vol. 2, parts 1–3.

41. For a detailed discussion, see Kaligian, *Armenian Organization and Ideology,* especially chap. 2.

42. "T'urk'ahay keank': Haykakan harts'ě ew Yeritasard T'urk'erě" [Turkish-Armenian life: The Armenian question and the Young Turks], part 1, *Haṛaj* (Tiflis) 22 (11 February 1906): 3–4; "T'urk'ahay keank': Haykakan harts'ě ew Yeritasard T'urk'erě" [Turkish-Armenian life: The Armenian question and the

Young Turks], part 3, *Haṛaj* 27 (18 February 1906): 3; "Haykakan harts'ĕ ew Yeritasard T'urk'erĕ" [The Armenian question and the Young Turks], part 4, *Haṛaj* 31 (23 February 1906): 3–4. Only part 6, in *Haṛaj* 44 (10 March 1906), bears the name of an author, A. Sis.

43. See also "Nor metodĕ" [The new method], part 2, *Yerkir* 10 (12 October 1906): 1.

44. "Voroshumner," 132–39.

45. See "T'urk'ahay keank': Pitlizi T'rk'akan sharzhumĕ" [Turkish-Armenian life: Bitlis's Turkish movement], *Arōr* (Tiflis) 6 (8 September 1907): 3; "Nshanner yerevum en" [Signs are appearing], part 1, *Haṛaj* 55 (24 March 1906): 1; "Nshanner yerevum en" [Signs are appearing], part 2, *Haṛaj* 57 (26 March 1906): 1; "Mkhitarakan nshanner" [Consoling signs], *Kovkasi Aṛawōt* (Tiflis), 32 (27 October 1907): 1; "Huzumner T'urk'iayum" [Agitations from Turkey], *Yerkir* 16 (18 October 1906): 1; "Artak'in tesut'iwn: Osmants'ineri kochĕ" [External view: The call of the Ottomans], *Yerkir* 20 (24 October 1906): 4. The last of these publications quotes from a brochure that circulated during the Erzurum revolts exhorting all peoples of Turkey to unite: "our fatherland's freedom and happiness is tied to mutual aid and unity of all Muslim and Christian nations," and if we stand up to demand liberty and justice, "we will find Armenians as comrades and support." *Vtak* also reports on the march of two hundred women in Erzurum against the arrest of a night watchman charged with speaking with an Armenian prisoner named Sedrak. See "Kanants' ts'oyts'" [Women's demonstration], *Vtak* 33 (28 December 1907): 2; "Na ēl art'nanum ē" [She too awakens], *Vtak* 34 (29 December 1907): 1. For a discussion of Young Turk (especially Sabaheddin's League of Private Initiative and Decentralization) and ARF collaboration in Erzurum, see Hanioğlu, *Preparation for a Revolution*, 94–119. For Sabaheddin and Armenians, see Kévorkian, *Armenian Genocide*, 24–29.

46. Ahmed Rıza to Comrades, "Chourai Umett, Mechveret; Comité Ottoman D'union et de progrès, Paris" [*Şûra-yı Ümmet* (The council of the community), *Meşveret* (Consultation); Ottoman Committee of Union and Progress, Paris], 17 July 1908, ARF Archives, C 873–146.

47. The ARF itself realized that its input was not appreciated and said as much in private and in public, as the contemporary press makes clear. For one of many examples, see letter to comrades in Geneva, August 1908, ARF Archives C 191–7. See also Kévorkian, *Armenian Genocide*, part 2.

48. "Menk' tanter enk' t'ē varts'vor Osmanean yerkrin mēj?" [Are we landlords or tenants in the Ottoman country?], *Zhamanak* (Istanbul) 190 (1/14 June 1909): 1; "Artak'in tesut'iwn: Tachik zhoghovrdakan ts'oyts'er Karinum" [External view: Turkish popular protests in Karin], *Haṛaj* 53 (22 March 1906): 3–4; "T'urk'ahay keank': Karini T'urk' sharzhumĕ" [Turkish-Armenian life: Karin's Turkish movement], *Vtak* 11 (2 December 1907): 4. The last two articles emphasize that the protesters are Turks and not Armenians or other Christian subjects. See also "Vaghean Tachkastanĕ" [Old Turkey], part 4, *Yerkir* 14 (17 October 1906): 1.

49. R. Zartarian, "Ĕnkerayin harts'er: Tirapetut'ean vogin" [Social questions: The spirit of dominance], *Zhamanak* 16 (1–14 November 1908): 1.

50. Garegin Khazhak, *Dēpi fēdērats'ia* (Tiflis: Aghanean, 1907), 331. For an earlier development of his ideas on federation, see Khazhak, "Kusakts'ut'ean biwreghats'um" [Party crystallization], *Yerkir* 31 (5 November 1906): 1–2 and *Yerkir* 32 (7 November 1906): 2.

51. *The Stanford Encyclopedia of Philosophy,* ed. Edward N. Zalta, s.v. "Federalism," by Andreas Føllesdal, Summer 2016, https://plato.stanford.edu /archives/sum2016/entries/federalism/.

52. Armenian spelling of the Russian федерация/federatsiya varied and often appeared as ֆէդէրացիա/fēdērats'ia or ֆէդէրացիա/federats'ia.

53. Ronald L. Watts, "Federalism, Federal Political Systems, and Federations," *Annual Review of Political Science* 1 (1998): 121.

54. See, for example, Holly Case, "The Strange Politics of Federative Ideas in East-Central Europe," *Journal of Modern History* 85, no. 4 (December 2013): 833–66, in which Case argues that a noticeably intimate relationship existed between nationalism and federalist schemes. Moreover, she maintains that an overriding and persistent theme in nineteenth-century federalism has been "The emphasis in early federalist schemes on the rights of nations—and later their territorial 'self-determination'. . . . " Case, 842.

55. "Mitingner ew zhoghovner: G. Khazhaki dasakhosut'iwně" [Meetings and assemblies: H. Khazhak's lecture], *Alik'* 13 (13 May 1906): 4; Y. Topchian, "Azgayin harts'ě ew fēdērats'ia" [The national question and federation], *Alik'* 55 (4 July 1906): 1–2; see also Y. Topchian, "Azgayin harts'ě ew fēdērats'ia" [The national question and federation], part 2, *Alik'* 57 (6 July 1906): 2.

56. "Namakner khmbagrut'ean" [Letters to the editorship], *Alik'* 15 (16 May 1906), 4.

57. See especially the series of articles titled "Dashnakts'ut'iwně ew nra k'aghak'akan-hasarakakan arzhek'ě" [The Federation and its political-public value] by Al. Rubeni. The same may be said about *Hosank',* also a Social Democrat (SD) paper published in Tiflis, 1906–7. In addition to criticism on ideological grounds, *Hosank'* also published reports of troublesome and injurious ARF activities. See, for example, issues 43 to 47 in January 1907. See also "Azgayin karavarut'iwn" [National government], *Murch* 10 (October 1906): 80–111; *Murch* 11–12 (November–December 1906): 78–104, which acquired some of its information from *Mshak* (Cultivator).

58. See "Heghap'okhakan mamulě" [The revolutionary press], *Drōshak* 9 (September 1907): 123.

59. *Kovkasi Aṛawōt* 22 (16 October 1907): 1; Mik. Hovhannisian [Mikayel Varandian], "T'ert'on: Dadarets'ēk!" [Feuilleton: Cease!], *Zang* (Tiflis) 3 (13 August 1906): 2; Mik. Hovhannisian [Mikayel Varandian], "Yerb kě dadaren?" [When will they cease?], *Zang* 17 (1 September 1906): 3.

60. Zavarian's lecture on decentralization and federation took place in the Armenian church in Pera, Istanbul, on 24 August 1908, only a month after the Young Turk Revolution. See S. Zavarian, preface to *Apakedronats'umě* [Decentralization] (Istanbul: Azatut'ean Matenadaran, 1908). See also Hrach Dasnabedian, *Simon Zavarean,* vol. 3 (Ant'ilias: Hrat. H.H. Dashnakts'ut'ean, 1997), 583–613.

61. Khazhak, *Dēpi fēdērats'ia,* 141, 277. Shakhatunian, *Fēdēralizm ew demōkratizm* [Federalism and democratism] (Tiflis: Ėlektropech. A. M. Tarumova, 1907), 16, 17, 19–33. As Watts sums it up, "As Forsyth (1989) and Wiessner (1993) have noted, the uniting of constituent units that are based on different ethnic nationalisms into some form of federal system appears to be one way of containing nationalist pressures for political fragmentation." See Watts, "Federalism, Federal Political Systems, and Federations," 131; Murray Forsyth, ed., *Federalism and Nationalism* (Leicester, UK: Leicester University Press, 1989); Siegfried Wiessner, "Federalism: An Architecture for Freedom," *European Law Review* 1, no. 2 (1993): 129–42.

62. Zavarian, *Apakedronats'umē,* 8, 31, 39, 47.

63. "Hoghi yeghbayr [Land brother], *Arōr* 10 (14 September 1907): 1. For references to "land brother" or "brother in land," see "T'urk'ahay keank': Tigranakerti sharzhumē" [Turkish-Armenian life: Tigranakert's movement], part 1, *Vtak* 29 (23 December 1907): 3.

64. "Hay-T'rk'akan hamerashkhut'iwn" [Armenian-Turkish solidarity], *Drōshak* 6–7 (June–July 1907): 82. See also Y. T. [Yervant Topchian], "T'urk'iayi shurj: Oruay harts'erē" [Regarding Turkey: The day's issues], *Gorts* 54 (13 November 1908), in which Topchian notes the necessity to work more diligently against nationalism and chauvinism, to gather around "the flag of solidarity," and to "shout again and again: We are brothers."

65. Nicholas Aroney, "Imagining a Federal Commonwealth: Australian Conceptions of Federalism, 1890–1901," *Federal Law Review* 30, no. 2 (2002): 268.

66. Watts, "Federalism, Federal Political Systems, and Federations," 132.

67. Shakhatunian, *Fēdēralizm ew demōkratizm,* 19.

68. Khazhak, *Dēpi fēdērats'ia,* 357, 267.

69. Rosa Luxemburg, "Federation, Centralization, and Particularism," in *The National Question: Selected Writings of Rosa Luxemburg,* ed. and trans. Horace B. Davis (New York: Monthly Review Press, 1976), 184.

70. In particular, Armenian federalists engage Montesquieu's *The Spirit of Laws,* James Bryce's *The American Commonwealth,* Dicey's *Law and Public Opinion in England,* Proudhon's *Du principe fédératif* [The principle of federation], probably Althusius's *Politica*—in which he develops his theory of federalism (although not identified in Zavarian)—Kropotkin's *Conquest of Bread and Fields, Factories and Workshops,* and Bakunin's *Federalism, Socialism, and Anti-Theologism.*

71. For a biographical sketch of Khazhak, see Lazian, *Heghap'okhakan dēmk'er,* 145–49.

72. Khazhak's discussion of the United States and Switzerland is especially detailed in chap. 6.

73. Bayly, *Birth of the Modern World,* 192.

74. Regarding Montesquieu, see Khazhak, *Dēpi fēdērats'ia,* 342–45. Khazhak translates from the original French and quotes all of the first chapter of book 9 of *De l'esprit des lois,* in which Montesquieu defines a "confederate republic":

This form of government is a convention by which several petty states agree to become members of a larger one, which they intend to establish. It is a kind of assemblage of societies, that constitute a new one, capable of increasing by means of further associations, till they arrive at such a degree of power as to be able to provide for the security of the whole body. . . . As this government is composed of petty republics, it enjoys the internal happiness of each; and with regard to its external situation, by means of the association, it possesses all the advantages of large monarchies. . . .

Khazhak, *Dēpi fēdērats'ia,* 342–43. Zavarian, too, brings in Montesquieu's *De l'esprit des lois.* See Zavarian, *Apakedronats'umĕ,* 12–13. *De l'esprit des lois* may be considered the "first attempt to conceptualise federalism in the modern political era." It left an "important legacy" that had a significant influence, for example, on the *Federalist Papers.* Frédéric Lépine, "A Journey through the History of Federalism: Is Multilevel Governance a Form of Federalism?," *L'Europe en formation* 363 (Spring 2012): 21–62 (30, 31). For Bakunin, see Khazhak, *Dēpi fēdērats'ia,* 333. For Bakunin and Proudhon, see Mikayel Varandian, *Hosank'ner* [Currents] (Geneva: Hratarakut'iwn H.H.D., 1910), 204, 211 ("Anarchism" section, 203–87). Varandian quotes especially from Bakunin's *Federalism, Socialism, Antitheologism* and *God and the State* in *Hosank'ner,* 236–42. For a discussion on Bakunin's views of "bottom-up" federalism as well as nations and states, see Michael Forman, *Nationalism and the International Labor Movement: The Idea of the Nation in Socialist and Anarchist Theory* (University Park: Pennsylvania State University Press, 1998), 22–41. For a comprehensive treatment of key anarchists, see Peter Marshall, *Demanding the Impossible: A History of Anarchism* (Oakland: PM Press, 2010). Bakunin is cited in Marshall, 236.

75. Shakhatunian draws most directly from Bryce (for the American model), Kautsky (regarding proletariat and federalism), and Jellinek as an advocate of federation. Zavarian, as we shall see below, directly references some like Montesquieu but not his other influences, probably because the booklet is only a slightly expanded version of his lecture.

76. According to Lépine, "Although the Ancient Greeks did not know the world [*sic*] 'federalism' and its derivatives, Montesquieu labels the idiosyncratic unions of Greek city-states as 'federative.'" Lépine, "History of Federalism," 30.

77. Zavarian, *Apakedronats'umĕ,* 3–4.

78. Zavarian, 5, 6. Here and elsewhere throughout the contemporary print, the terms *Turkey* and *the Ottoman Empire* are often used interchangeably.

79. Zavarian, 7.

80. Zavarian, 8.

81. Zavarian, 9, 10, 11.

82. Alexander Semyonov, Marina Mogilner, and Ilya Gerasimov refer to Kovalevsky as a "cosmopolitan scholar-globetrotter, who connected academic circles in St. Petersburg, Moscow, and Khar'kov (his native city in modern-day Urkraine) with Vienna, Berlin, London, Stockholm, and Chicago." See "Russian Sociology in Imperial Context," in *Sociology and Empire: The Imperial Entanglements of a Discipline,* ed. George Steinmetz (Durham: Duke University Press, 2013), 64. Zavarian, *Apakedronats'umĕ,* 12, 13.

83. As Watts contends, "Although federations have often been characterized as decentralized political systems, what distinguishes federations from decentralized unitary systems is not just the scope of decentralized responsibilities but the constitutional guarantee of autonomy for the constituent governments in the responsibilities they perform." Watts, "Federalism, Federal Political Systems, and Federations," 124.

84. Zavarian, *Apakedronats'umĕ*, 13, 24–25.

85. Zavarian, 21.

86. Zavarian, 27.

87. Zavarian, 28–30.

88. For a discussion of Demolins's ideas and Sabaheddin, see Stefano Taglia, *Intellectuals and Reform in the Ottoman Empire: The Young Turks on the Challenges of Modernity* (London: Routledge, 2015), 82–93; for a discussion of Sabaheddin and decentralization, see Taglia, 94–98. *Gorts* reports on a lecture given by Sabaheddin on decentralization and private initiative. See "Ishkh. Sabaheddinĕ ew apakendronats'man harts'ĕ" [Prince Sabaheddin and the decentralization issue], *Gorts* 2 (12 September 1908): 2. Sabaheddin's "Apakedronats'man sistemĕ ew kristonia ew mahmetakan azgabnakut'iwnĕ" [Decentralization system and Christian and Muslim populace] appears in *Yerkri Dzaynĕ* 4–16 (28 January 1907): 4–5 and *Yerkri Dzaynĕ* 5–17 (4 February 1907): 4–5. For the Austrian model for the Ottoman Empire, see also R. Zartarian, "Kordean hangoyts'ĕ" [The Gordian knot], *Zhamanak* (Istanbul) 54 (16/29 December 1908): 1; "Azgut'iwnneri harts'ĕ T'iwrk'iayum" [The nationalities question in Turkey], part 2, *Horizon* 27 (3 September 1909): 1.

89. Zavarian, *Apakedronats'umĕ, 30.

90. Zavarian, 31. See also Y. T. [Yervant Topchian], "T'urk'iayi shurj: Oruay harts'erĕ" [Regarding Turkey: the day's issues], part 5, *Gorts* 5 (17 September 1908): 1; "Azgut'iwnneri harts'ĕ T'iwrk'iayum" [The nationalities question in Turkey], part 2, *Horizon* 27 (3 September 1909): 1; "Miats'eal nahangner Osmanean kaysrut'ean: Osmanean zhoghovurdneru dashnakts'ut'iwn" [United states of the Ottoman empire: The federation of Ottoman peoples], *Zhamanak* (Istanbul) 114 (28 February/13 March 1909): 1. The last of these articles reported on the establishment of Eastern Nations/Ethnicities Federative Association, whose purpose was to establish solidarity among Ottoman peoples. It printed its program in full, proposing independent and federated states to put an end to tyranny and ethnic animosities, to take measures against separatism, and to act as a force against external attacks. It was signed by founder-president Konstanten Rokkas.

91. R[upen] Zartarian, "Anjatoghut'ean khrtvilakĕ" [The scarecrow of separatism], *Zhamanak* (Istanbul), 80 (19 January 1909): 1; Shahuni, "Mer datavornerĕ" [Our judges], *Zhamanak* 228 (15/28 July 1909): 1.

92. Tigran Zaven, "Ĕsēk', pataskhanets'ēk': T'urk' mamulin ew azatakannerun" [Say it, reply: To the Turkish press and the liberals], *Surhandak* 117 (17/30 October 1908): 1.

93. From Western Bureau to Simon [Zavarian], Alexandria, 18 January 1901, ARF Archives B 41–41.

94. Hanioğlu, *Preparation for a Revolution*, 83, 88–89.

95. Hanioğlu, 90.

96. George Gawrych, *The Crescent and the Eagle: Ottoman Rule, Islam and the Albanians, 1874–1913* (London: I. B. Tauris, 2006), 144; Hanioğlu, *Preparation for a Revolution*, 53–54. According to an ARF member, Aram-Ashot (Sarkis Minasian), who was one of the Balkan delegates to the ARF's Fourth General Congress in Vienna, the original editorial board of the paper included Turks, Armenians, Albanians, and Macedonians. See Session 85, 16 April 1907, in *Niwt'er*, 3:235–36.

97. Živković, general introduction, in Živković and Plavšić, *Balkan Socialist Tradition*, 7, 70; Blagovest Njagulov, "Early Socialism in the Balkans: Ideas and Practices in Serbia, Romania and Bulgaria," in *Entangled Histories of the Balkans*, vol. 2, *Transfers of Political Ideologies and Institutions*, ed. Roumen Daskalov and Tchavdar Marinov (Leiden: Brill, 2014), 199–280 (217–18); Fikret Adanır, "The National Question and the Genesis and Development of Socialism in the Ottoman Empire: The Case of Macedonia," in Tunçay and Zürcher, *Socialism and Nationalism in the Ottoman Empire*, 33; Raymond Detrez, *Historical Dictionary of Bulgaria*, 3rd ed. (London: Rowman & Littlefield, 2015), 75, 107. On different views regarding Balkan federation as well as Macedonian versus Balkan ideas of federation, see L. S. Stavrianos, *Balkan Federation: A History of the Movement toward Balkan Unity in Modern Times* (Hamden, CT: Archon Books, 1964), in particular chapters 5 and 6.

98. Njagulov, "Early Socialism in the Balkans," 266.

99. Andreja Živković, "The Revolution in Turkey and the Balkan Federation—Introduction," in *The Balkan Socialist Tradition and the Balkan Federation, 1871–1915*, Revolutionary History 8, no. 3, ed. Andreja Živković and Dragan Plavšić (London: Porcupine Press, 2003), 102–3. See also Dimitûr Blagoev, "The Revolution in Turkey and Social Democracy," in Živković and Plavšić, 112.

100. Rakovsky, "The Turkish Revolution." See also Christian Rakovsky, "Manifesto of the Socialists of Turkey and the Balkans" (October 1912) in Živković and Plavšić, 208.

101. Andreja Živković, "6: The Balkan Federation and Balkan Social Democracy—Introduction," in Živković and Plavšić, 155.

102. Živković, general introduction, in Živković and Plavšić, 8.

103. Živković, general introduction.

104. Njagulov, "Early Socialism in the Balkans," 267. For Serbian views on federation, see James Robertson, "Imagining the Balkans as a Space of Revolution: The Federalist Vision of Serbian Socialism, 1870–1914," *East European Politics and Societies and Cultures* 31, no. 2 (May 2017): 402–25.

105. Tchavdar Marinov, "We, the Macedonians: The Paths of Macedonian Supra-nationalism (1878–1912)," in *We, the People: Politics of National Peculiarity in Southeastern Europe*, ed. Diana Mishkova (Budapest: Central European University Press, 2009), 122.

106. Marinov.

107. Njagulov, "Early Socialism in the Balkans," 268–74.

108. Njagulov, 278. For the Workers' Federation of Thessaloniki, see Ibrahim Yalimov, "The Bulgarian Community and the Development of the Socialist Movement in the Ottoman Empire during the Period 1876–1923," and Paul

Dumont, "A Jewish, Socialist and Ottoman Organization: The Workers' Federation of Salonica," in Tunçay and Zürcher, *Socialism and Nationalism in the Ottoman Empire,* 99, 64. For relations between the Workers' Federation of Thessaloniki and Armenians, see Dumont, "A Jewish, Socialist and Ottoman Organization," 63.

109. Adanır, "The National Question and the Genesis and Development of Socialism in the Ottoman Empire," 41. Tchavdar Marinov, "Famous Macedonia, the Land of Alexander: Macedonian Identity at the Crossroads of Greek, Bulgarian and Serbian Nationalism," in *Entangled Histories of the Balkans,* vol. 1, *National Ideologies and Language Policies,* ed. Roumen Daskalov and Tchavdar Marinov (Leiden: Brill, 2013), 305. For a novel study on Macedonian nationhood, see İpek Yosmaoğlu, *Blood Ties: Religion, Violence, and the Politics of Nationhood in Ottoman Macedonia, 1878–1908* (Ithaca, NY: Cornell University Press, 2013).

110. Dimo Hadzhi Dimov, "Our Political Standpoint: The Principle of Autonomy, Regional Self-Government and the Balkan Federation," in Živković and Plavšić, *Balkan Socialist Tradition,* 115. See also Živković, "4: The Revolution in Turkey and the Balkan Federation—Introduction," in Živković and Plavšić, 103.

111. "Unity or Solidarity with Armenian revolutionary and foreign elements," Inscription of the Third General Congress, in *Niwt'er,* 2:118; Decisions of the Fourth General Congress, in *Niwt'er,* 3:304–5. See also "H.H. Dashnakts'ut'ean Ch'orrord Ĕndhanur Zhoghovi Voroshumnerĕ," 72. For a more detailed study of Armenian-Macedonian relations, see Moumdjian, "Rebels with a Cause," 136. See also Duncan M. Perry, "The Macedonian Revolutionary Organization's Armenian Connection," *Armenian Review* 42, no. 1/165 (Spring 1989): 61–70. Perry focuses on the 1893–1903 period. For a more recent study that has as one of its foci the ARF Military Academy in Bulgaria in the context of Armenian-Macedonian cooperation, see Varak Ketsemanian, "Straddling Two Empires: Cross-Revolutionary Fertilization and the Armenian Revolutionary Federation's Military Academy in 1906–07," *Journal of the Ottoman and Turkish Studies Association* 4, no. 2 (November 2017): 339–63.

112. See ARF Archives B 1466–1; "D'zhgoh tarreri hamakhmbumn" [Assembly of discontented elements], *Drōshak* 12 (December 1906): 178–79.

113. S. Sapah-Giwlian, "Sahmani yerku koghmerum" [On the two sides of the border], *Hnch'ak* 4–5 (April–May 1908): 25–30.

114. "Ch'orrord Ĕndhanur Zhoghovi Voroshumnerĕ" [Decisions of the Fourth General Congress], in *Niwt'er,* 3:305. See also "H.H. Dashnakts'ut'ean Ch'orrord Ĕndhanur Zhoghovi Voroshumnerĕ," 72.

115. "Osmanean Miut. ew Harajdimut. Komitēn ev Hnch'akean kusakts'ut'iwnĕ" [The Ottoman Unity and Progress Committee and the Hnch'akean party], *Surhandak* 68 (30 August/2 September 1908): 2. For SDHP's decision to work legally in the constitutional Ottoman Empire, see its decisions from the Sixth Congress in Istanbul in 1909. Kitur, *Patmut'iwn* 1:323–29.

116. Zavarian, *Apakedronats'umĕ,* 31.

117. Watts, "Federalism, Federal Political Systems, and Federations," 133.

118. Watts, 133.

119. Zavarian, *Apakedronats'umĕ*, 34.

120. Zavarian, 34–35. See also "P'ok'ramasnut'ean iravunk'ĕ" [The right of the minority], *Horizon* (Tiflis) 9 (12 August 1909): 1. See also A. Ab., "Proports'ional ĕntrut'iwnner" [Proportional elections], part 1, *Zang* (Tiflis) 1 (11 August 1906): 1–2; "Proports'ional ĕntrut'iwnner" [Proportional elections], part 2, *Zang* 5 (17 August 1906): 2; "Proports'ional ĕntrut'iwnner" [Proportional elections], part 3, *Zang* 8 (20 August 1906): 2.

121. According to Kautsky, "the most powerful of the threads uniting the nation, is language." See Karl Kautsky, "Nationality and Internationality Part 1," trans. Ben Lewis, *Critique* 37, no. 3 (June 2009): 371–89 (377).

122. Zavarian, *Apakedronats'umĕ*, 41; see also Zavarian, 46. See also "Hasarakagitakan—7: Lezun ew patmut'iwnĕ azgeri ēvoluts'iyayi mēj" [Social scientific—7: Language and history in the evolution of nations], *Drōshak* 1 (January 1910): 10–11.

123. Zavarian, *Apakedronats'umĕ*, 42. Catholicos Mgrtich/Mkrtich Khrimian, affectionately known as Khrimian Hayrik (Father Khrimian), served as Catholicos of All Armenians from 1892 to 1907 and led the Armenian delegation to the Berlin Congress of 1878.

124. Zavarian, 43, 48.

125. Zavarian, 49.

126. Zavarian, 49, 50.

127. Zavarian, 50.

128. Shakhatunian, *Fēdēralizm ew demōkratizm*, 15, 19–33, 66.

129. Shakhatunian, 63.

130. Shakhatunian, 66. Khazhak, too, cites Georg Jellinek throughout his book, including in his chapter on the "Future of Federation," in which Khazhak explicitly calls on Jellinek's optimism that federation will continue to play a role in the future, adding that this phrase is not metaphysical but is born out of meticulous research—for example, his *Recht des modernen Staates*. Khazhak, *Dēpi fēdērats'ia*, 362.

131. Shakhatunian does not bring up Bauer but only Renner and only by his pen name, Synopticus. Shakhatunian, *Fēdēralizm ew demōkratizm*, 66. Forman credits "a Southern Slav delegate by the name of Kristan who introduced the personality principle at the 1899 Brunn Congress." The resolution, which was not adopted, espoused the concept that "The principle of a free society finds its parallel in the separation of the idea of nation from that of territory." The concept reappeared in Otto Bauer's *Die Nationalitätenfrage und die Sozialdemokratie* [The national question and social democracy] (Vienna: Verlag der Wiener Volksbuchhandlung Ignaz Brand, 1907).

For the Jewish Bund and autonomy, see also Ian Reifowitz, "Otto Bauer and Karl Renner on Nationalism, Ethnicity and Jews," *Journal of Jewish Identities* 2, no. 2 (2009): 1–19; Roni Gechtman, "Jews and Non-Territorial Autonomy: Political Programmes and Historical Perspectives," *Ethnopolitics: Formerly Global Review of Ethnopolitics* 15, no. 1 (2016): 66–88; Bill Bowering, "From Empire to Multilateral Player: The Deep Roots of Autonomy in Russia," in *Minority Accommodation through Territorial and Non-Territorial Autonomy,* ed. Tove H. Malloy and Francesco Palermo (Oxford: Oxford University Press, 2015), 133–60.

132. Alexander Osipov, "Non-Territorial Autonomy during and after Communism: In the Wrong or Right Place?," *Journal on Ethnopolitics and Minority Issues in Europe* 12, no. 1 (2013): 9. See also Forman, *Nationalism and the International Labor Movement*, 95–109.

133. Shakhatunian, *Fēdēralizm ew demōkratizm*, 87–89.

134. Khazhak, *Dēpi fēdērats'ia*, 272.

135. Khazhak, 273–76. Khazhak specifically cites Springer (Renner), *Der Kampf der oesterreichischen Nationen um den Staat* [The struggle of the Austrian nations for the state] (1902), in the original German, and Karl Kautsky, *Der Kampf der Nationalitäten und das Staatsrecht in Oesterreich* [The struggle of nationalities and state law in Austria] (1897), in Russian translation.

136. Shakhatunian, *Fēdēralizm ew demōkratizm*, 90. Khazhak, *Dēpi fēdērats'ia*, 141, 272. For Khazhak, national-territorial autonomy was also the only just and beneficial government for the proletariat. Khazhak, 139, 284.

137. Khazhak, *Dēpi fēdērats'ia*, 140.

138. Khazhak, 171.

139. Zavarian centers on an Ottoman federation and Shakhatunian on a "Transcaucasian Federation." Zavarian, *Apakedronats'umě*, 31; Shakhatunian, *Fēdēralizm ew demōkratizm*, 114–20.

140. "Dashnakts'ut'ean hrahangě, petakan dumayi patmagavornerin" [The Federation's instruction to the delegates of the federal duma], n.d., ARF Archives B 16–145; in Russian, B 16–146.

141. Khazhak, *Dēpi fēdērats'ia*, 314, 315.

142. Khazhak, 316–17. Khazhak provides the following numbers for Armenians in the Caucasus, totaling 1,309,518: Yerevan province—510,975; Kars region—92,497; Gandzak province—309,858; Tiflis province—265,985; Baku province—88,520; Batumi region—27,670; Kutais province—3,824; Black Sea region—7,689; Zakatala/Zakatali region—2,500. See Khazhak, 321. He also identifies the areas with an Armenian majority. Khazhak, 322.

143. Khazhak, 318–19, 324.

144. Khazhak, 323.

145. Forman, *Nationalism and the International Labor Movement*, 83, 84. See Luxemburg's 1908 and 1909 articles from Rosa Luxemburg, "The National Question and Autonomy," in Davis, *National Question*, 267.

146. Khazhak, *Dēpi fēdērats'ia*, 329. Khazhak cites Rosa Luxemburg's "Chevo mi khotim" [What we want] from the Social Democracy of the Kingdom of Poland and Lithuania (SDKPL or SDKPiL) program, in Russian, 1906.

147. A. Walicki, "Rosa Luxemburg and the Question of Nationalism in Polish Marxism (1893–1914)," *Slavonic and East European Review* 61, no. 4 (October 1983): 574. See also Davis, *National Question*, 16, in which Davis discusses how Luxemburg, in the sixth and last article of her 1908–9 series, attempted to come up with self-government and cultural autonomy for Poles without reliance on the principle of self-determination. Luxemburg acknowledged that each case had to be considered with its particularities in mind.

148. Khazhak, *Dēpi fēdērats'ia,* 333, 334. In a critique of Polish patriotic socialists, which could also have been made against their Armenian counterparts, Luxemburg points to an effort to make nationalist demands but through an appeal to international socialism "by calling upon the names of Marx and Engels and other prominent socialists who succeeded them. A long list of big names in the high court of socialism was made to serve in default of any sound argument in support of the social-patriotic program." See Rosa Luxemburg, "*Foreword to the Anthology:* The Polish Question and the Socialist Movement," for a book published in 1905 in Kraków, in Davis, *National Question,* 68–69.

149. Khazhak, *Dēpi fēdērats'ia,* 37, 38, 330, 340; see also Shakhatunian, *Fēdēralizm ew demōkratizm,* 113, 114.

150. Khazhak's translation was published by Haraj press in Tiflis, 1906. See Anahide Ter Minassian, "The Role of the Armenian Community in the Foundation and Development of the Socialist Movement in the Ottoman Empire and Turkey, 1876–1923," in Tunçay and Zürcher, *Socialism and Nationalism in the Ottoman Empire,* 195. For Kautsky's words in the original German, see Karl Kautsky, "Die Nationalitätenfrage in Russland," *Leipziger Volkszeitung* 98 (29 April 1905): 17. For a discussion of views on federalism in Russia and Kautsky in particular, see Dimitri Sergius Von Mohrenschildt, *Toward a United States of Russia: Plans and Projects of Federal Reconstruction of Russia in the Nineteenth Century* (Plainsboro, NJ, London, Toronto: Associated University Presses, 1981), 226.

151. See, for example, Shakhatunian, *Fēdēralizm ew demōkratizm,* 94, 96–106.

152. Khazhak, *Dēpi fēdērats'ia,* 147.

153. Khazhak, 280.

154. Khazhak, 311.

155. Khazhak, 325, 371. Khazhak even exclaims that Marxism, addressed objectively, leads to federation. Khazhak, 294.

156. Khazhak, 6–8. See also "Hay Hegh. Dashanakts'ut'iwn: pahanjnerě" [Armenian Rev. Federation: Demands], *Drōshak* 9–10 (September–October 1908): 129–30.

157. Khazhak, *Dēpi fēdērats'ia,* 108.

158. Khazhak, 110.

159. Khazhak, 114, 190; Shakhatunian, *Fēdēralizm ew demōkratizm,* 15.

160. Stora-Kēt, "Panasirakan: Avtonomia t'ē federats'ia" [Philological: Autonomy or federation], *Khat'abala* 6 (1906): 43–46.

161. Khazhak, *Dēpi fēdērats'ia,* 142–43. See also Shakhatunian, *Fēdēralizm ew demōkratizm,* 113, 114; Varandian, *Hosank'ner,* 154–56. For the program of the Russian Social Democratic Labor Party in English, see Harcave, appendix to *Russian Revolution of 1905,* 263–68; for the program of the Russian Socialist Revolutionary Party, see Harcave, 268–73.

162. Arnold, "Grakhosut'iwn" [Book review], *Aniv* 2 (9 March 1908): 9–14.

163. See Rosa Luxemburg, "National Question and Autonomy," in Davis, *National Question,* 102–3. Khazhak, *Dēpi fēdērats'ia,* 142–43. See also Pro-

gram of the Russian Social Democratic Labor Party, in Harcave, *Russian Revolution of 1905*, 265, point 9.

164. Davis, *National Question*, 12.

165. Luxemburg, in Davis, *National Question*, 100.

166. Luxemburg, in Davis, *National Question*, 123; Karl Kautsky, "Nationality and Internationality Part 2," trans. Ben Lewis, *Critique* 38, no. 1 (February 2010): 143–63.

167. From a report of a lecture by Armenian Social Democrat Stepan Shahumian, Y. Topchian, "Azgayin harts'ě ew fēdērats'ia" [The national question and federation], part 1, *Alik'* 55 (4 July 1906): 1–2. See also B. Ishkhanian, "K'aghak'akan kendronats'man ew fēdērats'iayi khndirě" [The issue of political centralization and federation], *Murch* (Tiflis) 11–12 (November–December 1905): 174–88. Ishkhanian was an Armenian Social Democrat and coeditor, with T. Iskhanian, of *Dzayn* (Tiflis, 1906–7). Both the Armenian Social Democrats and the ARF criticized Ishkhanian extensively and even accused him of plagiarizing economist Karl Bücher and Karl Kautsky in his brochure, *Tntesakan zargats'man fazerě* [The phases of economic development], which also appeared in *Murch* 9 (September 1905): 24–37; *Murch* 10 (October 1905): 24–39; *Murch* 11–12 (November–December 1905): 25–41. See "Goghut'ean, tgitut'ean ew t'hasut'ean ardiwnk'" [The consequence of theft, ignorance, and immaturity], *Hosank'* 4 (19 November 1906): 2–3; "T'ert'on: Mi grakan talani aṛit'ov" [Feuilleton: On the occasion of a literary plunder], part 2, *Yerkir* 15 (18 October 1906): 1. Ishkhanian responded to some of his critics. See, for example, B. Ishkhanian, "Im pataskhaně demagogiayi arhestavorin" [My response to the artisan of demagogy], part 2, *Dzayn* 8 (19 November 1906): 120–24.

168. Y. Topchian, "Azgayin harts'ě ew fēdērats'ia," part 2, *Alik'* 56 (5 July 1906): 1. See also Topchian's series of articles: Y.T. [Yervant Topchian], "T'urk'iayi shurj: Oruay harts'erě" [Regarding Turkey: The day's issues], *Gorts* 2 (12 September 1908): 1; *Gorts* 3 (13 September 1908): 1; *Gorts* 4 (14 September 1908): 1; *Gorts* 5 (17 September 1908): 1, and others. The last two articles focus on Prince Sabaheddin, his organ *Terakki*, and his League of Private Initiative and Decentralization's positive views on decentralization. See also "Vaghean Tachkastaně," [Old Turkey], part 3, *Yerkir* 13 (15 October 1906): 1. Topchian also lectured on unions, the national question, and federation in Kars in July 1906. See "Zhoghovner ew mitingner: Y. Topchiani dasakhosut'iwnnerě Karsum" [Assemblies and meetings: Y. Topchian's lectures in Kars], *Alik'* 73 (27 July 1906): 3. See also "Kendronatsum ew apakendronats'um" [Centralization and decentralization], *Drōshak* 2 (February 1908): 18–21.

169. Khazhak, *Dēpi fēdērats'ia*, 295.

170. Y. Topchian was killed under suspicious circumstances in the summer of 1909. See "Yeghishe Topchian," *Drōshak* 9 (September 1909): 128.

171. Y. Topchian, "T'ert'on: Azgayin harts'ě ew fēdērats'ia," part 3, *Alik'* 57 (6 July 1906): 2. Topchian's series is on a lecture by Shahumian, which was followed by a lively debate on the pros and cons of federation and involved Shahumian as well as others, one of whom exclaimed, in anger or exasperation, "You [referring to the ARF] are wolves in sheep's clothing and we must

everywhere fight against you." See also Mik[ayel] Hovhannisian, "Federats'ia ew avtonomia" [Federation and autonomy], *Yerkir*, published in six parts from 53 (2 December 1906) to 64 (17 December 1906). A similar discussion of SD infallibility and even the phrase "Rome's Pope" appears in a book review of Karl Kautsky's *Karl Marx and His Historical Significance* in an Armenian Socialist Revolutionary paper, with the additional descriptive of "clean as the first snow untouched by feet." Arnold, "Grakhosut'iwn" [Book review], *Aniv* 12 (18 May 1908): 9–13 (10).

172. Y. Topchian, "Azgayin harts'ĕ ew fēdērats'ia," part 2, *Alik'* 55 (4 July 1906): 1–2.

173. Khazhak, *Dēpi fēdērats'ia*, 280. As Forman explains, "International-ism, however, never meant the simple abrogation of the nation. Rather, it implied, often simultaneously, a critique of the ideology of the nation-state and support for national self-determination or national autonomy. This internation-alism proposed complex views of the very idea of the nation." Forman, *Nation-alism and the International Labor Movement*, 3–4.

174. Khazhak, *Dēpi fēdērats'ia*, 362, 370, 371.

175. For a study of how Iranian Armenians saw themselves and what they sought in Iran, see Houri Berberian, "Traversing Boundaries and Selves: Iranian Armenian Identities during the Iranian Constitutional Revolution," *Compara-tive Studies of South Asia, Africa, and Middle East* 25, no. 2 (Summer 2005): 279–96.

176. Varandian, *Hosank'ner*, 3.

CHAPTER 4. CONNECTED THROUGH AND BEYOND READING

1. "Dashnakts'utiwnĕ anveradardz kerpov gnum ē dēpi sots'ializmĕ; usti p'okhel ayd ughin annpatak ē ew anōgut." Giwlkhandanian, *Bagui derĕ*, 204–5. *Federation* refers to the Armenian Revolutionary Federation.

2. For a critique of national(ist) history's "teleocratic" tendency to displace or marginalize events that did not lead to its telos of the nation-state or the nation, see Sebouh D. Aslanian, "From Autonomous to Interactive Histories: World History's Challenge to Armenian Studies," in *Words and Worlds in Motion: Armenians in the Mediterranean and Beyond*, ed. Kathryn Babayan and Michael Pifer (New York: Palgrave Macmillan, 2018), 81–125.

3. Khuri-Makdisi, *Eastern Mediterranean*, 8.

4. Khuri-Makdisi, 169.

5. Anderson, *Under Three Flags*, 1.

6. Stephen F. Jones, *Socialism in Georgian Colors: The European Road to Social Democracy, 1883–1917* (Cambridge, MA: Harvard University Press, 2005), 29.

7. Khuri-Makdisi, *Eastern Mediterranean*, 112.

8. "T'ert'on: Dasakargayin kṛiv" [Feuilleton: Class struggle], Part 4, *Alik'* 10 (9 May 1906): 2. The quotation is in reference to utopian socialism in particular and applied here more generally to socialism.

9. "1908–1909," *Drōshak* 1 (January 1909): 1–8 (2–5).

10. Bayly, *Birth of the Modern World*, 284.

11. Bayly, 323.

12. Riegg, "Beyond the Caucasus," chap. 6; Önol, *Tsar's Armenians*, 18. See Önol, chap. 1, for an account of the confiscation.

13. Riegg demonstrates how, despite majority opposition in the Council of Ministers to Golitsyn's proposal of confiscation, the tsar sided with the minority, led by Golitsyn. See Riegg, "Beyond the Caucasus," chap. 6. The high commissioner is also referred to as the governor-general. In 1881 Alexander II replaced the viceroyalty with the office of the high commissioner but reinstated it in 1905. Thus, Golitsyn was the last high commissioner.

14. For the trials, see Önol, *Tsar's Armenians*, chapter 2. For a contemporary account, see E. Aknouni [Khachatur Malumian], *Political Persecution: Armenian Prisoners of the Caucasus (A Page of the Tzar's Persecution)*, trans. A.M. and H.W. (New York: 1911), n.p.; E. Aknuni [Khachatur Malumian], *Boghoki dzayn: Kovkasahay k'aghak'akan bantarkialnerĕ (ts'arakan halatsank'i mi ēj)* [The voice of protest: Caucasian Armenian political prisoners (A page from tsarist persecution)] (Beirut: Ghukas Karapetean, 1978). For a study of Ottoman prisons and Armenian prisoners, see Nanor Kebranian, "Imprisoned Communities: Punishing Politics in the Late Ottoman Empire," in *Ottoman Armenians: Life, Culture, Society*, vol. 1, ed. Vahé Tachjian (Berlin: Houshamadyan, 2014), 114–43.

15. Fourth Regional Congress of Caucasus, 1904, Session 2, in *Niwt'er*, 2:213; "Nakhagits kovkasean gortsunēut'ean" [Plan for Caucasian activity], June 1905, in *Niwt'er*, 2:232–34. For text of the decisions, see, for example, "Heghap'okhakan dashn ts'arizmi dēm" [Revolutionary pact against tsarism], *Drōshak* 12 (December 1904): 181–84; *Heghap'okhakan dashn: mijkusakts'akan khorhrdazhoghovneri voroshumnerĕ* [Revolutionary pact: Decisions of the interparty council meetings] (Geneva: Drōshak Tparan, 1905). See also a circular sent out by the ARF's Western Bureau, 10 January 1905, in *Niwt'er*, 2:225–26. The new struggle on the Caucasian front was also helped by attempts at Armenian interparty solidarity. "Miut'iwn kam hamerashkhut'iwn hay heghap'okhakan ew otar tarreru het" [Unity or solidarity with Armenian revolutionary and foreign elements], Third General Congress (February–March 1904, Sofia), in *Niwt'er*, 2:118–19. See also Circular by the Western Bureau of the Dashnakts'ut'iwn, 30 November 1904, in *Niwt'er*, 2:202–3. See also "Heghap'okhakan kusaktsut'iwnneri dashn ts'arizmi dēm" [Pact of revolutionary parties against tsarism], *Drōshak* 5 (May 1905): 65–69. For the decisions of the Fourth General Congress, see *Drōshak* 5 (May 1907): 66–69.

16. See "XVIII Tari" [18th year], *Hnch'ak* 1 (January 1905): 1–3; "Bagui gortsadulĕ" [The Baku strike], *Hnch'ak* 1 (January 1905): 3–4; "Heghap'okhut'iwn Ṙusastanum" [Revolution in Russia], *Hnch'ak* 2 (February 1905): 11; "Kazmakerpuats kṙiv" [Organized battle], *Hnch'ak* 3 (20 February 1905): 17–18. For Armenian worker and peasant participation in the Russian Revolution, see, for example, Ts. P. Aghayan, *Revolyuts'ion sharzhumnerĕ Hayastanum, 1905–1907 t'.t'.* [Revolutionary movements in Armenia, 1905–1907] (Yerevan: Haykakan SAR Gitut'iwnneri Akademia, 1955); V[artan] A[ram] Parsamyan, *Revolyuts'ion sharzhumnerĕ Hayastanum, 1905–1907 t'.t'.* [Revolutionary movements in Armenia, 1905–1907] (Yerevan: Petakan Hamalsaran, 1955).

17. Kitur, *Patmut'iwn S.D. Hnch'akean Kusaktsut'ean*, 1:293. For similar perceptions, see also "Hnch'akean Kusakts'ut'iwně" [The Hnch'akean Party], *Hnch'ak* 1–2 (January–February 1906): 1–3.

18. The group, Social-Democratic Hnch'akean Party, Anzali Branch, Iran Group (Ferqeh-ye Sosial-Demokrat-e Sho'bah-ye Anzali, Dasteh-ye Iranian), was formed in January 1911 and included important Iranian political figures like its president, Hosein Mo'tamed (subsequently Majles delegate Key Ostovan), and its secretary, Abu al-Qasem Rezazadeh (subsequently member of the Gilan Republic). See Berberian, *Armenians and the Iranian Constitutional Revolution*, 148.

19. For further elaboration, see "Mi k'ani akamay khosk'er" [A few obligatory words], *Hnch'ak* 3 (March 1906): 21–24.

20. Regarding the factional split, see Kitur, *Patmut'iwn*, 1:270–86. See also Anahide Ter Minassian, "Le mouvement révolutionnaire arménien, 1890–1903" [The Armenian revolutionary movement, 1890–1903], *Cahiers du monde russe et soviétique* 14, no. 4 (October–December 1973): 536–607 (591n68); Minassian, *Nationalism and Socialism*, 9–11.

21. For the split, see Ter Minassian, *Nationalism and Socialism*, 45–47. For Mihran's role as informant, see Önol, *Tsar's Armenians*, 53–54.

22. Augusta Dimou, *Entangled Paths towards Modernity: Contextualizing Socialism and Nationalism in the Balkans* (Budapest: Central European University Press, 2009), 157.

23. Dimou, *Entangled Paths towards Modernity*, 4, 160.

24. Adanır, "National Question," 35.

25. For a comparative analysis of the ARF programs, see Gerard Libaridian, "Revolution and Liberation in the 1982 and 1907 Programs of the Dashnaktsutiun," in *Transcaucasia: Nationalism and Social Change*, ed. R.G. Suny (Ann Arbor: University of Michigan, 1983).

26. For the SDHP program, see *Hnch'ak* 11–12 (October–November 1888): 2–5.

27. The ARF asserted the fundamentality of nationhood but objected to chauvinism and national superiority even in its party program. For text of the 1907 program, see *Niwt'er*, 3:315–28; *Drōshak* 5 (May 1907).

28. Varandian, *Hosank'ner*, 146–47.

29. See, for example, the use of "our country" to refer to the Caucasus: "Azgayin harts'ě ew fēdērats'ia" [The national question and federation], part 2, *Alik'* 56 (5 July 1906): 1; Varandian, *Hosank'ner*, 172. For "our fatherland" in reference to the Ottoman Empire, see Zavarian, *Apakedronats'umě*, 50; circular from ARF Karin [Erzurum] Central Committee, 22 March 1909, ARF Archives, C 762–31. See also *Yerkri Dzayně*, edited by Tigran Zaven. According to Anahide Ter Minassian, "opposed to all separatism, Tigran Zaven was a partisan with a firm belief in Ottomanism" and a "fervent defender of a cooperation between Armenians and Turks" who "thought that the Armenian question, as well as the Macedonian and Arab questions, could be solved by a united front of all the oppressed peoples in the empire." Ter Minassian, "Role of the Armenian Community," 135; see, for example, Tigran Zaven, "Inch'

enk' uzum anel?" [What do we want to do?], *Yerkri Dzaynĕ* 1 (8 October 1906): 1.

30. Armenian-Turkish solidarity, harmonious coexistence, and news, programs, and declarations/letters by the Young Turks, including Ahmed Rıza and Prince Sabaheddin, dominate every issue of *Yerkri Dzaynĕ*. As for Iran, see "Zhoghovrdakan sharzhumĕ Parskastanum ew Parskahayerĕ" [The popular movement in Persia and Persian-Armenians], *Vtak* 20 (13 December 1907): 1–2; for more examples, see the following issues of the Tabriz *Zang*: 8 (3 May 1910), 12 (1 July 1910), 17 (5 August 1910), 29 (29 October 1910), 1 (13 January 1911), 8 (March 1911); see also the following issues of *Arawōt*: 6 (27 September 1909), 11 (1 November 1909), 13 (15 November 1909), 19 (27 December 1909), 39 (16 May 1910), 45 (27 June 1910), 46 (4 July 1910), 115 (4 September 1911). See also Berberian, "Iranian Armenian Identities," 289.

31. Revolutionaries often employed this motto from the nineteenth-century French novel *The Three Musketeers*, by Alexandre Dumas, when calling for solidarity. Regarding Ottoman solidarity, see, for example, H[arutiwn] Shahrigian, *Mer Havatamkĕ* [Our credo] (Beirut: Hamazgayin Vahē Sēt'ean Tparan, 1981), 28–29; regarding Caucasian solidarity, see "Kovkasi bolor azgut'iwnnerin" [To all the nationalities of the Caucasus], *Drōshak* 3 (March 1905): 43–44.

32. Alexander Vezenkov, "Formulating and Reformulating Ottomanism," in *Entangled Histories of the Balkans*, vol. 1, *National Ideologies and Language Policies*, ed. Roumen Daskalov and Tchavdar Marinov (Leiden: Brill, 2013), 241–71 (250). See also Vezenkov, "Reconciliation of the Spirits and Fusion of the Interests: 'Ottomanism' as an Identity Politics," in *We, the Macedonians: Politics of National Peculiarity in Southeastern Europe*, ed. Diana Mishkova (Budapest: Central European University Press, 2009), 47–77. For the Macedonian case, see Marinov, "We, the Macedonians," 128–29.

33. Vezenkov, "Formulating and Reformulating Ottomanism," 251, 252, 255.

34. "Mejlis" [Majles], *Arawōt* 81 (6 March 1911); "Vortegh ē azgeri iravahavasarutiunĕ ?" [Where is the peoples' equality of rights?] and "Mejlisē ew Hay patkamavorĕ" [The majles and the Armenian delegate], *Arawōt* 83 (20 March 1911); "Vtangavor kats'utiwn" [Dangerous situation], *Zang* 4 (6 May 1910); "Mer irakan drut'iwnits'—datarannerĕ" [From our real situation—the courts"], *Arawōt* 13 (15 November 1909): 2; Minutes of Azerbaijan Central Committee, Session 54, 31 July 1907, 520/b; Meeting of Azerbaijan Central Committee, 19 August 1908, 475/10; Report of Vrezhstan [Azerbaijan] Central Committee, 1908–1909, 476/141; Minutes of Azerbaijan Central Committee, Session 44, 19 August 1908, 540/b. See also Berberian, "Iranian Armenian Identities," 280.

35. Berberian, "Iranian Armenian Identities," 291. The quotation from *Iran-e Now* (New Iran), 16 February 1910, is cited in Mohamad Tavakoli-Targhi's "Refashioning Iran: Language and Culture during the Constitutional Revolution," *Iranian Studies* 23 (1990): 140.

36. "Oruan mtatsumner: Zinvor piti ĕllan t'ē voch'" [The day's thoughts: Will they be soldiers or not], *Zhamanak* 85 (24 January/6 February 1909): 1.

37. Erik J. Zürcher, "The Ottoman Conscription System in Theory and Practice, 1844–1918," *International Review of Social History* 43 (1998): 444. For a discussion of conscription and Armenians during the Tanzimat, see Masayuki Ueno, "'For the Fatherland and the State': Armenians Negotiate the Tanzimat Reforms," *International Journal of Middle East Studies* 45 (2013): 93–109 (95).

38. Dikran Arpiarian, "Hayeru zinvoragrut'iwně" [The conscription of Armenians], *Zhamanak* 134 (24 March/6 April 1909): 1.

39. "Menk' tantēr enk' t'ē vartzvor Osmanean yerkrin mēj?" [Are we landlords or tenants in the Ottoman country?], *Zhamanak* (Istanbul) 190 (1/14 June 1909): 1. See also Y. T. [Yervant Topchian], "T'urk'iayi shurj: Oruay harts'erě" [Regarding Turkey: The day's issues], part 1, *Gorts* 1 (11 September 1908): 1; Shahrigian, *Mer Havatamkě*, 10, 58, 59. Gerard Libaridian makes an important point regarding Ottoman Armenian life and its historiography: "Often overlooked is the fact that these parties were active players in Ottoman political life, so active, in fact, that by 1908 they were widely considered as having replaced the church as the main intermediary between the Ottoman authorities and their Armenian subjects. They worked with Young Turk and other Ottoman organizations, took part in Ottoman elections following the Young Turk Revolution in alliances with other Ottomans, held seats in parliament, and deliberated on matters relevant to the whole empire." Gerard J. Libaridian, "What Was Revolutionary about Armenian Political Parties in the Ottoman Empire?," in Suny, Göçek, and Naimark, *Question of Genocide*, 82.

40. "Menk' tantēr enk' t'ē vartzvor Osmanean yerkrin mēj?," *Zhamanak*, 1.

41. Y. T., "T'urk'iayi shurj: Oruay harts'erě," 1. See also "K'aghak'akan tesut'iwn: zhamanakakits' knchirner, 2: Gaghap'arě ew nra artahaytut'iwnnerě" [Political view: Contemporary knots, 2: The idea and its expressions], *Drōshak* 7 (July 1909): 92–96 (93), in which the ARF clarifies that the Ottoman Empire is not a nationalist state *(Nationalstaat)* but a state of nationalities *(Nationalitatenstaat)* similar to Austria and Russia.

42. Vezenkov, "Formulating and Reformulating Ottomanism," 255, 257, 259. For a treatment of Ottoman Jewish response and engagement with Ottomanism, see Julia Philips Cohen, *Becoming Ottoman: Sephardi Jews and Imperial Citizenship in the Modern Era* (Oxford: Oxford University Press, 2014). For the Greek case, see Sia Anagnostopoulou, "The 'Nation' of the Rum Sings of Its Sultan: The Many Faces of Ottomanism," in *Economy and Society on Both Shores of the Aegean,* ed. Lorans Tanatar Baruh and Vangelis Kechriotis (Athens: Alpha Bank Historical Archives, 2010).

43. Der Matossian, *Shattered Dreams*, 7. In this insightful study, Der Matossian discusses Ottomanism in depth, as an "ambiguous" concept with multiple and often conflicting meanings, and also discusses its ultimate failure.

44. Vezenkov, "Formulating and Reformulating Ottomanism," 255, 257, 259.

45. For differing Russian views of Caucasian Armenians, see Riegg, "Beyond the Caucasus," chap. 6; Riegg, "Imperial Challengers: Tsarist Responses to Armenian Raids into Anatolia, 1875–90," *Russian Review* 76, no. 2 (2017): 253–71; and Önol, *Tsar's Armenians*. Not all Russian officials viewed Armenians strictly or primarily as seditious rebels. Vorontsov-Dashkov, for example,

held that "There is no separatism among the Armenians of the Caucasus." Ilarion Vorontsov-Dashkov, *Vsepoddanneishii otchet za vosem' let upravleniia Kavkazom* (Saint Petersburg: Gosudarstvennaia tipografiia, 1913), 7, cited in Riegg, "Beyond the Caucasus," chap. 6.

46. Zaven, "Inch' enk' uzum anel," 2; T. Zaven, "Mer hegap'okhut'iwně" [Our revolution], *Yerkri Dzayně* 11 (17 December 1907): 1. See also "Seghmenk' shark'eră" [Let us close the ranks] (29 November 1908), in Teodik, *Amēnun tarets'oyts'ě* [Everyone's yearbook], 3rd year (Istanbul, 1909), 377. According to Istanbul-born writer and philologist Teodik (Teodoros Lapchinchian), the Russian government hindered the publication of *Yerkri Dzayně* after the reinstatement of the Ottoman constitution in 1908. Teodik, *Amēnun tarets'oyts'ě*, 376.

47. Garegin [Kozikian], "Iravazurk dasakargi pahanjě ch'ē" [It is not the demand of the proletarian class], *Surhandak* 119 (2 November 1908): 1.

48. Karl Marx and Friedrich Engels, *Manifesto of the Communist Party*, authorized English translation, ed. and annot. Friedrich Engels (Chicago: Charles H. Kerr, 1906), 41. For "fatherlandless," see "Umn ē hayrenik'ě?" [Whose is the fatherland?], *Kovkasi Arawōt* 11 (3 October 1907): 1.

49. For an English translation of Hervé's speech, see "Anti-patriotism," 1906, accessed 27 September 2017, https://www.marxists.org/archive/herve/1905/anti-patriotism.htm.

50. S. Sapah-Giwlian, "Skzbunk'ayin khndirner" [Issues of principle], *Hnch'ak* 9–10 (September–October 1907): 111–13. Sapah-Giwlian's article was also in response to charges of SDHP duality. See also "Hakasakan t'rich'k'eră Marksizmi ēvoluts'iayi měj" [Contradictory flights in the evolution of Marxism], *Drōshak* 4 (April 1908): 54–56; "K'aghak'akan tesut'iwn: zhamanakagits' knchirner, 2: Gaghap'arě ew nra artahaytut'iwnnerě" [Political view: Contemporary knots, 2: The idea and its expressions], *Drōshak* 7 (July 1909): 92–96.

51. "Astichanakan zijumner" [Gradual retreats], *Vtak* 26 (20 December 1907): 1.

52. "Hasarakakan harts'eru shurjě" [Regarding public issues], *Apagay* (Istanbul) 16 (14 August 1910): 3–5.

53. "Umn ē hayrenik'ě?," 1.

54. "Umn ē hayrenik'ě?"

55. Mik. Hovhannisian [Mikayel Varandian], "Yerb kě dadarēn?" [When will they cease?], *Zang* (Tiflis) 19 (3 September 1906): 2.

56. See, for example, "Kronikon: Heghap'okhakan mamulits'—Heghap'okhakan nats'ionalizmě ew sotsi'al-demokratia" [Chronicon: From the revolutionary press—revolutionary nationalism and social-democracy], *Hnch'ak* 8 (August 1904): 84–87; "Ho yertak', vardapetk'?" [Where are you going, masters?], *Dzayn* 2 (8 October 1906): 18; "Natsionalizmi dēm" [Against nationalism], *Hosank'* (Tiflis) 39 (17 January 1907): 1; "Nahanjetsēk' yet dēpi Tajkastan" [Retreat to Turkey], *Hosank'* 44 (24 January 1907): 1. See also Victor, "Banasirakan: H.H. Dashnakts'ut'iwně" [Study: A.R. Federation], *Hosank'* 57 (8 February 1907): 2–3. According to a *Hnch'ak* article, "It is the work of Social-Democracy, especially with us in the Caucasus, to fight unceasingly

against nationalism and annihilate it from its roots." See "Nats'ionalizmĕ Kov-kasum" [Nationalism in the Caucasus], *Hnch'ak* 7 (July 1905): 57–59. These are only a sampling of the many examples—far too many to list.

57. Varandian and Sapah-Giwlian wrote impassionedly about the ARF and SDHP positions, respectively. See Varandian, *Hosank'ner,* 153–56; S. Sapah-Giwlian, "Menk' ew mer knnadatnerĕ" [We and our critics], *Hnch'ak* 9–10 (September–October 1906): 91–95; S. Sapah-Giwlian, "Kay yerkuorakanut'iwn (dualizm) mer davanats skzbunk'eri mēj?" [Is there dualism (dualism) in our professed principles?], *Hnch'ak* 2 (February 1907): 15–19; S. Sapah-Giwlian, "Azgayin iravunk'ner ew voch' t'ē aṛandznashnorhumner" [National rights and not privileges], *Hnch'ak* 3–4–5 (October–November–December 1910): 26–31.

58. M.H. [Mikayel Varandian], "Miatarr ew aylatarr" [Homogeneous and heterogenous], part 2, *Yerkir* 26 (31 October 1906): 2.

59. Varandian's reference is to Karl Kautsky, *Die Agrarfrage. Eine Übersicht über die Tendenzen der modernen Landwirthschaft und die Agrarpolitik der Sozialdemokratie* [The agrarian question. A review of the tendencies in modern agriculture and the agrarian policy of Social-democracy] (Stuttgart: Dietz, 1899).

60. "Hakasakan t'ṛich'k'erĕ Marksizmi evolutsi'ayi mēj" [Contradictory flights in the evolution of Marxism], *Drōshak* 4 (April 1908): 54–56. The article identifies Wilhelm Liebknecht as the German Social Democrat who was the most loyal follower of reformist socialism and its interpreter. It quotes from his 1897 Hamburg declaration emphasizing the importance of working on practical ground.

61. "K'aghak'akan tesut'iwn: zhamanakakits' knchirner, 1: Azgayin nshanabanĕ [Political view: Contemporary knots, 1: The national slogan], *Drōshak* 6 (June 1909): 74–79. See also also "K'aghak'akan tesut'iwn: zhamanakagits' knchirner, 2: Gaghap'arĕ ew nra artahaytut'iwnnerĕ" [Political view: Contemporary knots, 2: The idea and its expressions], *Drōshak* 7 (July 1909): 92–96.

62. The reference to Kropotkin is to his *Mutual Aid: A Factor of Evolution* (1902). "Hasarakagitakan: Azgayin ĕnkerakts'ut'iwnneri tsagumĕ" [Social scientific: The dawn of national associations], part 4, *Drōshak* 8 (August 1909), 108–12 (108). See also "Hasaragitakan: Azgayin arzhek'ner [Social scientific: National values], part 8, *Drōshak* 2 (February 1910): 24–28.

63. This is reflected in the decisions of the Fourth General Congress (Vienna, February–May 1907). For the text of the 1907 program, see Hrach Dasnabedian, comp., ed., *Niwt'er,* 3:315–28; *Drōshak* 5 (May 1907).

64. S. Sapah-Giwlian, "Menk' ew mer k'nnadatnerĕ" [We and our critics], *Hnch'ak* 9–10 (September–October 1906): 91–95.

65. Sapah-Giwlian, 95.

66. Endizhen, "Sots'ializm ew panarmenizm" [Socialism and pan-Armenian-ism], *Hnch'ak* 12 (December 1906): 118–20.

67. Endizhen, 120.

68. S. Sapah-Giwlian, "Sots'ializm ew azgut'iwn" [Socialism and national-ity], *Hnch'ak* 6 (June 1907): 59–60.

69. For a discussion of the views of Marx and Engels on nations, see Forman, *Nationalism and the International Labor Movement*, 41–60. Forman explains that their conception of the "'sovereign right belonging to every nation' was never about the establishment of states in the name of human groupings defined around descent, language, race, or any other such characteristic. It was a call for democratic republicanism. Since Marx and Engels perceived the nation as a society exercising political power, as a nation-state, its political form was of great importance. In practice, this meant that nationalities—that is, nations understood in terms of shared orientations emerging from an organic development out of a common history—had no a priori claims to the support of progressive forces." Forman, 60.

70. Georges Renard, *Le socialisme à l'œuvre: Ce qu'on a fait, ce qu'on peut faire* [Socialism at work: What we did, what we can do] (Paris: Édouard Cornély et Cie, 1907). See English translation of passage by John Spargo, "Socialism and Internationalism," *Atlantic Monthly* 120 (September 1917): 300–312 (303). See also S. Sapah-Giwlian, "Sots'ializm ew azgut'iwn," 61, 63. Sapah-Giwlian further draws from a rather eclectic mix of Jules Ferri, Garibaldi, Victor Hugo, and others.

71. S. Sapah-Giwlian, "Skzbunk'ayin khndirner" [Issues of principle], *Hnch'ak* 9–10 (September–October 1907): 111–24; Shahrigian, *Mer Havatamkĕ*, 81. Shahrigian (pseudonyms Adom and Nitra) was a prominent ARF member, lawyer, and activist in Baku and Istanbul and an admirer of Kropotkin. He was also the author of several Armenian and Turkish books, including *Petakan veranorogut'iwnn u hoghayin harts'ĕ* [Governmental reform and the land question] (Istanbul: Tparan A. Shahēn, 1910), *Ōsmanean Kaysrut'ean ankman patmut'iwnĕ: yeritasard-t'urk'eru veranoroguogh dprots'ĕ* [The history of the fall of the Ottoman Empire: The revived school of the Young Turks] (Istanbul: Gratun P. Palents', 1913), *Barenorogumneru harts'ĕ* [The question of reforms] (Istanbul: Tparan "Sanchagchean," 1914). He also coauthored a book with S. Sirenis and Celâl Nuri İleri, *Osmanlı İmparatorluğunun tarih-i tedennisi* [The history of the decline of the Ottoman Empire] (Dersaadet/Istanbul: Edep Matbaası, 1331 [1915]). The last book was published in the same year that Shahrigian became one of the first victims of the Armenian Genocide.

72. Jones, *Socialism in Georgian Colors*, 29. On nationalism and socialist thought, see Ephraim Nimni, *Marxism and Nationalism: The Theoretical Origins of a Political Crisis* (London: Pluto Press, 1991); Erica Benner, *Really Existing Nationalisms: A Post-Communist View of Marx and Engels* (New York: Oxford University Press, 1995); Horace B. Davis, *Nationalism and Socialism: Marxist and Labor Theories of Nationalism to 1917* (New York: Monthly Review Press, 1967); and Forman, *Nationalism and the International Labor Movement*.

73. Jones, *Socialism in Georgian Colors*, 47, 198, 227.

74. Jones, 47, 77, 283.

75. Jones, 160, 283.

76. Dimou, *Entangled Paths towards Modernity*, 159.

77. "Inch'u Dashnakts'ut'iwnĕ kaykayvum ē?" [Why is the Federation dissolving?], part 2, *Hosank'* 13 (8 December 1906): 1.

78. "Ayd kez khrat, gaylatsuk, vor ch'p'ordzes mkner vorsalu" [Advice for you, pike, not to try to hunt for mice], *Hosank'* 50 (31 January 1907): 2.

79. The Armenian SD newspaper, referring to its diversity, called the ARF's position "this way or that way." See "Vorn ē iskakan Dashnakts'ut'iwnĕ?" [Which is the real Federation?], *Hosank'* 71 (25 February 1907): 3. "Vorn ē iskakan Dashnakts'ut'iwnĕ?" [Which is the real Federation?], *Hosank'* 71 (25 February 1907): 3. See also Meg.-Hos., "Khazhakizm" [Khazhakism], *Hosank'* 58 (9 February 1907): 2–3.

80. I am borrowing the terms from Jones's *Socialism in Georgian Colors*.

81. The Socialist Revolutionaries, too, were charged with synthesis, "only a euphemism for eclecticism." See Manfred Hildermeier, *The Russian Socialist Revolutionary Party before the First World War*, trans. from the German (Münster: Lit Verlag; New York: St. Martin's Press, 2000), 67, 96.

82. The criticism was not confined to the press or meetings; it affected the lives and relationships of workers too. For example, an ARF worker pleaded with the Central Committee to take steps against what he reported as the constant derision of the ARF by SDHP and other SD workers in factories, leading sometimes to clashes and the drawing of guns among workers. Letter to the Sixth Central Committee, 8 May 1905, ARF Archives B 376–60. Signature of author is illegible.

83. M.H. [Mikayel Hovhannisian/Mikayel Vardanian], "T'ert'on: Nakhagitsĕ" [Feuilleton: The protocol], *Yerkir* 29 (3 November 1906): 2.

84. "Ashkhatavorneri keank'its': Harstaharuats ashkhatank'" [From the life of workers: Exploited labor], *Haraj* 1 (17 January 1906): 3–4.

85. See, for example, a series of articles in the ARF Tiflis press: "Dasakargayin kriv" [Class struggle], appearing in the pages of *Haraj, Alik'*, and *Zang* in 1906 and *Kovkasi Arawōt* in 1907; "Sots'ialisti namaknerĕ" [The letters of a socialist] in *Drōshak* in 1907 and 1908, and a few others in February–March 1910 and January–February 1911; Shen, "Mer ashkhatavorut'ean k'aghak'akanut'iwnĕ" [Our labor's politics], *Arawōt*, November 1909–January 1910; "Sots'ializm ew T'urk'ia" [Socialism and Turkey], *Haraj* (Erzurum), December 1909, and *Yerkri Dzaynĕ*, 1906 and 1907. See also *Nor Ōrer*, 1908–9, with contributions by Smbat Smbatian and D. Ananun (David Ter Danielian). The latter is the author of *Rusahayeri hasarakakan zargats'umĕ* [The social development of Russian Armenians], vol. 1: 1800–1870, vol. 2: 1870–1900, and vol. 3: 1901–1918 (Baku: Hratarakut'iwn Tigran Budagheani, 1914–26). According to Ter Minassian, Tigran Zaven, the editor of *Yerkri Dzaynĕ*, "used a pure class discourse to resolve the ideological incompatibilities between the Young Turks and the Armenian socialists," focusing on classes—not nations— "oppressors and oppressed, exploiters and exploited." See Ter Minassian, "Role of the Armenian Community," 136. For SD articles, some of which even instructed readers on how to wage class struggle, see *Aniv*, March–April 1908. For a series of articles on the development of economic stages, Engels, Marx and Marxism, Social Democracy, and other related matters, see the leftist paper *Murch*, May 1905–March 1907. See also the series by N., "Banasirakan: Utopiakan ew gitakan sots'ializm" [Study: Utopian and scientific socialism], in SDHP's paper *Zang* (Tabriz), 12 (1 July 1910): 2; 13 (8 July 1910): 2–3; 14 (15 July

1910): 2–3. Further on the left, see Kadmos, "Ěnkervarakan harts'er" [Socialist questions], Part A, *Nor Hosank'* 5 (16 May 1909): 35–37; Part B, *Nor Hosank'* 6 (6 June 1909): 43; and Part C, *Nor Hosank',* 7 (27 June 1909): 51–52. The author of the last article is Yesalem [Garegin Kozikian].

I discussed public lectures in the "Federation" section. Here are a few more examples: "Zhoghovner ew ěnkerut'iwnner: P[aron] Khazhaki 'Dasakhosut'iwně'" [Meetings and societies: Mr. Khazhak's "lecture"], *Ankakh Mamul* [Independent Press] (Tiflis) 16 (19 December 1907): 3, where the author, in reference to Khazhak's discussion of nation and class, mockingly remarks, "only in Armenian circles can one talk about something he himself does not understand." See also "Normal hangist" [Normal rest], *Apagay* 46 (4 May 1907): 3; "Zhoghovner ew mitingner: Dashnakts'ut'iwně ew Tachkahaykakan datě" [Assemblies and meetings: The Federation and the Turkish-Armenian cause], *Alik'* 82 (6 August 1906): 5. The ARF also hosted a series of lectures on a number of issues after the reinstatement of the Ottoman constitution: (1) solidarity and the Paris Congress; (2) revolution and the establishment of the constitution in Turkey; (3) ARF's activities (historical glance); (4) the constitution and its fundamental principles (5) the principle of equality of ethnicities and the federal regime; (6) the country's contemporary economic and political situation; (7) parliamentary electoral struggle; (8) ARF's program and tactic; (9) the foundation of socialist doctrine; (10) the latest movements of Caucasian Armenians; (11) strikes and labor organizations; (12) revolutionary figures; (13) decentralization and parties in Turkey. See "Hraparakayin atenakhosut'iwnner" [Public orations], *Surhandak* 59 (8/21 August 1908), 2. The following issues announce individual lectures.

86. H. Artanoysh, "Kareli ē ěnkervarakan ěllal achaparelov?" [Is it possible to be socialist in haste?], *Zhamanak* 257 (19 August/1 September 1909): 1.

87. Mik. Hovhannisian [Mikayel Varandian], "Dadaretsēk'!" [Cease!], part 2, *Zang* (Tiflis) 5 (17 August 1906): 2–3. Here, Varandian writes that in the 1890s, Armenian intellectuals were under the influence of Russian and European currents, especially Narodnaya Volya, which had socialism as an ideal goal. See also M. H. [Mikayel Hovhannisian/Varandian], "T'ert'on: Nakhagitsě" [Feuilleton: The protocol], part 2, *Yerkir* 30 (4 November 1906): 2–3.

88. V. Araratski, "Sots'ialisti namaknerě: arajin namak" [Socialist's letters: First letter], *Drōshak* 6–7 (June–July 1907): 87–89. See also "Tsragrayin harts': Dashnakts'ut'ean tsragiře" [Programmatic question: The Federation's program], *Drōshak* 9 (September 1907): 124–27.

89. V. Araratski, "Sots'ialakan tesut'iwn: Sots'ialisti namaknerě" [Socialist view: The letters of a socialist], *Drōshak* 9 (September 1907): 127–30. For similar demands made earlier, see *Drōshak* 1 (January 1905): 6, which lists twenty-eight demands and is followed by announcements from Socialist Revolutionaries and Social Democrats (6–7). *Hosank',* too, carried similar demands. See "Sots'ializm ew demōkratizm" [Socialism and democratism], *Hosank'* 5 (28 November 1906): 1.

90. "Tsragrayin harts': Dashnakts'ut'ean tsragiře" [Programmatic matter: The program of the Dashnakts'ut'iwn], *Drōshak* 9 (September 1907): 124–27. For the text of the 1907 program, see *Niwt'er,* 3:315–28; *Drōshak* 5 (May 1907). For the Hnch'aks, see S. Sapah-Giwlian, "Sots'ializm ew haykakan

khndir" [Socialism and Armenian issue], *Hnch'ak* 1 (January 1907): 3–8. See also S. Sapah-Giwlian, "Kay yerkuorakanut'iwn (dualizm) mer davanats skzbunk'eri mēj?" [Is there dualism (dualism) in our professed principles?], *Hnch'ak* 2 (February 1907): 15–19.

91. Jones, *Socialism in Georgian Colors,* 283.

92. See SDHP program in *Hnch'ak* 11–12 (October–November 1888): 2–5.

93. S. Sapah-Giwlian, "Skzbunk'ayin khndirner" [Issues of principle], *Hnch'ak* 9–10 (September–October 1907): 111–24. See also "Mer dirk'ě" [Our position], *Hnch'ak* 12 (December 1904): 105–7.

94. See "XVIII tari," 1–3.

95. Sapah-Giwlian, "Sots'ializm ew haykakan khndir," 3–8. See also Sapah-Giwlian, "Kay yerkuorakanut'iwn (dualizm) mer davanats skzbunk'eri mēj," 15–19. For a critique of Sapah-Giwlian's approach, see Monist, "Sots'ializmě Hnchak'ean aknots'ov" [Socialism through Hnch'akean lenses], *Yerkri Dzaynĕ* 15 (15 April 1907): 3–4. On socialism in the Ottoman Empire, see T. Zaven, "Kay ardiok' gortsunēut'ean hogh" [Is there perhaps ground for activity], part 5, *Yerkri Dzaynĕ* 28 (9 December 1907): 1–4; A. Nazatetian, "Sotsi'alistakan t'ē demokratakan gortsunēut'iwn" [Socialist or democratic activity], *Yerkri Dzaynĕ* 30 (23 December 1907): 8.

96. The series ran in the February and March 1907 issues of *Hosank'*. See, in particular, A. Ch. [Arshavir Chilinkirian], "Parskastani hasarakakan k'aghak'akan keank'its'" [From Persia's public political life], *Hosank'* 56 (7 February 1907): 2 and *Hosank'* 76 (6 March 1907): 2. See also Arsh[avir] Chilinkirian, "Parskakan sharzhumnerě" [The Persian movements], National Archives of Armenia, Fond 87/Tsutsak 287/Gorts 298, pp. 91–100. Chilinkirian, writing in Tabriz, critiques a series of articles that appeared in the ARF newspaper, *Aṛawōt,* 20, 21, 22, 23 (1907).

97. See Berberian, *Armenians and the Iranian Constitutional Revolution,* 86–89. For a more detailed discussion of the role of Armenian Social Democrats, see also Janet Afary, "Social Democracy and the Iranian Constitutional Revolution of 1906–1911," in *A Century of Revolution: Social Movements in Iran,* ed. John Foran (Minneapolis: University of Minnesota Press, 1994); Cosroe Chaqueri, "The Role and Impact of Armenian Intellectuals in Iranian Politics 1905–1911," *Armenian Review* 41, no. 2 (Summer 1988): 1–51; Chaqueri, *Origins of Social Democracy,* 147–72. One of Chilinkirian's articles, titled "Sahmanadrakan Parskastaně ew ir karik'nerě" (Constitutional Persia and its needs], also appeared in a series in the Tiflis-based *Mshak,* nos. 13–15, from 21 January to 23 January 1910. See also an English translation of another article by Chilinkirian in Cosroe Chaqueri, ed., *The Armenians of Iran: The Paradoxical Role of a Minority in a Dominant Culture: Essays and Documents* (Cambridge, MA: Center for Middle Eastern Studies of Harvard University, 1998), 193–239, which also appeared in the original Armenian in *Mshak* in 1909. For the letter to Kautsky, see "Lettre de A. Tchilinkirian à K. Kautsky," Tabriz, 16 July 1908, in *La social-démocratie en Iran,* 19–22. For a Persian translation, see Khosrow Shakeri [Cosroe Chaqueri], ed., *Asnad-e tarikhi-e jonbesh-e kargari, sosiyal-*

demukrasi va komunisti-e Iran (1903–1963) [Documents of the history of the labor/social democratic and communist movement in Iran (1903–1963)], vol. 6 (Florence: Mazdak, n.d.), 36. For an English translation, see John Riddell, ed., *Lenin's Struggle for a Revolutionary International: Documents: 1907–1916* (New York: Monad Press, 1984), 60–61, and Chaqueri, *Armenians of Iran*, 313–16. For letters to Plekhanov, see "A. Tchilinkirian à G. Plekhanov," Tabriz, 10 December 1908, Chaqueri, *La social-démocratie en Iran*, 50–51. An English translation appears in Chaqueri, *Armenians of Iran*, 335–37; Karakhanian à G. Plekhanov," Tabriz, 15 September 1905, in Chaqueri, *La social-démocratie en Iran*, 33–34. An English translation appears in Chaqueri, *Armenians of Iran*, 311–12; "Khacaturian [Khachaturian] à G. Plekhanov," undated, in Chaqueri; *La social-démocratie en Iran*, 39. An English translation, dated 19 November 1908, appears in Chaqueri, *Armenians of Iran*, 324–30. "T. Dervitch [Tigran Darvish/Ter-Hakobian] à G. Plekhanov," 3 December 1908, in Chaqueri, *La social-démocratie en Iran*, 44–49. An English translation appears in Chaqueri, *Armenians of Iran*, 338–44. Ter Hakobian was a frequent contributor to the constitutionalist paper *Iran-e Now*. See Afary, *Iranian Constitutional Revolution*, 268.

98. Tigran Zaven, "Ashkhatank'i azatut'iwně" 2 [The freedom of labor, part 2], *Surhandak* 96 (23 September/6 October 1908): 1. Zaven describes the Ottoman worker's situation as "remarkable" because the capitalists are foreign. When the capital and the labor are born of the same place, then profit remains in the country and serves the "fatherland's prosperity and progress," but when the capital is foreign, the profit "milked" from the worker's "blood-sweat" goes to countries like Germany and France, filling their "purses" or being "spilled on the sidewalks of those countries."

99. "Khacaturian [Khachaturian] à G. Plekhanov," undated, in Chaqueri, *La social-démocratie en Iran*, 39–41. See also S.-D., "Inch' piti anen sots'.-demokratneř Parskastanum?" [What will the Soc. Democrats do in Persia?], part 1, *Zang* (Tabriz) 13 (8 July 1910): 1–2; part 2, *Zang* 14 (15 July 1910): 1–2; part 3, *Zang* 16 (29 July 1910): 1–2; part 4, *Zang* 17 (5 August 1910): 2; part 5, *Zang* 18 (12 August 1910): 2; part 6, *Zang* 19 (19 August 1910): 1.

100. "Protocole no. 1 de la Conference des Social-Democrates de Tabriz, 1908," in Chaqueri, *La social-démocratie en Iran*, 35–36. For a Persian translation, see Chaqueri, *Asnad*, 6:50. An English translation appears in Chaqueri, *Armenians of Iran*, 331–34.

101. Afary, *Iranian Constitutional Revolution*, 246–47.

102. Kitur lists the names of those who seceded from the SDHP and settled in Tabriz. See Kitur, *Patmut'iwn*, 1:294. Pilosian's letter to Taqizadeh, dated 19 August 1909, confirms that plans to form the Democrat party had already taken shape on Taqizadeh's return in November 1908 from London to Tabriz and before his departure to Tehran in July or August 1909. Ettehadieh Nezam Mafi gives the date of Taqizadeh's return to Tabriz as Rajab 1327 *(qamri)*, which may be July or August 1909. See Mansoureh Ettehadieh Nezam Mafi, *Peydayesh va tahavvol-e ahzab-e siyasi-ye mashnitiyat: dowreh-ye avval va dovvom-e majles-e showra-ye melli* [Appearance and evolution of political

parties of constitutionalism: The first and second period of the National Consultative Assembly] (Tehran: Gustardah Press, 1982), 199. This is further supported by a letter from ARF member Vahan Zakarian to Yeprem Khan, wherein Zakarian states that the foundations of the party were put into place on Taqizadeh's return to Tabriz. For Zakarian's letter, see A[ndre] Amurian, comp., ed., *Dashnakts'ut'iwn, Yep'rem, parskakan sahmanadrut'iwn, H.H.D. kendronakan arkhiv* [A.R. Federation, Yeprem, Persian constitution, A.R.F. central archive] (Tehran: Alik', 1976), 1:254–62. For Pilosian's letter, see Iraj Afshar, ed., *Owraq-e tazehyab-e mashrutiyat va naqsh-e Taqizadeh* [Newly found constitutional papers and the role of Taqizadeh] (Tehran: Bahman, 1980), 238–40. See also G. Astghuni [Grigor Yeghikian], "Chshmartut'iwnner Parskastani heghap'okhakan sharzhumneri masin (akanatesi hishoghut'iwnnerits')" [Truths about the Persian revolutionary movements (from the memoirs of an eyewitness)], *Yeritasard Hayastan* 9, no. 46 (12 August 1913): 226. Pilosian to Taqizadeh, 19 August 1909, in Afshar, *Owraq*, 238–40. For program and regulations of the Democrat party, see Mansoureh Ettehadieh Nezam Mafi, ed., *Majmu'eh-ye motun va asnad-e tarikhi* [Collection of historical texts and documents], vol. 4 (Tehran: Naqsh-e Jahan, 1982), 3–19.

103. Ter Hacobian [Hakobian] to Taqizadeh, 1 November 1910, in Afshar, *Owraq*, 315.

104. Afary, *Iranian Constitutional Revolution*, 269. For a discussion of Ter Hakobian's series of articles titled "Terror," which appeared in *Iran-e Now* from 18 December 1910 to 4 January 1911, see Afary, 293–98.

105. Afary, 275, 388n81. See also Janet Afary, "Armenian Social Democrats and *Iran-i Naw*: A Secret Camaraderie," in *Reformers and Revolutionaries in Modern Iran: New Perspectives on the Iranian Left* (London and New York: Routledge/Curzon, 2004). In response to the *London Times*, which accused *Iran-e Now* of being run by Armenians and Russians, the paper denied that it had any Armenians on its staff. See Edward G. Browne, *The Persian Revolution, 1905–1909*, ed. Abbas Amanat with essays by Abbas Amanat and Mansour Bonakdarian (1910; Washington, DC: Mage, 1995), 443.

106. Astghuni [Yeghikian], "Inch'pēs kazmvets' Parskastani S.D. Kusakts'ut'iwnĕ" [How Persia's S.D. Party was organized], in S.D. Hnch'akean Kusaktsut'ean Fransayi Shrjan, ed., *Hushardzan nuiruats Sots'ial Demokrat Hnch'akean Kusakts'ut'ean k'arasunameakin* [Memoria dedicated to the fortieth anniversary of the Hnch'akean Party] (Paris: H.B. Tiwrapean, 1930), 192–93. A meeting between Naser al-Molk and Yeghikian may have taken place in January or February 1911 when the regent was in Anzali. See Cosroe Chaqueri, "The Role and Impact of Armenian Intellectuals in Iranian Politics, 1905–1911," *Armenian Review* 41, no. 2 (Summer 1988): 23. The Socialist International Bureau received information about the organization on 29 October 1910. See "Bulletin Périodique du B[ureau] S[ocialiste] I[nternationale]" [Periodic bulletin of the S[ocialist] I[nternational] B[ureau]], no. 7, 1911, p. 37, in Chaqueri, *Social-démocratie en Iran*, 229.

107. Astghuni [Yeghikian], "Inch'pēs kazmvets' Parskastani S.D. Kusakts'ut'iwnĕ," 194.

108. *Encyclopædia Iranica,* s.v. "Ełikean (Yaqikiyan), Grigor E.," by Aram Arkun, vol. 8, fasc. 4, 15 December 1988, 364–65 (print); 13 December 2011, www.iranicaonline.org/articles/elikean-yeqikian.

109. Mikayel Varandian, *H. H. Dashnakts'ut'ean patmut'iwn* [History of A. R. Federation] (Paris: Navarre, 1932).

110. Varandian, *Hosank'ner,* 307, 311–12, 318–21, 323, 345–47.

111. Varandian, 333.

112. Varandian, 203–87, in particular 204, 205, 274, 275, 276, 279. Varandian mentions the short run of *Hamaynk '(Community),* the organ of a small group of Armenian anarchists active in the 1890s, positing that anarchism "remained spurious and unfamiliar to the Armenian milieu." See Varandian, 287.

113. Varandian, 33, 34. Varandian is quoting and translating from Marx and Engels's *Die Klassenkämpfe in Frankreich 1848 bis 1850* [The class struggles in France, 1848 to 1850] (Berlin, 1895). See also Varandian, 44–45. In a work published four years later, Varandian surveys the history of protest beginning with the French Revolution but focusing on the nineteenth-century European socialist movements. See Mikayel Varandian, *Boghokě noragoyn patmut'ean měj* [Protest in recent history] (Geneva: ARF Press, 1914).

114. Varandian, *Hosank'ner ,* 27–28, 51.

115. Varandian, 47, 49, 52, 53.

116. Varandian, 57. For a similar discussion of revisionism, Bernstein, Jaurès, and others, see "Sots'ialakan tesut'iwn: Skzbunk' ew taktika" [Social view: Principle and tactic], *Drōshak* 6 (June 1908): 84–87.

117. Varandian, *Hosank'ner,* 71–76.

118. Varandian also discusses the German SD resolutions against reformism in meetings at Dresden in 1903 and then modified with the contributions of Adler and Vandervelde at the Socialist International Amsterdam 1905. See Varandian, *Hosank'ner,* 56–57, 59–67, 85, 88. Kautsky and Plekhanov wanted Jaurès expelled from socialism's ranks over his defense of socialist statesmen, like Millerand and Waldeck-Rousseau, who entered government. See Varandian, 63.

119. Varandian, 85, 107–13. See also "Resolution Adopted at the Seventh International Socialist Congress at Stuttgart," August 18–24, 1907 (Berlin: Vorwärts, 1907), 64–66, accessed 27 September 2017, https://www.marxists.org /history/international/social-democracy/1907/militarism.htm.

120. Irving Howe, cited in Geoffrey Kurtz, "A Socialist State of Grace: The Radical Reformism of Jean Jaurès," *New Political Science* 28, no. 3 (2006): 402. See also Geoffrey Kurtz, *Jean Jaurès: The Inner Life of Social Democracy* (University Park: Pennsylvania State University Press, 2014). For a brief discussion of Jaurès and Armenians, see Madeleine Rebérioux, "Jean Jaurès and the Armenians," *Armenian Review* 44, no. 2/174 (1991): 1–11.

121. Kurtz, "Socialist State of Grace," 404, 405.

122. Kurtz, 406. Varandian, like Khazhak and many other ARF thinkers, criticized the "dogmatism," "phraseology," "economism," and "proletarian fire worship" of European and especially Russian and Georgian SDs, the latter having been "baptized in the social-democratic pond." See Kurtz, 179–81.

123. Kurtz, "Socialist State of Grace," 406.

124. Kurtz, 406, 408, 410.

125. Kurtz, 416, 418.

126. See Kévorkian, *Armenian Genocide,* for such encounters, attempts at collaboration, and conflict, especially Parts 1 and 2.

127. Ter Minassian, "Role of the Armenian Community," 149.

128. Tigran Zaven, "Ashkhatank'i azatut'iwně" 1 [Freedom of labor, part 1], *Surhandak* 95 (22 September/5 October 1908): 1. For news of the translation, see *Surhandak* 103 (1/14 October 1908): 2. Starting in October 1908, under Tigran Zaven's editorship, *Surhandak* went further to the left, declaring that the paper defends the interests of the majority "working, exploited and suffering class." See *Surhandak* 93 (19 September/2 October 1908) and 94 (20 September/3 October 1908).

129. Ter Minassian, "Role of the Armenian Community," 154.

130. *Nor Hosank'* 1 (28 March 1909): 2; Eliminor, "Patcharner ew hetevank'ner" [Reasons and consequences], *Nor Hosank'* 1 (28 March 1909): 3–4.

131. Ter Minassian, "Role of the Armenian Community," 144.

132. Ter Minassian, 203n68. Tarpinian's series of twelve articles, R. Tarpinian, "H.H. Dashnakts'ut'iwně ew anor k'aghak'akanut'iwně T'urk'ioy měj" [The A.R. Federation and its politics in Turkey], appeared on the first page of *Azatamart.* See part 1, 418 (21 October/3 November 1910); part 2, 420 (22 October/4 November 1910); part 3, 422 (26 October/8 November 1910); part 4, 425 (29 October/11 November 1910); part 5, 427 (31 October/13 November 1910); part 6, 430 (4/17 November 1910); part 7, 433 (7/20 November 1910); part 8 (11/24 November 1910); part 9, 438 (13/28 November 1910); part 10, 444 (20 November/3 December 1910); part 11, 447 (24 Nov/7 December 1910); part 12, 468 (18/31 December).

133. Tarpinian, "H.H. Dashnakts'ut'iwně," part 3, 1. See also part 10, 1.

134. Tarpinian, "H.H. Dashnakts'ut'iwně," part 4, 1.

135. Adom [Shahrigian], "H.H. Dashnakts'ut'ean k'aghak'akanut'iwně T'urk'ioy měj" [A.R. Federation's politics in Turkey], *Azatamart* 476 (28 December 1910/10 January 1911): 1. See also Ter Minassian, "Role of the Armenian Community," 147.

136. For a nuanced discussion of the Broad socialists on this issue, see Dimou, *Entangled Paths towards Modernity,* 224–39.

137. Adom, "H.H. Dashnakts'ut'ean k'aghak'akanut'iwně T'urk'ioy měj," 1. Tigran Zaven, writing a few years earlier on the issue of Turkey's preparation for socialist activity, argued that the ground for a socialist party in Turkey existed but only as long as the primary arena of activity covered not just one part of Turkey—for example, the Armenian provinces—but worked in all of the Ottoman Empire as an international party. See T. Zaven, "Sots'ialistakan t'ē demokratakan" [Socialist or democratic] part 1, *Yerkri Dzayně* 31 (30 December 1907): 2–4. For parts 2 and 3 of the article, see *Yerkri Dzayně* 1 (13 January 1908): 1–3 and 2 (20 January 1908): 1–3.

138. Hildermeier, *Russian Socialist Revolutionary Party,* 230.

139. Hildermeier, 67.

140. Varandian, *Hosank'ner,* 123.

141. K[ristapor] Mikayelian, "Bekorner im husherits'" [Fragments from my memoirs], *Hayrenik' Amsagir* 2, no. 10 (August 1924): 54–62. This posthumously published memoir mentions the formation of a Tiflis Narodnaya Volya group, in the 1880s, composed of two Armenian men, one Armenian woman, two Georgian men, and one Georgian woman.

142. Jones, *Socialism in Georgian Colors*, 159.

143. Jones, 166; Hildermeier, *Russian Socialist Revolutionary Party*, 61. Plekhanov and other SDs gave the intelligentsia a subsidiary role in developing a socialist consciousness, convinced that workers must develop their own struggle without external intervention. See Robert Mayer, "Plekhanov, Lenin and Working-Class Consciousness," *Studies in East European Thought* 49 (1997): 159–85. For a similar Armenian SD point of view, see Zarmayr, "Hay ashkhatavor giwghats'iut'iwně ew intelijents'ian" [The Armenian working peasantry and the intelligentsia], *Aniv* 1 (2 March 1908): 6–8. See also E., "Proletaristě ew intelijents'ian ěst Kautsku" [The proletariat and the intelligentsia according to Kautsky], *Murch* 11–12 (November–December 1906): 119–27, which concludes that, on the whole, the intelligentsia's interests differ from those of the working class.

144. Njagulov, "Early Socialism in the Balkans," 245–47, 277.

145. "Sots'ialistakan intelijents'ia ew heghap'okhut'iwně" [The socialist intelligentsia and the revolution], *Drōshak* 2–3 (February–March 1909): 37–39.

146. Tsarist Spy Service "Okhrana's" Report about the A.R. Federation, in *Niwt'er*, 2:326, 328.

147. *Niwt'er*, 2:329.

148. *Niwt'er*, 2:325, 331, 333.

149. Although the report says the meeting took place in the editorial offices of *Gorts* in Baku, the report is by the Tiflis gendarmerie chief, and *Gorts* was published in Tiflis in 1908–9. The report also contains a list of agreed-upon targets. See Document 8, secret police report on an interparty meeting held in Baku, 16 February 1909, Indexed 4162, Chief of the Tiflis Provincial Gendarmerie Directorate (9 February 1909, 28/2), no. 1556, in Yeghiayan, *Armenians and the Okhrana*, 20. For a report, compiled on 17 December 1909 and listing 115 terror acts attributed to the ARF, see Document 19, "List of ARF victims compiled by Chief Prosecutor Lizhin, in Yeghiayan," *Armenians and the Okhrana*, 70–83. Another report provides a clue regarding informants Russian authorities employed to acquire information. See Document 9, MVD report on the recruiting of an Armenian informant, 23 March 1909, Indexed 7877, Ministry of Interior, re: informant Avanesiants, in Yeghiayan, *Armenians and the Okhrana*, 22–32.

150. Hildermeier, *Russian Socialist Revolutionary Party*, 52.

151. Hildermeier, 53–54. See, for example, the poem "P'ark'ahabekich'nerun" [Praise to the terrorists], *Drōshak* 8 (August 1905): 115–16. Among the Party of Socialist Revolutionaries' more high-profile assassinations were Minister of Interior Vyacheslavovich von Plehve (April 1904) and Governor-General of Moscow Sergei Aleksandrovich (February 1905); among the ARF's was Governor of Baku Mikhail Nakashidze (May 1905), as well as the attempted assassinations of Sultan Abdul-Hamid (1905). High Commissioner in the Caucasus

Grigorii Sergeyevich Golitsyn (1896–1904), who saw to the confiscation of Armenian Church properties in 1903, survived an assassination attempt by the SDHP in 1903. In 1905 he left his position and the region and was replaced by Illarion Ivanovich Vorontsov-Dashkov. For a list of ARF victims compiled by tsarist authorities, see Document 19 in Yeghiayan, *Armenians and the Okhrana*, 64–83. This report attributes Golitsyn's attempted assassination to the ARF. Stephen Riegg argues that Golitsyn's predecessor, High Commissioner Sergei Sheremetev (1890–96), had already established the foundation for the seizure of Armenian Church properties. See Riegg, "Beyond the Caucasus," chap. 6.

152. Such works include V. Chernov, *About the Theory of the Class Struggle*, trans. M. Har (1907), and *The Proletariat and the Hard-Working Farmers*, trans. A. Mehrabian (1907); Ter Minassian, "Role of the Armenian Community," 194–96n33, 200–201n47.

153. The ARF replaced the term *proletariat* with the more comprehensive term *worker* and included peasants within that understanding. See, for example, Khazhak, *Dēpi fēdērats'ia,* 279, and, of course, the ARF press and programs.

154. Hildermeier, *Russian Socialist Revolutionary Party,* 75, 77, 79, 88.

155. "Sots'ialistakan inteligentsi'a ew heghap'okhut'iwnĕ," 38. I have not come across similar discussion of land socialization for Iran.

156. Tarpinian, "H.H. Dashnakts'ut'iwnĕ" [The A..R. Federation], part 8, *Azatamart* 436 (11/24 November 1910): 1.

157. V. Araratski, "Sots'ialakan tesut'iwn: sots'ialisti namaknerĕ" [Social view: The letters of a socialist], 4th letter, *Drōshak* 11–12 (November–December 1907): 167–70. See also 5th letter, *Drōshak* 1 (January 1908): 6–9.

158. V. Araratski, "Sots'ialakan tesut'iwn: sots'ialisti namaknerĕ" [Social view: The letters of a socialist], 6th letter, *Drōshak* 2 (February 1908): 21–24.

159. *Drōshak* printed the Party of Socialist Revolutionaries' demands in V. Araratski, "Heghap'okhakan Ṛusastanĕ: K'aghak'akan kusaktsut'iwnner Ṛusastanum" [Revolutionary Russia: Political parties in Russia], part 2, *Drōshak* 5 (May 1906): 73–76. A comparison of Party of Socialist Revolutionaries and ARF demands demonstrates the commonalities, which included replacing a standing army with a popular militia. For more on popular militias, see *Drōshak* 9 (September 1909): 126–28; *Drōshak* 10–11 (October–November 1909): 144–47; Mikayel Varandian, *Hamazhoghovrdakan banak* [Popular militia] (Geneva: A.R. Federation, 1909). For more on SR views, see M.H. [Mikayel Hovhannisian/Mikayel Vardanian], "T'ert'on: Nakhagitsĕ" [Feuilleton: The protocol], parts 3 and 4, *Yerkir* 33 (8 November 1906): 2 and *Yerkir* 35 (19 November 1906): 2; H.P. [Hayrapet Panirian], "Giwghats'in ew sots'ial demokrat'ean" [The peasant and Social Democracy], parts 1 and 2, *Aṛawōt* 25 (7 February 1910): 2 and *Aṛawōt* 26 (14 February 1910): 2–3. On SDs and their differences with SRs, especially regarding historical process, economic determinism, and the role of the peasantry, see, for example, part 3 of the same series, *Drōshak* 8 (August 1906): 124–26; V. Araratski, "Kusaktsut'iwnner Ṛusastanum" [Parties in Russia], part 4, *Drōshak* 10 (October 1906): 152–55. For the SD view on the peasantry, see "Giwghats'iut'iwnĕ ew azatagrakan

sharzhumě" [The peasantry and the liberation movement], *Hosank'* 19 (17 December 1906): 1; S.S.G. [Stepan Sapah-Giwlian], "Sots'ializm ew yerkragort-sakan khndirner" [Socialism and agricultural questions], part 1, *Hnch'ak* 8 (August 1907): 95–98.

    160. Jones, *Socialism in Georgian Colors*, 77, 103, 158.

    161. Khuri-Makdisi, *Eastern Mediterranean*, 29.

    162. Eastern Bureau circular, ARF Archives, B 16–150. From a report presented to the Second International in Stuttgart in 1907. See "Kusaktsut'ean gortsunēut'enēn (mi kani p'aster)" [From the party's activity (a few proofs)], *Drōshak* 9 (September 1907): 137.

    163. *Hnch'ak* appeared in London from 1887 to 1892 and 1894 to 1904, in Athens from 1892 to 1894, and in Paris from 1904 to 1915.

    164. For the French Armenophile movement, see Claire Mouradian, ed., *Arménie, une passion française: Le mouvement arménophile en France (1878–1923)* [Armenia, a French passion: The Armenophile movement in France] (Paris: Magellan, 2007); Edmond Khayadjian, *Archag Tchobanian et le mouvement arménophile en France* [Archag Tchobanian and the Armenophile movement in France] (Marseille: Centre national de documentation pédagogique, 1986).

    165. Quillard visited Istanbul in late 1908 to meet with ARF members with the intention of establishing a newspaper there with the support of Prince Saba-heddin. In the end, the ARF decided against this paper and published its own, *Azatamart* [Battle for freedom] later in 1909. See "Kiarě Polsum" [Quillard in Istanbul], *Gorts* 62 (23 November 1908): 1.

    166. See, for example, Kévorkian, *Armenian Genocide*, Part 1, chap. 2. See also the firsthand account by S[tepan] Sapah-Giwlian, *Pataskhanatunerě* [The responsibles] (Providence: Yeritasard Hayastan, 1916).

    167. A. Aharonian, "T'ert'on: Haykakan harts'ě ew Haagayi II hamazhogově," 1 [Feuilleton: The Armenian question and the Hague conference], part 1, *Arōr* 3 (5 September 1907): 2; for parts 2, 3, and 4, see 4 (6 September 1907): 2; 5 (7 September 1907): 2; and 6 (8 September 1907): 2.

    168. "Khaghaghut'ean kongresner ew hakamilitarizm" [Peace congresses and antimilitarism], *Drōshak* 9 (September 1907): 121. Victor Berard, Pierre Quillard, Anatole France, and Francis de Pressensé also intervened on behalf of Aharonian when he was imprisoned by the Russian state from early 1909 to 1911. See Yervand Pampukian, ed., *Niwt'er* (Beirut: Hamazgayin Vahē Sēt'ean Tparan, 2012), 9:232–42. Regarding Aharonian's arrest and imprisonment, see also Document 10, intelligence questions regarding Aharonian, 8 May 1909, in Yeghiayan, *Armenians and the Okhrana*, 32–34; for a sympathetic portrayal by an official of the secret police, see Document 11, 21 July 1909, no. 24682, in Yeghiayan, 35–38. For more Okhrana reports on Aharonian, including details about his life and surveillance, see documents in Yeghiayan, 84–86, 134, 167–209.

    169. Rostom to Western Bureau, 13/20 January 1907, probably from Vienna, *Rostom Namakani*, 417; Rostom to Western Bureau, 20 January 1907, probably from Vienna, *Rostom Namakani*, 418; Rostom to Western Bureau, 3 July 1907, *Rostom Namakani*, 423. Contacts took place before and beyond

these kinds of appeals; for example, Kristapor Mikayelian met with Quillard in Paris in 1904. See Mikayelian to Western Bureau, 9 July 1904, in *K'ristap'or Mik'ayeleani namaknerě*, 332 (original in ARF Archives, 1268–49).

170. R. Lernian, "Mijazgayin sots'ializtakan hamagumarě" [International socialist congress], *Arōr* 1 (2 September 1907): 2–3.

171. Ego, "T'ert'on: Internats'ionali zhamadravayrits'" [Feuilleton: From the International's rendezvous], *Arōr* 2 (4 September 1907): 2.

172. Varandian also recounted a conversation with Austrian Social Democrat Engelbert Pernerstorfer, who took issue with Varandian's comparison of Young Turk chauvinism with Austrian chauvinism. According to Varandian, Pernerstorfer argued that he did not believe the Austrians had the same "appetite" for hegemony and were only interested in preserving their own national particularity, adding that he himself was a socialist but also a patriot: "Along with being a socialist, I never forget that I belong to the German nation . . . " In response, Varandian qualified his statement, explaining that his comparison applied only to the pan-Germans and that the ARF was in full agreement with his views, even translating and publishing his work on the national question, a detail that seemed to please Pernerstorfer. "VII Michazgayin Sots'ialistakan kongres" [VII: International socialist congress], *Drōshak* 8 (August 1907): 110–14; "Mijazgayin Sots'ialistakan biwroyi X hamagumarě" [International socialist bureau's 10th congress], *Drōshak* 9–10 (September–October 1908): 148–51; "Sots'ialakan: VIII Mijazgayin Sots'ialistakan kongres" [Socialist: VIII International socialist congress], *Drōshak* 7–9 (July–September 1910): 83–94. The other ARF representatives were Nikol Duman, Shirakuni, and Barseghian. Varandian seems to have headed the delegation and to have been the one to speak to the congresses.

173. "Sots'ialakan: VIII Mijazgayin sots'ialistakan kongres," 83–94. The report appeared in German translation in 1910; see Ter Minassian, "Role of the Armenian Community," 193–94.

174. "Mijkusakts'ayin khorhrdazhoghov" [Interparty council meeting], *Drōshak* 7–9 (July–September 1910): 91. Similar meetings were held much earlier in 1905. For minutes of meetings (including disagreements) and correspondence in Russian between combinations of ARF, SDHP, Social Democrats, Socialist Revolutionaries, and others during the Russian revolutionary period, see documents in ARF Archives, Part B, Files 1714–2, 1714–3, 1714–4, 1714–5, 1714–6, 1714–7, 1714–8, 1714–13, 1714–16.

175. "Heghap'okhakan dashn ts'arizmi dēm," 181–84; *Heghap'okhakan dashn: mijkusakts'akan khorhrdazhoghovneri voroshumnerě* [Revolutionary pact: Decisions of the interparty council meetings] (Geneva: Drōshak Tparan, 1905). See also a circular sent out by the ARF's Western Bureau, 10 January 1905, in *Niwt'er*, 2:225–26; "Prizyv Kavkazskogo soyuznogo komiteta RSDRP, Tiflisskogo komiteta sotsialistov federalistov 'Sakartvelo,' Tiflisskogo komiteta eserob Kavkazskogo komiteta partii Dashnaktsutyun k grazhdanam protiv tsarskogo samoderzhaviya" [RSDRP Caucasian union, Sarkartvelo social federalist Tiflis committee, SR Tiflis committee, Federation (ARF) party Caucasian committee's call to citizens against tsarist autocracy], 2 February 1905, Fond 1457/Fond 4047, Catalog 1, Doc. 22, National Archives of Armenia. (Both fond numbers appear.)

176. "Heghap'okhakan kusakts'ut'iwnneri dashn ts'arizmi dēm" [Pact of revolutionary parties against tsarism], *Drōshak* 5 (May 1905): 65–69.

177. Kévorkian, *Armenian Genocide*, part 1, chap. 2. See also the firsthand account by Stepan Sapah-Giwlian of his own, SDHP's, and, to some extent, ARF relations with the Young Turks in his *Pataskhanatunerĕ*.

178. "Mijkusakts'ayin kongren" [Interparty congress], *Drōshak* 1 (January 1908): 1–2. For the actual announcement of participants in the congress, see "Haytararagir Osmanean kaysrut'ean ĕnddimadir tarreru kongrein, gumaruats yevropayi mēj" [Declaration of the Ottoman Empire's oppositional elements congress, convoked in Europe], *Drōshak* 1 (January 1908): 2–4. Signatories: Union and Progress Ottoman Committee (official organs: *Şûra-yı Ümmet* and *Meşveret*); ARF (*Drōshak*); Ottoman Union of Private Initiative, Decentralization, and Constitution (*Terakki*); Jewish Committee of Egypt (*La Vera*); editorial board of *Khilafet;* editorial board of *Armenia;* editorial board of *Ṛazmik;* editorial board of *Hayrenik';* committee "Ahti Osmani" (Egypt). See also "K'aghuats'k'ner kongrei voroshumnerēn" [Excerpts from the decisions of the congress], *Drōshak* 1 (January 1908): 4–5.

CHAPTER 5. "THE EGOISM OF THE CURED PATIENT"

1. Rostom to Mikayel Varandian, in *Ṛostom Namakani,* 521 (original in ARF Archives, 1738–18). Given the contents, the letter was clearly written after the 1908 reinstatement of the constitution in the Ottoman Empire, but it is hard to identify the exact date and place from which he was writing, although Dasnabedian suggests 1910 and Erzurum without explaining his reasoning. Rostom was in Tabriz, Van, and Istanbul during 1909 and in Istanbul and Erzurum in 1910. He mentions writing to Istanbul regarding the expenses of *Azatamart,* which began publication in 1909. It is likely, therefore, that he was indeed writing from Erzurum sometime in 1910.

2. Rostom to Western Bureau, Istanbul section, in *Ṛostom Namakani,* 522–23 (original in ARF Archives, 99–82). Undated but presumed to have been written in 1910 or after.

3. Anderson, *Under Three Flags,* 2.

4. Libaridian, "What Was Revolutionary about Armenian Political Parties in the Ottoman Empire?," 83. For a call for "shared history," see "Introduction: Ottoman History's Black Hole," in *The Ottoman East in the Nineteenth Century: Societies, Identities and Politics,* ed. Yaşar Tolga Cora, Dzovinar Derderian, and Ali Sipahi (London: I. B. Tauris, 2016), 1–15.

5. Milan Kundera, "Part Eight: Paths in the Fog," in *Testaments Betrayed: An Essay in Nine Parts,* trans. Linda Asher (New York: Harper-Perennial, 1996), 237.

Bibliography

PRIMARY SOURCES

Archives

Armenian Revolutionary Federation, Watertown, Massachusetts
Bibliothèque Nubar, Paris
British Library, London
Mkhitarist Monastery Archives, Vienna
Mesrop Mashtots Institute of Ancient Manuscripts (Matenadaran), Archives of
   the Catholicosate, Yerevan
National Archives, Kew, United Kingdom
National Archives of Armenia, Yerevan
National Library of Armenia, Yerevan

Newspapers

Alik' [Wave], Tiflis, 1906
Aniv [Wheel], Baku, 1908
Ankakh Mamul [Independent press], Tiflis, 1906
Apagay [Future], Tiflis, 1907
Apagay [Future], Istanbul, 1910
Aṛawōt [Morning], Baku, 1909
Aṛawōt [Morning], Tabriz, 1909–12
Arōr [Plough], Tiflis, 1907
Azatamart [Battle for freedom], Istanbul, 1909–11
Drōshak [Banner], Geneva, 1905–12
Dzayn [Voice], Tiflis, 1906–7
Gorts [Work], Tiflis, 1908–9
Haṛaj [Forward], Tiflis, 1906

Haṛaj [Forward], Erzurum, 1909–11
Hnch'ak [Bell], Paris, 1888, 1905–12
Hosank' [Current], Tiflis, 1906
Khat'abala [Trouble], Tiflis, 1906–11
Kovkasi Aṛawōt [Caucasus's morning], Tiflis, 1907
Murch [Hammer], Tiflis, 1905–7
Nor Alik' [New wave], Tiflis, 1907
Nor Hosank' [New current], Tiflis, 1909
Nor Ōrer [New days], Baku, 1908
Surhandak [Messenger], Istanbul, 1908
Vtak [Brook/Stream], Tiflis, 1907
Yerkir [Country], Tiflis, 1906
Yerkri Dzaynĕ [The voice of country], Tiflis, 1906–8
Zhamanak [Time], Tiflis, 1906–7
Zhamanak [Time], Istanbul, 1908–9
Zang [Bell], Tiflis, 1906
Zang [Bell], Tabriz, 1910–12

Collected Published Documents

Afshar, Iraj, ed. *Owraq-e tazehyab-e mashrutiyat va naqsh-e Taqizadeh* [Newly found constitutional papers and the role of Taqizadeh]. Tehran: Bahman, 1980.

Amurian, A[ndre] [Andre Ter Ohanian], comp. and ed. *Dashnakts'ut'iwn, Yep'rem, parskakan sahmanadrut'iwn, H.H.D. kendronakan arkhiv* [A.R. Federation, Yep'rem, Persian constitution, A.R.F. central archive]. Vol. 1. Tehran: Alik', 1976.

Dasnabedian, Hrach, comp. and ed. *Niwt'er H.H. Dashnakts'ut'ean patmut'ean hamar* [Materials for the history of the A.R. Federation]. Vols. 1–4. Beirut: Hamazgayin Vahē Sēt'ean Tparan, 1972–2007.

———, comp. and ed. *K'ristap'or Mik'ayeleani namaknerĕ* [K'ristap'or Mik'ayelean's letters]. Beirut: Hamazgayin Vahē Sēt'ean Tparan, 1993.

———, comp. and ed. *Rostom namakani: Mahuan ut'sunameakin aṛt'iw* [Rostom Letters: On the occasion of the eightieth anniversary of his death]. Beirut: Hamazgayin Vahē Sēt'ean Press, 1999.

———, comp. and ed. *Simon Zavarean.* 2 vols. Ant'ilias: Hrat. H.H. Dashnakts'ut'ean, 1997.

Hushamatean Hay Heghap'okhakan Dashnakts'ut'ean albom-atlas, vol. 1, *Diwts'aznamart* [Commemorative album-atlas of the Armenian Revolutionary Federation, vol. 1, Heroic combat]. Glendale, CA: ARF Central Committee, 1992.

Pambukian, Yervant, comp. and ed. *Niwt'er H.H. Dashnakts'ut'ean patmut'ean hamar* [Materials for the history of the A.R. Federation]. Vols. 5–12. Beirut: Hamazgayin Vahē Sēt'ean Tparan, 2007–17.

Rostom: Mahuan vat'sunameakin aṛt'iw [Rostom: On the sixtieth anniversary of his death]. Beirut: Hamazgayin Vahē Sēt'ean Tparan, 1979.

Yeghiayan, Vartkes, ed. *The Armenians and the Okhrana, 1907–1915: Documents from the Russian Department of Police Archives.* Los Angeles: Center for Armenian Remembrance, 2016.

Other Primary Sources

Aknouni [Khachatur Malumian]. *Political Persecution: Armenian Prisoners of the Caucasus (A Page of the Tzar's Persecution)*, trans. A. M. and H. W. New York: 1911, n.p.

Aknuni, E. [Khachatur Malumian]. *Boghoki dzayn: kovkasahay k'aghak'akan bantarkialnerě (ts'arakan halatsank'i mi ēj)* [The voice of protest: Caucasian Armenian political prisoners (A page from tsarist persecution)]. Beirut: Ghukas Karapetean, 1978.

Astghuni, G. [Grigor Yeghikian]. "Chshmartut'iwnner Parskastani heghap'okhakan sharzhumneri masin (akanatesi hishoghut'iwnnerits')" [Truths about the Persian revolutionary movements (from the memoirs of an eyewitness)]. *Yeritasard Hayastan* [Young Armenia] 9, no. 46 (12 August 1913).

Chaqueri, Cosroe, ed. *La social-démocratie en Iran: Articles et documents annotés et presentés.* Florence: Mazdak, 1979.

Giwlkhandanian, A[braham]. *Bagui derě mer azatagrakan sharzhman mēj* [Baku's role in our liberation movement]. Tehran: Alik', 1981.

Heghap'okhakan dashn: Mijkusakts'akan khorhrdazhoghovneri voroshumnerě [Revolutionary pact: Decisions of the interparty conferences]. Geneva: Drōshak Tparan, 1905.

Khazhak, Garegin. *Dēpi fēdērats'ia* [Toward federation]. Tiflis: Aghanean, 1907.

Nezam Mafi, Mansoureh Ettehadieh, ed. *Majmu'eh-ye motun va asnad-e tarikhi* [Collection of historical texts and documents]. Vol. 4. Tehran: Naqsh-e Jahan, 1982.

"The Ottoman Constitution, Promulgated the 7th Zilbridje, 1293 (11/23 December 1876)." *American Journal of International Law* 2, no. 4, Supplement: Official Documents (October 1908): 367–87.

Papazian, Vahan. *Im Husherě* [My memoirs]. Vol. 1. Boston: Hayrenik', 1950.

Papazian, Vahan. *Im Husherě* [My memoirs]. Vol. 2. Beirut: Hamazgayin, 1952.

"Resolution adopted at the Seventh International Socialist Congress at Stuttgart." International Socialist Congress at Stuttgart, August 18–24, 1907. Berlin: Vorwärts Publishers, 1907. https://www.marxists.org/history/international/social-democracy/1907/militarism.htm.

Sapah-Giwlian, S[tepan]. *Pataskhanatunerě* [The responsibles]. Providence, RI: Yeritasard Hayastan, 1916.

Shahrigian, H[arutiwn]. Adom. *Mer havatamkě* [Our credo]. Beirut: Hamazgayin, 1981.

Shakeri, Khosrow [Cosroe Chaqueri]. *Asnad-ye tarikhi-e jonbesh-e kargari, sosyal-demokrasi va komunisti-ye Iran. 1903–1963.* [Documents of the history of the labor/social democratic and communist movement in Iran, 1903–1963]. Vol. 6. Florence: Mazdak, n.d.

Shakhatunian, A. *Fēdēralizm ew demōkratizm* [Federalism and democratism]. Tiflis: Ėlektropech. A. M. Tarumova, 1907.

Teodik. *Amēnun tarets'oyts'ě* [Everyone's yearbook]. 3rd year. Istanbul, 1909.

Varandian, Mikayel. *Hosank'ner* [Currents]. Geneva: Hratarakut'iwn H.H.D., 1910.

Zavarian, S[imon]. *Apakedronatsumĕ.* Istanbul: Azatut'ean Matenadaran, 1908.

Zaven, T[igran], comp. *T'iwrk' sahmanadrut'iwnĕ ew Yeritasard T'iwrk' kusakts'ut'iwnnerĕ* [The Turkish constitution and the Young Turk parties]. Tiflis: Tparan Epokha, 1908.

SECONDARY SOURCES

Abdulifard, Firaydun. *Tarikh-e post dar Iran az sadarat-e Amir Kabir ta vizarat-e Amin al-Dowlah. 1267–1297 h.q.* [A history of postal service in Iran: From the premiership of Amir-Kabir to the ministry of Amin al-Dowlah, 1888–1918]. Tehran: Hirmand, 1996.

Abrahamian, Ervand. *History of Modern Iran.* New York: Cambridge University Press, 2008.

Adanalyan, M.L. "Azganuer Hayuhyats' Ĕnkerut'iwnĕ" [Patriotic Armenian women's society]. *Patma-banasirakan handes* [Historical-Philological Review] 4, no. 87 (1979): 255–59.

Adanır, Fikret. "The National Question and the Genesis and Development of Socialism in the Ottoman Empire: The Case of Macedonia." In *Socialism and Nationalism in the Ottoman Empire, 1876–1923,* edited by Mete Tunçay and Erik J. Zürcher, 27–48. London: I.B. Tauris, 1994.

Afary, Janet. "Armenian Social Democrats and *Iran-i Naw:* A Secret Camaraderie." In *Reformers and Revolutionaries in Modern Iran: New Perspectives on the Iranian Left,* edited by Stephanie Cronin, 67–84. London: Routledge/Curzon, 2004.

———. *The Iranian Constitutional Revolution, 1906–1911: Grassroots Democracy, Social Democracy, and the Origins of Feminism.* New York: Columbia University Press, 1996.

———. "Social Democracy and the Iranian Constitutional Revolution of 1906–1911." In *A Century of Revolution: Social Movements in Iran,* edited by John Foran, 21–43. Minneapolis: University of Minnesota Press, 1994.

Aghayan, Ts. P. *Revolyuts'ion sharzhumnerĕ Hayastanum, 1905–1907 t'.t'.* [Revolutionary movements in Armenia, 1905–1907]. Yerevan: Haykakan SAR Gitut'iwnneri Akademia, 1955.

AHR Conversation: On Transnational History with C.A. Bayly, Sven Beckert, Matthew Connelly, Isabel Hofmeyr, Wendy Kozol, and Patricia Seed. *American Historical Review* 111, no. 5 (December 2006): 1441–64.

Al-Muwaylihi, Ibrahim. *Spies, Scandals, and Sultans: Istanbul in the Twilight of the Ottoman Empire.* Translation of *Ma Hunalik.* Translated and introduced by Roger Allen. London: Rowman and Littlefield, 2008.

Altstadt, Audrey. *The Azerbaijani Turks: Power and Identity under Russian Rule.* Stanford, CA: Hoover Institution Press, 1992.

Altstadt-Mirhadi, Audrey. "Baku: The Transformation of a Muslim Town." In *The City in Late Imperial Russia,* edited by Michael F. Hamm, 283–318. Bloomington: Indiana University Press, 1986.

Amirahmadi, Hooshang. *The Political Economy of Iran under the Qajars: Society, Politics, and Foreign Relations, 1799–1921.* London: I.B. Tauris, 2012.

Amurian, Andre. *H.H. Dashnakts'ut'iwně Parskastanum, 1890–1918* [The A.R. Federation in Persia, 1890–1918]. Tehran: Alik', 1950.

———. *Heghap'okhakan Yep'remi vodisakaně* [Revolutionary Yeprem's odyssey]. Tehran: Alik', 1972.

Anagnostopoulou, Sia. "The 'Nation' of the Rum Sings of Its Sultan: The Many Faces of Ottomanism." In *Economy and Society on Both Shores of the Aegean,* edited by Lorans Tanatar Baruh and Vangelis Kechriotis, 79–106. Athens: Alpha Bank Historical Archives, 2010.

Anderson, Benedict. *Under Three Flags: Anarchism and the Anti-Colonial Imagination.* London: Verso, 2005.

Armenian Review 47, nos. 1–2 (Spring/Summer 2001).

Aroney, Nicholas. "Imagining a Federal Commonwealth: Australian Conceptions of Federalism, 1890–1901." *Federal Law Review* 30, no. 2 (2002): 265–94.

Artinian, Vartan. *The Armenian Constitutional System in the Ottoman Empire, 1839–1863: A Study of Its Historical Development.* Self-published, Istanbul, 1988.

Ascher, Abraham. *The Revolution of 1905.* Vol. 1, *Russia in Disarray.* Stanford, CA: Stanford University Press, 1988.

———. *The Revolution of 1905.* Vol. 2, *Authority Restored.* Stanford, CA: Stanford University Press, 1994.

———. *The Revolution of 1905: A Short History.* Stanford, CA: Stanford University Press, 2004.

Aslanian, Sebouh D. "From Autonomous to Interactive Histories: World History's Challenge to Armenian Studies." In *Words and Worlds in Motion: Armenians in the Mediterranean and Beyond,* edited by Kathryn Babayan and Michael Pifer, 81–125. New York: Palgrave, 2018.

———. "Port Cities and Printers: Reflections on Early Modern Global Armenian Print Culture." *Book History* 17, no. 1 (2014): 51–93.

Astghuni, G. [Grigor Yeghikian]. "Inch'pēs kazmvets' Parskastani S.D. Kusakts'ut'iwně" [How Persia's S.D. Party was organized]. In *Hushardzan nuirvats Sots'ial Demokrat Hnch'akean Kusakts'ut'ean k'aṛasunameakin* [Memoria dedicated to the fortieth anniversary of the Hnch'akean Party], edited by S.D. Kusaktsut'ean Fransayi Shrjan, 81–125. Paris: H.B. Tiwrapean, 1930.

Ateş, Sabri. *The Ottoman-Iranian Borderlands: Making a Boundary, 1843–1914.* Cambridge: Cambridge University Press, 2013.

Ayalon, Ami. *Reading Palestine: Printing and Literacy, 1900 –1948.* Austin: University of Texas Press, 2004.

Aytekin, E. Attila. "Tax Revolts during the Tanzimat Period (1839–1876) and before the Young Turk Revolution (1904–1908): Popular Protest and State Formation in the Late Ottoman Empire." *Journal of Policy History* 25, no. 3 (2013): 308–33.

Azgayin hayrenasirakan heghap'okhakan yergaran [National patriotic revolutionary songbook]. Beirut: Hamazgayin Vahē Sēt'ean Tparan, 2004.

Barkhutariants, Makar. *Patmut'yun Aghuanits'* [History of the Albanians]. Vol. 1. 1860. Ējmiatsin: Tparan Mayr At'oṛoy Srboy Ějmiatsni, 1902.

Barsoumian, Hagop. *Armenian Amira Class of Istanbul.* Yerevan: American University of Armenia Press, 2007.

Bast, Oliver. "'Sheer Madness' or 'Railway Politics' Iranian Style? The Controversy over Railway Development Priorities within the Persian Government in 1919–1920 and British Railway Imperialism, Iran." *Journal of the British Institute of Persian Studies* 55, no. 1 (2017): 62–72.

Bayat, Mangol. *Iran's First Revolution: Shi'ism and the Constitutional Revolution of 1905–1909.* Oxford: Oxford University Press, 1991.

Bayly, C. A. *The Birth of the Modern World, 1780–1914.* Malden, MA: Blackwell, 2004.

Bayraktaroğlu, Sena. "Development of Railways in the Ottoman Empire and Turkey." MA thesis, Boğaziçi University, 1995.

Bazilevich, K. V. *The Russian Posts in the XIX Century.* Translated by David M. Skipton. Millersville, MD: Rossica Society of Russian Philately, 1987.

Bektas, Yakup. "The Sultan's Messenger: Cultural Constructions of Ottoman Telegraphy, 1847–1880." *Technology and Culture* 41, no. 4 (October 2000): 669–96.

Benner, Erica. *Really Existing Nationalisms: A Post-Communist View of Marx and Engels.* New York: Oxford University Press, 1995.

Bentley, Jerry H. "Cross-Cultural Interaction and Periodization in World History." *American Historical Review* 101 (1996): 749–70.

———. "The Task of World History." In *The Oxford Handbook of World History,* edited by Jerry H. Bentley, 2–10. Oxford: Oxford University Press, 2011.

———. "The New World History." In *A Companion to Western Historical Thought,* edited by Lloyd Kramer and Sarah Maza, 393–416. Malden, MA: Blackwell, 2002.

———. "Why Study World History." *World History Connected* 5, no. 1 (2013). http://worldhistoryconnected.press.uillinois.edu/5.1/bentley.html.

Berberian, Houri. "Armenian and Iranian Collaboration in the Constitutional Revolution: The Agreement between Dashnakists and Majles Delegates, 1908." Annotated translation with introduction. In *The Modern Middle East: A Sourcebook for History,* edited by Camron Michael Amin, Benjamin C. Fortna, and Elizabeth B. Frierson, 339–43. Oxford: Oxford University Press, 2006.

———. *Armenians and the Iranian Constitutional Revolution of 1905–1911: "The Love for Freedom Has No Fatherland."* Boulder: Westview Press, 2001.

———. "Armenian Women and Women in Armenian Religion." In *Encyclopedia of Women and Islamic Cultures,* edited by Suad Joseph and Afsaneh Najmabadi, 10–14. Vol. 2. Leiden: Brill Academic Publishers, 2005.

———. "Armenian Women in Turn-of-the-Century Iran: Education and Activism." In *Iran and Beyond: Essays in Honor of Nikki R. Keddie,* edited by Rudi Matthee and Beth Baron, 70–98. Costa Mesa, CA: Mazda, 2000.

———. "Connected Revolutions: Armenians and the Russian, Ottoman, and Iranian Revolutions in the Early Twentieth Century." In *"L'ivresse de la liberté": La révolution de 1908 dans l'Empire* ["The intoxication of freedom": The 1908 revolution in the Ottoman Empire], edited by François Georgeon, 487–510. Louvain, Belgium: Peeters, 2012. Russian translation: http://hamatext.com/articles/item/71-vzaimosvyazannye-revolyutsii; http://hamatext.com/articles/item/72-vzaimosvyazannye-revolyutsii-2.

———. "Traversing Boundaries and Selves: Iranian Armenian Identities during the Iranian Constitutional Revolution." *Comparative Studies of South Asia, Africa, and Middle East* 25, no. 2 (Summer 2005): 279–96.

———. "Nest of Revolution: The Caucasus, Iran, and Armenians." In *Russia and Iran: Ideology and Occupation,* edited by Rudi Matthee and Elena Andreeva, 95–121. London: I. B. Tauris, 2018.

Bonakdarian, Mansour. *Britain and the Iranian Constitutional Revolution of 1906–1911: Foreign Policy, Imperialism, and Dissent.* Syracuse, NY: Syracuse University Press, 2006.

———. "Iranian Nationalism and Global Solidarity Networks 1906–1918: Internationalism, Transnationalism, Globalization, and Nationalist Cosmopolitanism." In *Iran in the Middle East: Transnational Encounters and Social History,* edited by H. E. Chehabi, Peyman Jafari, and Maral Jefroudi, 77–129. London: I. B. Tauris, 2015.

Bowering, Bill. "From Empire to Multilateral Player: The Deep Roots of Autonomy in Russia." In *Minority Accommodation through Territorial and Non-Territorial Autonomy,* edited by Tove H. Malloy and Francesco Palermo, 133–60. Oxford: Oxford University Press, 2015.

Brower, Daniel R. "Urban Revolution in the Late Russian Empire." In *The City in Late Imperial Russia,* edited by Michael F. Hamm, 319–54. Bloomington: Indiana University Press, 1986.

Browne, Edward G. *The Persian Revolution, 1905–1909.* 1910. New edition edited by Abbas Amanat with essays by Abbas Amanat and Mansour Bonakdarian. Washington, DC: Mage, 1995.

Campos, Michelle. *Ottoman Brothers: Muslims, Christians, and Jews in Early Twentieth-Century Palestine.* Stanford, CA: Stanford University Press, 2011.

Carey, James W. "Technology and Ideology: The Case of the Telegraph." In *Communication as Culture: Essays on Media and Society,* edited by David Thorburn, 155–77. Boston: Unwin Hyman, 1989.

Carmont, Pascal. *The Amiras: Lords of Ottoman Armenia.* London: Gomidas Institute, 2012.

Case, Holly. "The Strange Politics of Federative Ideas in East-Central Europe." *Journal of Modern History* 85, no. 4 (December 2013): 833–66.

Çetinkaya, Doğan. *The Young Turks and the Boycott Movement: Nationalism, Protest and the Working Classes in the Formation of Modern Turkey.* London: I. B. Tauris, 2013.

Chaqueri, Cosroe, ed. *The Armenians of Iran: The Paradoxical Role of a Minority in a Dominant Culture: Essays and Documents.* Cambridge, MA: Center for Middle Eastern Studies of Harvard University, 1998.

———. *The Left in Iran, 1905–1940.* Revolutionary History 10, no. 2. London: Merlin Press, 2010.

———. *Origins of Social Democracy in Modern Iran.* Seattle: University of Washington Press, 2001.

———. "The Role and Impact of Armenian Intellectuals in Iranian Politics 1905–1911." *Armenian Review* 41, no. 2 (Summer 1988): 1–51.

Chehabi, H. E., and Vanessa Martin, eds. *Iran's Constitutional Revolution: Popular Politics, Cultural Transformations and Transnational Connections.* London: I. B. Tauris, 2010.

Coene, Frederik. *The Caucasus: An Introduction.* London: Routledge, 2010.

Cohen, Julia Philips. *Becoming Ottoman: Sephardi Jews and Imperial Citizenship in the Modern Era.* Oxford: Oxford University Press, 2014.

Cora, Yaşar Tolga, Dzovinar Derderian, and Ali Sipahi, eds. *The Ottoman East in the Nineteenth Century: Societies, Identities and Politics.* London: I.B. Tauris, 2016.

Cresswell, Tim. *On the Move: Mobility in the Modern Western World.* New York: Taylor and Francis, 2006.

Daskalov, Roumen, and Tchavdar Marinov, eds. *Entangled Histories of the Balkans.* Vol. 1, *National Ideologies and Language Policies.* Leiden: Brill, 2013.

Dasnabedian, Hrach. *H.H. Dashnakts'ut'ean kazmakerpakan karoyts'i holovoyt'ĕ* [The evolution of the A.R. Federation's organizational structure]. Beirut: Hamazgayin Vahē Sēt'ean Tparan, 1974.

Davis, Horace B. *Nationalism and Socialism: Marxist and Labor Theories of Nationalism to 1917.* New York: Monthly Review Press, 1967.

Davis, Horace B., ed. and trans. *The National Question: Selected Writings of Rosa Luxemburg.* New York: Monthly Review Press, 1976.

Davison, Roderic H. "The Advent of the Electric Telegraph in the Ottoman Empire." In *Essays in Ottoman and Turkish History, 1774–1923: The Impact of the West,* 133–65. Austin: University of Texas Press, 1990.

———. *Reform in the Ottoman Empire, 1856–1876.* Princeton, NJ: Princeton University Press, 1963.

Der Matossian, Bedross. "From Bloodless Revolution to Bloody Counterrevolution: The Adana Massacres of 1909." *Genocide Studies and Prevention* 6, no. 2 (Summer 2011): 152–73.

———. "Ottoman Armenian Kesaria/Kayseri in the Nineteenth Century." In *Armenian Kesaria/Kayseri and Cappadocia,* edited by Richard G. Hovannisian, 187–209. Costa Mesa, CA: Mazda, 2013.

———. *Shattered Dreams of Revolution: From Liberty to Violence in the Late Ottoman Empire.* Stanford, CA: Stanford University Press, 2014.

Detrez, Raymond. *Historical Dictionary of Bulgaria.* 3rd ed. London: Rowman & Littlefield, 2015.

Deutschmann, Moritz. "Cultures of Statehood, Cultures of Revolution: Caucasian Revolutionaries in the Iranian Constitutional Movement, 1906–1911." *Ab Imperio: Studies of New Imperial History and Nationalism in the Post-Soviet Space* 2 (2013): 165–90.

———. *Iran and Russian Imperialism: The Ideal Anarchists, 1800–1914.* London: Routledge, 2016.

Douki, Caroline, and Philippe Minard. "Histoire global, histoire connectées: Un changement d'échelle historiographique" [Global history, connected histories: A historiographic change of scale]. *Revue d'histoire moderne and contemporaine* 54, no. 4 (2007): 7–21.

Elmar, H. [Hovsep Hovhannisian]. *Yep'rem.* Tehran: Modern, 1964.

Fakhra'i, Ibrahim. *Gilan dar jonbesh-e mashrutiyat* [Gilan in the constitutional movement]. Tehran: Ketabha-ye Jibi, 1974.

Faroqhi, Suraiya, Bruce McGowan, Donald Quataert, and Sevket Pamuk. *An Economic and Social History of the Ottoman Empire.* Vol. 2. Cambridge: Cambridge University Press, 1997.

Farro [Hovsep Hovhannisian]. "Grishayi husherě" [Grisha's memoirs]. *Hayrenik' Amsagir* 3, no. 4 (February 1925): 90–92.

Fletcher, Joseph. "Integrative History: Parallels and Interconnections in the Early Modern Period, 1500–1800." In *Studies on Chinese and Islamic Inner Asia*, 37–57. London: Variorum, 1995.

Floor, Willem. "The Chapar-Khāna System in Qajar Iran." *Iran* 39 (2001): 257–91.

Foran, John. *Taking Power: On the Origins of Third World Revolutions*. Cambridge: Cambridge University Press, 2005.

Forman, Michael. *Nationalism and the International Labor Movement: The Idea of the Nation in Socialist and Anarchist Theory*. University Park: Pennsylvania State University Press, 1998.

Forsyth, Murray, ed. *Federalism and Nationalism*. Leicester, UK: Leicester University Press, 1989.

Garsoian, Nina. "Iran and Caucasus." In *Transcaucasia, Nationalism, and Social Change: Essays in the History of Armenia, Azerbaijan, and Georgia*, edited by Ronald Grigor Suny. Rev. ed. Ann Arbor: University of Michigan Press, 1999.

Gechtman, Roni. "Jews and Non-Territorial Autonomy: Political Programmes and Historical Perspectives." *Ethnopolitics: Formerly Global Review of Ethnopolitics* 15, no. 1 (2016): 66–88.

Geddes, Barbara. "Authoritarian Breakdown: Empirical Test of a Theoretic Arguments." Paper presented at the annual meeting of the American Political Science Association, Atlanta, September 1999. http://eppam.weebly.com /uploads/5/5/6/2/5562069/authoritarianbreakdown_geddes.pdf.

Geertz, Clifford. *Islam Observed: Religious Development in Morocco and Indonesia*. Chicago: Chicago University Press, 1971.

Gelofiants, Sokrat Khan. *Kayts: S. D. Hnch'. Kusakts'ut'ean gortsunēut'iwnits' togh p'asterě khosin* [Spark: Let the evidence from the S.D. Hnch. Party activity speak]. Providence, RI: Yeritasard Hayastan, 1915.

Gelvin, James. *The Modern Middle East*. 4th ed. Oxford: Oxford University Press, 2016.

Georgeon, François. *Abdülhamid II: Le sultan calife (1876–1909)*. Paris: Fayard, 2003.

———, ed. *"L'ivresse de la liberté": La révolution de 1908 dans l'Empire ottoman* ["The intoxication of freedom": The 1908 revolution in the Ottoman Empire]. Louvain, Belgium: Peeters, 2012.

Giwlkhandanian, Abraham. *Kovkas: yerkirě, zhoghovurdě, patmut'iwně* [Caucasus: The country, people, history]. Vol. 1. Paris: Librairie Universitaire J. Gamber, 1943.

Gladwell, Malcolm. *The Tipping Point: How Little Things Can Make a Big Difference*. New York: Back Bay Books/Little, Brown, 2000.

Gocheleishvili, Iago. "Georgian Sources on the Iranian Constitutional Revolution, 1905–1911: Sergo Gamdlishvili's Memoirs of the Gilan Resistance." In *Iranian-Russian Encounters: Empires and Revolutions since 1800*, edited by Stephanie Cronin, 207–30. London: Routledge, 2013.

———. "Introducing Georgian Sources for the Historiography of the Iranian Constitutional Revolution (1905–1911)." In *Iran's Constitutional Revolution:*

Popular Politics, Cultural Transformations and Transnational Connections, edited by H.E. Chehabi and Vanessa Martin, 45–66. London: I.B. Tauris, 2010.

Goldstone, Jack A. "Comparative Historical Analysis and Knowledge Accumulation in the Study of Revolutions." In *Comparative Historical Analysis in the Social Sciences,* edited by James Mahoney and Dietrich Rueschemeyer, 41–90. Cambridge: Cambridge University Press, 2003.

———. "East and West in the Seventeenth Century: Political Crises in Stuart England, Ottoman Turkey, and Ming China." *Comparative Studies in Society and History* 30, no. 1 (January 1988): 103–42.

———. "Is Revolution Individually Rational? Groups and Individuals in Revolutionary Collective Action." *Rationality and Society* 6, no. 1 (January 1994): 139–66.

———. *Revolution and Rebellion in the Early Modern World.* Berkeley: University of California Press, 1993.

Gould, Eliga H. "Entangled Histories, Entangled Worlds: The English-Speaking Atlantic as a Spanish Periphery." *American Historical Review* 112, no. 3 (June 2007): 764–86.

Grant, Bruce. *The Captive and the Gift: Cultural Histories of Sovereignty in Russia and the Caucasus.* Ithaca, NY: Cornell University Press, 2009.

Grant, Bruce, and Lale Yalçın-Heckmann. Introduction to *Caucasus Paradigms: Anthropologies, Histories and the Making of a World Area,* edited by Bruce Grant and Lale Yalçın-Heckmann. Münster: Lit, 2007.

Gregorian, Vartan. "Impact of Russia on the Armenians and Armenia." In *Russia and Asia: Essays on the Influence of Russia on the Asian Peoples,* edited by Wayne S. Vucinich, 167–218. Stanford, CA: Hoover Institution Press, 1972.

Grew, Raymond. "The Case for Comparing Histories." *American Historical Review* 85, no. 4 (October 1980): 763–78.

Gruzinski, Serge. "Les mondes *mêlés* de la monarchie catholique et autre 'connected histories'" [The entangled worlds of the Catholic monarchy and other "connected histories"]. *Annales* 56, no. 1 (January–February 2001): 85–117.

Gurr, Ted. *Why Men Rebel.* Princeton, NJ: Princeton University Press, 1970.

Gutman, David. "Travel Documents, Mobility Control, and the Ottoman State in an Age of Global Migration, 1880–1915." *Journal of the Ottoman and Turkish Studies Association* 3, no. 2 (November 2016): 347–68.

Haag-Higuchi, Roxane. "A Topos and Its Dissolution: Japan in Some 20th-Century Iranian Texts." *Iranian Studies* 29, nos. 1–2 (Winter/Spring 1996): 71–83.

Hakimian, Hassan. "Wage Labor and Migration: Persian Workers in Southern Russia, 1880–1914." *International Journal of Middle East Studies* 17, no. 4 (November 1985): 443–62.

Hamm, Michael F., ed. *The City in Late Imperial Russia.* Bloomington: Indiana University Press, 1986.

———. "Continuity and Change in Late Imperial Kiev." In *The City in Late Imperial Russia,* edited by Michael F. Hamm, 79–122. Bloomington: Indiana University Press, 1986.

Hanioğlu, M. Şükrü. *Preparation for a Revolution: The Young Turks, 1902–1908.* Oxford: Oxford University Press, 2001.

———. *The Young Turks in Opposition.* Oxford: Oxford University Press, 1995.

Harper, T.N. "Empire, Diaspora and the Language of Globalism, 1850–1914." In *Globalization in World History,* edited by A.G. Hopkins, 156–57. London: Pimlico, 2002.

Harvey, David. *The Condition of Postmodernity: An Enquiry into the Origins of Cultural Change.* Cambridge: Blackwell, 1989.

Harcave, Sidney. *The Russian Revolution of 1905,* originally published as *First Blood.* London: Collier, 1964.

Haupt, Heinz-Gerhard, and Jürgen Kocka. "Comparative History: Methods, Aims, Problems." In *Comparison and History: Europe in Cross-National Perspective,* edited by Deborah Cohen and Maura O'Connor, 23–39. London: Routledge, 2004.

Haupt, Heinz-Gerhard. "Comparative History—A Contested Method." *Historisk Tidskrift* 127, no. 4 (2007): 697–714.

Headrick, Daniel R. *The Tentacles of Progress: Technology Transfer in the Age of Imperialism, 1850–1940.* New York: Oxford University Press, 1988.

Heywood, Anthony. "Socialists, Liberals and the Union of Unions in Kyiv during the 1905 Revolution: An Engineer's Perspective." In *The Russian Revolution of 1905: Centenary Perspectives,* edited by Jonathan D. Smele and Anthony Heywood, 177–95. London: Routledge, 2005.

Hildermeier, Manfred. *The Russian Socialist Revolutionary Party before the First World War.* Transl. from German. New York: St. Martin's Press, 2000.

Hillis, Faith. *Children of Rus': Right-Bank Ukraine and the Invention of a Russian Nation.* Ithaca, NY: Cornell University Press, 2003.

Hovhannisian, Hovsep. *Husher* [Memoirs]. Yerevan: Abolon, 1995.

Hovhannisian, Richard G. "The Historical Dimension of the Armenian Question, 1878–1923." In *The Armenian Genocide in Perspective,* edited by Richard G. Hovhannisian, 19–42. New Brunswick, NJ: Transaction, 1987.

Howard, Nicole. *The Book: The Life Story of a Technology.* Baltimore: Johns Hopkins University Press, 2009.

Hugill, Peter J. *Global Communications since 1844: Geopolitics and Technology.* Baltimore: Johns Hopkins University Press, 1999.

Inchikyan, H.G., ed. *Merdzavor ew Mijin Arewelk'i yerkrner ew zhoghovurdner* [Countries and peoples of the Near and Middle East]. Vol. 8, *Iran.* Yerevan: Haykakan SSH Gitut'yunneri Akademia, 1975.

Innis, Harold A. *The Bias of Communication.* Toronto: University of Toronto Press, 1951.

———. *Empire and Communications.* Toronto: University of Toronto Press, 1972.

Ipekian, Gaspar, comp. "*Hamazgayini*" ōrats'oyts-tarets'oyts' 1951 [Hamazgayin's almanac-annuary 1951]. Beirut: Hamazgayin, 1956.

Issawi, Charles. "European Economic Penetration, 1872–1921." In *The Cambridge History of Iran,* edited by Peter Avery, Gavin Hambly, and Charles Melville, 590–607. Cambridge: Cambridge University Press, 1991.

Jones, Stephen F. *Socialism in Georgian Colors: The European Road to Social Democracy, 1883–1917.* Cambridge, MA: Harvard University Press, 2005.

Kaligian, Dikran Mesrob. *Armenian Organization and Ideology under Ottoman Rule, 1908–1914.* Rev. ed. New Brunswick, NJ: Transaction Publishers, 2011.

Kankruni, Hrant. *Hay heghap'okhut'iwnĕ Osmanean b̦natirut'ean dēm (1890–1910)* [The Armenian revolution against Ottoman despotism (1890–1910)]. Beirut: G. Doniguean et Fils, 1983.

Kansu, Aykut. *The Revolution of 1908 in Turkey.* Leiden: Brill, 1997.

Karakışla, Yavuz Selim. "Sultan Il. Abdülhamid'in istibdat döneminde (1876–1909): Hafiyelik ve jurnalcilik" [During Sultan Abdülhamid II's period of tyranny (1876–1909): Spying and reporting]. *Toplumsal Tarih* [Social history] 119 (November 2003): 12–21.

Karbelashvili, Andre. "Europe-India Telegraph 'Bridge' via the Caucasus." *Indian Journal of History of Science* 26, no. 3 (1991): 277–81.

Kasravi, Ahmad. *Tarikh-e hijdah saleh-ye Azerbaijan* [The eighteen-year history of Azerbaijan]. Vol. 1. Tehran: Amir Kabir, 1978.

———. *Tarikh-e mashrutah-ye Iran* [History of the constitution of Iran]. Vol. 2. Tehran: Amir Kabir, 1984.

Kautsky, Karl. "Nationality and Internationality Part 1." Translated by Ben Lewis. *Critique* 37, no. 3 (June 2009): 371–89.

———. "Nationality and Internationality Part 2." Translated by Ben Lewis. *Critique* 38, no. 1 (February 2010): 143–63.

Kayalı, Hasan. *Arabs and Young Turks: Ottomanism, Arabism, and Islamism in the Second Constitutional Period of the Ottoman Empire, 1908–1918.* Berkeley: University of California Press, 1997.

Kaynar, Erdal. "Ahmed Rıza (1858–1930): Histoire d'un vieux Jeune Turc" [Ahmed Rıza (1858–1930): History of an old Young Turk]. PhD diss., École des Hautes Études en Sciences Sociales, Paris, 2012.

Kazemzadeh, Firuz. *Russia and Britain in Persia, 1864–1914: A Study in Imperialism.* New Haven: Yale University Press, 1968.

Keddie, Nikki R. "The Economic History of Iran, 1800–1914, and Its Political Impact: An Overview." *Iranian Studies* 5, nos. 2/3 (Spring–Summer 1972): 58–78.

———. *Iran: Religion, Politics and Society: Collected Essays.* New York: Frank Cass, 1980.

———. "Iranian Revolutions in Comparative Perspective." *American Historical Review* 88, no. 3 (June 1983): 579–98.

———. *Modern Iran: Roots and Results of Revolution.* New Haven: Yale University Press, 2003.

———. *Religion and Rebellion in Iran: The Tobacco Protest of 1891–92.* London: Frank Cass, 1966.

———. ed. *Debating Revolutions.* New York: New York University Press, 1995.

Ketsemanian, Varak. "Straddling Two Empires: Cross-Revolutionary Fertilization and the Armenian Revolutionary Federation's Military Academy in

1906–07." *Journal of the Ottoman and Turkish Studies Association* 4, no. 2 (November 2017): 339–63.

Kévorkian, Raymond. *The Armenian Genocide: A Complete History.* London: I. B. Tauris, 2011. First published in France in 2006.

Khachaturian, Lisa. *Cultivating Nationhood in Imperial Russia: The Periodical Press and the Formation of a Modern Identity.* New Brunswick, NJ: Transaction Publishers, 2009.

Khayadjian, Edmond. *Archag Tchobanian et le mouvement arménophile en France* [Archag Tchobanian and the Armenophile movement in France]. Marseille: Centre national de documentation pédagogique, 1986.

Khuri-Makdisi, Ilham. *The Eastern Mediterranean and the Making of Global Radicalism, 1860–1914.* Berkeley: University of California Press, 2010.

Kimmel, Michael S. *Revolution: A Sociological Interpretation.* Philadelphia: Temple University Press, 1990.

King, Charles. *The Ghost of Freedom: A History of the Caucasus.* Oxford: Oxford University Press, 2008.

Kirakosian, A. *Hay parberakan mamuli matenagitut'yun, 1794–1967: hamahavak' ts'ank* [Bibliography of Armenian periodical press, 1794–1967: Compiled catalog]. Yerevan: Hanrapetakan Gradaran, 1970.

Kitur, Arsen. *Patmut'iwn S. D. Hnch'akean Kusakts'ut'ean* [History of the S. D. Hnch'akean Party]. 2 vols. Beirut: Shirak Press, 1962.

Kocka, Jürgen. "Comparison and Beyond." *History and Theory* 42 (February 2003): 39–44.

Koçunyan, Aylin. "Long Live Sultan Abdulaziz, Long Live the Nation, Long Live the Constitution!" In *Constitutionalism, Legitimacy and Power: Nineteenth-Century Experiences,* edited by Kelly Grotke and Markus Prutsch, 189–210. Oxford: Oxford University Press, 2014.

———. "Historicizing the 1908 Revolution: The Case of *Jamanak.*" In *The Young Turk Revolution and the Ottoman Empire: The Aftermath of 1908,* edited by Noémi Lévy and François Georgeon, 236–64. London: I. B. Tauris, 2017.

Kowner, Rotem, ed. *The Impact of the Russo-Japanese War.* London: Routledge, 2007.

Kundera, Milan. "Part Eight: Paths in the Fog." In *Testaments Betrayed: An Essay in Nine Parts,* 197–238. Translated from the French by Linda Asher. New York: Harper-Perennial, 1996.

Kuran, Timur. "Now Out of Never: The Element of Surprise in the East European Revolution of 1989." *World Politics* 44, no. 1 (1991): 7–48.

Kurtz, Geoffrey. *Jean Jaurès: The Inner Life of Social Democracy.* University Park: Pennsylvania State University Press, 2014.

———. "A Socialist State of Grace: The Radical Reformism of Jean Jaurès." *New Political Science* 28, no. 3 (2006): 401–18.

Kurzman, Charles. *Democracy Denied, 1905–1915: Intellectuals and the Fate of Democracy.* Cambridge, MA: Harvard University Press, 2008.

———. *The Unthinkable Revolution in Iran.* Cambridge, MA: Harvard University Press, 2004.

Lazian, Gabriel. *Heghap'okhakan dēmk'er* [Revolutionary figures]. Aleppo: Hamazgayin, 1990.

Lépine, Frédéric. "A Journey through the History of Federalism: Is Multilevel Governance a Form of Federalism?" *L'Europe en formation* 363 (Spring 2012): 21–62.

Levine, Philippa. "Is Comparative History Possible?" *History and Theory* 53 (October 2014): 331–47.

Levonian, Garegin. *Hayots' parberakan mamulĕ, 1794–1934* [The Armenian periodical press, 1794–1934]. Yerevan: Melkonean Foundation, 1934.

Libaridian, Gerard J. "Revolution and Liberation in the 1982 and 1907 Programs of the Dashnaktsutiune." In *Transcaucasia. Nationalism and Social Change,* edited by Ronald Grigor Suny, 187–98. Ann Arbor: University of Michigan, 1983.

———. "What Was Revolutionary about Armenian Political Parties in the Ottoman Empire?" In *A Question of Genocide: Armenians and Turks at the End of the Ottoman Empire,* edited by Ronald Grigor Suny, Fatma Müge Göçek, and Norman M. Naimark, 82–112. Oxford: Oxford University Press, 2011.

Lloyd's Register of British and Foreign Shipping. Vol. 2. London, 1905.

Malkhas [Artashes Hovsepian]. *Aprumner* [Life experiences]. Boston: Hayrenik', 1931.

Marinov, Tchavdar. "We, the Macedonians: The Paths of Macedonian Supranationalism (1878–1912). In *We, the People: Politics of National Peculiarity in Southeastern Europe,* edited by Diana Mishkova, 107–37. Budapest: Central European University Press, 2009.

———. "Famous Macedonia, the Land of Alexander: Macedonian Identity at the Crossroads of Greek, Bulgarian and Serbian Nationalism." In *Entangled Histories of the Balkans,* edited by Roumen Daskalov and Tchavdar Marinov. Vol. 1, *National Ideologies and Language Policies,* 273–330. Brill: Leiden, 2013.

Marshall, Peter. *Demanding the Impossible: A History of Anarchism.* Oakland: PM Press, 2010.

Massey, Doreen. "Politics and Space-Time." *New Left Review* 196 (November–December 1992): 65–84.

Mayer, Robert. "Plekhanov, Lenin and Working-Class Consciousness." *Studies in East European Thought* 49 (1997): 159–85.

Marx, Karl. *Grundrisse: Foundations of the Critique of Political Economy (Rough Draft).* Harmondsworth, UK: Penguin, 1973.

Marx, Karl, and Friedrich Engels. *Manifesto of the Communist Party.* Authorized English translation. Edited and annotated by Friedrich Engels. Chicago: Charles H. Kerr, 1906.

McNeill, J.R., and William H. McNeill. *The Human Web: A Bird's-Eye View of World History.* New York: W.W. Norton, 2003.

Melson, Robert. *Revolution and Genocide: On the Origins of the Armenian Genocide and the Holocaust.* Chicago: University of Chicago Press, 1996.

Miller, Burton Richard. *Rural Unrest during the First Russian Revolution: Kursk Province, 1905–1906.* Budapest: Central European University Press, 2013.

Minassian, Gaïdz. "Les relations entre le Comité Union et Progrès et la Fédération Révolutionnaire Arménienne à la veille de la Première Guerre mondiale d'après les sources arméniennes" [Relations between the Committee of Union and Progress and the Armenian Revolutionary Federation on the eve of the first world war according to Armenian sources]. *Revue d'histoire arménienne contemporaine* 1 (1995): 45–99.

Mitchell, Timothy. *Carbon Democracy: Political Power in the Age of Oil*. London: Verso, 2011.

Moumdjian, Garabet K. "Rebels with a Cause: Armenian-Macedonian Relations and Their Bulgarian Connection, 1895–1913." In *War and Nationalism: The Balkan Wars, 1912–1913, and Their Sociopolitical Implications*, edited by Hakan Yavuz and Isa Blumi, 132–75. Salt Lake City: University of Utah Press, 2013.

———. "Struggling for a Constitutional Regime: Armenian-Young Turk Relations in the Era of Abdulhamid II, 1895–1909." PhD diss., UCLA, 2012.

Mouradian, Claire, ed. *Arménie, une passion française: Le mouvement arménophile en France (1878–1923)* [Armenia, a French passion: The Armenophile movement in France]. Paris: Magellan, 2007.

Moore, Barrington, Jr. *Social Origins of Dictatorship and Democracy*. Boston: Beacon Press, 1966.

Moore, Will. "Rational Rebels: Overcoming the Free-Rider Problem." *Political Research Quarterly* 48 (June 1995): 417–54.

Morison, John. "Russia's First Revolution." *History Today* 38 (December 2000). https://www.historytoday.com/john-morison/russias-first-revolution.

Muller, Edward N., and Karl-Dieter Opp. "Rational Choice and Rebellious Collective Action." *American Political Science Review* 80, no. 2 (June 1986): 471–88.

Nalbandian, Louise. *The Armenian Revolutionary Movement: The Development of Armenian Political Parties Through the Nineteenth Century*. Berkeley: University of California Press, 1963.

The New Oxford Annotated Bible with the Apocrypha. 3rd ed. Oxford: Oxford University Press, 2001.

Nezam Mafi, Mansoureh Ettehadieh. *Peydayesh va tahavvol-e ahzab-e siyasi-ye mashnitiyat: dowreh-ye avval va dovvom-e majles-e showra-ye melli* [Appearance and evolution of political parties of constitutionalism: The first and second period of the National Consultative Assembly]. Tehran: Gustardah Press, 1982.

Nichanian, Marc. "Zabel Yesayan, Woman and Witness, or the Truth of the Mask." *New Perspectives on Turkey* 42 (2010): 31–53.

Nimni, Ephraim. *Marxism and Nationalism: The Theoretical Origins of a Political Crisis*. London: Pluto Press, 1991.

Njagulov, Blagovest. "Early Socialism in the Balkans: Ideas and Practices in Serbia, Romania and Bulgaria." In *Entangled Histories of the Balkans*, edited by Roumen Daskalov and Tchavdar Marinov. Vol. 2, *Transfers of Political Ideologies and Institutions*, 199–280. Brill: Leiden, 2014.

Ogle, Vanessa. *The Global Transformation of Time, 1870–1905*. Cambridge, MA: Harvard University Press, 2015.

Okan, Ayşegül. "The Ottoman Postal and Telegraph Services in the Last Quarter of the Nineteenth Century." MA thesis, Boğaziçi University, 2003.

Osipov, Alexander. "Non-Territorial Autonomy during and after Communism: In the Wrong or Right Place?" *Journal on Ethnopolitics and Minority Issues in Europe* 12, no. 1 (2013): 7–26.

Osterhammel, Jürgen. *The Transformation of the World: A Global History of the Nineteenth Century.* Translated by Patrick Camiller. Princeton, NJ: Princeton University Press, 2014.

Panossian, Razmik. *The Armenians: From Kings and Priests to Merchants and Commissars.* New York: Columbia University Press, 2006.

Parker, Geoffrey. *Global Crisis: War, Climate Change and Catastrophe in the Seventeenth Century.* New Haven: Yale University Press, 2013.

Parsa, Misagh. *States, Ideologies, and Social Revolutions: A Comparative Analysis of Iran, Nicaragua, and the Philippines.* Cambridge: Cambridge University Press, 2000.

Parsamyan, V[artan] A[ram]. *Revolyuts'ion sharzhumnerĕ Hayastanum, 1905–1907 t'.t'.* [Revolutionary movements in Armenia, 1905–1907]. Yerevan: Petakan Hamalsaran, 1955.

Pepinov, Fuad. "The Role of Political Caricatures in the Cultural Development of the Meshketian (Ahiska) Turks." In *Islamic Art and Architecture in the European Periphery: Crimea, Caucasus, and the Volga-Ural Region,* edited by Barbara Kellner-Heinekele, Joachim Gierlichs, and Brigitte Heuer, 159–64. Wiesbaden: Harrassowitz Verlag, 2009.

Polasky, Janet. *Revolutions without Borders: The Call to Liberty in the Atlantic World.* New Haven: Yale University Press, 2015.

Quataert, Donald. "Ottoman Workers and the State, 1826–1914." In *Workers and Working Classes in the Middle East: Struggles, Histories, Historiographies,* edited by Zachary Lockman, 21–40. Albany, NY: SUNY Press, 1994.

———. "Transportation." In *An Economic and Social History of the Ottoman Empire, 1300–1914,* 791–823. Cambridge: Cambridge University Press, 1994.

Ra'in, Isma'il. *Yep'rem Khan Sardar* [Commander Yep'rem Khan]. Tehran: Zarin, 1971.

Rapp, Stephen H. "Recovering the Pre-National Caucasian Landscape." In *Mythical Landscapes Then and Now: The Mystification of Landscapes in Search for National Identity,* edited by Ruth Büttner and Judith Peltz, 13–52. Yerevan: Antares, 2006.

Rebérioux, Madeleine. "Jean Jaurès and the Armenians." *The Armenian Review* 44, 2/174 (1991): 1–11.

Reifowitz, Ian. "Otto Bauer and Karl Renner on Nationalism, Ethnicity and Jews." *Journal of Jewish Identities* 2, no. 2 (2009): 1–19.

Reynolds, Michael A. *Shattering Empires: The Clash and Collapse of the Ottoman and Russian Empires, 1908–1918.* Cambridge: Cambridge University Press, 2011.

Riddell, John, ed. *Lenin's Struggle for a Revolutionary International: Documents: 1907–1916.* New York: Monad Press, 1984.

Riedler, Florian. "Armenian Labour Migration to Istanbul and the Migration Crisis of the 1890." In *The City in the Ottoman Empire: Migration and the Making of Urban Modernity,* edited by Ulrike Freitag, Malte Fuhrmann, Nora Lafi, and Florian Riedler, 160–76. London: Routledge, 2011.

Riegg, Stephen. "Imperial Challengers: Tsarist Responses to Armenian Raids into Anatolia, 1875–90." *Russian Review* 76, no. 2 (2017): 253–71.

———. "Beyond the Caucasus: The Russian Empire and Armenians, 1801–1914." Unpublished manuscript, 2017.

Roberts, Steven. "The Indo-European Telegraph Company." http://atlantic-cable.com/CableCos/Indo-Eur/.

Robertson, James. "Imagining the Balkans as a Space of Revolution: The Federalist Vision of Serbian Socialism, 1870–1914." *East European Politics and Societies and Cultures* 31, no. 2 (May 2017): 402–25.

Rowe, Victoria. *A History of Armenian Women's Writing 1880–1922*. Amersham, UK: Cambridge Scholars Press, 2003.

Rowley, Alison. *Open Letters: Russian Popular Culture and the Picture Postcard, 1880–1922*. Toronto: University of Toronto Press, 2013.

Rubin, Michael. "The Culture of Telegraph Workers in Iran." In *Iran: Questions et connaissances. Actes du IVe congrès européen des études iraniennes, organisé par la Societas Iranologica Europaea* [Proceedings of the 4th European Congress of Iranian Studies; organized by Societas Iranologica Europaea], edited by Maria Szuppe, 349–69. Vol. 2. Leuven: Peeters, 2002.

———. "The Formation of Modern Iran, 1858–1909: Communications, Telegraph and Society." PhD diss., Yale University, 1999.

Sablinsky, Walter. "The All-Russian Railroad Union and the Beginning of the General Strike in October, 1905." In *Revolution and Politics in Russia: Essays in Memory of B. I. Nicolaevsky*, edited by Alexander and Janet Rabinowitch with Ladis K. D. Kristof, 113–33. Bloomington: Indiana University Press, 1977.

Sapah-Giwlian, Beruz. *Kensagrut'iwn Step'an Sapah-Giwleani* [Biography of Stepan Sapah-Giwlean]. Union City, NJ: Elmas-Satin, 1936.

Sapah-Giwlian, Stepan. *Yeritasard T'urk'ia* [Young Turkey]. Paris: A. H., 1908.

———. *Ewropayi k'aghak'akan drut'iwně Berlini dashnadrut'iwnits' hetoy* [Europe's political situation after the Berlin treaty]. Ruschuk [Ruse], Bulgaria: A. H., 1898.

———. *Sots'ializm ew hayrenik'* [Socialism and fatherland]. Providence, RI: Tparan Yeritasart Hayastani, 1916.

Sargent, Leslie. "The 'Armeno-Tatar War' in the South Caucasus, 1905–1906: Multiple Causes, Interpreted Meanings." *Ab Imperio* 4 (2010): 143–69.

Schedewie, Franziska. "Peasant Protest and Peasant Violence in 1905: Voronezh Province, ostrogozhskii Uezd." In *The Russian Revolution of 1905: Centenary Perspectives*, edited by Jonathan D. Smele and Anthony Heywood, 137–55. London: Routledge, 2005.

Schenk, Frithjof Benjamin. "'This New Means of Transportation Will Make Unstable People More Unstable': Railways and Geographical Mobility in Tsarist Russia." In *Russia in Motion: Cultures of Human Mobility since 1850*, edited by John Randolph and Eugene M. Avrutin, 218–34. Chicago: University of Illinois Press, 2012.

Schivelbusch, Wolfgang. *The Railway Journey: The Industrialization of Time and Space in the Nineteenth Century*. Berkeley: University of California Press, 2014.

Seigel, Micol. "Beyond Compare: Comparative Method after the Transnational Turn." *Radical History Review* 91 (Winter 2005): 62–90.

Selbin, Eric. *Revolution, Rebellion, Resistance: The Power of Story*. London: Zed Books, 2010.

———. "Stories of Revolution in the Periphery." In *Revolution in the Making of the Modern World: Social Identities, Globalization, and Modernity*, edited by John Foran, David Lane, and Andreja Zivkovic, 130–48. London: Routledge, 2008.

Semyonov, Alexander, Marina Mogilner, and Ilya Gerasimov. "Russian Sociology in Imperial Context." In *Sociology and Empire: The Imperial Entanglements of a Discipline*, edited by George Steinmetz, 53–82. Durham, NC: Duke University Press, 2013.

Sewell, William, Jr. "Ideologies and Social Revolutions: Reflections on the French Case." *Journal of Modern History* 57 (1985): 57–85.

Seyf, Ahmad. "Obstacles to the Development of Capitalism: Iran in the Nineteenth Century." *Middle Eastern Studies* 34, no. 3 (July 1998): 54–82.

Shanin, Teodor. *Russia, 1905–07: Revolution as a Moment of Truth*. Vol. 2, *The Roots of Otherness: Russia's Turn of Century*. London: Macmillan, 1986.

Shuster, W. Morgan. *The Strangling of Persia*. London: T. Fisher Unwin, 1913.

Siefert, Marsha. "'Chingis-Khan with the Telegraph': Communications in the Russian and Ottoman Empires." In *Comparing Empires: Encounters and Transfers in the Long Nineteenth Century*, edited by Jörn Leonhard and Ulrike von Hirschhausen, 78–108. Oakville, CT: Vandenhoeck & Ruprecht, 2011.

Skocpol, Theda. *States and Social Revolutions: A Comparative Analysis of France, Russia, and China*. Cambridge: Cambridge University Press, 1979.

Smele, Jonathan D., and Anthony Heywood, eds. *The Russian Revolution of 1905: Centenary Perspectives*. London: Routledge, 2005.

Sohrabi, Nader. "Historicizing Revolutions: Constitutional Revolutions in the Ottoman Empire, Iran, and Russia, 1905–1908." *American Journal of Sociology* 100, no. 6 (May 1995): 1383–1447.

———. *Revolution and Constitutionalism in the Ottoman Empire and Iran*. Cambridge: Cambridge University Press, 2011.

Spargo, John. "Socialism and Internationalism." *Atlantic Monthly* 120 (1917): 300–312.

Spector, Ivan. *The First Russian Revolution: Its Impact on Asia*. Englewood Cliffs, NJ: Prentice Hall, 1962.

Stavrianos, L. S. *Balkan Federation: A History of the Movement Toward Balkan Unity in Modern Times*. Hamden, CT: Archon Books, 1964.

Stein, Jeremy. "Reflections on Time, Time-Space Compression and Technology in the Nineteenth Century." *TimeSpace: Geographies of Temporality*, edited by Jon May and Nigel Thrift. London: Routledge, 2001.

Stepanian, Hovak. "Nikol Duman: mahuan 15-ameaki artiw" [Nikol Duman: On the occasion of the 15th anniversary of his death]. *Hayrenik' Amsagir* 8, no. 12 (October 1930): 148–60.

Stepanyan, Gevorg S. *Armenians of Baku Province in the Second Half of the 19th Century: Historical-Demographic Study*. Yerevan: Lusakn, 2013.

Struck, Bernhard, Kate Ferris, and Jacques Revel. "Introduction: Space and Scale in Transnational History." *International History Review* 33, no. 4 (December 2011): 573–84.

Subrahmanyam, Sanjay. "Connected Histories: Notes towards a Reconfiguration of Early Modern Eurasia." *Modern Asian Studies* 31, no. 3 (July 1997): 735–62.

———. "Holding the World in Balance: The Connected Histories of the Iberian Overseas Empires, 1500–1640." *American Historical Review* 112, no. 5 (December 2007): 1359–85.

Suny, Ronald Grigor. *The Making of the Georgian Nation.* 2nd ed. Bloomington: University of Indiana Press, 1994.

———. "Tiflis: Crucible of Ethnic Politics, 1860–1905." In *The City in Late Imperial Russia,* edited by Michael Hamm, 249–82. Bloomington: Indiana University Press, 1986.

———. *Looking toward Ararat: Armenia in Modern History.* Bloomington: Indiana University Press, 1993.

Svolik, Milan W. *The Politics of Authoritarian Rule.* Cambridge: Cambridge University Press, 2012.

Tachjian, Vahé, ed. *Ottoman Armenians: Life, Culture, Society.* Vol. 1. Berlin: Houshamadyan, 2014.

Taglia, Stefano. *Intellectuals and Reform in the Ottoman Empire: The Young Turks on the Challenges of Modernity.* London: Routledge, 2015.

Ter Minassian, Anahide [Anaïde]. "Aux origines du marxisme arménien: Les spécifistes" [At the origins of Armenian Marxism: The specifists]. *Cahiers du monde russe et soviétique* 19, nos. 1–2 (January–June 1978): 67–117.

———. *Nationalism and Socialism in the Armenian Revolutionary Movement, 1887–1912.* Cambridge, MA: Zoryan Institute, 1984.

———. "The Role of the Armenian Community in the Foundation and Development of the Socialist Movement in the Ottoman Empire and Turkey, 1876–1923." In *Socialism and Nationalism in the Ottoman Empire and Modern Turkey,* edited by Mete Tunçay and Erik J. Zürcher, 109–56. London: I. B. Tauris, 1994.

Tilly, Charles. "Does Modernization Breed Revolution?" *Comparative Politics* 5 (1973): 425–47.

———. *From Mobilization to Revolution.* Reading, MA: Addison-Wesley, 1978.

Toksöz, Meltem. "'Are They Not Our Workers?' Socialist Hilmi and His Publication *İştirak:* An Appraisal of Ottoman Socialism." In *The Young Turk Revolution and the Ottoman Empire: The Aftermath of 1908,* edited by Noémi Lévy and François Georgeon, 286–317. London: I. B. Tauris, 2017.

Torpey, John. *The Invention of the Passport: Surveillance, Citizenship and the State.* Cambridge: Cambridge University Press, 2000.

Trevor-Roper, Hugh. "The General Crisis of the Seventeenth Century." *Past & Present* 26 (1959): 31–64.

Tunçay, Mete, and Erik J. Zürcher, eds. *Socialism and Nationalism in the Ottoman Empire and Modern Turkey.* London: I. B. Tauris, 1994.

Ueno, Masayuki. "'For the Fatherland and the State': Armenians Negotiate the Tanzimat Reforms." *International Journal of Middle East Studies* 45 (2013): 93–109.

Ury, Scott. *Barricades and Banners: The Revolution of 1905 and the Transformation of Warsaw Jewry.* Stanford, CA: Stanford University Press, 1912.

Van Inwegen, Patrick. *Understanding Revolution.* Boulder: Lynne Rienner, 2011.

Varandian, Mikayel. *Boghokĕ noragoyn patmut'ean mēj* [Protest in recent history]. Geneva: ARF Press, 1914.

———. *Simon Zavarean: Gtser ir Keank'ēn* [Simon Zavarean: Sketches from his life]. Boston: Hayrenik', 1927.

———. *H.H. Dashnakts'ut'ean patmut'iwn* [History of A.R. Federation]. Paris: Navarre, 1932.

Vezenkov, Alexander. "Formulating and Reformulating Ottomanism." In *Entangled Histories of the Balkans,* edited by Roumen Daskalov and Tchavdar Marinov. Vol. 1, *National Ideologies and Language Policies,* 241–71. Leiden: Brill, 2013.

———. "Reconciliation of the Spirits and Fusion of the Interests: 'Ottomanism' as an Identity Politics." In *We, the Macedonians: Politics of National Peculiarity in Southeastern Europe,* edited by Diana Mishkova, 47–77. Budapest: Central European University Press, 2009.

Von Mohrenschildt, Dimitri Sergius. *Toward a United States of Russia: Plans and Projects of Federal Reconstruction of Russia in the Nineteenth Century.* Plainsboro, NJ, London, Toronto: Associated University Presses, 1981.

Walicki, Andrzej. "Rosa Luxemburg and the Question of Nationalism in Polish Marxism, 1893–1914." *Slavonic and East European Review* 61, no. 4 (October 1983): 565–82.

Watts, Ronald L. "Federalism, Federal Political Systems, and Federations." *Annual Review of Political Science* 1 (1998): 117–37.

Wenzlhuemer, Roland. *Connecting the Nineteenth-Century World: The Telegraph and Globalization.* Cambridge: Cambridge University Press, 2015.

Werner, Michael, and Bénédicte Zimmermann. "Beyond Comparison: Histoire Croisée and the Challenge of Reflexivity." *History and Theory* 45 (February 2006): 30–50.

Westwood, J.N. *A History of Russian Railways.* London: George Allen and Unwin, 1964.

Wickham-Crowley, Timothy. *Guerrillas and Revolution in Latin America: A Comparative Study of Insurgents and Regimes Since 1956.* Princeton, NJ: Princeton University Press, 1992.

Wiessner, Siegfried. "Federalism: An Architecture for Freedom." *European Law Review* 1, no. 2 (1993): 129–42.

Williams, Beryl. "Russia 1905." *History Today* 55 (5 May 2005): 1–6.

———. "1905: The View from the Provinces." In *The Russian Revolution of 1905: Centenary Perspectives,* edited by Jonathan D. Smele and Anthony Heywood, 34–54. London: Routledge, 2005.

Wilson, A.C. "A Thousand Years of Postal and Telecommunications Services in Russia." *New Zealand Slavonic Journal* (1989–90): 135–66.

Yazdani, Sohrab. "The Question of the Iranian *Ijtima'iyun-i Amiyun* Party." In *Iranian-Russian Encounters: Empires and Revolutions since 1800*, edited by Stephanie Cronin, 189–206. London: Routledge, 2013.

Yosmaoğlu, İpek. *Blood Ties: Religion, Violence, and the Politics of Nationhood in Ottoman Macedonia, 1878–1908*. Ithaca, NY: Cornell University Press, 2013.

———. "Chasing the Printed Word: Press Censorship in the Ottoman Empire, 1876–1913." *Journal of Turkish Studies* 27, nos. 1/2 (2003): 15–49.

Zagorin, Perez. *Rebels and Rulers*. Vol. 1. Cambridge: Cambridge University Press, 1982.

Zeitlian, Sona. *Hay knoj derě hay heghap 'okhakan sharzhman měj* [The role of the Armenian woman in the Armenian revolutionary movement]. Los Angeles: Hraztan Sarkis Zeitlian Publications, 1992.

Živković, Andreja, and Dragan Plavšić, eds. *The Balkan Socialist Tradition and the Balkan Federation, 1871–1915*. Revolutionary History 8, no. 3. London: Porcupine Press, 2003.

Zürcher, Erik J. "The Ottoman Conscription System in Theory and Practice, 1844–1918." *International Review of Social History* 43 (1998): 437–49.

———. *The Young Turk Legacy and Nation Building: From the Ottoman Empire to Ataturk's Turkey*. London: I. B. Tauris, 2010.

Index